THE FREE SOILERS

Frederick J. Blue

THE FREE SOILERS
Third Party Politics
1848-54

UNIVERSITY OF ILLINOIS PRESS
Urbana Chicago London

© 1973 by the Board of Trustees of the University of Illinois
Manufactured in the United States of America
Library of Congress Catalog Card No. 72-86408
ISBN 0-252-00308-x

For Judy

Contents

Preface

In 1885, John Bigelow noted the significance of the Free Soil movement in which he had played a minor role: "It is one of the most important chapters of our national history but one which is in great danger of being overlooked."[1] Historians for the most part have overlooked the Free Soil party as Bigelow feared, for the only previous extended account was written by Theodore C. Smith in 1897, *The Liberty and Free Soil Parties in the Northwest* (New York, 1897). Smith's work includes an extremely useful and detailed account of state and local affairs, but only in the Great Lakes region, and it puts little emphasis on national events. The recent study by Joseph G. Rayback, *Free Soil: The Election of 1848* (Lexington, Kentucky, 1970) also deals with the Free Soil party in its initial year but only as a part of a presidential campaign and from the perspective of all three parties involved, with little emphasis on state and local issues. Hence the need remains for a more extended account of the role of the Free Soil party in national issues as well as the relevant state and local issues of the late 1840s and early 1850s.

The party suffered the fate of virtually all third parties in American history. After a promising beginning in 1848 when it placed the major parties on the defensive, it won relatively few votes and even fewer elections and was often ignored by the major parties. In calling for the containment although not the abolition of slavery, it presented a message that the voters of the North were not yet prepared to hear. Unable to sustain itself between national elections, it almost disappeared before 1852. Yet the members were finally rewarded with a measure of success when the Republican party adopted their containment policy and used it to establish itself as a major party. In the course of its six-year

[1] John Bigelow to Henry B. Dawson, November 11, 1885, in Bigelow Papers, New York Historical Society.

history the Free Soil party thus played an important role which we should not continue to overlook.

Many of the leaders of the Free Soil movement differed little in motive from the major party politicians they challenged for power. Although they professed to be dedicated to the containment of slavery, they usually acted instead like politicians in quest of a job. Hence they were willing to compromise their principles if it meant political advancement. For many, free soil was not an end in itself but a very practical means to improve their positions. Nor was the Free Soil party more than a temporary device which could be used for this same end until the proper time for reentry into the two-party system presented itself. On the other hand, the party also included many dedicated idealists who were more interested in preventing the spread of slavery than in immediate political office. It was this group which helped to preserve the party's independence when the initial enthusiasm of 1848 had worn off. It was also this group whose dedication to the principle of free soil distinguished the party from the Democratic and Whig parties with which it had broken. Thus the Free Soil movement included a constant struggle between the idealist and the politician. Yet on the issue of race almost all Free Soilers demonstrated how similar they were to Democrats and Whigs, sharing the racism of northern society and with it the desire to avoid any contact with the black population.

What follows is essentially a leadership study rather than one stressing the grass roots following. Such an approach is justified because the Free Soil movement was not characterized by a spontaneous groundswell of popular support but was one dominated by a few at the top. In a society which was still somewhat elitist and deferential, the average voter continued to take his cues from the political leaders he respected. Fortunately the Free Soil leadership was a highly articulate group which left extensive writings recording its strategy and feelings. Hence this study is based primarily on the writings of the major participants including Martin Van Buren, Charles Francis Adams, Salmon P. Chase, Joshua Giddings, Gamaliel Bailey, Charles Sumner, and John P. Hale.

Throughout this study emphasis has been placed on the national phase of the party's history rather than the purely state and local, since the party directed itself primarily to the national issue of slavery in the territories and had little to say about most local issues. Often failing to perceive the importance of state and local questions in winning elections, the party usually did not challenge the firmly entrenched Democrats and Whigs on problems which were of great significance to many voters. Only when state events are necessary for an understanding of the larger movement, as in Ohio, New York, Massachusetts, and Wisconsin, are they discussed in any detail. In these cases an account of the role of Free Soilers in state politics adds greatly to an understanding of the motives of the men involved. The transition of the Free Soil and Whig parties into the Republican party in 1854 and 1855 is treated only in a summary manner because this belongs more properly in a study of the Republican party.[2] While the Free Soilers provided an important element of leadership in the Republican party and helped formulate that party's position advocating the containment of slavery, the history of the Free Soil party actually ends with the passage of the Kansas-Nebraska bill in May, 1854.

The valuable assistance and suggestions of several people have made this work possible. I am indebted to Professor Richard N. Current of the University of North Carolina at Greensboro, who supervised the project in its original form as a doctoral dissertation at the University of Wisconsin. I am also grateful to Professor Robert V. Bruce of Boston University and Professor Chaplain Morrison for the constructive and appropriate criticisms they offered in early stages of the project. My special thanks go to Professors Dominic J. Capeci of Southwest Missouri State College and James P. Ronda of Youngstown State University, who were so generous with their time in reading the entire manuscript and offering valuable suggestions on revisions. This work has benefited greatly from their encouragement and advice.

Special thanks go to the library staff of the State Historical Society of Wisconsin, where much of the research was done, and especially to Ruth Davis, who willingly lent her time and expert knowledge in locating research material. I am also appreciative of the cooperation extended me by the staffs of the Library of Congress, the Massachu-

---

[2] For a full discussion of the varied elements of the early Republican party see Eric Foner, *Free Soil, Free Labor, Free Men: The Ideology of the Republican Party before the Civil War* (New York, 1970).

setts Historical Society, the New Hampshire Historical Society, Houghton Library at Harvard University, and the Ohio Historical Society. Finally I am indebted to my wife Judy for her encouragement and patience as well as for her many hours of assistance in the project.

THE FREE SOILERS

1

Salmon P. Chase
Prepares the Liberty Party
for Coalition

The immediate origins of the Free Soil party lay in the explosive issue of slavery in the territories — an issue which reached crisis proportions in 1848 with the acquisition of new lands from Mexico. When the Democratic and Whig parties refused to take a positive stand against the extension of slavery into these territories, many northerners of various political backgrounds felt that strong action was necessary. As a result they united to form the Free Soil party and prepared for an active campaign for national and state office. The origins of the Free Soil party were more complex, however, than simply opposition to slavery in the Mexican War territories. As a third party organization, it was the immediate successor of the Liberty party, which existed throughout the 1840s. The Free Soil party adopted much of the Liberty party's platform and absorbed many of its leaders and supporters. It was not as advanced a group as the Liberty party, however, for it was tempered by former Whigs and Democrats who were unwilling to go beyond the containment of slavery. At the same time, the Liberty party itself, under the guidance of Salmon P. Chase of Ohio, moved in a direction whereby it was ready by 1848 to cooperate with other more moderate groups. In that year, factions in both major parties broke away and joined with the Liberty men to create the Free Soil party. In order to comprehend fully this new party one must first understand its background and the reasons that these three very different groups could cooperate.

The antislavery movement was extremely diverse in its composition

and approach. As a result, those who have described the various de-
grees and methods of opposition to slavery have rarely agreed on the
meaning of the important terms used. Their definitions have often
reflected their own value judgments, and hence it is necessary to clarify
the meaning of the key terms as they are used in this study. These definitions will attempt to conform to those used by the opponents of slavery themselves despite the varied use of the terms both before the Civil
War and now. In addition, the use of such terms as "radical," "extremist," and "conservative" will be omitted wherever possible because of
the difficulty of avoiding modern connotations and value judgments
which these words almost automatically imply.

The word antislavery is used in a general way to describe any or
all aspects of opposition to slavery, whether practiced by William Lloyd
Garrison, who sought an immediate uncompensated end to slavery
everywhere, or Martin Van Buren, who wanted merely to prevent its
expansion. The term abolitionist is used to apply only to those who
were morally opposed to slavery wherever it existed. The abolitionist
not only opposed the extension of slavery into new territories but also
argued that it should be abolished in the slave states. Some abolitionists
like Garrison opposed political activity of any kind while others like
James Birney favored it as long as it remained true to their principles.
For the most part those abolitionists favoring the political approach did
not join the Free Soil party, feeling that it did not go far enough and
was too ready to compromise with the major parties.[1] The term anti-
extensionist will be used to describe those who were not willing to interfere with slavery in the South but were willing to resist its expansion
into federally owned territories as well as to call for its elimination in
the District of Columbia. The anti-extensionists, including men like
Salmon P. Chase and Charles Sumner, made up the bulk of the Free
Soil party. While there was a great deal of disagreement within each of
these two antislavery groups concerning the proper tactics to be followed, for the most part all of those involved can be classified as either
abolitionists or anti-extensionists.[2]

---

[1] The best description of the attitude of Garrison and other abolitionists toward
participation in politics is found in Aileen S. Kraditor, *Means and Ends in American Abolitionism: Garrison and His Critics on Strategy and Tactics, 1834-1850*
(New York, 1969), especially 118-85.
[2] Politicians of the antebellum period who opposed the antislavery movement

Throughout the 1830s the abolition movement was apolitical. The only political activity of the abolitionists of any kind was the policy adopted by some in the late 1830s of questioning candidates concerning their antislavery views. They would then either vote for those with whom they most agreed or abstain if no candidate seemed acceptable. After discovering that mere interrogation of candidates brought no appreciable results, a small faction reluctantly turned to third-party activity. In so doing they at first were a highly idealistic group which stressed the need for moral opposition to slavery everywhere. They naively believed that their ideological approach could win supporters in a political system which had rarely stressed ideology. It was not long, however, before many were convinced that a more politically realistic approach was necessary. Their movement would then gradually be taken over by those who believed that only by using the methods of the major parties could they have any effect on the voters. With this lesson learned, political considerations began to take precedence over ideology and political naiveté gave way to political reality.

Late in 1839, a small group of abolitionists formed the Liberty party and in 1840 nominated a former slaveholder turned abolitionist, James G. Birney, for president. The Liberty campaign of 1840 was largely lost in the excitement surrounding the candidacy of William Henry Harrison and the meaningless uproar over hard cider and log cabins. Fewer than 7,000 Americans supported Birney, and only in Massachusetts did the Liberty vote reach 1 percent of the total. Birney even failed completely to attract a significant number of abolitionists, who numbered at this time approximately 250,000.[3] Their traditional opposition to political activity of any kind, plus the inexperience and naiveté of the Liberty leaders, meant that significant third-party agitation still lay in the future.

---

in any form frequently lumped all of its members together, whether abolitionist or merely anti-extensionist, under the rubric "abolitionist." Most often this implied a negative connotation and was used to describe a person whom the speaker or writer wished to present as a dangerous agitator. Many historians, whether intentionally or not, have adopted this definition and have thus perpetuated the confusion which still exists.

[3] W. Dean Burnham, *Presidential Ballots, 1836-1892* (Baltimore, 1955), 26; Edward Stanwood, *A History of the Presidency from 1788 to 1897* (Boston and New York, 1898), 203; Louis Filler, *The Crusade against Slavery, 1830-1860* (New York, 1960), 67.

The Liberty party grew slowly during the next four years, for most northerners were not yet ready to face the slavery issue and support an ideological party; to many the third party appeared to be forcing an issue that was better left alone. Slavery was not yet of significant relevance to the average northern farmer or worker, and this single-minded party took no stand on any of the topics of more immediate interest such as the tariff, the national bank, public lands, and internal improvements. Nor could the idealistic Liberty men compete against the flamboyant and colorful campaign techniques of their Democratic and Whig opponents.

The election of 1844 demonstrated both the strength and weakness of the Liberty party as well as a change in emphasis away from idealism in the direction of political realism. With its antislavery appeal it won the support of an increasing but still small percentage of both abolitionists and anti-extensionists. The party again nominated James G. Birney but adopted a platform which hedged somewhat on outright abolition. Rather than directly calling for federal interference with slavery in the states, a position which many of the members endorsed, the platform merely demanded "the absolute and unqualified divorce of the General Government from slavery." Liberty leaders had apparently decided that this was a politically attainable goal while emancipation was not. They also realized that it would have a wider appeal among northern voters. According to the platform, which was in large part influenced by the thinking of Salmon P. Chase of Ohio, slavery existed solely by virtue of state law, and Congress had no authority to establish the institution in the territories or continue it in the District of Columbia. The party condemned the three-fifths clause of the Constitution and called the fugitive slave laws unconstitutional and void.[4] Most important, its failure to demand immediate emancipation reflected Chase's growing influence and a significant trend for the future of antislavery politics.

The major issue of the campaign of 1844 was the annexation of

[4] Kirk H. Porter and Donald Bruce Johnson (comps.), *National Party Platforms, 1840-1960* (Urbana, Ill., 1961), 4-8; Eric Foner, *Free Soil, Free Labor, Free Men: The Ideology of the Republican Party before the Civil War,* 79-80; Theodore C. Smith, *The Liberty and Free Soil Parties in the Northwest,* Vol. VI of Harvard Historical Studies (New York, 1897), 70.

Texas. Although many northerners viewed annexation as a southern plot to extend slavery, only the Liberty men openly opposed it and took an anti-extension position.[5] The Whigs were officially silent on the issue, but northern members sought Liberty support for their perennial candidate Henry Clay in order to defeat James K. Polk and annexation. Clay, however, as a slaveholder, was the Whig least likely to attract Liberty votes. He straddled the fence on the Texas issue by attempting to divorce slavery from annexation. Not wishing to alienate southern Whigs, he said he would support annexation if it would not jeopardize the Union. Realizing the vulnerability of their own candidate in the North, the Whigs waged an effective campaign of rumor and innuendo against Birney, the former planter aristocrat.[6]

Birney's 62,000 votes proved to be one of the high points in the Liberty party's history although the total disappointed many. Unfortunately for the anti-extension movement, a more important result was that the Liberty votes indirectly elected James K. Polk and thus made possible the immediate annexation of Texas. Whigs pointed out that had Clay won in New York he would have won the election. Birney's vote here was more than 15,000 whereas Polk's plurality in the state was only 5,000. Since most of the Liberty vote came from counties which in 1840 had given large Whig majorities, the Whigs concluded accurately that Birney's candidacy gave the state to Polk.[7] This was a reliable conclusion despite the fact that in 1844 the Liberty party actually lost votes from its 1843 showing in the race for governor when there had been no Texas annexation issue. The important point was that enough people had switched from Whig to Liberty

[5] The Liberty platform did not specifically mention Texas, because when it was adopted the issue had not yet become prominent. The party's members, however, opposed annexation and made this emphatically clear during the campaign. See Porter and Johnson (comps.), *National Party Platforms,* 4-8.

[6] Smith, *The Liberty and Free Soil Parties,* 77-79; Edgar A. Holt, "Party Politics in Ohio, 1840-1850," *Ohio Archaeological and Historical Quarterly,* XXXVIII (1929), 99; Betty Fladeland, *James Gillespie Birney: Slaveholder to Abolitionist* (Ithaca, N.Y., 1955), 244-46; George W. Julian, *Political Recollections, 1840-1872* (Chicago, 1884), 36-43.

[7] John D. Hicks, "The Third Party Tradition in American Politics," *Mississippi Valley Historical Review,* XX (1933), 9; Burnham, *Presidential Ballots,* 31; George W. Roach, "The Presidential Campaign of 1844 in New York State," *Proceedings of the New York State Historical Association,* XXXVI (1938), 171.

sometime prior to 1844 to prevent Henry Clay from carrying the state.[8]
Liberty leaders could not deny that the majority of Liberty votes in
1844 had been Whig in earlier elections. The results in Massachusetts
also pointed this out fairly conclusively; the same was true in Ohio,
where most Liberty votes were cast in the Western Reserve, a stronghold of Whig and anti-extension support.[9] In their anger the Whigs
ignored all other possible causes of Clay's defeat, including his indeci-
siveness on the Texas issue, and they laid the blame solely on the Liberty party. In the words of the New York *Express,* "There has never
been a vote of any fragment of a party so extensively disastrous in its
consequences, or so pernicious to the ostensible objects of its authors."[10]
The election thus had the unavoidable result of antagonizing many
who sympathized with the anti-extension movement.

The campaign did reveal, however, that the Liberty party was not
dominated by men determined to destroy slavery immediately and
everywhere as their critics charged. Their platform had not called for
federal action to end slavery in the southern states, and the party had
not received the support of such controversial abolitionists as the uncompromising William Lloyd Garrison. Garrison continued to oppose
all third-party activity.[11] But these facts were largely ignored by major
party politicians, who continued their abusive attacks unabated.

The election of 1844 had thus isolated and weakened the Liberty
party because of its controversial role in determining the outcome. Although the party did manage to recoup some of its losses in the elections of 1846 and increase its total vote to close to 75,000, it had little
impact in most areas.[12] The only real Liberty strength was in the New
England states and in New York, but even there the outlook for the
future was not bright.[13] Northern voters had not yet been sufficiently

---

[8] In 1843 the Liberty party won 4.5 percent of the vote in the gubernatorial
race or a total of 16,097 votes. In 1844 James G. Birney polled only 3.3 percent
of the vote or 15,812 votes. See Lee Benson, *The Concept of Jacksonian Democracy: New York as a Test Case* (Princeton, 1961), 135-36, 261-62.

[9] Smith, *The Liberty and Free Soil Parties,* 80-85; *National Era* (Washington),
March 11, 1852.

[10] Quoted in *Niles' Register* (Baltimore), December 21, 1844.

[11] Kraditor, *Means and Ends in American Abolitionism,* 158-60; Bertram Wyatt-
Brown, *Lewis Tappan and the Evangelical War against Slavery* (Cleveland, 1969),
270-71.

[12] Smith, *The Liberty and Free Soil Parties,* 97.

[13] William G. Bean, "Party Transformations in Massachusetts with Special
Reference to the Antecedents of Republicanism, 1848-1860" (Ph.D. dissertation,

moved by the question of slavery to desert their traditional parties and support one dedicated solely to antislavery.

Despite the increase in total vote in 1846, many Liberty members now understood more fully the political ineffectiveness of their organization. They had achieved little by following their adopted course, and some now demanded a change in tactics in order to achieve more immediate and practical results. One Liberty faction, led by the Ohioans, desired some kind of alliance with Democratic or Whig forces because of the futility of further third-party agitation. Even before the 1844 election Salmon P. Chase and Gamaliel Bailey had organized a drive to remove Birney from the ticket because of his uncompromising defense of abolitionism. They had sought to replace him with a figure of greater prestige and more moderate attitude.[14] Less ideological emphasis was necessary if political results were to be achieved. The results of 1844 and the continued isolation of the Liberty party since then were the necessary lessons to show them that a new approach was needed.

Soon after the election of 1844, Birney's followers began urging his nomination for 1848, but this time Chase and Bailey were better prepared to resist. In 1845, they organized a convention in Cincinnati which made no mention of immediate abolition. The members looked instead toward a "union of all sincere friends of Liberty and Free Labor" and sought "to divorce the National Government from Slavery; to prohibit slaveholding in all places of exclusive National jurisdiction." Chase favored a coalition with northern Democrats, but because this was not immediately feasible he worked instead to delay as long as possible any Liberty nominations for the 1848 election. Chase hoped he might still obtain some kind of agreement with anti-extension elements of the major parties.[15]

Harvard University, 1922), 5n; Benson, *The Concept of Jacksonian Democracy,* 135.

[14] Chase to Joshua Giddings, January 21, 1843, in Giddings-Julian Correspondence, Library of Congress; Dwight L. Dumond (ed.), *Letters of James Gillespie Birney, 1831-1857* (New York, 1938), II, 661, 662.

[15] For a thorough discussion of Chase's role in developing the idea that slavery was a local institution with which the federal government could have no connection, see Foner, *Free Soil, Free Labor, Free Men,* 78-102; Cincinnati *Weekly Herald,* June 25, 1845; Joseph G. Rayback, "The Liberty Party Leaders of Ohio: Exponents of Antislavery Coalition," *Ohio State Archaeological and Historical Quarterly,* LVII (1948), 173.

There were many Liberty men who maintained their idealism and did not share this interest in coalition. The New York abolitionist William Goodell expressed the views of many of his party when he attacked the willingness of Chase and others of his faction to compromise: "The old party attachments of many who joined the Liberty party were not broken off. They were not steady in their adhesion to the Liberty party. . . . Why should they [Democrats and Whigs] quit their party, when those who had done so, were evidently on tip-toe for an opportunity to get back into it."[16]

Compromise with either the Democratic or Whig parties was the last thing that James Birney and his supporters wanted, for they knew it would mean abandoning their interest in immediate abolition in favor of anti-extensionism. On the contrary, they were gradually adopting the highly controversial thesis that the Constitution was an anti-slavery document. With this approach one could more easily argue that Congress had the authority to abolish slavery in the southern states. In addition, Birney now supported a more general reform party, an idea which would further factionalize the Liberty party. He argued that the Liberty party would have to broaden its platform to include a variety of current reform issues, for "We must be prepared to take on ourselves *all* the administration of government or *none* of it."[17]

This development meant that there were now three factions within the Liberty party. The Chase group, which stressed practical politics, wanted an anti-extension coalition, while the Birney faction idealistically sought to maintain Liberty identity but to broaden its appeal with other reform issues. Finally, the old guard of the party agreed with Birney on the need for an independent Liberty party but felt that the original one-idea antislavery platform was still the proper approach.

The Birney group, while small in numbers, was nevertheless determined enough on abolitionism and general reform to break with the other two factions and follow an independent course. This decision would make it easier later for the Chase faction to lead the remaining Liberty men into an anti-extension coalition. Birney himself suffered a paralytic stroke in August, 1845, and leadership of his faction fell to

---

[16] William Goodell, *Slavery and Antislavery* (New York, 1853), 472.

[17] Birney to Lewis Tappan, September 12, 1845, in Lewis Tappan Papers, Library of Congress.

William Goodell and the wealthy New York philanthropist, Gerrit Smith. In June, 1847, they broke with the main body of the Liberty party and held a convention of their own at Macedon Lock, New York.[18] That convention nominated Smith for president. Although they would make a later effort to win the main body of Liberty men to their point of view, they felt that they had seceded from the Liberty party and they thus adopted a new name, the Liberty League. They broadened the original Liberty party platform to include such demands as free trade, free public lands, and the abolition of legalized monopolies, and they argued that the Constitution made slavery illegal everywhere. The Liberty party had thus divided, but in losing Smith's Liberty League, the party lost its most uncompromising and idealistic element. Undoubtedly this loss represented a victory for those who stressed political success, for it placed the party in a better position to join later the broader Free Soil movement.[19]

The remaining Liberty party members were far from united on the proper course to take during the campaign of 1848. They still had to decide whether to continue as an independent party or to seek alliance with another group. If they agreed to remain separate they had to determine whom and when to nominate as well as to define their position on slavery. The old guard of the party, centered mostly in the East, urged continued independence and pushed for an early convention to avoid being swallowed up later in a larger movement. Salmon P. Chase led the Ohio faction in urging that the convention be postponed until the summer of 1848 to allow time to work out an agreement with other anti-extension elements.[20] In his efforts Chase had the backing of several important Liberty newspapers. Gamaliel Bailey, who had first edited an antislavery paper in Cincinnati, established the *National Era* in Washington in 1847 and used it to spread Chase's ideas and gain their acceptance by Liberty men throughout the coun-

[18] Goodell, *Slavery and Antislavery*, 473; The call for the convention is included in Dumond (ed.), *Letters of Birney*, II, 1047-57.

[19] E. S. Gilbert to Smith, June 14, 1847, *Calendar of the Gerrit Smith Papers* (Albany, 1942), II; Fladeland, *James G. Birney*, 263; Goodell, *Slavery and Antislavery*, 475, 477; Ralph V. Harlow, *Gerrit Smith: Philanthropist and Reformer* (New York, 1939), 178-79. For a complete discussion of the split within the Liberty party see Kraditor, *Means and Ends in American Abolitionism*, 153-57.

[20] Cincinnati *Weekly Herald*, June 30, July 7, 21, 1847; Rayback, "The Liberty Party Leaders," 176.

try. Bailey's successor on the Cincinnati *Weekly Herald,* Stanley
Matthews, also endorsed the Chase position, which sought to appeal
to discontented Whigs and Democrats.[21]

Salmon P. Chase, the key figure in this movement, led a strange and
shifting political course that is not easily explained. There was, on the
one hand, his dedicated opposition to slavery. But more important,
on the other hand, his frequent moves from one political party to
another in the 1840s and early 1850s revealed him to be a political
opportunist. Chase's role in the factional struggles of the Liberty party
shows both sides of his makeup, although his opportunistic desire for
political power and prestige clearly took precedence over his dedication
to the anti-extension cause. Originally a Whig, he joined the Liberty
party in the early 1840s, bringing a highly pragmatic approach to the
idealistic program of the third party. The ambitious Chase, who by
the mid-1840s leaned toward the Democrats on other issues, was willing to unite with whichever major party would adopt a strong anti-
extension position. Concerning one possible cooperative effort with the
Whigs of Ohio in 1846, Chase wrote, "Were the Whig party to adopt
Liberty principles and measures as paramount in importance, I should
give to its candidates, if honest and capable, a cordial support. . . ."
But he concluded with a pessimistic note: "My fear is that if there
were no party distinctly and earnestly antislavery, parties divided
by other questions would, as they always have, compromise away
Liberty."[22]

Yet Chase continued to think in terms of a broad union of all anti-
extensionists which would be more effective than the Liberty party.
In a letter to Senator John P. Hale of New Hampshire, he reviewed
the past history of the Liberty party and its antislavery agitation and
predicted for it "no prospect of greater future progress, but rather of

---

[21] The *National Era* was the first national Liberty party newspaper, although it
spoke primarily for the Chase faction. See *National Era,* April 15, 22, 29, July 1,
1847; Cincinnati *Weekly Herald,* April 21, 1847.

[22] Chase to Giddings, August 15, 1846, in Chase Papers, Library of Congress.
See also Chase to Giddings, October 20, 1846, in Edward G. Bourne *et al.* (eds.),
"Diary and Correspondence of Salmon P. Chase," *Annual Report of the American
Historical Association, 1902* (Washington, 1903), II, 108-11. In this letter Chase
notes the continuing need for a Liberty party as long as the Whigs and Democrats
refuse to take a strong anti-extension position.

less." Consequently, he was ready to try a new tactic and proposed to Hale "an anti-slavery league, operating upon both parties from without, aided by the antislavery men already in the ranks of the two parties and those who would come in from the Liberty party." He argued that such a nonpartisan league would be able in the shortest time to "accomplish the great work of overthrowing slavery."[23]

Nothing came immediately of his suggestion, for most anti-extension Democrats and Whigs would not be ready to cooperate until their own parties' positions for the 1848 campaign left them little choice. Throughout 1847, Chase continued to seek postponement of a Liberty presidential nomination, feeling that "with the developments of the winter recommending it, we could form a powerful party of Independents in the spring." He expressed himself willing to sacrifice the third party at any time if a more effective agent to overthrow slavery could be found. In June, 1847, he wrote revealingly: "I have always regarded the Lib. organization as a means to this end. I now regard it as nothing more." Chase clearly saw the possibility of a more powerful third party but feared that premature Liberty action might preclude it.[24]

Chase's efforts to postpone a Liberty meeting until 1848 failed, however, for the general committee of the party, balloting by states, voted seven to five to hold a convention at Buffalo in October, 1847. The breakdown of the vote revealed that seven eastern states favored the early convention while the remaining five states, under Chase's leadership, opposed.[25] Yet if there had to be an early convention Chase was determined that its platform and candidate would be such that subsequent cooperation with anti-extension Whigs and Democrats might still be feasible. Only in such cooperation could his hopes for political advancement be realized.

The search for such a candidate soon centered on John P. Hale, who had begun his political career as a Democrat but had broken

[23] Chase to Hale, May 12, 1847, quoted in Robert B. Warden, *An Account of the Private Life and Public Services of Salmon Portland Chase* (Cincinnati, 1874), 312-15.

[24] Chase to Sumner, September 22, 1847, Chase to John Thomas, June 24, 1847, Chase to Joshua Leavitt, June 16, 1847, in Bourne (ed.), "Chase Correspondence," 116-24.

[25] Rayback, "The Liberty Party Leaders," 177; *National Era,* July 21, 1847.

with the party in 1845. Hale had been elected to the Senate by the New Hampshire legislature in a political bargain with the aid of Liberty, Whig, and Independent Democratic support.[26] Third-party interest in his candidacy placed Hale in a serious dilemma, however. He agreed with the Liberty party's anti-extension position, but Liberty identification might label him an extremist and harm his Senate career before it even started. During the summer of 1847, Hale remained undecided and received conflicting advice. New England Liberty leaders urged a close identification with the third party, while Massachusetts anti-extension Whigs like Charles Sumner and Charles Francis Adams advised him that a Liberty nomination would do him no good. Hale attempted to escape his dilemma by indicating support for Chase's efforts to postpone a Liberty nomination until spring. While he would oppose being the party's candidate, "If all his friends wished him to accept the nomination and it were tendered to him he would accept it."[27] Publicly Hale did not make his position clear before the convention assembled, however, and the delegates acted not knowing whether he would accept a nomination or not.

At the convention Chase introduced a motion to postpone the nominations until the spring of 1848, and thus allow time for a broader anti-extension movement to develop, but he was defeated by a combination of Liberty Leaguers and the old guard by a vote of 144 to 72. This was his last defeat, however, for Chase and his midwestern supporters joined forces with the old guard to control the writing of the platform and the choice of the candidate. Such a combination was possible because of the lack of sympathy felt by the old guard for either the ideas or leadership of the Liberty League.[28] Having secured the

[26] For an account of Hale's early career see Richard H. Sewell, *John P. Hale and the Politics of Abolition* (Cambridge, 1965), 36-85; Vincent Y. Bowditch, *Life and Correspondence of Henry Ingersoll Bowditch* (Boston, 1902), I, 184-87.

[27] H. B. Stanton to Hale, July 6, 1847, Amos Tuck to Hale, August 2, 1847, in Hale Papers, New Hampshire Historical Society; H. B. Stanton to Chase, August 6, 1847, in Chase Papers, Library of Congress; Richard H. Sewell, "John P. Hale and the Liberty Party, 1847-1848," *New England Quarterly*, XXXVII (1964), 200-223; Sumner to Giddings, July 28, 1847, in Giddings Papers, Ohio Historical Society; C. F. Adams Manuscript Diary, July 29, 1847, Adams Papers, Massachusetts Historical Society. The *National Era*, September 2, 1847, supported Hale for the nomination. See also Sewell, *John P. Hale*, 89-93.

[28] Cincinnati *Weekly Herald*, November 3, 1847; Rayback, "The Liberty Party Leaders," 177.

principle of an early nomination, which they felt would guarantee Liberty independence, the old guard was then willing to cooperate with Chase in opposing further League efforts.

Before the Chase wing took control, the members of the Liberty League, led by Smith and Goodell, made one final attempt to persuade the majority to have slavery everywhere labeled unconstitutional and to expand the platform into other reform areas. The convention, however, voted down their suggestions, and instead the chief antislavery plank read: "It is the duty of the antislavery men in Congress to propose and vote for acts to repeal the Slave Code of the District of Columbia; to repeal the act of 1793 relating to fugitives from service; to provide against the introduction of slavery in any territory, and such other laws as may be necessary and expedient to withdraw the support of the government from slavery and to array the powers of the general government, on the side of Liberty and free labor." Unlike members of the League, Chase and most other Liberty members felt that slavery, while unconstitutional in the territories, was nevertheless legal in the states no matter how evil it might be. Their position was that the federal government must divorce itself from all connection with slavery, an institution which they said existed solely by virtue of state law. From a pragmatic point of view this was an approach which might be acceptable to a substantial number of northern Whigs and Democrats. The platform did note, however, that the "establishment of peaceful emancipation throughout the Union" remained the eventual goal of the Liberty party.[29]

The Chase faction's second victory came when the convention easily nominated John P. Hale over the League's candidate Gerrit Smith by a vote of 103 to 44. The choice of Hale was largely the result of Chase's efforts, for he and his supporters were determined that if they must nominate they would present the right kind of man. Yet they could not have secured Hale's nomination on their own, and in this effort they were aided by many of the easterners, including Joshua Leavitt and Lewis Tappan, who had demanded the early convention. Only the Liberty League opposed Hale's nomination, the others realizing that

[29] Cincinnati *Weekly Herald*, November 3, 1847; Fladeland, *James G. Birney*, 266; Harlow, *Gerrit Smith*, 181.

having a prominent candidate was perhaps more important than that candidate's past political independence. The Chase faction thus gained substantially from the proceedings. Defeated at the outset in having the nomination postponed, they then secured what they desired in both platform and candidate.[30]

Hale responded very hesitantly to news of his nomination, but in so doing, proved he was the kind of candidate Chase had sought in order to broaden the third-party appeal. The New Hampshire senator waited two months before answering and even then his acceptance was reluctant and provisional. He wrote that his decision to run was against his better judgment and only at the urging of friends. Hale also announced that if a more general anti-extension coalition formed of the kind Chase advocated, he would gladly step aside and "enroll myself among the humblest privates who will rally under such a banner." Thus he proved that Chase's position had triumphed in the long run. His actions indicated also that he had come so completely under Chase's influence that the Ohioan could manipulate him at will in order to achieve his own political aims. Hale's nomination and acceptance and the subsequent break with the League faction marked the official end of the kind of immediate abolitionism which had dominated the Liberty party during its early years. In its place there was now both a party and a candidate that would respond readily to subsequent coalition attempts based on anti-extensionism. The way had been smoothed for the absorption of the Liberty party into the larger Free Soil movement when the time came in 1848.[31]

Such a development was made even more feasible when the Liberty League announced that it could not accept either the platform or candidate of the Liberty party. The League held another of its own conventions in 1848, at which time the dwindling membership again proved its antislavery idealism by nominating Gerrit Smith and approving his abolition and general reform views. The League remained in the campaign as a separate party, but it represented a very small

[30] The proceedings of the convention were published in the *National Era*, November 11, 1847. See also Smith, *The Liberty and Free Soil Parties*, 118-20; Harlow, *Gerrit Smith*, 177-80; Sewell, *John P. Hale*, 92-94.

[31] The *National Era* of January 27, 1848, printed Hale's acceptance letter. See also Rayback, "The Liberty Party Leaders," 178; Sewell, *John P. Hale*, 95-96.

minority of the original Liberty organization.[32] Factionalism had divided the Liberty party, but the loss of the League was not mourned
by the Chase men, who could now direct their full efforts toward cooperation with anti-extension Whigs and Democrats and what they
hoped would be ultimate political success. In the meantime, while
Chase was successfully readying the Liberty party for coalition, events
in the two major parties were taking place which would soon provide
factions from each willing to negotiate with the Liberty leaders.

[32] Birney to L. Tappan, July 10, 1848, Dumond (ed.), *Letters of Birney,* II,
1108-9; Harlow, *Gerrit Smith,* 182-87. See also *Proceedings of the National Liberty
Convention* (Utica, 1848).

2

Fragmentation and Realignment: The Roots of Free Soil

Long before the issue of abolitionism versus anti-extensionism divided the Liberty party, the Democratic and Whig parties were experiencing internal difficulties of their own. The issue in both major parties was the proposed annexation of Texas and how it related to the larger question of slavery in the territories. While all of the Liberty factions could agree on anti-extensionism in Texas, Democrats and Whigs could not. With no abolition elements to be concerned with, each major party nevertheless had a growing faction opposed to the expansion of slavery. And each had a strong southern wing with important northern allies determined to resist the anti-extensionists. The resulting controversy over slavery first in Texas and then in the Mexican War territories prepared the anti-extensionist faction in each to break with its parent party in 1848 and unite with the Liberty coalitionists.

Slavery had been an established institution in Texas ever since the first United States citizens moved into this Mexican region in the early 1820s. After Texas gained its independence in 1836 southerners had continued to come, many of them bringing slaves. Thus when the Texans began their drive for annexation and statehood there was little doubt that if accepted by the United States Texas would be a slave state. For this reason those opposed to the extension of slavery had little alternative but to oppose annexation. Slavery and Texas were almost synonymous, for the Texans themselves as well as other southerners would consider annexation under no other terms.

In April, 1844, President Tyler sent a treaty to the Senate, drawn up by Secretary of State John C. Calhoun, providing for the annexation of the Republic of Texas. Although the Senate ultimately rejected the treaty because of the slavery controversy, the presidential campaign of 1844 brought that question and the larger one of the expansion of slavery into even greater prominence. In the process, the issue precipitated major splits within the Democratic and Whig parties. Martin Van Buren had been considered the logical candidate for the Democratic party in 1844, and as the convention neared he apparently had the support of a majority of the delegates. Everyone expected Henry Clay to be his Whig opponent. As Texas annexation and slave expansion became the burning issue, politicians pressed both men to explain their positions. Van Buren had visited Clay in 1842, and after that meeting rumors spread that the two had agreed to remain silent on the Texas problem and thus avoid it as a campaign issue.[1] But the controversy surrounding Calhoun's treaty would prevent such evasion.

Van Buren especially was under great pressure from many Democrats to support annexation. While Clay faced little opposition in winning the Whig nomination despite his announced opposition to the Texas treaty,[2] failure to endorse annexation would probably cost Van Buren the support of the strong southern and western factions at the Democratic convention. Andrew Jackson, still influential among Democrats in his retirement, made it clear that he favored immediate annexation. On the other hand, because Texas had become inextricably connected with the issue of the extension of slavery, Van Buren had to consider the mounting political pressure in the North opposing

[1] There is no written evidence of any agreement, but Clay later asserted that he and Van Buren would take "common ground" on the Texas issue. Clay to Crittenden, April 21, 1844, in Crittenden Papers, quoted in James C. Paul, *Rift in the Democracy* (Philadelphia, 1951), 38-39. See also Stanwood, *A History of the Presidency*, 209; Holmes Alexander, *The American Talleyrand: The Career and Contemporaries of Martin Van Buren, Eighth President* (New York, 1935), 392; Alto L. Whitehurst, "Martin Van Buren and the Free Soil Movement" (Ph.D. dissertation, University of Chicago, 1932), 17-26.

[2] Clay's letter opposing annexation was printed in the *Niles' Register*, May 4, 1844. Sentiment in favor of Texas annexation was not as strong in the more northern-oriented Whig party as it was in the Democratic organization, and hence Clay's position, while distasteful to some southern Whigs, pleased enough northern delegates to assure him the nomination. For an example of northern Whig opinion see Kinley J. Brauer, *Cotton Versus Conscience: Massachusetts Whig Politics and Southwestern Expansion, 1843-1848* (Lexington, Ky., 1967), 86-89.

the entrance into the Union of another slave state. Van Buren thus
stood to lose support whatever he decided.[3]

On April 20, 1844, with the Democratic convention only a month
away and the Senate nearing a decision on the Texas treaty, Van
Buren announced his opposition to immediate annexation, a step he
knew might cost him his party's nomination. In a letter first published
in the Washington *Globe*, Van Buren equivocated on some points in
his typical evasive manner but was conclusive on others. The crafty
Democrat failed to mention that northern opposition to the extension
of slavery was a major factor in his decision and instead explained that
annexation would be an act of aggression against Mexico which would
lead to war.[4] But the immediate and vehement reaction of northern
and southern Democrats revealed that slavery as well as westward
expansion and war with Mexico were on many people's minds. Jackson expressed shock and disapproval of the letter while Van Buren's
New York colleague Senator Silas Wright wrote, "I never felt more
proud of him than at that moment." At the same time, Wright noted
that support for Van Buren's nomination was rapidly falling away.[5]

The dramatic Democratic convention of 1844 brought Van Buren's
defeat and exactly the kind of expansionist platform that he had feared.
It also resulted in increased dissension within the Democratic party.
Realizing the effect Van Buren's letter might have on his candidacy,
other Democratic aspirants for the nomination seized on the issue to
appeal to the strong annexation sentiment of the delegates, many of
whom had been originally pledged to Van Buren before his Texas
letter. The most serious challenge came from Lewis Cass, the drab and

[3] Stanwood, *A History of the Presidency*, 209-10; Alexander, *The American Talleyrand*, 395-96; Jackson to Martin Van Buren, February 12, 1843, in Van Buren
Papers, Library of Congress. For the reaction of a typical northerner against annexation see E. W. Goodwin to Martin Van Buren, April 12, 1844, *ibid*.

[4] Martin Van Buren to William Hammett, April 20, 1844, in Van Buren Papers.
In typical Van Buren style, the letter was intricate, long, and cryptic. Although
few readers could struggle through the six and a half columns that it covered in
the *Globe*, most realized that Van Buren opposed annexation if it meant war with
Mexico.

[5] Paul, *Rift in the Democracy*, 116; Silas Wright to B. F. Butler, May 15, 1844,
in Butler Papers, Princeton University; Wright to Martin Van Buren, May 13,
1844, in Van Buren Papers; Jackson to the Washington *Union*, May 13, 1844;
Jackson to Francis P. Blair, Sr., May 7, 11, 1844, in Blair Papers, Library of
Congress.

unimpressive senator from Michigan who was a bitter rival of Van Buren.[6] When, after many ballots, the convention found itself hopelessly deadlocked between Cass and Van Buren, the delegates finally turned to a dark horse, James K. Polk of Tennessee.[7] Benjamin Butler, Van Buren's close adviser, helped direct the New York delegation to Polk in a final effort to defeat Cass. Realizing that they could not block the party's rush toward annexation and slavery extension, the New Yorkers agreed reluctantly to support a man enthusiastically pledged to expansion and Texas in order to defeat their bitter enemy, the equally expansionist-minded Lewis Cass. In comparison to Cass, they considered the stern and determined Polk the lesser of two evils, and they were willing to accept him partly because he had played no role in the movement to dump Van Buren.[8]

In both its nomination and platform, the Democratic party had demonstrated the increasing ascendency of its southern and western wings and had accelerated the isolation and alienation of its anti-extension faction. It had nominated James K. Polk, a Tennessee slaveholder and avowed expansionist, and its platform called for "the re-annexation of Texas at the earliest practicable period." The platform repeated the planks originally adopted in 1840 stating that the federal government was one of limited powers and could not interfere with slavery in the states. In addition, the platform urged that all efforts by abolitionists "to induce Congress to interfere with questions of slavery" would lead to alarming and dangerous consequences. These efforts, it continued, tended to "endanger the stability and permanency of the Union and ought not to be countenanced by any friend to our political institutions."[9] Thus the party reaffirmed its commitment to

[6] Paul, *Rift in the Democracy*, 156-57; John A. Garraty, *Silas Wright* (New York, 1949), 264-70; Alexander, *The American Talleyrand*, 398; Whitehurst, "Martin Van Buren," 39.

[7] The best account of the Democratic convention and the maneuvering leading to Polk's nomination is found in Charles Sellers, *James K. Polk, Continentalist, 1843-1846* (Princeton, 1966), 67-107. See also Wright to Martin Van Buren, June 2, 1844, in Van Buren Papers; Wright to Flagg, June 8, 1844, in Flagg Papers, New York Public Library.

[8] Polk's views on annexation were expressed in a letter to Salmon P. Chase, April 23, 1844, and published well in advance of the convention in the Washington *Globe* on May 6, 1844. For Polk's role in the pre-convention events, see Sellers, *James K. Polk*, 67-73, 107.

[9] Porter and Johnson (comps.), *National Party Platforms*, 3-4.

slavery in the South and added its enthusiastic support for Texas and the expansion of slavery. Of equal significance, the rejection of Van Buren and the adoption of the Texas plank had left a legacy of bitterness and discontent among the New Yorker's followers which would make party harmony in the future almost impossible.

Polk's surprising victory over Henry Clay meant that the new administration would be one fully committed to expansion and slavery. It also meant that further unrest in the North would be inevitable. Those Democrats unhappy with the administration's policies soon had all the evidence they needed to prove that proslavery groups had captured the party. In March of 1845, even before Polk was inaugurated, Congress annexed Texas by joint resolution. Before the year was over Texas entered the Union as a slave state with the active backing of the president. When annexation led to the Mexican War in 1846, many northerners of both parties concluded that the major purpose of the war was to extend slavery into new areas to be acquired from Mexico. They agreed that the spread of slavery must stop and that Congress must take the necessary steps to assure its cessation.

President Polk quickly confirmed their fears when he sought funds from Congress to purchase additional territory in concluding a peace treaty with Mexico. In so doing, he galvanized the anti-extension elements in Congress into action, and they retaliated by introducing the Wilmot Proviso. A device to halt the spread of slavery, the Proviso would lead directly to the formation of the Free Soil party, a party which would appeal to the growing anti-extension sentiment throughout the North. In August, 1846, a group of northern Democrats already angry with the president over other policies introduced the Proviso as an amendment to the president's appropriation bill, providing that "as an express and fundamental condition to the acquisition of any territory from the Republic of Mexico . . . neither slavery nor involuntary servitude shall ever exist."[10] None of the northern Democrats behind this move, including David Wilmot of Pennsylvania, Preston King of New York, Jacob Brinkerhoff of Ohio, and John Wentworth of Illinois were abolitionists, but each was an anti-extensionist. The Wilmot Proviso was thus devised as a means to shift the issue from opposition to slavery per se to the more practical and imme-

---

[10] *Congressional Globe,* 29th Cong., 1st Sess., 1217.

diate matter of opposition to the expansion of slavery. It thus helped place the slavery issue on a level where anti-extensionist politicians as well as abolitionists could oppose it.

The Wilmot Proviso and the issue of slavery in the territories would be directly before Congress for most of 1847; it would be the major issue of the Free Soil election of 1848; and it would delay the organization of California and New Mexico until 1850. Yet the Proviso's introduction into congressional debates was a rather commonplace maneuver which might have occurred automatically to many members. Its language contained little originality; it was similar to the clause in the Northwest Ordinance of 1787 which banned slavery in the Great Lakes territories. It had been offered as an amendment in relation to the Texas bill, and two days before Wilmot took his action, another Democrat from Pennsylvania, Rep. James Thompson, had proposed that the same principle be included in the Oregon territorial bill. Because slavery was already an established institution in Texas and would not become a major issue in Oregon, the earlier amendments had not caused as great a controversy as the Wilmot Proviso created.[11] In Congress it received bipartisan northern support. Seized on by many to relieve their frustrations against the president and the increasingly unpopular Mexican War, it would completely disrupt an otherwise successful Polk administration.

At first the Proviso surprisingly did not create much discussion. The New York *Herald* viewed it as abolitionist "sound and fury, signifying nothing." The determined President Polk, however, was angered and noted in his diary that it was "a mischievous and foolish amendment." He showed his lack of sympathy toward northern anti-extension sentiment when he wrote: "What connection slavery had with making peace with Mexico it is difficult to conceive." A slaveholder himself, Polk was, however, more concerned with adding new territories than he was with extending slavery. His clear purpose was to keep the slave issue out of politics, where it could only cause further division in his own party and perhaps thwart his expansionist aims. The slave extension question had been kept out of Congress since Missouri's entrance into the Union twenty-five years earlier. Since then Washington poli-

[11] *Ibid.*, 1200, 1217; Sellers, *James K. Polk*, 479.

ticians had succeeded in evading the topic, although the Texas episode had revived it for many. Yet the strong-willed president, who was bent on territorial expansion on the one hand and party unity on the other, was unwilling to see these priorities diverted by the growing anti-extensionist sentiment. His was not a calculated policy to block northern policies but rather one of the choice of priorities in which his own plans clearly took precedence over anti-extensionism. Much to Polk's distress, however, Congress took no action on the appropriation bill before it adjourned in August, thanks to the opposition and delaying tactics of anti-extension northerners.[12] The issue was thus left to the next session of Congress, but in the ensuing months the Proviso was widely discussed in the press and at public meetings throughout the country. Anti-extensionism had become the major topic of the day.

At the new session of Congress which convened in December, 1846, Polk again pressed for passage of the appropriation bill without the Proviso but found himself faced with an even more determined northern opposition. Still hoping to avoid the slavery issue, the president sought to convince anti-extensionist Democrats that he was not interested in the spread of slavery. On January 4, 1847, however, Preston King of New York called for the passage of an amendment which expanded on the principle of the original Proviso. King asked Congress to declare that slavery should not exist in any territory thereafter acquired, not just Mexican War territories. Northern anti-extension feelings were intensifying and the president became more convinced of the seriousness of the situation. He noted that "the movement of Mr. King today, if persisted in, will be attended with terrible consequences to the country, and cannot fail to destroy the Democratic party, if it does not ultimately threaten the Union itself. . . . The slavery question . . . is a firebrand in the body." The president, still unwilling to yield to the anti-extension movement, argued that "there is no probability that any territory will ever be acquired from Mexico in which slavery could ever exist."[13]

    [12] New York *Herald*, August 11, 1847; Milo M. Quaife (ed.), *The Diary of James K. Polk* (Chicago, 1910), II, 75, 115; Sellers, *James K. Polk*, 476-78.
    [13] Richard R. Stenberg, "The Motivation of the Wilmot Proviso," *Mississippi Valley Historical Review*, XVIII (1932), 541n; Quaife (ed.), *Diary of James K. Polk*, II, 288-90, 299, 308-9, 320; *Congressional Globe*, 29th Cong., 2nd Sess., 105, 114ff, Appendix, 139.

By early 1847, sentiment in both North and South concerning the Wilmot Proviso had developed to the point that the party unity which President Polk so earnestly sought appeared unattainable. The intense logician, John C. Calhoun, speaking in the Senate, gave the southern answer when he insisted that the territories were the "common property of the States." He then introduced resolutions stating that Congress could make no law forbidding an American from bringing his slaves into any territory. Although his efforts to unite the South in a proslavery movement transcending party lines were frustrated, he nevertheless succeeded in arousing the southern public to the possible implications of the territorial issue. One by one, southern state legislatures agreed to resist the Proviso and oppose any presidential candidate who did not disavow it. There were even threats that the end of the Union was at hand if the Proviso should become law.[14]

While Congress and state legislatures debated the Wilmot Proviso all talk of compromise was ruled out. Proslavery and anti-extensionist factions had taken such opposite positions that an all-out showdown appeared inevitable. Finally, after months of debate, the House defeated the Proviso, and Polk's appropriation bill passed without the amendment in March of 1847.[15] Despite its defeat, however, the Proviso remained the leading topic of conversation in political circles for months to come and would be the key issue in the election of 1848. Factionalism, brought on in large part by the Wilmot Proviso debates, was increasingly dividing both Democrats and Whigs.

Other events closely related to the extension issue during the Polk administration had served to hurry the process of fragmentation in both parties. Polk's election and his subsequent use of his patronage power had been an early cause of unrest among the Van Buren faction of New York Democrats still smarting from its failure to win the nomination for the former president. In order to help Polk's chances for

[14] Richard K. Cralle (ed.), *The Works of John C. Calhoun* (New York, 1857), IV, 339-49; Avery Craven, *The Coming of the Civil War* (Chicago, 1942), 232-34. For a description of Calhoun's Southern Rights Movement, see Chaplain W. Morrison, *Democratic Politics and Sectionalism: The Wilmot Proviso Controversy* (Chapel Hill, 1967), 38-51.

[15] Quaife (ed.), *The Diary of James K. Polk*, II, 334-35; *Congressional Globe*, 29th Cong., 2nd Sess., 541-43, 555-56, 572-73. The House reversed its earlier approval of the Proviso as seven northern Democrats changed their positions and six more failed to vote.

carrying New York in 1844, Silas Wright had agreed to give up a safe seat in the Senate and seek the potentially explosive office of governor.[16] Wright's candidacy had clearly strengthened the national ticket in New York, and Polk had carried the state by a narrow margin in a victory which proved decisive in his election to the presidency.[17]

The outcome of the election had clearly obligated Polk to the Van Buren wing of the New York Democratic party. Realizing that he could not have won New York without the aid of Van Buren and Wright, the new president had written thanking them for having "contributed so largely to secure my election" and asking for advice in filling several key cabinet posts. As a result the Van Buren faction had logically expected to play a conspicuous role in the new administration, and the evidence indicates that Polk held similar expectations, at least at first.[18] There followed long and involved negotiations between the Van Buren wing and the president-elect concerning cabinet posts — negotiations which finally ended in a schism. These exchanges were complicated by Polk's desire to avoid entanglement with any one of the major Democratic factions and to control his own administration free of commitments. On the other hand, many Democrats, including the Van Buren faction, took a rather patronizing attitude toward Polk and, thinking they could dominate him, unwisely lectured him on cabinet choices.[19] The results only added to the growing discontent of the New York faction, and a greater willingness on their part to challenge the national party leadership later.

The cabinet negotiations between Polk and the New Yorkers included the offer of the post of secretary of the treasury to Silas Wright

[16] Martin Van Buren to Jackson, September 16, 1844, in Van Buren Papers; New York *Evening Post*, August 21, 1844; Whitehurst, "Martin Van Buren," 54-55; Garraty, *Silas Wright*, 293-308; *Niles' Register*, August 3, 1844. The Democratic party of New York was hopelessly divided on state issues, but until 1844, Wright had been able to remain friendly with both sides. As senator, he avoided local issues, but as governor he could remain aloof no longer.

[17] Wright defeated his Whig opponent for governor, Millard Fillmore, by 10,000 votes, while Polk carried the state by only half that margin. See Garraty, *Silas Wright*, 326.

[18] Polk to Martin Van Buren, January 4, 1845, in Van Buren Papers; Joseph G. Rayback, "Martin Van Buren's Break with James K. Polk: The Record," *New York History*, XXXVI (1955), 51-52.

[19] Martin Van Buren to Polk, January 18, 1845, in Polk Papers, Library of Congress; Sellers, *James K. Polk*, 163-65.

and his subsequent rejection of it because of his recent election as governor.[20] The negotiations also included Polk's rejection of Van Buren's advice to appoint Benjamin Butler as secretary of state or Azariah C. Flagg for the treasury post. For these two key positions Polk chose instead bitter rivals of the Van Buren faction, James Buchanan to be secretary of state and Robert J. Walker of Mississippi for the treasury.[21] With this accomplished Polk tried to placate the New Yorkers with the position of secretary of war, which he offered to Butler. When the ambitious Butler rejected what he considered an inferior position, Polk unwisely appointed William L. Marcy, the leading member of the rival New York Democratic faction.[22] With the announcement of Marcy's appointment, it seemed to the Van Buren men that the president had surrendered completely to their political enemies.

The net result of Polk's patronage policy was to intensify already existing divisions within the Democratic party and to turn many against the administration. Polk had sought to satisfy the Van Buren wing, but had succeeded only in antagonizing it. It is true, however, that the determined president was under extreme pressures from other important factions in the party, and he logically wanted men in his

[20] Polk to Wright, December 7, 1844, Wright to Polk, December 20, 1844, in Polk Papers; Rayback, "Martin Van Buren's Break," 52-53; Martin Van Buren to Polk, January 18, 1845, in Polk Papers; Sellers, *James K. Polk*, 178.

[21] Wright to Polk, January 21, 1845, Polk to Martin Van Buren, January 4, 20, 1845, in Polk Papers; Martin Van Buren to Polk, January 18, 1845, Wright to Martin Van Buren, January 17, 1845, in Van Buren Papers; Norman A. Graebner, "James K. Polk: A Study in Federal Patronage," *Mississippi Valley Historical Review*, XXXVIII (1952), 618; Sellers, *James K. Polk*, 179-80.

[22] Polk to Martin Van Buren, February 22, 25, 1845, Martin Van Buren to Polk, February 27, 1845, B. F. Butler to Polk, February 27, 1845, Mrs. Butler to Martin Van Buren, nd, Butler to Martin Van Buren, February 28, 1845, in Van Buren Papers; Butler to Polk, February 27, 1845, in Polk Papers. The available evidence indicates that members of the anti–Van Buren faction were responsible for Polk's appointment of Marcy after Butler had rejected the post. Former Governor William C. Bouck and Edwin Crosswell both warned Polk against appointing any man suggested by Van Buren or Wright. See Bouck and Crosswell to Polk, February 18, 1845, in Polk Papers; Martin Van Buren to Polk, March 1, 1845, in Van Buren Papers. Concerning the Van Burenites' anger with Polk, see Smith Van Buren to Martin Van Buren, March 2, 3, 1845, in Van Buren Papers. In an effort to ease the hurt, Polk offered the ministry at London to Van Buren, but the latter refused. See Polk to Butler, May 5, 1845 and Martin Van Buren to George Bancroft, May 12, 1845, in Van Buren Papers; Sellers, *James K. Polk*, 200-204.

cabinet who represented his own point of view. He may have questioned how well the New York group could do this and he noted in his diary: "I cannot proscribe all others of the Democratic party in order to gain their good will."[23] Yet no matter how justifiable Polk's patronage policies may have been, he had unwittingly given the Van Buren men another reason for bolting the party in 1848. They could now take up the anti-extension cause more freely and willingly.

The interests of midwestern Democrats, like those of the Van Burenites, ranked rather low in Polk's priorities; as a result there would be a growing dissatisfaction with the president in that region as well. Ohio Democrats had felt they had a claim to a place in Polk's cabinet but were disappointed when they were passed by in favor of southern appointees.[24] More important, the president seemed bent on satisfying the territorial interests of the slaveholding South in regard to Oregon. In the view of many midwesterners, the president willingly accepted a compromise with Great Britain instead of pushing for the extreme northern boundary of Oregon, which the party had promised in its 1844 platform and which Polk had endorsed in his inaugural address. Realistically, however, Polk could not have expected any more of the disputed territory without recourse to war, for the proposed treaty already favored the United States.[25] In addition, the president deeply disappointed midwestern Democrats on the issue of federal aid for internal improvements. Many had assumed without good reason that Polk would support such a program, which would especially benefit the Great Lakes area. As a result the three Polk vetoes of river and harbor bills came as a deep shock to midwesterners and only added further cause for unrest.[26] Finally, when the issue of the expansion of

[23] Quaife (ed.), *The Diary of James K. Polk,* I, 104; III, 74; II, 405; see also Graebner, "James K. Polk," 626-27.

[24] The Ohioans had wanted Samuel Medary appointed Postmaster General, but instead Polk chose his own close friend Cave Johnson of Tennessee. Johnson to Polk, February 26, 1845, in Polk Papers; Graebner, "James K. Polk," 621.

[25] Porter and Johnson (comps.), *National Party Platforms,* 3-4; James D. Richardson, *A Compilation of the Messages and Papers of the Presidents, 1789-1897* (Washington, 1897), IV, 373-82. For the reaction of the Midwest to Polk's effort to compromise in Oregon see Holt, "Party Politics in Ohio," 121-22.

[26] Holt, "Party Politics in Ohio," 122; Theodore C. Pease, *The Frontier State, 1818-1848,* Vol. II of *The Centennial History of Illinois* (Springfield, Ill., 1918), 330; Arthur Charles Cole, *The Era of the Civil War, 1848-1870,* Vol. III of *The Centennial History of Illinois* (Springfield, Ill., 1919), 20-25.

slavery, first in Texas and then in the Mexican War territories, was added to the issues of Polk's patronage policies, Oregon, and internal improvements, there was ample reason for many midwestern Democrats to become discontented. Because the president did not feel the Midwest important enough to risk antagonizing Democrats in other sections, his policies served to intensify the already deepening schism in his party and gave further impetus to a third-party movement.

Those divisive issues of the Polk administration not directly related to slave extension provide additional insight into the background of the Wilmot Proviso. The Proviso was introduced by members of Polk's own party motivated at least in part by other issues. It was the result of the cooperative effort of several Democrats including Wilmot, King, Brinkerhoff of Ohio, and Wentworth of Illinois, all of whom had been alienated by one or more of the president's policies.[27] All were no doubt upset over the pro-southern orientation of Polk's southwestern expansion policies, but in addition, Wilmot, Brinkerhoff, and King felt that they had been treated badly in patronage distribution. Wentworth was a leading advocate of federal assistance for internal improvements, and Polk's river and harbor vetoes turned him against the administration. To members of the Van Buren faction like King, the Proviso provided the opportunity to exploit northern resentment against Polk and the South already created by the Oregon, patronage, and internal improvements issues.[28] All four men could doubtless see the potential

[27] Charles B. Going, *David Wilmot, Free Soiler* (New York, 1924), 117-41. Going argues that Wilmot was the sole author and was motivated by his hatred of slavery. Other explanations are offered in Craven, *The Coming of the Civil War,* 223-25; Stenberg, "The Motivation of the Wilmot Proviso," 535-41; Graebner, "James K. Polk," 627-28; Ernest P. Muller, "Preston King: A Political Biography," (Ph.D. dissertation, Columbia University, 1957), 364; Milo M. Quaife, *The Doctrine of Non-Intervention with Slavery in the Territories* (Chicago, 1910), 12-16. For Wilmot's own account of the Proviso's origin see *National Era,* October 21, 1847. By 1846, Wilmot had become disenchanted with the pro-southern orientation of the Polk administration and had joined the Van Buren faction. See Morrison, *The Wilmot Proviso Controversy,* 16-17, 180-81n.

[28] Clark E. Persinger, "The 'Bargain of 1844' as the Origin of the Wilmot Proviso," *Annual Report of the American Historical Association* (1911), I, 187-95; Graebner, "James K. Polk," 628. As early as September, 1846, Brinkerhoff claimed to be the co-author of the Proviso. See Brinkerhoff to Glesner, September 16, 1846, in *Ohio Statesman* (Columbus), October 2, 1846; Brinkerhoff to Henry Wilson, April 4, 1868, in the New York *Times,* April 23, 1868; Henry Wilson, *History of the Rise and Fall of the Slave Power in America* (Boston, 1874), II, 16. Wilson gives further support to Brinkerhoff's story. He and some later writers

of a Northeast-Midwest Democratic alliance, and thus all four had ample reason to initiate and support the Proviso completely aside from their anti-extension principles. With all four sincerely desirous of stopping the spread of slavery, a mixture of politics and principle thus combined to produce a highly significant challenge to Polk's policies.

When Preston King introduced his strengthened version of the Wilmot Proviso in Congress, observers predicted that it was a move of greater political significance than first met the eye. Many supposed and stated accurately that it was the work of the supporters of New York Governor Silas Wright. The first issue of the *National Era* carried King's bill and speech and said that they "may be regarded as defining the position of the Northern and Western sections of the Democratic party." The highly regarded Wright was already widely mentioned as the presidential candidate of the anti-extension faction for 1848, and rumors spread that King's speech was a calculated move to further Wright's chances.[29] With more and more northern Democrats alienated from the president and seizing on the Proviso to express their frustrations, Wright's potential candidacy was becoming an increasing threat to party unity.

Yet Wright's chances were not without their difficulties. His administration in Albany had been beset by problems from the outset as the opposing Democratic faction, known as the Hunkers,[30] resisted his every move. The Hunkers had won a major victory with the appointment of Marcy to Polk's cabinet, but the result was to increase the

---

assumed that Brinkerhoff persuaded Wilmot to introduce the Proviso because the latter was held in high regard by southerners and it would thus receive a better hearing. For King's role see Muller, "Preston King," 363-88. For Wentworth's role see Don E. Fehrenbacher, *Chicago Giant: A Biography of "Long John" Wentworth* (Madison, 1962), 244n. The only evidence to support Wentworth's claim that he was one of the originators of the Proviso is his own statement in the *Weekly Chicago Democrat*, January 30, 1849. See also Sellers, *James K. Polk*, 479-81.

[29] *National Era*, January 7, May 27, 1847; *Niles' Register*, January 16, 1847; Albany *Argus*, August 27, 1847; Wright to Dix, January 19, 1847, in R. H. Gillet, *The Life and Times of Silas Wright* (Albany, 1874), II, 1916; See also Garraty, *Silas Wright*, 392-94; Muller, "Preston King," 387-88; Quaife, *Non-Intervention*, 22.

[30] The group's success in attaining Marcy's appointment and other important patronage posts had earned them their name because it was said they "hunkered" after Polk's patronage. See Allan Nevins, *Ordeal of the Union* (New York, 1947), I, 190.

bitterness between the two factions as each fought for control of the state party.[31] In 1846, they withheld their support in Wright's reelection bid, and as a result he was soundly defeated by his Whig opponent. The Hunker inaction was due as much to their assumption that Wright was interested in the presidency on an anti-extension platform as it was to state issues, for as a group they agreed with Polk's position and wished to do nothing which might antagonize southern members of their party. Predictably, the governor's defeat caused some of his supporters in Congress, like Preston King, to press even harder for the Wilmot Proviso. The Proviso was thus the final impetus for the complete break of the two New York factions in 1847.[32]

Another indirect result of the New York election was to make Wright more popular than ever among the anti-extensionists for they now succeeded in picturing him as a martyr. Northern Democrats who supported the Wilmot Proviso looked to him as the most attractive presidential candidate for 1848, the man who could regain for them their waning influence in the Democratic party. And interest in Wright was not confined to Democrats, for Salmon P. Chase informed Preston King that the Liberty party was ready to support Wright on a Wilmot Proviso platform. By the summer of 1847, the Wright boom was well underway with many anti-extension elements both within and outside of the Democratic party actively supporting him.[33]

In August, 1847, the country was shocked to learn of the sudden and unexpected death of Silas Wright, who was stricken with a heart

[31] Garraty, *Silas Wright*, 338-39; Ivor D. Spencer, *The Victor and the Spoils: A Life of William L. Marcy* (Providence, 1959), 175-76; Walter L. Ferree, "The New York Democracy: Division and Reunion, 1847-1852" (Ph.D. dissertation, University of Pennsylvania, 1953), 13-14. See also William H. Seward to Chase, February 2, 1847, in Chase Papers, Library of Congress.

[32] Garraty, *Silas Wright*, 378-80; Whitehurst, "Martin Van Buren," 98-102; Ferree, "The New York Democracy," 22-26; Quaife (ed.), *Diary of James K. Polk*, II, 218; De Alva S. Alexander, *A Political History of the State of New York* (New York, 1906), II, 119.

[33] Wright to Martin Van Buren, November 10, 1846, in Van Buren Papers; Ferree, "The New York Democracy," 18-19; John Bigelow, *The Life of Samuel J. Tilden* (New York, 1895), I, 116; Thomas Corwin to Oran Follett, February 7, 1847, in E. S. Hamlin (ed.), "Selections from the Follett Papers," *Quarterly Publication of the Historical and Philosophical Society of Ohio*, IX (1914), 90-91; Chase to King, July 15, 1847 in Bourne (ed.), "Chase Correspondence," 120-22; King to Chase, August 16, 1847, in Chase Papers, Historical Society of Pennsylvania.

attack. Following the usual eulogies, many politicians now unrealistically assumed that had Wright lived, he would have been the candidate of a united Democratic party in 1848. Indeed, many who had hesitated to support him while he still lived announced rather hypocritically after his death that he alone could have united the warring factions of the party. To his anti-extension supporters, however, Wright's death was a severe blow. With former president Van Buren in political retirement, the loss of Wright left the group without a leader and unprepared for the coming political struggles. As Wilmot told King: "Silas Wright had left behind him no living man in whom is contained the same elements of strength and moral grandeur of character. He was the man for the crisis."[34]

Wright's death removed the last major hope of his supporters to reorient the Democratic party in the direction of anti-extensionism. As a result, his demise played a major role in their eventual secession from the party. At the state party convention in Syracuse in September, following a struggle between the factions for control of the party, the Hunkers triumphed and quickly nominated their own candidates for state office. More important, they also prevented discussion of the Wilmot Proviso. For them the need for national party unity during the coming election year took precedence over what little anti-extension sentiment they might have felt. But their opponents fought back, and in the confusion of the convention, one of the delegates invoked the memory of Silas Wright and spoke of doing him justice. A Hunker replied: "It is too late; he is dead!" As if to highlight the split within New York Democrats, James Wadsworth defiantly retorted: "Though it may be too late to do justice to Silas Wright, it is not too late to do justice to his assassins."[35]

---

[34] See John Niles to Gideon Welles, September 13, 1847, in Welles Papers, Library of Congress; E. A. Maynard to Martin Van Buren, August 31, 1847, Wilmot to Preston King, September 25, 1847, in Van Buren Papers; Garraty, *Silas Wright,* 407; J. D. Hammond, *The Life and Times of Silas Wright* (Syracuse, 1848), 722-31.

[35] Henry B. Stanton, *Random Recollections* (Johnstown, N.Y., 1885), 33; Albany *Evening Atlas,* October 9, 12, 1847; Albany *Argus,* October 4, 1847; *The Syracuse Convention: Its Spurious Organization and Oppressive and Anti-Republican Action. Remarks of John Van Buren, Etc., Etc.,* Albany *Atlas* Extra (October, 1847); Ferree, "The New York Democracy," 80-85; Herbert Donovan, *The Barnburners: A Study of the Internal Movements in the Political History of New York and of the Resulting Changes in Political Affiliations* (New York, 1925), 93-94.

In anger, the anti-extensionists threatened to withhold support from the state Democratic ticket, and as a result they received the name Barnburners. Like the Dutch farmer who burned down his barn to get rid of the rats, critics charged that they were willing to destroy the Democratic party to get their own way. To some, the term Barnburner defined a grasping selfish politician who sought to control the state Democratic party, with political power and patronage his only goal — a man motivated by a rule or ruin attitude. To many others, however, the term represented a renewed emphasis on the Wilmot Proviso, for after the Syracuse convention all other issues were of secondary importance. The refusal of the Hunkers to consider the Proviso at the convention served only to magnify its importance and surround its proponents with the aura of martyrdom. John Van Buren summed up the results of that meeting by declaring that the vote of the state had been put up "at the slave auction, to the highest bid of southern aspirants for the Presidency. For this purpose it was necessary to silence the vote of the state on the great question of Freedom and to give its mute assent to the aggression of the slave powers."[36]

It was John Van Buren, the former president's flamboyant and politically ambitious son, who directed Barnburner strategy in the ensuing months. Unwilling to accept the advice of older leaders, often including his own father, "Prince John" arranged for a mass protest meeting. Martin Van Buren, still placing party loyalty first, had complained that "the call of some of our well meaning friends for a *Mass State* meeting is so unwise and so directly playing into the hands of their opponents" that it should not meet. But young Van Buren was determined.[37] The mass convention assembled in late October in the railroad station in the New York town of Herkimer. David Wilmot opened the meeting by attacking the extension of slavery and stressing the importance of his Proviso. John Van Buren delivered the major address, a strong indictment of the actions of the Hunker majority at the Syracuse con-

[36] Ferree, "The New York Democracy," 107; Donovan, *The Barnburners*, 32-33. See also Nevins, *Ordeal of the Union*, I, 190. Nevins suggests that the name Barnburner was an allusion to the recent Dorrite incendiarism in Rhode Island.

[37] King to Azariah Flagg, October 8, 15, 1847, in Flagg Correspondence, Columbia University; Albany *Evening Atlas*, October 9, 1847; Martin Van Buren to Flagg, October 12, 1847, in Van Buren Papers; Whitehurst, "Martin Van Buren," 114-15; Morrison, *The Wilmot Proviso Controversy*, 81-84.

vention. Although the members resolved not to make separate nominations for the approaching state election, Van Buren charged that
the Syracuse ticket had been nominated by fraud. He announced that
he would not support it, and the popular reaction showed that many
others would follow his example. Hoping to use the issue to regain
control of the state party, the Barnburners proclaimed themselves to be
the true Democratic party of New York. Their defection, however,
clearly strengthened Hunker claims to legitimacy in the minds of national Democratic politicians. Significantly for the future, the Herkimer meeting adopted a resolution opposing any Democratic nominee
for the presidency in 1848 who favored the extension of slavery. When
the state elections resulted in a predictable sweep for the Whigs, John
Van Buren attempted to justify his course at Herkimer to his father:
"Mr. W. [Wright] is dead and I assume that you are sincere in not
wishing to return to public life. I can therefore, hurt no one but myself — and on my own account I will never submit to imposition and
rascality a moment."[38]

The split deepened in the ensuing months as each faction sought to
arrange matters so that its delegates would be the only ones admitted
at the party's national convention in 1848. Such recognition would
help each to legitimize its claims to be the true Democratic party of
New York. Some very practical political considerations thus combined
with anti-extension principle to motivate the Barnburners. They still
considered themselves Democrats, but would be willing to remain so
only if they could regain control of the state party machine.[39]

In at least two other important states there were also indications by
the end of 1847, that anti-extension sentiment was threatening Democratic unity. In Ohio where many Whigs supported the Wilmot Proviso, Democrats wavered in their loyalty to President Polk. Many had
been upset by the president's Oregon compromise, and a growing faction had joined with Jacob Brinkerhoff in support of the Wilmot
Proviso. While the majority continued to stand behind the adminis-

---

[38] O. C. Gardiner, *The Great Issue or the Three Presidential Candidates* (New
York, 1848), 50-72; Albany *Evening Atlas,* October 27, 1847; *Niles' Register,*
October 30, 1847; Donovan, *The Barnburners,* 96-97; John Van Buren to Martin
Van Buren, November 13, 1847, in Van Buren Papers.

[39] Glyndon Van Deusen, *Horace Greeley, Nineteenth-Century Crusader* (Philadelphia, 1953), 119; Donovan, *The Barnburners,* 97; Albany *Argus,* November 1,
1847.

tration, there were indications that the party was dividing into organized factions over the issue.[40] Democratic difficulties in Massachusetts dated back at least as far as 1844 when the party had divided into Van Buren and anti–Van Buren factions over the presidential nomination. The quarrel here involved patronage and party control as well as the extension of slavery. Marcus Morton led the faction attempting to hold Democrats loyal to Van Buren and to give the party an anti-extension character. At the state convention in September, 1847, Morton's group was defeated when its opponents tabled an anti-extension motion.[41] The frustrations of the anti-extensionists in Ohio and Massachusetts only added to the unrest among northern Democrats as the election of 1848 approached.

The same two states, Massachusetts and Ohio, were the scene of serious divisions within Whig ranks, and again practical considerations combined with anti-extension principle to create unrest. In Massachusetts where the discord was more significant, factionalism within the Whig party had begun as soon as Texas became an issue in national politics. While virtually all Massachusetts Whigs opposed annexation, there were differences in motivation. The manufacturing group, including older established politicians who dominated the party, feared westward expansion and the resulting loss of Massachusetts influence in national affairs. More specifically, they feared that increased southern influence in Congress would endanger the principle of protective tariffs on which the textile industry depended. On the other hand, they sought to maintain their southern Whig allies and avoid antagonizing their suppliers of cotton. By the late 1830s a younger faction of Whigs made up of men on the make began to challenge the established manufacturing elite for control. They added a new element to the anti-Texas movement, a moral opposition to the extension of slavery. This approach was naturally resisted by the manufacturers who feared it would endanger their southern alliance.[42] Also involved in the deepen-

---

[40] Francis P. Weisenburger, *The Passing of the Frontier,* Vol. III of *The History of Ohio* (Columbus, 1941), 436-50.

[41] Arthur B. Darling, *Political Changes in Massachusetts, 1824-1848: A Study of Liberal Movements in Politics* (New Haven, 1925), 342-45; Boston *Post,* September 22, 1847; Bean, "Party Transformations in Massachusetts," 27-28.

[42] The best and most complete account of Massachusetts Whig politics in the 1840s and the motivations of the two factions is provided in Brauer, *Cotton Versus Conscience,* 1-29.

ing factionalism, in addition to the issue of slave extension, was a struggle for political control of the Whig party and a challenge to the manufacturing group which dominated the economic life of Massachusetts.

While the two factions united behind Clay in 1844 in their common opposition to annexation, their basic differences in approach soon came to the surface. Not yet wishing to break with the manufacturing group, the anti-extension faction, known as the Young Whigs, nevertheless felt strongly about the moral issue of slavery and refused to continue to appease southern Whigs by avoiding it. They were also becoming increasingly upset over their secondary role in Whig politics. Whigs in both factions had at first remained completely aloof from the abolitionists, not only those of the Garrisonian approach who refrained from politics but also those who became involved in the Liberty party. The anti-extension Whigs felt that the Liberty party would never be strong enough to combat slavery effectively, and they joined with other Whigs in denouncing the third party's role in the election of 1844. Also involved in their attitude, however, was the feeling that the only road to political and social leadership in Massachusetts was through the Whig party.[43] Yet following Clay's defeat, the increasingly explosive issue of slave extension and the frustration brought on by their subordinate role in the Whig party combined to sharpen their differences with the manufacturing group and led to an eventual break.

As Congress again took up the Texas issue in early 1845 the anti-extension Whigs, unable to move the manufacturing group to firm opposition, tried to seize the initiative by calling a nonpartisan state convention of all persons who opposed annexation. Most of the manufacturing faction, led by Abbott Lawrence, Nathan Appleton, and Robert Winthrop, boycotted the meeting in fear that the abolitionists might seize control and obtain stringent resolutions which would antagonize their southern allies. The Young Whigs, led by Charles Francis Adams, Charles Sumner, John G. Palfrey, and Henry Wilson, worked successfully to prevent such an abolitionist takeover, and in the end the delegates adopted the Whig address which strongly denounced annexation. While the Young Whigs remained as much interested in control of their party as they did in anti-extensionism, lines

[43] *Ibid.*, 24-26.

of communication had been opened with Massachusetts abolitionists. An anti-Texas committee was soon created to continue joint agitation even should annexation be accomplished.[44]

Even after Congress officially annexed Texas, the Massachusetts anti-Texas committee continued the struggle, hoping that the lawmakers might still be persuaded to reject statehood for Texas because of its proslavery constitution. Although the Young Whigs feared the increasing influence of abolitionists on their committee, the deepening dispute with members of their own party had forced them to continue their informal association of anti-extension elements. The opposing Whig faction, on the other hand, was now ready to acquiesce in Texas annexation and statehood in its efforts to maintain their southern Whig connections unimpaired.[45]

The anti-Texas movement culminated in November, 1845, with a mass meeting in Boston which drew up another petition to Congress on the Texas question. Congress promptly tabled it, however, and in December admitted Texas as a slave state without a serious struggle. The Liberty party and abolitionist elements in Massachusetts now pressed the Young Whigs to join them in the formation of a more general antislavery league to keep the men of the committee together, but the latter were not yet ready for a complete break from the Whig party. They still opposed third-party agitation, fearing that an alliance of this kind would jeopardize their hopes of eventually displacing the manufacturers in the Whig leadership. The committee thus quietly disbanded, but the groundwork had been laid for future cooperation.[46]

The beginning of the Mexican War and the introduction of the Wilmot Proviso in 1846 gave the Young Whigs of Massachusetts the opportunity to renew their anti-extension movement. By this time also

[44] Henry Wilson charged later that Daniel Webster had been the instigator of the meeting but had lost interest when he found it did not meet with the approval of the Cotton Whigs. See Boston *Commonwealth*, July 14, 1852; David Donald, *Charles Sumner and the Coming of the Civil War* (New York, 1960), 136-37; Frank Otto Gatell, *John Gorham Palfrey and the New England Conscience* (Cambridge, 1963), 122-23; Brauer, *Cotton Versus Conscience*, 114-29.

[45] J. Daniel Loubert, "The Orientation of Henry Wilson (1812-1856)" (Ph.D. dissertation, Boston University, 1952), 42; Gatell, *John Gorham Palfrey*, 125-26; Donald, *Charles Sumner*, 139.

[46] Edward L. Pierce, *Memoir and Letters of Charles Sumner* (Boston, 1894), III, 103-4; Donald, *Charles Sumner*, 140-41. See also Martin B. Duberman, *Charles Francis Adams, 1807-1886* (Boston, 1960), 102-10.

the two Whig factions of the state had received highly revealing names. During a legislative debate, when it was suggested that agitation over the Proviso would injure Massachusetts business interests, a Young Whig, Ebenezer R. Hoar, responded that it was time that the legislature began to represent the conscience as well as the cotton of the Commonwealth. The anti-extension men gladly accepted the name Conscience Whig to distinguish themselves from the Cotton Whigs.[47] They also purchased a newspaper, the Boston *Daily Whig,* to continue their agitation more effectively. Charles Francis Adams assumed editorial responsibilities, using the paper to attack the Cotton Whigs for their southern connections and their support of the Mexican War.[48]

The Whig party's state conventions of 1846 and 1847 furthered the process of driving the Conscience faction into open rebellion. In the 1846 meeting only the dramatic appearance of the imposing Daniel Webster to argue the cause of Whig unity rather than sectional agitation prevented the Conscience men from pushing through a Wilmot Proviso resolution.[49] The results were naturally disillusioning to the anti-extension faction, and the *Daily Whig* charged that the convention had been the tool of manufacturing interests. John Quincy Adams concluded that "there are two divisions of the party, one based on public principle and the other upon manufacturing and commercial interests."[50] At the 1847 state convention the Conscience men lost again, this time with the defeat of their resolution, "that the Whigs of Massachusetts will support no men as candidates for the Offices of President and Vice President, but those who are known by their acts or declared opinions to be opposed to the extension of slavery."[51] This

[47] Boston *Atlas,* February 4, 27, September 30, October 15, 1846; George F. Hoar, *Autobiography of Seventy Years* (New York, 1903), I, 134; Wilson, *The Slave Power,* II, 115-18.

[48] C. F. Adams, Diary, May 23, 1846 in Adams Papers; Boston *Daily Whig,* June 1, July 9, 16, August 20, 1846; Donald, *Charles Sumner,* 142-46; Charles Francis Adams, Jr., *Charles Francis Adams* (Boston, 1900), 50-51.

[49] Wilson, *The Slave Power,* II, 120; Boston *Daily Whig,* September 24, 28, October 1, 1846; C. F. Adams, Diary, September 20, 1846, in Adams Papers; Donald, *Charles Sumner,* 147-48.

[50] C. F. Adams, Diary, September 20, 1846, in Adams Papers; Boston *Daily Whig,* September 29, 1846; J. Q. Adams, Diary, September 23, 1846, in Adams Papers, Massachusetts Historical Society.

[51] The convention actually did adopt a statement endorsing the Wilmot Proviso in all but name. The Cotton Whigs would have much preferred the position of the

latest rebuff convinced many Conscience members, including Adams and Sumner, that they had attended their last political gathering as Whigs.[52] It was becoming increasingly clear that only if the national Whig party should take the highly improbable step of endorsing the Wilmot Proviso and nominating a candidate pledged to it would the Conscience Whigs remain loyal.

With the deepening discord within Massachusetts Whig circles, many old friendships came to an abrupt end, and Conscience Whigs frequently found themselves ostracized from Boston social circles where they had once been respected members. This breaking of friendships brought on by the personalizing of attacks served to hasten the movement of Whigs into different political camps. Even before the convention of 1846, articles in the Boston *Daily Whig* had led to violent exchanges with members of Boston's foremost families. John G. Palfrey had written a series of articles in which he had harsh words for many of the Cotton Whigs and had thus strained relations with old friends. Charles Sumner got into heated arguments with Nathan Appleton and Robert Winthrop and was barred from Appleton's home. His furious exchange with Winthrop over the latter's House vote in favor of the Mexican War bill brought an end to all contact between the two men for the next sixteen years. Even the more cautious and respected Charles Francis Adams did not escape completely from these social pressures.[53] The Conscience Whigs having risked their positions in Boston society and having been ostracized as a result, thus had one more reason to challenge the manufacturing group for control of the Whig party.

national Whig party which sought to avoid the Proviso by calling for the acquisition of no territory at all from Mexico. The increasing demand for anti-extensionism in Massachusetts, however, forced them to endorse the Proviso in principle. Boston *Daily Whig*, October 2, 16, 1847; Brauer, *Cotton Versus Conscience*, 207-8, 216-18.

[52] C. F. Adams, Diary, August 11, September 25, 28, 29, 1847, in Adams Papers; Sumner to Chase, October 1, 1847, in Chase Papers, Library of Congress; Frank O. Gatell, "Palfrey's Vote, the Conscience Whigs, and the Election of Speaker Winthrop," *New England Quarterly*, XXXI (1958), 221.

[53] Sumner to Appleton, August 11, 22, 1846, and Appleton to Sumner, August 20, 1846, in Appleton Papers, Massachusetts Historical Society; Appleton to Palfrey, October 15, 24, 1846, Palfrey to Appleton, October 17, 1846, in Palfrey Papers, Harvard University; Winthrop to Sumner, August 7, 17, 1846, in Sumner Papers, Harvard University; Donald, *Charles Sumner*, 146; Gatell, *John Gorham Palfrey*, 133-34; C. F. Adams, Diary, August 11, 1846, in Adams Papers.

Another incidence of the growing rift in the Massachusetts Whig
party came when Congressman John G. Palfrey tried to block the
election of Robert Winthrop to be speaker of the House. Palfrey and
two other anti-extension Whigs, Joshua Giddings of Ohio and Amos
Tuck of New Hampshire, agreed to support no one who would not
endorse the Wilmot Proviso. Before the voting in the House, Palfrey
had addressed a note to Winthrop asking his position on the problems
of the Mexican War and slavery in any territory acquired as a result
of the war. When Winthrop refused to make any pledges as to what
his position would be as speaker, the three Whigs determined to withhold their votes.[54] The House finally elected Winthrop, but the votes
of the three dissident Whigs were the subject of much heated discussion and all three men were widely abused by the Whig press.[55] In
retaliation, Giddings charged that Winthrop had urged members of
the party to vote for the Mexican War bill which authorized the enlist-
ment of volunteers for the war and appropriations for its expenses. The
Ohio Whig thus argued that he was justified in opposing Winthrop
because he could support no man who advocated a war which was in
Giddings's mind clearly one to extend slavery. Although Winthrop's
supporters denied he had tried to influence anyone's vote, the evidence
indicates that Giddings's charges were correct, and the Cotton Whigs
could not deny that Winthrop had supported the war himself. This
in itself was enough for Giddings and Palfrey to justify opposition.
Although Speaker Winthrop tried to remain aloof from the controversy

[54] Palfrey to Winthrop, December 5, 6, 1847, in Winthrop Papers, Massachu-
setts Historical Society; Winthrop to Palfrey December 5, 1847, in Palfrey Papers;
Congressional Globe, 30th Cong., 1st Sess., 2; George W. Julian, *The Life of
Joshua R. Giddings* (Chicago, 1892), 221-22; Gatell, "Palfrey's Vote," 221; Gatell,
John Gorham Palfrey, 143.

[55] Massachusetts Cotton Whigs tried to exploit the fact that John Quincy Adams
had supported Winthrop and had even urged Palfrey to do so too. Charles Francis
Adams reacted bitterly to the actions of his father in this incident but felt that
the former president, old and feeble at the time, was simply being used by the
Cotton men to create divisions within the Conscience ranks. The younger Adams
remained faithful to his anti-extension principles and stood behind Palfrey despite
the abuse that the congressman was subjected to. See C. F. Adams, Diary, December 7, 9, 13, 1847, C. F. Adams to Palfrey, December 11, 30, 1847; J. Q. Adams
to C. F. Adams, December, 1847, in Adams Papers; Gatell, "Palfrey's Vote," 229-
30; Boston *Atlas,* December 9, 1847; Palfrey to Sumner, December 25, 1847, in
Palfrey Papers.

with Palfrey and Giddings, he assigned both men to committees where they could least effectively agitate on the extension question.[56]

The Winthrop controversy helped to focus attention on the growing isolation of the small anti-extension bloc in Congress and also served to bring its members into closer cooperation with each other. Both major parties regarded congressmen holding strong anti-extension convictions as unreliable agitators who endangered the political status quo. They gave these legislators as little recognition as possible, and Washington society frequently ostracized them. Consequently, they gravitated toward an informal group of their own. Included in the group in 1847 were Giddings, Palfrey, Amos Tuck, Joseph Root of Ohio, Senator John P. Hale, and Gamaliel Bailey, editor of the *National Era*. Their gatherings had an important effect in bringing anti-extension leaders in Congress to a mutual understanding and agreement on strategy, although they had the negative effect of allowing their opponents to isolate them more easily. The meetings were also significant because they put anti-extensionists from the East and West in contact with each other whereby they could discuss the possibilities of united action in the coming campaign of 1848. This opportunity was especially important in bringing together disaffected Whigs from Massachusetts and Ohio.[57]

Joshua Giddings led those Whigs of Ohio most upset over the extension issue and therefore most willing to cooperate with men in other areas with a similar disposition. A dedicated idealist who was less concerned than most with practical political considerations, Giddings was unable to develop the anti-extension faction of Ohio into a clearly defined group with unified objectives and goals like the Conscience Whigs of Massachusetts. Outside of Giddings's own Western Reserve, the majority of Ohio's Whigs were more concerned with party loyalty than they were with the Wilmot Proviso. The situation was further complicated by the desire of two leading Ohioans, Senator Thomas Corwin and Supreme Court Justice John McLean, to win the Whig

[56] Julian, *Joshua Giddings,* 227-34; Boston *Atlas,* January 27, 1848; Boston *Daily Whig,* March 18, 1848; Sumner to Giddings, February 3, 1848, C. F. Adams to Giddings, February 10, 17, 1848, Giddings Papers; James B. Stewart, *Joshua R. Giddings and the Tactics of Radical Politics* (Cleveland, 1970), 141-46, 149-51.

[57] Adams to Palfrey, December 23, 1847, in Adams Papers; Julian, *Joshua Giddings,* 236-37; Gatell, *John Gorham Palfrey,* 151-52.

presidential nomination with the help of backing from anti-extension Whigs. The apparent support of the Wilmot Proviso by each at first allowed the Giddings faction to become interested in their candidacies.[58]

Senator Corwin had first aroused their interests with a speech in February, 1847, vehemently denouncing America's role in the Mexican War. With presidential aspirations in mind he dramatically criticized the seizure of Mexican territory: "If I were a Mexican, I would tell you, 'Have you not room in your own country to bury your dead men? If you come into mine we will greet you with bloody hands and welcome you to hospitable graves.' " This bitter tirade called attention to the struggle over slavery in any territory which might be obtained as a result of the war.[59] The Giddings men were delighted with Corwin's speech and immediately began to urge his candidacy.

The favorable reaction of anti-extension Whigs was not confined to Ohio, for many Whigs feared that their party might choose an opponent of the Proviso. Many of the Conscience Whigs corresponded regularly with the Ohio men, and both groups now agreed that Corwin was the best possibility for nominating a man of their views. Adams and Wilson urged the Ohio senator to proclaim full support of the Wilmot Proviso, implying that in such event they were ready to campaign actively for him.[60] The interest in Corwin's candidacy was aimed at heading off the growing possibility that the party would nominate General Zachary Taylor, the Louisiana slaveholder, who was directing American armies in a war which many Whigs felt was being waged to extend slavery. Henry Wilson called on the Ohio Whigs to resist the Taylor boom even "if it breaks the party to pieces." Wilson suggested bolting the party should a southern slaveholder be nominated, and Whigs in the Western Reserve under Giddings's leadership, announced that they could not support Taylor. Giddings noted that the Taylor movement "has shaken my confidence in the Whig party more than anything that has previously happened."[61] Although he was still

---

[58] Holt, "Party Politics in Ohio," 143-47; Stewart, *Joshua Giddings*, 127-28.

[59] *Congressional Globe*, 29th Cong., 2nd Sess., Appendix, 216-17.

[60] Henry Wilson to Giddings, February 24, 1847, C. F. Adams to Giddings, February 22, 1847, in Giddings Papers; Ashtabula *Sentinel*, April 19, May 10, 1847; Holt, "Party Politics in Ohio," 160.

[61] Wilson to Giddings, February 6, 1847, Giddings Papers; Cleveland *American*, May 26, 1847, quoted in Smith, *The Liberty and Free Soil Parties*, 108-9; Giddings to Oran Follett, July 26, 1847, in "Follett Papers, III," X, 33.

very hesitant to bolt the party, only the choice of an anti-extension Whig like Corwin could keep him loyal.

Thomas Corwin was not the Wilmot Proviso advocate that many had hoped he was, however. His opposition to the Mexican War and expansion stemmed from a far different motive than did that of Giddings, for his primary concerns were the strength and permanence of the Union and the unity of the Whig party. He felt that the war, by raising the extension issue, endangered both, and he thus was as much opposed to the Wilmot Proviso as he was to the addition of new slave territories.[62] As a loyal Whig he also realized that a Wilmot Proviso candidate was not likely to win the endorsement of a united party. With Taylor the leading candidate, Corwin apparently hoped to make himself a compromise choice in case a deadlock should develop at the convention. In a September speech, he therefore appealed for Whig unity and attacked the Proviso, calling it a "dangerous issue." Noting the movement to bolt the party should a slaveholder be nominated, Corwin told Sumner that all Whigs must abide by the majority decision reached at the convention.[63]

Anti-extension Whigs were naturally disappointed in Corwin but still hoped that a suitable candidate could be found. Charles Francis Adams noted in his diary: "Mr. Corwin is evidently a sluggish timid politician, but I fear not equal to the commanding attitude in which we would place him. We must do with what we have." Although Giddings was not yet ready to give up on Corwin, Adams concluded that nothing could be done with the old Whig party.[64] Temporarily the anti-extensionists looked to Judge McLean as the man who might head off a Taylor nomination. Yet McLean was not interested in their support if it meant antagonizing the main body of the Whig party. He took a very cautious position on slavery and extension, arguing that

[62] Norman Graebner, "Thomas Corwin and the Election of 1848: A Study in Conservative Politics," *Journal of Southern History*, XVII (1951), 162-79.

[63] Cleveland *Herald*, September 28, 1847; Corwin to Giddings, August 19, October 12, 1847, in Giddings Papers; Corwin to Sumner, September 20, October 25, 1847, E. S. Hamlin to Sumner, October 26, 1847, in Sumner Papers; Corwin to John J. Crittenden, September 2, 1847, in Corwin Papers, Ohio Historical Society; Stewart, *Joshua Giddings*, 127, 133-34.

[64] C. F. Adams, Diary, September 8, 1847, and Giddings to C. F. Adams, November 11, 1847, in Adams Papers; Sumner to Giddings, November 1, 1847, in Giddings Papers.

the Wilmot Proviso was inherent in the Constitution and therefore did not have to be put into law. His noncommittal position would neither satisfy anti-extension Whigs completely nor turn them against him. But many correctly surmised that his political ambitions were stronger than his anti-extension convictions and that he was thus not a man on whom they could depend.[65]

With these developments in 1847, the anti-extension factions of the Whig party in Ohio and Massachusetts became more discouraged with the prospects of their party endorsing the Wilmot Proviso. By early 1848, Conscience Whigs debated a break with the party in order to join with anti-extensionists of other parties, should the proper opportunity present itself. Most would not be ready for the final break until after the Whigs had nominated; but discussions on the question were frequent, and there were signs of cooperation with Liberty men and rebelling Democrats. Gamaliel Bailey, whose *National Era* had endorsed Corwin's candidacy until the latter announced his opposition to the Wilmot Proviso, remained ready for a coalition of anti-extension elements while Salmon P. Chase expressed the view that the Liberty nomination of Hale in October, 1847, was not necessarily final and could be reconsidered if a broader based party were organized. Adams had become so disgusted with the Whig party that he was hopeful that the New York Barnburners, the Liberty party and the anti-extension Whigs of Massachusetts and Ohio might reach some common ground for cooperation in the 1848 campaign. Sumner predicted accurately that "the antislavery sentiment will be the basis of a new organization."[66]

The Conscience men did have some reason to be optimistic, for they had received an overture from Albany inquiring whether John Quincy Adams and Martin Van Buren might take the lead in an anti-extension convention. Although former President Adams expressed pleasure at the proposal, he pleaded that he was too old and infirm to take an

---

[65] Palfrey to C. F. Adams, January 13, 1848, in Adams Papers; Holt, "Party Politics in Ohio," 171; Francis P. Weisenburger, *The Life of John McLean, A Politician on the United States Supreme Court* (Columbus, 1937), 127-32; Weisenburger, *The Passing of the Frontier*, 460.

[66] *National Era*, September 30, 1847; C. F. Adams to Palfrey, December 11, 1847, in Adams Papers; Sumner to Chase, October 1, 1847, February 7, 1848, in Chase Papers, Library of Congress; Sumner to George Sumner, November 1, 1847, quoted in Pierce, *Charles Sumner*, III, 157.

active part. For his part, Van Buren remained in political retirement although he privately supported the anti-extension movement.[67] Nevertheless, the groundwork had been laid. Liberty men and anti-extension Democrats and Whigs had begun to think of abandoning their old parties to join in a new organization pledged to the Wilmot Proviso.

[67] Sumner to Giddings, November 1, December 1, 1847, in Giddings Papers.

3

The Free Soilers
Organize

In early 1848 neither the anti-extensionists of the Democratic party nor those of the Whig party had a potential leader who could arouse enthusiastic and united support. The obvious choice of many had been Silas Wright, for his firmness had expressed northern determination to oppose the spread of slavery. Wright's death in August, 1847, left a void which was not easily filled. Martin Van Buren had remained in the background throughout 1847, and the Liberty candidate, Senator John P. Hale, had only a limited reputation and could not be expected to command much Democratic or Whig support. John Quincy Adams, long in failing health, died in February, 1848, leaving only younger and less known Whigs to continue his crusade.[1] Unfortunately, there was now no one of significant national reputation in the anti-extension ranks to provide leadership, and for the time being the three groups were somewhat confused and disorganized.

The Barnburners of New York finally acted to end this confusion in a series of moves that led to their complete withdrawal from the national Democratic party and to the renewed political leadership of Martin Van Buren. Following the state elections in 1847, both Barnburners and Hunkers strove to confirm their claims that they were the true Democrats of the state by devising schemes for choosing delegates to the party's national convention which would exclude the other faction and establish their own claims to legitimacy. The split in the party

[1] Samuel Flagg Bemis, *John Quincy Adams and the Union* (New York, 1956), 534-38; Brauer, *Cotton Versus Conscience,* 226.

had already gone too far for either faction to be seriously interested in reaching an accommodation. Each was determined to control the state organization by itself.[2]

The Barnburner insistence on sole recognition by the national convention reveals much about their degree of commitment to the principle of anti-extension. Although they reaffirmed their devotion to the Wilmot Proviso, regaining control of the party clearly took precedence. When they chose their delegates to the Baltimore convention in February, 1848, at a meeting in Utica, John Van Buren stressed above all his group's party loyalty and its claims to be the legitimate representative of New York Democrats. Both Van Buren and the Barnburner platform pointed out that while they endorsed the Wilmot Proviso as the answer to the territorial issue, they would not insist on the national party or its candidate supporting this position. The Utica platform noted that the Barnburners did not have "any desire to prescribe a test in the Presidential canvass which might prevent the union of all who sustain the general principles of the Democratic creed."[3] The previous autumn at Herkimer they had agreed to support no candidate who favored the extension of slavery but now, sobered by the loss of political power and the approach of a presidential election, they considered party control in New York to be more important.

In April, Martin Van Buren combined anonymously with his son John and Samuel J. Tilden to publish an address known later as the "Barnburner Manifesto" or the "First Gun for Free Soil." Although it included a ringing defense of the Wilmot Proviso and the power of Congress to prohibit slavery in the territories, it also again defended the Barnburner delegates as the legal spokesmen of the New York Democratic party. Most important, it reasserted their uncompromising demand that they alone be admitted at Baltimore.[4] Van Buren later

[2] Ferree, "The New York Democracy," 137; Gardiner, *The Great Issue,* 74; Whitehurst, "Martin Van Buren," 118.

[3] Albany *Evening Atlas,* February 27, 1848.

[4] "Address of the Democratic Members of the Legislature of the State of New York," Albany *Evening Atlas,* April 14, 1848. The address is also found in the Van Buren Papers. Concerning the authorship of the document see Bigelow, *Samuel J. Tilden,* I, 119; Alexander Clarence Flick, *Samuel Jones Tilden: A Study in Political Sagacity* (New York, 1939), 82-83; John Bigelow (ed.), *Writings and Speeches of Samuel J. Tilden* (New York, 1885), II, 535-74. See also Martin Van Buren to John Van Buren, May 3, 1848, in Van Buren Papers.

suggested to his son that the Barnburners should withdraw from the convention if they were not granted sole representation. All attempts by the convention to extract a pledge from the delegation to support the nomination as an inducement for admission "should be repelled as insulting" and they must reject any effort to diminish the strength of the delegation by dividing it with the Hunkers.[5]

As the national convention approached, Martin Van Buren took a more active role in the Barnburner movement, and as a result party politics received more attention than the Wilmot Proviso. Throughout 1847 Van Buren had merely acquiesced in his son John's agitation or, as in the case of the Herkimer meeting, had advised against it. In early 1848, "the Little Magician" became an active behind-the-scenes participant, however, for the prospect of continued Hunker ascendency in New York was too much for a politician of Van Buren's nature to accept without a fight. In addition, in his mind the actions of the Polk administration required a Barnburner answer. Although the "Barnburner Manifesto" emphasized that the anti-extension faction had no candidate of its own, many Barnburners insisted that they should campaign for Martin Van Buren.[6] John Van Buren took the lead in forming plans to present his father's name, and he even suggested that if the convention rejected his suggestion, the delegation should bolt and make a separate nomination.[7]

Van Buren's answer to his son's request was a firm no. He pointed out that John's proposal would reveal a lack of sincerity and indicate that vengeance was all that the Barnburners considered. Such action would be a "rash and unadvised step which would give the Democracy of other free states to assume that you are indifferent to the general

[5] Martin Van Buren to John Van Buren, May 3, 1848, in Van Buren Papers.

[6] Thomas Hart Benton had urged an endorsement of Van Buren, but the former president was clearly opposed to such a step. See Dix to Flagg, January 16, February 3, 1848, in Flagg Papers, Columbia University. See also Whitehurst, "Martin Van Buren," 125; Ferree, "The New York Democracy," 120-23.

[7] John Van Buren to Martin Van Buren, April 20, 1848, in Van Buren Papers. Both Van Burens mentioned Zachary Taylor as a possible candidate should the Barnburners be forced to secede. This was because Taylor's political inclinations were not yet known, and he had indicated guarded approval of some Barnburner views. See *Niles' Register,* July 10, 1847. The February Utica convention had singled out Senators Thomas Hart Benton of Missouri and John A. Dix of New York for special praise. Dix was described as "a most worthy successor of the late lamented Silas Wright." See Albany *Evening Atlas,* February 27, 1848.

success of the party. . . ." Van Buren noted that the preceding five years had made his nomination and election impossible and that he had no desire to be president again.[8] Still a loyal Democrat, his response revealed that although he thought the Barnburners should bolt the party before accepting a Hunker takeover, he was not interested in forwarding his own candidacy to avenge his rejection by the Democracy four years earlier.

Despite Barnburner opposition to the two leading Democratic contenders, Lewis Cass and James Buchanan, Van Buren did not suggest that these opponents of the Wilmot Proviso be proscribed. If given full admission to the convention, the Barnburners should accept any nominee except James K. Polk. If, then, Van Buren did not seek revenge upon the national party, he certainly did want revenge upon the president. He noted that Polk's treatment of the Barnburners on patronage questions should not be overlooked. The president, he felt, had willfully humbled Silas Wright in order to lessen Wright's chances for the presidency.[9] Thus with Martin Van Buren in a key advisory role, the Barnburners went to Baltimore hoping to avenge Polk's actions and to obtain a Wilmot Proviso plank in the party's platform. Most important, however, they were intent on regaining control of the New York Democratic party.

At the Baltimore convention, the Barnburners made good their threat to secede when their terms were not met. After preliminary maneuvering the convention witnessed a bitter floor fight between the Barnburner and Hunker delegations, each claiming to be the only genuine representatives of New York Democrats. Each argued that its delegates were the only New York representatives chosen in a fair and open manner. In an effort to discredit their opponents, the Hunkers labeled the Barnburners political abolitionists, a charge which Preston King vehemently denied in an emotional speech. He argued that while the Barnburners did oppose the extension of slavery and would stand by the Wilmot Proviso, the convention should rule only on the validity of their credentials, not on their anti-extension principles. The Hunkers

[8] Martin Van Buren to John Van Buren, May 3, 1848, in Van Buren Papers. See also Joseph G. Rayback, "Martin Van Buren's Desire for Revenge in the Campaign of 1848," *Mississippi Valley Historical Review*, XL (1954), 707-16.

[9] Martin Van Buren to John Van Buren, May 3, 1848, in Van Buren Papers.

had the support of most of the delegates due to their willingness to placate the South on issues related to slavery, yet the convention was determined not to threaten party harmony by antagonizing either New York group. A united Democratic party in New York was essential for victory in 1848. In what it realized would probably be a futile effort to achieve this unity, the convention, in an extremely close decision, agreed to recognize both delegations and let them share the state's votes. Neither group was satisfied with the outcome, however, and each announced it would take no further part in the convention.[10] Yet before the Barnburners walked out of the proceedings they watched in silence, refusing to vote, as the party chose its candidate for president.

With the future success of the party already jeopardized by the New York feud, the convention finished the issue for the Barnburners by nominating Lewis Cass. The Michigan senator had played a key role in denying Martin Van Buren the nomination in 1844 and appeared willing to go to almost any length to win the nomination. He was, in the words of a contemporary, a politician who "supports measures because others do whose support he desires." Like many northern Democrats, he had been an early supporter of the Wilmot Proviso. Yet when that measure began to threaten a party schism, he abandoned it in the interest of unity and political expediency.[11]

To win the 1848 nomination, Cass knew he must oppose the Barnburners and the Proviso. Accordingly, late in 1847 he wrote a public letter in which he argued that slavery in the territories was a matter for the residents to decide, for Congress lacked the constitutional authority to interfere. Although this theory was not original with Cass, he more than anyone else was responsible for its widespread popularity.[12] Cass's doctrine could effectively appeal to moderates on both

[10] Butler to Martin Van Buren, May 29, 1848, in Van Buren Papers; New York *Herald*, May 24-27, 1848; *Proceedings of the Democratic National Convention, Held at Baltimore, May 22, 1848* (Washington, 1848), n.p.; Morrison, *The Wilmot Proviso Controversy*, 130-37; Joseph G. Rayback, *Free Soil: The Election of 1848* (Lexington, Ky., 1970), 186-90.

[11] Gideon Welles to ———, February 27, 1847, in Welles Papers; *Congressional Globe*, 29th Cong., 2nd Sess., 551.

[12] Quaife, *Non-Intervention*, 45-62; Frank B. Woodford, *Lewis Cass: The Last Jeffersonian* (New Brunswick, N.J., 1950), 253. Cass's public letter, which was written to A. O. P. Nicholson on December 24, 1847, was first published in the Washington *Daily Union*, December 30, 1847.

sides, for it evaded the question of slavery by leaving it up to the people of the territories. Thus the senator strove to be all things to all people; at a time when both major parties sought to avoid the most controversial issue before the country, his ambiguous letter had the effect of winning for him the Democratic nomination.

When the convention chose Cass on the fourth ballot, the Barnburners immediately denounced the entire proceedings. They then dramatically marched out of the convention in a body, leaving a stunned group of delegates to continue without them.[13] The convention had chosen the Barnburners' bitter enemy, a man who in their eyes had evaded the slavery issue in order to win the nomination. The party had surrendered again to southern domination and chosen a colorless, weak, party hack who had favored Texas annexation and now opposed the Wilmot Proviso. His nomination was scarcely less objectionable to them than Polk's would have been. This, coming on top of the failure of the convention to meet their most important demand, sole representation of New York Democrats, was more than they could accept.[14] They thus left the Hunkers to represent New York in a weakened national party and formalized the schism which had been developing for several years.

After choosing for vice-president another avowed opponent of the Wilmot Proviso, William O. Butler of Kentucky, the party then adopted a platform which effectively dodged the issue of slavery in the territories. It repeated the planks from its 1840 and 1844 platforms which said that Congress could not interfere with slavery in the states, but it said nothing about extension, the only real issue of the day.[15] The platform was, however, understood to repudiate the Proviso and could thus appeal to all but a few southerners who insisted on a positive guarantee of territorial slavery. Yet the Democrats hoped that by not mentioning the issue, they could keep the defection of anti-extensionists to a minimum.

[13] *Niles' Register*, December 13, 1848; Rayback, *Free Soil*, 191.
[14] Butler to Martin Van Buren, May 29, 1848, in Van Buren Papers. For a later expression of Van Buren's attitude toward Cass and his policies see Martin Van Buren, *Inquiry Into the Origin and Course of Political Parties in the United States* (New York, 1867), 354; Albany *Evening Atlas*, May 29, 1848.
[15] *Proceedings of the Democratic National Convention, 1848*, n.p.; Porter and Johnson (comps.), *National Party Platforms*, 11.

As the Whig party prepared to assemble in convention in Philadelphia it too was faced with a potential secession of its anti-extension wing, but it seemed even less interested than the Democrats had been in conciliating the dissenters. The major concern of the party instead was which of two slaveholders it would nominate for president, Zachary Taylor, the frontrunner, or its perennial candidate, Henry Clay. With the signing of the Treaty of Guadalupe Hidalgo ending the Mexican War in early 1848, the question of slavery in the newly acquired areas of California and New Mexico became all the more urgent. Most observers logically assumed that both Taylor and Clay would oppose the application of the Wilmot Proviso to these regions. With this unhappy prospect facing them, anti-extension Whigs in Ohio and Massachusetts concentrated their efforts on trying to find an acceptable alternative candidate.

By early 1848, the anti-extensionists had centered their efforts on Judge John McLean and hoped for a Taylor-Clay deadlock which might force the convention to accept a compromise candidate. That they would show such interest in a man whose anti-extension sentiments they had little confidence in is indicative of how desperate they were to stop the Taylor boom and of how deficient the Whig party was in prominent candidates who supported their views. In Ohio, even Liberty party leaders like Salmon P. Chase and E. S. Hamlin, the editor of the Cleveland *True Democrat,* indicated interest in McLean despite his refusal to endorse the Wilmot Proviso. In Massachusetts, the Conscience Whigs also had misgivings but considered him to be the only prominent Whig who still might publicly support their opposition to the extension of slavery. John G. Palfrey, among others, tried to persuade McLean to endorse their views, for the Conscience Whigs at that point were more concerned with the Wilmot Proviso principle than they were with political considerations. Judge McLean refused to make a commitment on slavery extension, but he continued to write letters to influential Whigs in the North bidding for their support. An expert in the art of politics, McLean preferred to straddle the fence, realizing that a definite position would most certainly alienate a large group of delegates.[16]

[16] Weisenburger, *John McLean,* 117-32; Chase to Sumner, February 19, 1848, Bourne (ed.), "Chase Correspondence," 128-32. McLean's position concerning

With the convention at hand and the selection of Taylor becoming more and more likely, the anti-extension Whigs became more determined than ever to nominate a man pledged to support the Wilmot Proviso. Most of them had never supported the "no territory" solution of Senator Corwin because they had enough of the spirit of manifest destiny to desire new lands. At the same time, they agreed that any new territory must be kept free of slavery. To carry out these sentiments the Massachusetts Conscience Whigs determined that their two representatives in the state delegation to the convention, Charles Allen and Henry Wilson, would actively oppose Taylor's nomination. At a meeting in Boston late in May, Adams, Sumner, Wilson, and others tentatively agreed that if the Whigs should nominate Taylor or any other candidate not pledged against slavery extension, they would withdraw from the party and nominate candidates of their own committed to the Wilmot Proviso.[17]

At their Philadelphia convention the Whigs did as expected and chose Taylor on the fourth ballot. The desired Taylor-Clay deadlock did not develop, and McLean's chances thus never materialized. Completely frustrated in their efforts to block the general's nomination, the two Conscience Whig delegates could do little except protest. Charles Allen rose to denounce the surrender of northern principles and warned, "The free states will no longer submit. I declare to this convention my belief that the Whig party is here and this day dissolved." John A. Bingham of Ohio then introduced a resolution in favor of the Wilmot Proviso but was immediately ruled out of order.[18]

slavery in the territories is explained in McLean to Palfrey, February 7, 1848, in Palfrey Papers. For Conscience Whig reaction to McLean see Palfrey to Adams, January 13, 1848, in Adams Papers. For McLean's maneuverings see McLean to John Teesdale, January 15, February 15, 24, 1848, in McLean Papers, Ohio Historical Society; McLean to Caleb Smith, March 23, April 15, May 10, 16, 1848, Palfrey to McLean, February 4, 1848, Caleb Smith to McLean, March 29, 1848, in McLean Papers, Library of Congress. See also Holt, "Party Politics in Ohio," 262-68.

[17] What the Conscience Whig reaction would be if the Whig party chose McLean on a non–Proviso platform was not clear, but presumably they would remain true to their principles and leave the party. Duberman, *Charles Francis Adams*, 136; Wilson, *The Slave Power*, II, 125; Pierce, *Charles Sumner*, III, 165; Brauer, *Cotton Versus Conscience*, 230-32.

[18] Wilson, *The Slave Power*, II, 136-37. The proceedings of the Whig convention are included in the *National Intelligencer*, June 8-12, 1848. See also Holman Hamilton, *Zachary Taylor: Soldier in the White House* (Indianapolis,

Thus the convention managers prevented a floor fight on the slavery issue and the anti-extensionists were powerless to divert the overwhelming majority from its determined course. The platform said little about the issues of the day and was especially silent on the most important issue, slavery extension. Although the majority would not support the Proviso, there could be little agreement on exactly where the party did stand on the territorial issue. Hence the platform confined itself to meaningless platitudes defending Taylor's qualifications as the Whig candidate.[19]

When the convention moved to nominate a man for vice-president, the anti-extensionists rose to protest the candidacy of the Boston industrialist Abbott Lawrence. An active Taylor supporter, Lawrence had commercial ties with the South and was expected to contribute at least a hundred thousand dollars to the Whig campaign. Some northerners opposed him partly because southerners endorsed him, and both the Webster and Clay backers turned against him because of his support of Taylor. Anti-extension elements argued bitterly that the party should not have "cotton at both ends of the ticket." An enraged Charles Allen declared, "You have put one ounce too much on the strong back of Northern endurance. You have presumed that the State which led on the first revolution for Liberty will now desert that cause for the miserable boon of the Vice-Presidency. Sir, Massachusetts will spurn the bribe."[20]

1951), 97; Oliver Dyer, *Great Senators of the United States Forty Years Ago, (1848-1849) With Personal Recollections and Delineations of Calhoun, Benton, Clay, Webster, General Houston, Jefferson Davis, and Other Distinguished Statesmen of that Period* (New York, 1889), 76. For McLean's role see Holt, "Party Politics in Ohio," 279; McLean to Teesdale, June 24, 1848, in McLean Papers, Ohio Historical Society; James Harvey to McLean, June 9, 1848, Elisha Whittlesey to McLean, June 12, 1848 and J. B. Mower to McLean, June 12, 1848, in McLean Papers, Library of Congress.

[19] Taylor had aroused considerable hostility among orthodox Whigs by his refusal to declare his support of Whig measures, and so the convention felt it necessary to emphasize his standing as a true Whig. The platform stated: "General Taylor in saying that, had he voted in 1844, he would have voted the Whig ticket, gives us the assurance — and no better is needed from a consistent and truth speaking man — that his heart was with us at the crisis of our political destiny." Realistically, little else could be said for the General. See Hamilton, *Zachary Taylor*, 97; Porter and Johnson (comps.), *National Party Platforms*, 14-15.

[20] Wilson, *The Slave Power*, II, 136-37; *Autobiography of Thurlow Weed*, ed. Harriet A. Weed (Boston, 1883), 578; Nevins, *Ordeal of the Union*, I, 194-96; Dyer, *Great Senators*, 79-80; William R. Lawrence (ed.), *Extracts from the Diary*

The convention ultimately rejected Lawrence and nominated Millard Fillmore of New York in a move designed more to placate the disappointed Clay followers than the Conscience Whigs. Many delegates felt that Lawrence could add little strength to the ticket. In addition, some Whigs believed that the anti-extension faction would bolt no matter who the vice-presidential candidate was, and they reasoned that the party could win without its support. The possibility that such support would be denied appeared good as Henry Wilson, referring to Taylor's nomination, warned that he would not be bound by the convention's proceedings. Amidst wild uproar, he declared, "Sir I will go home; and so help me God, I will do all I can to defeat the election of that candidate."[21]

The Democratic and Whig conventions proved to be the final impetus necessary to force the anti-extension factions into secession. Each had waited until the delegates had acted, for each included men who were loyal party followers who clearly preferred to remain in the fold. But neither could endure any longer what it felt was the culmination of a flagrant and calculated disregard for its legitimate interests and principles. Each now felt that these interests could only be protected through separate action. As a result each moved quickly to carry out its threats. On their way home from the Democratic convention the Barnburners announced that they would hold a convention late in June to nominate a separate slate of candidates. At a tremendous rally in City Hall Park in New York attended by twelve thousand, they shouted their determination to bolt the party.[22] In a similar way, anti-extension Whigs took the first step to put their angry words into actions

and *Correspondence of the Late Amos Lawrence* (Boston, 1855), 257. See also Hugh Maxwell to Appleton, May 16, 1848, in Appleton Papers; Thomas O'Connor, *Lords of the Loom: The Cotton Whigs and the Coming of the Civil War* (New York, 1968), 79.

[21] Wilson, *The Slave Power*, II, 136-37; *Reunion of the Free Soilers of 1848-1852 at the Parker House, Boston, Massachusetts, June 28, 1888* (Cambridge, 1888), 15; Webster to Appleton, June 10, 1848, in Appleton Papers; Robert J. Rayback, *Millard Fillmore: Biography of a President* (Buffalo, 1959), 184-86; Brauer, *Cotton Versus Conscience*, 234-36.

[22] Albany *Evening Atlas*, May 29, June 2, 1848; Dyer, *Great Senators*, 61-62. There is some evidence to suggest that the Barnburners were still interested in having Zachary Taylor lead their movement as an independent candidate since his position on the territorial issue was somewhat ambiguous. In order to persuade Taylor to run as an independent the Barnburners would have first to bring about his defeat in the Whig convention. For this purpose they invited northern Whig

even before they returned home. Henry Wilson immediately assembled some fifteen disaffected Philadephia delegates and proposed holding a national convention of all persons opposed to the extension of slavery and to the election of the Democratic and Whig candidates. The group then chose a committee to make plans for such a convention to be held in Buffalo in early August. That committee in turn quickly decided to try to interest Liberty party leaders such as Salmon P. Chase and thus expand into a broader northern movement.[23] The first steps had been taken to launch a new party pledged to oppose the extension of slavery.

The actions of the Democratic and Whig nominating conventions set in motion a series of June rallies and conventions of anti-extension leaders throughout the North and West, for neither party had considered its anti-extension wing important enough to grant it the concessions necessary to keep it loyal. The *National Era* spoke for many northerners when it noted: "We had thought that the Baltimore Convention, in respect to servility to slavery, reckless tyranny over individual freedom and disregard of order and decorum, had placed itself beyond competition," but compared to the Whig convention, it was "the very spirit of Freedom and Order embodied."[24]

With northern sentiments rising, Salmon P. Chase was the first to act in organizing a convention to protest the nominations. Many Ohioans appeared ready for a new party and Chase worked feverishly to activate these feelings. In the Western Reserve, hundreds of Whigs quickly repudiated Taylor and Fillmore, and eight Whig newspapers declared their opposition.[25] Chase, anticipating the probable results of the national conventions even before they met, had called for an independent free territory mass convention to meet in Columbus on

---

delegates on their way to their national convention in Philadelphia to stop in New York and attend their rally. There they hoped to persuade the delegates that a northern Whig candidate could do better than Taylor. In this manner Taylor would be freed for a third-party nomination, Cass would be defeated and the Barnburners could elect their own state ticket. See New York *Herald,* June 13, 1848; Morrison, *The Wilmot Proviso Controversy,* 146.

23 Wilson, *The Slave Power,* II, 142-44; Wilson to L. V. Bell in the Boston *Commonwealth,* July 14, 1852; Loubert, "Henry Wilson," 63-65; Stanley Matthews to Chase, June 12, 1848, in Chase Papers, Library of Congress.

24 *National Era,* June 15, 1848.

25 Smith, *The Liberty and Free Soil Parties,* 128; Albert G. Riddle, "The Rise of Antislavery Sentiment on the Western Reserve," *Magazine of Western History,* VI (1887), 145-56.

June 21. He was in complete command of the situation because Joshua Giddings, his only potential rival in Ohio, had refused to join in the planning before the Whig convention. Chase, the expert manipulator, carefully arranged the rally to coincide with a Liberty party meeting also being held in Columbus. Overlooking no detail, Chase planned that after an appropriate period he would lead his Liberty followers into a "spontaneous" alliance with the larger group meeting next door.[26] He had already contacted John P. Hale, who had agreed privately to withdraw as the Liberty candidate should a more far-reaching movement develop. With this promise secured, he convinced the Liberty group that fusion was desirable, and the two meetings combined. Over one thousand delegates attended including prominent Whigs, Democrats, and Liberty men; others such as Joshua Giddings sent letters supporting the movement. After listening to enthusiastic addresses, the members repudiated the Taylor and Cass nominations, adopted strong anti-extension resolutions and recommended the holding of a free soil national convention in Buffalo in August.[27] Ohio, under Chase's leadership, was thus the first state to act, but New York and Massachusetts were quick to follow.

Ever since the Barnburners had bolted the Democratic convention in Baltimore, they had been planning their own convention to be held in Utica on June 22. The major purpose of such a meeting would be to make separate nominations. John Van Buren had taken the responsibility of making arrangements and notifying Barnburner leaders throughout the state, most of whom agreed that separate nominations were desirable. Yet like the Conscience Whigs, the Barnburners had difficulty in finding a prominent man willing to lead a third-party ticket. Few politicians were willing to stake their futures on a movement with such doubtful chances of success. At first many Barnburners

[26] Giddings to Chase, April 7, 1848, in Chase Papers, Historical Society of Pennsylvania; Weisenburger, *The Passing of the Frontier*, 463; Smith, *The Liberty and Free Soil Parties*, 129-34.

[27] Chase to Hale, June 15, 1848, in Bourne (ed.), "Chase Correspondence," 134-36; Hale to Chase, June 8, 14, 1848, in Chase Papers, Historical Society of Pennsylvania; Holt, "Party Politics in Ohio," 288-90; Erwin H. Price, "The Election of 1848 in Ohio," *Ohio Archaeological and Historical Society*, XXXVI (1927), 242; *Addresses and Proceedings of the State Independent Free Territory Convention of the People of Ohio, Held at Columbus, June 20, 21, 1848* (Cincinnati, 1848), n.p.; Stewart, *Joshua R. Giddings*, 153-54.

preferred Thomas Hart Benton, but after an initial period of indecision Benton finally endorsed Cass and urged others to do so.[28] Many then turned to Senator John A. Dix of New York, who was prominent enough to have great vote-getting potential. But Dix opposed any third-party nomination and noted privately that it would be best just to vote against Cass and let Taylor win. This strategy, he felt, would be the best method for ousting the Hunkers from control of the New York Democratic party. Dix would not consent to run despite the urging of Preston King, John Van Buren, and others.[29]

All speculation over a candidate would be unnecessary, however, if the Barnburners could persuade Martin Van Buren to accept the nomination. All agreed that he could attract more votes than any other Democrat, but he had long since announced his retirement from active politics. As the pressure on Van Buren to run increased, he consistently refused. In his reply to New York City delegates on a request that he accept the nomination, "the Little Magician" expressed his "determination never again to be a candidate for public office." But he agreed that the Barnburners were justified in seceding from the Democratic party and taking whatever action they deemed fit at the Utica convention. Six months earlier he had advised against secession, but the possibility of using a third-party movement to regain lost political influence now seemed more feasible. He noted that the illegal rejection of the Barnburner delegation at Baltimore and the nomination of Lewis Cass, whose territorial policy was simply an appeal for southern support, left them no choice.[30]

[28] Despite Benton's dislike for Cass, he advised his friends that any third-party movement would be a mistake. He explained his views to Van Buren in a letter and then accompanied Cass on a campaign visit to New York. There Benton talked with Barnburner leaders and tried to convince them of the value of coming to terms with the national party. See Benton to Martin Van Buren, May 29, 1848, in Van Buren Papers; Morrison, *The Wilmot Proviso Controversy*, 147-48; Elbert B. Smith, *Magnificent Missourian: The Life of Thomas Hart Benton* (Philadelphia, 1958), 239; Thomas Hart Benton, *Thirty Years View* (New York, 1857), II, 723.

[29] Welles to Martin Van Buren, June 5, 1848, Flagg to Martin Van Buren, June 19, 1848, Blair to Martin Van Buren, June 26, 1848, in Van Buren Papers; Ferree, "The New York Democracy," 194-96; Dix to Flagg, June 5, 1848, in Flagg Papers, Columbia University; Dix to Butler, June 20, 1848, in Butler Papers; John Van Buren to Chase, June 8, 1848, in Chase Papers, Library of Congress.

[30] Samuel Waterbury and others to Martin Van Buren, June 16, 1848, Martin Van Buren to Samuel Waterbury, June 20, 1848, in Van Buren Papers; Gardiner, *The Great Issue*, 109-16.

When the convention opened, Van Buren's letter declining to run was read. It was clear from the letter, however, that unlike Senator Dix, Van Buren no longer opposed a third-party movement. The delegates correctly surmised that Van Buren was too much of a politician to remain on the sidelines while the Hunkers improved their position. They definitely wanted Van Buren, for in the words of one Barnburner, he was "the democratic statesman best qualified by talent and experience." The reading of his letter at Utica including his strong denunciation of the Baltimore proceedings was all that the delegates needed. Disregarding his expressed wish, they chose him by acclamation and hoped that their unity behind him would persuade him to reconsider.[31]

After nominating Senator Henry Dodge of Wisconsin for vice-president the convention then turned to adopting a platform. The finished product revealed that the delegates still considered themselves Democrats and that the Wilmot Proviso was not the only thing which motivated them. In an effort to show their loyalty they explained that only the "arbitrary and insulting conditions" imposed on them at Baltimore had forced them to withdraw, and "the democracy of New York" was therefore fully justified in making its own nominations. In this way they could rationalize that they were the only true New York Democrats. With equal determination, they forcefully endorsed the Wilmot Proviso: "We are uncompromisingly opposed to the extension of slavery by any action of the federal government to territories now free."[32]

[31] Before they made their final decision the delegates voted on an informal ballot and gave Van Buren sixty-nine votes to fourteen for former Lieutenant Governor Addison Gardiner and two for Dix. John Van Buren and several others voted for Gardiner in order to prevent charges that they were trying to pressure the delegates into nominating the elder Van Buren. See New York *Daily Tribune,* July 1, 1848; John Van Buren to Martin Van Buren, June 26, 1848, in Van Buren Papers.

[32] *Proceedings of the Utica Convention for the Nomination of the President of the United States Held at Utica, N.Y., June 22, 1848,* n.p.; Gardiner *The Great Issue,* 121-37 prints the address of the Utica convention which reviewed the causes of the appearance of factions in the New York Democracy. The address emphasized the alleged treason to Silas Wright by the Hunkers and the Polk administration. The rest of the document dealt with the necessity of limiting slavery extension. See Martin Van Buren to Dix, June 20, 1848, in Dix Papers; Albany *Evening Atlas,* June 23, 24, 1848; Charles Benton to Henry Dodge, June 27, 1848, in Charles Benton Papers, State Historical Society of Wisconsin; John Van Buren to Martin Van Buren, June 26, 1848, in Van Buren Papers.

The possibility of cooperation between the Barnburners and the other anti-extension groups became more likely when, on June 29, Senator Dodge announced that he would not accept the Utica nomination for vice-president. Since the convention had made no provision for informing the candidates officially of their selection, Dodge waited about a week and then, assuming he would not be notified, published a letter in the Polk administration's newspaper, the Washington *Daily Union*, declining the nomination. He explained that, despite his strong belief in the Wilmot Proviso, he would go along with the Wisconsin Democrats in supporting Cass's candidacy. Again practical politics had proven stronger than principle, but the way was now open to replace Dodge with a candidate of one of the two other factions and to broaden the appeal of the movement.[33]

The national Democratic party, and especially the Hunker faction of New York, was clearly disconcerted by the Utica proceedings. Led by the Albany *Argus,* they immediately charged that the Barnburners had acted solely out of a desire for political revenge. Realizing that a separate nomination would probably be disastrous to the Cass cause as well as their own, William Marcy complained of the Barnburners: "If they cannot be everything, they are determined that no Democrat shall be anything." The New York *Herald* feared that the movement would destroy the Democratic party and the nation, while President Polk characterized Van Buren's course as "selfish, unpatriotic and wholly inexcusable."[34]

The Whig party also had cause for alarm as the Conscience faction of Massachusetts held its protest rally and revealed its growing popular appeal. Five thousand attended their meeting in Worcester on June 28. Some of them were attracted by the chance to hear Joshua Giddings, whom the Massachusetts leaders had persuaded to give a key address. Sumner also made an impassioned speech in which he insisted that the old Whig issues were now subordinate to that of the Wilmot Proviso. He called the Taylor nomination a Cotton Whig conspiracy between "the lords of the lash and the lords of the loom." The speeches of Sum-

---

[33] New York *Tribune,* July 1, 1848; Welles to Martin Van Buren, July 3, 1848, in Van Buren Papers; Boston *Post,* July 3, 1848.

[34] Marcy to Wetmore, June 10, 1848, in Marcy Papers, Library of Congress; Albany *Argus,* June 27, 28, 1848; New York *Herald,* June 26, 1848; Quaife (ed.), *The Diary of James K. Polk,* III, 502.

ner and Giddings, which called for a new anti-extension party, were the highlights of a convention filled with ardent and righteous oratory. The rally thus proved to be the successful climax to the entire Conscience Whig movement. Following the addresses, those present choose delegates to go to the Buffalo convention. In an attempt to appeal for Liberty and Democratic support they divided the delegation equally among the three parties. The gathering had an air of excitement, and even the normally cautious, such as Adams, were thoroughly moved by its sincerity and predicted the possibility of ultimate victory.[35] There remained, however, the problem of agreeing with the other factions on candidates.

For a while after the June rallies, there was some question whether Martin Van Buren would accept the Barnburner nomination in view of his stated desire to remain in political retirement. John Van Buren tried to pressure his father into accepting by telling him that the Barnburners were determined to support him whether he wanted them to or not. He wrote: "I do not see anything in the Constitution which enables you to forbid our balloting for you." The former president ended the speculation on July 4 by tacitly accepting when a group of Barnburners held a strategy session with him. Having already committed himself to the wisdom of the Utica movement and the need for a break from the Cass Democrats, he was now convinced by the Barnburner arguments that his name would draw the support of more Wilmot Proviso Democrats than any other. Political considerations were clearly the major factors in his decision to accept the nomination. He knew that the national Democratic party and the Hunker faction would be punished in the process and would be forced to grant the Barnburners their proper place of influence in the future. As he became increasingly caught up in the spirit of the younger Barnburners around him and the excitement of another political campaign, he made his decision to lead their crusade.[36]

[35] Sumner to Chase, June 12, 1848, in Chase Papers, Library of Congress; Adams to Giddings, June 15, 1848, Sumner to Giddings, June 17, 23, 1848, Giddings Papers; *The Works of Charles Sumner* (Boston, 1875), II, 81; Adams, Diary, June 28, 1848, in Adams Papers; Boston *Daily Whig*, June 29, 30, 1848; Wilson, *The Slave Power*, II, 146-47.

[36] The only official acceptance of the nomination by Van Buren came late in July when he wrote to the chairman of the Industrial Congress, meeting in Phila-

Van Buren was, however, insistent that the Barnburners seek out
the active support of the Liberty and Conscience Whig factions in the
movement to maximize its effectiveness. Some Barnburners, including
Samuel Tilden, whose sole purpose was to defeat Cass to regain control
of the state party and who were not interested in a national movement,
had argued that the movement should be confined to former Democrats. In framing their call for the Buffalo convention the conferees
accepted Van Buren's view when he noted: "I had supposed that we
wanted every man who was opposed to the extension of slavery. . . . Is
not the vote of Gerrit Smith just as weighty as that of Judge Martin
Grover?"[37]

Although the Barnburners expressed a willingness to cooperate with
Whigs and Liberty men, it was generally understood that they would
accept no other candidate for president than Martin Van Buren. David
Dudley Field made this clear when he observed: "We have nominated
him against his consent and wishes, but having placed him in the position, we cannot, under any circumstances, abandon him." Field continued that the Barnburners would gladly give a Liberty or Conscience
Whig leader second place on the ticket, "but we must have nothing
to do with it if a different candidate for the Presidency is named."
Even though Van Buren informed the New York delegation to the
Buffalo convention that he would gladly acquiesce should the convention choose another candidate, the Barnburners were determined to
accept no other. As Tilden informed Chase, "It will not under any
circumstances be practical to change the position of the Democracy
of this state."[38] Because Van Buren's influence in a new party would
be too great to be ignored and because he would have the largest contingent of supporters at Buffalo, the Barnburners could assume that the
other factions would have to acquiesce on the candidate for president.
In addition, while the Conscience Whigs and Liberty men continued

delphia, saying he could not refuse to accept. Van Buren to A. E. Bovay, July 20,
1848, in Van Buren Papers, quoted in Albany *Evening Atlas,* July 26, 1848;
John Van Buren to Martin Van Buren, June 26, 1848, in Van Buren Papers;
L. E. Chittenden, *Personal Reminiscences, 1840-1890, Including Some Not Hitherto
Published of Lincoln and the War* (New York, 1893), 11-16.

[37] Chittenden, *Personal Reminiscences,* 11-16.

[38] Field to Samuel F. Lyman, July 26, 1848, in Charles Benton Papers; Martin
Van Buren to New York delegates, August 2, 1848, in Van Buren Papers; Tilden
to Chase, July 29, 1848, in Bourne (ed.), "Chase Correspondence," 469.

to struggle to find a prominent candidate of their own, the Barnburners had seized the initiative and were first to organize and name a candidate. This would greatly strengthen their hand in their demand for the retention of Van Buren.

Opposition to Van Buren was based primarily on the contradictions between his past record and free-soil principles. As vice-president, in 1834, he cast the deciding vote in the Senate for a bill to suppress abolitionists literature in the slave states. As president, he opposed the abolition of slavery in the District of Columbia without the consent of the slave states. In the *Amistad* case he tried, through an executive order, to force the black mutineers back into slavery. He endorsed the gag rule, a rule many northerners considered to be a gross infringement upon freedom of speech. He insisted that slavery in the South be left to the discretion of the southerners.[39] On the other hand, Van Buren had a consistent record in opposing the extension of slavery into newly acquired territories. In 1820, he supported a New York legislative resolution calling for the admission of Missouri as a free state. In 1844, seeking northern support, he opposed the immediate annexation of Texas, thus angering proslavery Democrats enough to deprive him of the presidential nomination. In 1848, he rejected the popular sovereignty ideas of Lewis Cass and instead supported the Wilmot Proviso as the best method to deal with slavery in the territories.[40]

Yet critics typically forgot Van Buren's record on slavery extension and remembered only his inconsistencies. The reputation of "the Little Magician" as a political opportunist was such that it was easy to assume that all of his actions were motivated by personal gain rather than principle. One dubious Liberty man noted: "He endorses with pleasure his proslavery administration, his most atrocious treatment of the poor Africans of the Amistad, his casting vote for the robbery of the mails. . . . How is it possible for an antislavery man to look one moment on such a ticket?"[41]

[39] Max M. Mintz, "The Political Ideas of Martin Van Buren," *Proceedings of the New York State Historical Association,* XLVII (1949), 422-48; *Inconsistency and Hypocrisy of Martin Van Buren on the Question of Slavery* (n.p., 1848), 4-14; Filler, *The Crusade against Slavery,* 167-69; Boston *Post,* August 16, 1848.

[40] Rayback, "Martin Van Buren's Desire for Revenge," 707-8; Mintz, "The Political Ideas of Martin Van Buren," 422-48.

[41] A. Willey to Chase, July 10, 1848, in Chase Papers, Library of Congress.

The part of Van Buren's record that most upset Liberty and Conscience Whig leaders was his position on slavery in the District of Columbia. In his letter to the Barnburner convention in Utica in June, he had noted that while he thought Congress had the power to abolish slavery in Washington, he was "very decidely opposed" to the use of this power by Congress. When Charles Francis Adams wrote to him to express his misgivings over this attitude and to ask for a less equivocal stand, Van Buren replied by standing firm on his Utica pronouncement. The Liberty newspaper, the *National Era,* said that it would be satisfied with Van Buren as the candidate if he would only leave the issue open instead of remaining committed to his old position. But Van Buren rationalized his unwillingness to change by explaining that it would look too much like "asking votes."[42] It was thus quite clear that the various factions would have difficulty in finding a common position on some important aspects of the slavery issue.

The Barnburners' unwillingness to compromise on Van Buren made the position of the Liberty party especially difficult, for it had already nominated John P. Hale the previous fall. Although Hale had privately expressed a willingness to withdraw should a broader movement be formed, the choice of Van Buren pleased few Liberty men. The *National Era* voiced their views when it noted: "We cannot but regret that the Utica convention did not take the lead in calling the Buffalo meeting, restricting itself merely to the recommendation of Mr. Van Buren as a candidate."[43]

Realistically most Liberty men knew, however, that they could not resist the Barnburners. Accordingly, Chase suggested to Hale that he publicly announce his withdrawal before the Buffalo meeting and allow the convention to make the final choice. The *National Era* also expressed a willingness to support any candidate the delegates agreed upon, providing Liberty principles were endorsed. Because of Hale's

---

[42] Martin Van Buren to Waterbury, June 20, 1848, quoted in Gardiner, *The Great Issue,* 114-15; Adams to Martin Van Buren, July 16, 1848, King to Martin Van Buren, July 12, 1848, in Van Buren Papers; Martin Van Buren to Adams, July 24, 1848, in Adams Papers; *National Era,* August 3, 1848; Martin Van Buren to Blair, July 26, 1848, in Blair Papers.

[43] Hale to Chase, June 14, 1848, in Chase Papers, Historical Society of Pennsylvania; Chase to Hale, June 24, 1848, in Chase Papers, New Hampshire Historical Society; *National Era,* July 13, 1848.

original reluctance to accept the Liberty nomination, he was ready to accept suggestions now that he step down. Accordingly, on July 13, the *National Era* reported that Hale would withdraw, but only on the condition that his Liberty supporters first approve.[44]

Quite understandably many of the Liberty leaders, including Lewis Tappan and Samuel Lewis, opposed any withdrawal before the Buffalo convention. They distrusted Van Buren and questioned the sincerity of Barnburner anti-extension views too much to concede the nomination without a fight. Hale, however, gave his supporters so little encouragement that even Samuel Lewis began to wonder after all if Van Buren might not be the best man on whom "to unite all of antislavery influence." Although some Liberty men, like Chase, were ready to endorse Van Buren, most were not.[45] Equally reluctant to accept Van Buren's candidacy, the Conscience Whigs also desperately sought an alternative. They did so, however, always with the unhappy feeling that the best they could realistically hope for was to balance the ticket with a vice-presidential candidate from their own ranks and to obtain an acceptable platform. Unlike the Liberty men, they could not even count on a substitute who was willing to lead the movement. In an effort to solve their dilemma they concentrated their efforts on Judge John McLean[46] but were embarrassed by the judge's unwillingness to commit himself. Throughout July, Ohio and Massachusetts leaders tried to persuade McLean to declare himself a candidate. McLean wavered. One day he wrote: "I am brought to the conclusion that I ought not go before the Buffalo convention as a candidate for the Presidency." Several days later he disclosed that he "might not refuse the nomination" if there were a "general upheaving" in his favor. McLean had apparently not decided whether he should risk his political future with the new party.

[44] Chase to Hale, June 15, 1848, in Chase Papers, New Hampshire Historical Society; *National Era*, July 6, 13, 1848; Hale to Lewis Tappan, July 6, 1848, in Hale Papers.

[45] Tappan to Hale, July 8, August 2, 1848, Samuel Lewis to Hale, July 10, 29, 1848, in Hale Papers; Sewell, *John P. Hale*, 98-99.

[46] Chase to McLean, August 2, 1848, in McLean Papers, Library of Congress; Adams to E. S. Hamlin, July 12, 1848, in Adams Papers; Stephen C. Phillips to Palfrey, July 17, 1848, in Palfrey Papers; Joshua Leavitt to Hale, July 1, 1848, in Hale Papers.

A politician with little interest in anti-extensionism, he would have to be convinced that the movement could be of practical value to him.[47] Nor surprisingly, McLean was not at all interested in the Conscience Whig suggestion that he accept the vice-presidential nomination on a Van Buren ticket. He was already under pressure from loyal Whigs who pointed out that if he expected to have a future in their party, he must either support Taylor or at the very least maintain a position of neutrality. On the other hand, Conscience Whigs were already promising that if he would agree to run with Van Buren in 1848, he would be the candidate for president in 1852. Sumner assured him: "Whatever may be the fate of the movement in 1848, it must surely succeed in the next election and all would gladly turn to you at that period as their chief." The appeals were to no avail. McLean lacked the courage to break out of the two-party system, although in continuing to pander to consensus politics, he attempted to rationalize his position on other grounds. He explained that "knowing Mr. Van Buren, I could never assent to identify myself with his political principles."[48]

As soon as the Conscience Whigs realized that they could not persuade McLean to run for vice-president, they began looking for some other acceptable Whig. Sumner suggested the president of Harvard, Edward Everett, although he was not surprised when Everett rejected the idea. Everett's reply included the basic argument against all third parties and one that would weaken the movement in 1848: "I think no one expects that the nominee of the Buffalo convention will be chosen. It is then a question between General Taylor and General Cass. I do not see how any Whig of whatever stamp can hesitate in that alternative." Other suggestions were made for vice-president, but there was no consensus. As the Buffalo convention opened, it appeared likely

[47] See Giddings to McLean, July 13, 1848, S. C. Phillips to McLean, July 17, 1848, E. S. Hamlin to McLean, July 24, 1848, McLean to James Briggs, July 31, 1848, in McLean Papers, Library of Congress; Dana to Jared Wilson, July 26, 1848, in Dana Papers; S. C. Phillips to Palfrey, July 30, 1848, in Palfrey Papers; McLean to Chase, August 2, 1848, in Chase Papers, Historical Society of Pennsylvania.

[48] Sumner to McLean, July 31, 1848, Stanton to Chase, July 28, 1848, Chase to McLean, August 2, 1848, Whittlesey to McLean, July 24, 1848, McLean to W. H. Denny, July 31, 1848, in McLean Papers, Library of Congress; Horace Greeley to Giddings, July 15, 1848, in Giddings Papers; Sumner to Adams, July 30, 1848, in Adams Papers; Weisenburger, *John McLean*, 136-38.

that the delegates would nominate Van Buren, but his running mate remained in question.[49]

The three June rallies in Columbus, Utica, and Worcester and subsequent events prior to the Buffalo convention revealed a very mixed assortment of people willing for one reason or another to cast their lots with a new party. These developments also indicated that there were many who were not yet ready to leave an established party and support a new organization which might prove unsuccessful and shortlived. It is almost impossible to generalize on what motivated men to join the new movement or not to because there was such a variety of causes and circumstances. A brief look at a limited number of the key figures, however, helps to reveal something of the complexity of human motivation. It also shows that there was a great deal of distrust among the factions, especially between the Conscience Whigs and Barnburners. In addition, there were factors such as practical political considerations, personal animosities and ambitions and provincialism, as well as anti-extensionist principle and idealism, which influenced the decisions of many.

The Hunkers could charge with some evidence that revenge was the dominant motive behind the Barnburner actions, but such an explanation is far from complete when one considers the role of Preston King in the movement.[50] King had been one of the original leaders in the House fight to approve the Wilmot Proviso, and at this point, compared to other anti-extensionists, he was somewhat of an idealist. Although he was moved in part by anger over Polk's patronage policies and the Hunker control of the Democratic party in New York, he never veered from his insistence that slavery must be kept out of the territories. At Herkimer, Baltimore, and Utica, King fought to justify the Barnburner movement, not only in terms of the desire to control the state party but more important in an effort to redirect the national Democratic party away from its southern proslavery domination toward an anti-extension stance. When the Baltimore convention proved that

<hr>

[49] Sumner to Everett, July 31, 1848, Everett to Sumner, August 4, 1848, in Everett Papers, Massachusetts Historical Society; Sumner to Adams, July 31, 1848, in Adams Papers.

[50] The only complete study of King's career is Ernest Muller's dissertation, "Preston King: A Political Biography."

would not be possible in 1848, a third-party movement was the only answer for King. While his feelings about a third party would change in time, during the campaign of 1848 he was one of the most dedicated anti-extensionists.

For many other Barnburner leaders, such as John Van Buren, state party control and the desire to avenge the party's treatment of Martin Van Buren were more important than the Wilmot Proviso. Although the younger Van Buren endorsed the Proviso, his interest in anti-extensionism was more a means than an end. His interest in the Proviso did not become apparent when it was first introduced in 1846, but rather not until the fall of 1847, when he realized it might be used to eliminate the Hunkers from party control. Revenge also crept into his thinking. He later explained his extensive activities in the Free Soil movement in terms of the story of a boy feverishly pitching hay, who when asked by a passerby why he was working so hard, replied, "Stranger, Dad's under there." What he implied was that this was the way to punish those who had wronged his father. A tall, impressive figure who was an especially effective orator, "Prince John" shared his father's sentiments that the Democratic party must not be permitted to sanction the spread of slavery.[51] For both Van Burens, however, such concern over anti-extensionism was motivated by political considerations. The Barnburner revolt in 1848 might be all the evidence necessary to convince national party leaders that its proslavery and pro-southern tendencies must be checked. Such evidence could then be used to reestablish Barnburner influence in the party both nationally and in New York.

Not all anti-extensionist Democrats were willing to join those bolting the party and enter a movement with such an uncertain future, for fear of jeopardizing their future political careers. Marcus Morton of Massachusetts was such a figure. A long-time supporter of Van Buren and a man who at least passively sympathized with the anti-extension movement, Morton now had close connections with the Polk administration as Collector of the Port of Boston. Several Barnburners had suggested

51 John Van Buren to Martin Van Buren, April 30, 1848, in Martin Van Buren Papers; John Van Buren to James S. Wadsworth, October 22, 1847, in Wadsworth Papers, Library of Congress; Donovan, *The Barnburners,* 112; Rayback, "Martin Van Buren's Desire for Revenge," 707-16; Morrison, *The Wilmot Proviso Controversy,* 82; Ferree, "The New York Democracy," 189-90.

that he accept the vice-presidential nomination of the Utica convention, but less than a week before the meeting, Morton attempted to rationalize why he could not accept. Although he supported the Barnburner position, he argued that he could not withdraw from the national party for fear of endangering the jobs of loyal Democrats under him in his collector's position. Nor was he willing to join in the rally at Worcester because so much of the anti-extension leadership in his own state had been assumed by the Conscience Whigs.[52] The traditional animosity of Democrats for Whigs would not easily be overcome. Although Morton was later to join the cause in a more limited capacity, his hesitancy was typical of many other northern Democrats and Whigs who let partisanship stand in the way and lacked both the courage and conviction needed to support the new party.

The most difficult problem for the Conscience Whigs to overcome in joining a larger movement was this same feeling of distrust of their political rivals and especially of Martin Van Buren. Charles Francis Adams was perhaps typical of the Conscience Whigs in his reaction. A lifelong Whig and the son of Van Buren's old nemesis, John Quincy Adams, the younger Adams would find it impossible to overcome his distrust of "the Red Fox of Kinderhook" completely. Since early June he had worked to prevent a Barnburner nomination, desiring instead that the choice of candidates should be left to a more inclusive convention. Adams's response to a suggestion that the Barnburners and specifically Van Buren would have to lead a third-party effort summed up his feelings: "We do not seek to make them Whigs. They ought not insist upon making us democrats, so far as obnoxious nominations are concerned."[53]

Yet Adams and other Conscience Whigs were so firmly dedicated to opposing the extension of slavery and breaking with the Cotton faction that they were relieved that the nomination of Zachary Taylor had given them an excuse for a formal break. Adams expressed elation that

[52] Morton to Field, June 17, 1848, Morton to Flagg, June 17, 1848, Morton to Martin Van Buren, June 24, 1848, Morton to B. F. Butler, June 26, 1848, in Morton Papers, Massachusetts Historical Society; Darling, *Political Changes in Massachusetts,* 334-37; Frank Otto Gatell, "Conscience and Judgment: The Bolt of the Massachusetts Conscience Whigs," *The Historian* (1958), 37-38.

[53] H. B. Stanton to Adams, June 6, 1848, Adams to Stanton, June 8, 1848, Palfrey to Adams, June 16, 1848, in Adams Papers.

the period of indecision was over and that a third party committed to their basic concern for the Wilmot Proviso could really begin.[54] As expected, the Worcester convention made no nomination, for the members hoped that at Buffalo they could agree on a substitute for Van Buren. Adams's close friend, Richard Henry Dana, a recent recruit to the Conscience cause, remarked, "All we ask is that we be not required to vote for a man identified with everything we have opposed through life, whose name we have rebelled against." Adams, however, was more easily reconciled to Van Buren's candidacy. He wrote to Palfrey: "On the whole things look better than we could have anticipated. The selection of Mr. V. B. is something of a trial but I do not know whether it may not be the means of raising up more friends to the cause than it deters." He and Sumner thus reluctantly accepted the Van Buren choice philosophically and began their search for a strong vice-presidential candidate to balance the ticket.[55] While the distrust would linger through the summer months, it would not destroy their commitment to anti-extensionism.

In their search for a substitute for Van Buren, some of the Conscience men hoped that Daniel Webster would refuse to support Taylor and instead accept a place in a new party. Yet an established position in the two-party system prevented Webster and many practical politicians like him from joining their movement and risking the loss of political influence should it fail. An early backer of the principle of the Wilmot Proviso, he had frequently been at odds with many of the Cotton Whigs. Despite his unwillingness to support the Conscience men in their earlier efforts to direct the Massachusetts party toward anti-extensionism, many still hoped that his own frustrations at the recent Whig convention might turn him toward separation. Noting Webster's silence on the Taylor nomination, the committee on resolutions at the Worcester convention made a bid for his support. Webster's son Fletcher attended the convention and invited Wilson and Allen to confer with his father. At this meeting, Webster reportedly praised the resolutions

---

[54] Adams, Diary, June 8, 27, 1848, Adams to Palfrey, June 10, 1848, in Adams Papers.

[55] Palfrey to Adams, July 4, 1848, Adams to Palfrey, July 2, 1848, in Adams Papers; Dana to Jared Wilson, July 26, 1848, in Dana Papers, Massachusetts Historical Society; Sumner to Chase, July 7, 1848, in Chase Papers, Library of Congress.

of the Worcester convention but refused any public endorsement. His silence lasted until September when he finally reluctantly acquiesced in the Taylor nomination. His decision no doubt relieved some Conscience men, including Palfrey and Adams, who had been highly critical of Webster's vacillating course in the past. Another factor in Webster's hesitancy was his unwillingness to join in a movement in which his former enemy Van Buren had a leading role. As the famed orator explained it, "I never proposed anything in my life of a general or public nature, that Mr. Van Buren did not oppose. Nor has it happened to me to support any important measure proposed by him. If he and I were now to find ourselves together under the Free Soil flag, I am sure that with his accustomed good humor, he would laugh. If nobody were present, we would both laugh. . . ."[56] For a man like Webster, who had dedicated his efforts to building an established position in the Whig party, however, Van Buren's role was more a rationalization than it was a real reason. Significantly, Webster had shown little sympathy for the movement before the New Yorker had assumed a position of leadership in it.

Fortunately for the Free Soilers there were northern Whigs with enough commitment to the Wilmot Proviso to be willing to risk their futures with a new party. Joshua Giddings of the Western Reserve of Ohio is an example of those who remained loyal to the Whig party until the Taylor nomination, giving it every possible chance to turn to anti-extensionism before bolting. Giddings had been an early congressional spokesman for the cause of the slave and in 1842 had been censured by the House for his outspoken defense of the slaves who had mutinied on the American ship the *Creole*. Yet Giddings had consistently turned down suggestions from Liberty party members to join their crusade. Despite his feud with the Cotton Whigs over his vote against Winthrop, he maintained his constant optimistic belief that the Whig party would nominate an anti-extension candidate in 1848. Completely dedicated to the Wilmot Proviso, Giddings idealistically refused to let political considerations change his decision to leave the

[56] Wilson, *The Slave Power*, II, 147-48; Moorfield Storey and Edward W. Emerson, *Ebenezer Rockwood Hoar: A Memoir* (Boston, 1911), 61-63; Sumner to Palfrey, June 8, 1848, in Palfrey Papers; Gatell, *John Gorham Palfrey*, 166; *Writings and Speeches of Daniel Webster* (Boston, 1903), XVI, 123-29.

Whig party following its Philadelphia convention. As a result, the somewhat naive and optimistic Giddings could not understand a political manipulator of Chase's nature whom he felt was using the movement more for political gain than because of a firm belief in its principles. Nor could he accept the Barnburners as he expressed his distrust of the "leading locos of New York."[57]

Despite this pervasive legacy of distrust and the great variety of motives, the three factions were about to unite in a new third party. Whether or not idealists like Giddings, Adams, and even King could work together with men motivated more by political considerations, such as John Van Buren, remained to be seen. Their differences helped to prevent their movement from being as effective as it might have been. Yet as they met in Buffalo, to a surprising degree they were able to cooperate sufficiently to put the Whigs and Democrats on the defensive.

A spontaneous, almost religious atmosphere surrounded the gathering at Buffalo, which opened on August 9. A crowd of about 20,000 packed a huge tent broiling under the August sun in the city park. Leaders had made a heroic effort to attract people by promising some of the most distinguished speakers of the day. Railroads had offered half fare from Albany to Buffalo for convention members. Antislavery men of every description from all the free states and three slave states (Virginia, Maryland, and Kentucky) attended. Several black men, including Frederick Douglass, were present. As one delegate noted cynically, "It was a motley assembly. Proslavery Democrats were there to avenge the wrongs of Martin Van Buren. Free Soil Democrats were there to punish the assassins of Silas Wright. Proslavery Whigs were there to strike down General Taylor because he had dethroned their idol, Henry Clay. . . . Antislavery Whigs were there, breathing the spirit of the departed John Quincy Adams. Abolitionists of all shades of opinion were there, from the darkest type to those of the milder hue, who shared the views of Salmon P. Chase." Yet whatever their motives and backgrounds, the speakers and the crowd exhibited a spirit of in-

[57] *Congressional Globe*, 27th Cong., 2nd Sess., 342-46; Giddings to Chase, April 7, 1848, in Chase Papers, Historical Society of Pennsylvania; Giddings to Follett, July 26, 1848, in "Follett Papers," X, 32-33; Stewart, *Joshua Giddings*, 73-74, 151-52, 153-55.

tense political excitement and expectation resembling the atmosphere of a revival meeting.[58]

It would have been impossible to satisfy fully such a varied group, yet the convention came close to achieving the impossible. Each of the three major factions had its favorite candidate — Van Buren, McLean, or Hale. Of the three, Hale was the most popular. Not only did he have Liberty support, but he appealed also to Democrats outside of New York and was the second choice of some Whigs. Had the tumultuous mass of delegates been allowed to vote at once on a candidate, Hale might have been chosen. But the convention leaders knew that the Barnburners, representing the strongest single element of the convention, would accept no one but Martin Van Buren and that the support of the New Yorkers was essential if the movement were to have any appreciable effect. Those in control, including Salmon P. Chase, Van Buren's old law partner Benjamin F. Butler, and Preston King, recognized the superior prestige and vote-getting ability of a former president, and they therefore arranged a delay in the proceedings so as to prevent the possibility of a Hale victory.[59]

As is often the case in third-party movements, while lofty idealism moved many of the participants, canny and practical politicians were pulling wires in the background. Thirty years later, Charles Francis Adams, the president of the convention, was mistaken when he wrote that no other convention had surpassed this one "for plain downright

[58] Numerous accounts of the convention are available. Among the more significant primary descriptions are: "Official Proceedings of the National Free Soil Convention Assembled at Buffalo, N.Y., August 9th and 10th, 1848," (Buffalo *Republic* Extra); Gardiner, *The Great Issue*, 137-41; Oliver Dyer, *Phonographic Report of the Proceedings of the National Free Soil Convention at Buffalo, N.Y., August 9th and 10th, 1848* (Buffalo, 1848); Adams, Diary, August 9, 10, 1848, in Adams Papers; Dana, Journal, August 9-11, 1848, in Dana Papers. Important secondary accounts include: Smith, *The Liberty and Free Soil Parties*, 138-43; Nevins, *Ordeal of the Union*, I, 206-8; Stanton, *Random Recollections*, 162-63; Donovan, *The Barnburners*, 105; Dyer, *Great Senators*, 95-103; John Hubbell, "The National Free Soil Convention of '48 Held in Buffalo," *Publications of the Buffalo Historical Society*, IV (1896), 147-62; Julian, *Political Recollections*, 57-58; Sewell, *John P. Hale*, 99-103; Rayback, *Free Soil*, 224-30; Charles H. Wesley, "The Participation of Negroes in Antislavery Political Parties," *Journal of Negro History*, XXIX (1944), 53. See Madison *Observer* (N.Y.), August 1, 1848, quoted in Harlow, *Gerrit Smith*, 186.

[59] "Official Proceedings of the National Free Soil Convention," 2; Dyer, *Great Senators*, 96; Smith, *The Liberty and Free Soil Parties*, 138-39.

honesty of purpose, to effect high ends without a whisper of bargain
and sale." Adams did not understand or at least was not willing to
admit what actually occurred behind the scenes. In order to forestall
an early vote, the Barnburners introduced a mass of preliminary business and allowed numerous speakers ample time. A committee on resolutions headed by Benjamin F. Butler then adjourned to draft a platform. As Adams himself noted in his diary: "When it was proposed
to proceed to nominate a candidate, there was evident a nervous flut-
tering which laboured to put it off."[60] In effect Adams was indirectly
admitting that there were factors more important than idealism which
controlled the events at Buffalo.

As it became apparent that the huge crowd would make it difficult
to transact business and also might unduly influence the delegates' decisions, Preston King, chairman of the committee on organization,
proposed that a special committee of conferees made up of the official
delegates would meet separately. After careful deliberation it would
make recommendations which the mass meeting could either accept
or reject. In order that the three factions be represented as fairly as
possible it had been decided beforehand that the delegates to the convention would include six at large from each state and three from each
congressional district, chosen so as to provide "equal representation to
each of the three former political parties." While the delegates delib-
erated, the mass convention, presided over by Charles Francis Adams,
would continue to meet under the big tent and listen to impassioned
antislavery speeches.[61] Thus while Adams and the twenty thousand
could feel they had a real role in the proceedings, the major decisions
of the convention were made behind closed doors by the four hundred
and sixty-six conferees. As Richard Henry Dana recorded of the latter's
meeting place: "It has no galleries, and none are admitted but delegates, not even reporters."[62]

Yet even before the conferees assembled at the Universalist Church,

---

[60] Adams, *Charles Francis Adams,* 90; "Official Proceedings of the National
Free Soil Convention," 2-3; Gardiner, *The Great Issue,* 138-39; Dyer, *Great
Senators,* 98-99; Adams, Diary, August 9, 1848, in Adams Papers; Ferree, "The
New York Democracy," 212-13.
[61] Richard Henry Dana, Jr., *Speeches in Stirring Times and Letters to a Son*
(Boston, 1910), 152; Gardiner, *The Great Issue,* 138.
[62] Dana, Journal, August 9, 1848, in Dana Papers.

a much smaller group of Liberty and Barnburner leaders had agreed on a compromise which would determine the outcome. At a meeting of the committee on organization the night before the convention opened, Salmon P. Chase, along with two other prominent Liberty leaders, Joshua Leavitt of Massachusetts and Henry B. Stanton of New York, had maneuvered to let those Barnburners with whom they most agreed on slavery issues propose the platform. In an attempt to arrange a bargain of strong resolutions in return for acquiescence in Van Buren's candidacy, Chase later explained his strategy: "Knowing Mr. Preston King's sentiment I took the liberty of calling upon him for a speech, and at its conclusion moved that he be requested to reduce its leading proposition to writing, and that his speech should be considered as the platform recommended by the meeting." Chase's proposal had the desired effect for the motion was unanimously approved.[63]

Ideological factors were thus considered in drafting a platform, but in return some very practical political necessities would determine the choice of the presidential candidate. It is safe to presume that Chase promised Liberty help in nominating Van Buren in return for Barnburner support for the King proposals. Realizing that the New Yorkers were more concerned about the candidate than the platform, Chase succeeded in having a prominent Barnburner propose a set of principles that Liberty men could endorse. He no doubt realized that many Barnburners were still concerned with using the movement to regain control of the New York Democratic party after the election and only with Van Buren in the lead could they make a strong enough showing in New York to make this possible. More concerned with politics than principle himself, Chase could easily accept without question the Barnburner motivation.[64] In order to assure the delegates that no bargain had been arranged and to give the appearance of a completely open convention, however, the committee members agreed with

[63] Chase to J. T. Trowbridge, March 21, 1864, quoted in Warden, *Salmon P. Chase,* 318-19; Chase to James W. Taylor, August 15, 1848, in Chase Papers, Historical Society of Pennsylvania; Dyer, *Phonographic Report,* 5; Morrison, *The Wilmot Proviso Controversy,* 152-53.

[64] Barnburner interest in using the state elections of 1848 to regain a foothold in the New York Democracy can be seen in Van Buren's letter to John A. Dix, October 2, 1848, in Dix Papers. See also Martin Van Buren to John Van Buren, May 3, 1848, in Van Buren Papers.

Van Buren's associate, Benjamin F. Butler, that the names of both Hale and Van Buren would be placed before the delegates. All would then abide by their decision. Thus the nominations of earlier Barn-burner and Liberty conventions were not to be considered binding. As Stanton later rationalized to Hale: "After becoming satisfied you could not be nominated . . . in order to bring the supporters of Mr. Van Buren to agree to give us a thorough Liberty platform . . . we agreed on our part to reconcile all our friends to his nomination (provided the choice fell on him) and make it harmonious and unanimous if possible."[65]

Before the delegates' meeting proceeded to nominate, it chose Chase as its chairman, and the committee on resolutions headed by Butler submitted the platform. Chase himself had taken most of the responsibility for its drafting, using his own and King's ideas. Together they had prepared a series of planks designed to appeal to every possible dissident group except the abolitionists. This adroit mixture, which included many planks unrelated to slavery, was summed up in the famous concluding slogan: "Free soil, free speech, free labor and free men!" To appeal to the Whigs the platform called for federal funds for internal improvements. To please Democrats, it demanded the election of all civil officials and a tariff for revenue only. In order not to needlessly antagonize potential Whig supporters, the tariff plank called for duties which would "raise revenue adequate to defray the necessary expenses of the Federal Government, and to pay annual installments of our debt and the interest thereon." To please farmers, eastern workers, and land reformers it called for a homestead bill to include a "free grant to actual settlers."[66]

On the most important issue of slavery, the platform was designed to satisfy the Liberty men. It endorsed the Wilmot Proviso by declaring that Congress had no power to extend slavery and must in fact prohibit its extension, thus returning to the principle of the Northwest Ordinance of 1787. Equally important, in reference to the District of Columbia, Chase used a concept he had long advocated: "It is the

[65] Smith, *The Liberty and Free Soil Parties,* 139; Dyer, *Great Senators,* 99; Stanton to Hale, August 20, 1848, Leavitt to Hale, August 22, 1848, in Hale Papers; Sewell, *John P. Hale,* 101.

[66] For the complete Free Soil platform, see Appendix A. For a complete discussion of the land reform issue see Rayback, *Free Soil,* 220-22.

duty of the Federal Government to relieve itself from all responsibility for the existence of slavery wherever that government possesses constitutional power to legislate on that subject and is thus responsible for its existence." The "slave power" should be confronted with a firm promise: "No more slave states, no more slavery territory and no more compromises with slavery anywhere." There were, however, differences in the positions of the Free Soil and Liberty parties on the issue of the power of the federal government to deal with slavery. While the Liberty platform of 1844 contained no direct demand that Congress eliminate slavery in the states, it did not include an outright denial of that power as did the Free Soil platform of 1848. In addition, the Free Soilers omitted any mention of the three-fifths and fugitive slave clauses of the Constitution which the Liberty platform had denounced. Nor did they include any demand for equal rights for blacks in the North. Thus while the new party was firm on the extension issue it did not conform to the necessary terms of those abolitionists who had formed the Liberty League. They had demanded an attack on slavery everywhere and an easing of racial discrimination. But the Liberty men present did not argue these points and were highly satisfied with the finished product.[67] From a practical point of view to include any of these proposals would alienate many more voters than it would please, and few Free Soil leaders were sufficiently ideologically inclined to go that far anyway.

Rather than debating the proposed platform, the delegates ratified it by acclamation and submitted it to the mass convention. There, as Adams noted, the resolutions "were vehemently applauded and after I put the question on them, there arose such a shout, and waving of hats, handkerchiefs, and all conceivable things as might have been distinctly heard in every part of Buffalo." Thus in neither convention was there any opportunity to debate the various planks, although the platform surely pleased most of the participants. The delegates' meeting then turned to the nominations, a procedure which allowed Richard Henry Dana to discover proof of the "determination and principle of the Convention." Dana noted, "We would not permit the subject

[67] Gardiner, *The Great Issue*, 138-40; Smith, *The Liberty and Free Soil Parties*, 140; Porter and Johnson (comps.), *National Party Platforms*, 13-14; Dyer, *Phonographic Report*, 5.

of the Presidency to be stirred, we would not suffer a man to speak on
the Presidency, until we had adopted a Platform of Principles." Like
Adams, Dana was unwilling to admit that a small group had already
struck a bargain and had left little choice to the delegates.[68]

When the convention proceeded to nominate, the first name mentioned was that of Judge John McLean. Immediately, Salmon P.
Chase withdrew the judge's name, explaining that this was McLean's
wish.[69] This action surprised and disappointed many Conscience Whigs,
and some charged later that Chase had acted without McLean's au-
thorization. Chase later wrote to McLean that he could have been
nominated had he permitted his name to be entered. Although both
Chase and McLean knew this was untrue, the judge's conduct before
the convention had been so vacillating and contradictory that all were
confused, and Chase probably acted in good faith when he removed
his name. More important, however, Chase was definitely in the Van
Buren camp by this time and definitely had an ulterior motive in wishing to see the bargain completed.[70]

Butler and Stanton, knowing that Van Buren's nomination had already been virtually assured, then explained rather hypocritically the
willingness of both the former president and John P. Hale to abide by
whatever decision the convention reached. Butler read a letter from
Van Buren offering to withdraw if it would help to achieve unity. This
supposedly open-handed gesture in abandoning the Utica nomination
made it possible for some Whigs to accept him more readily, for as
Dana explained it, "This was the turning point of the Convention for
me. Mass. Whigs had determined not to go into the ballot unless
the Democrats came in on equal terms and took with us the chances of
the nomination." Butler then launched into a long discourse designed
to convince the members that Van Buren would be nothing less than
a providential candidate. He would surely accept a nomination if the

---

[68] Adams, Diary, August 10, 1848, in Adams Papers; Dana, Journal, August
10, 1848, in Dana Papers; Dana, *Speeches in Stirring Times,* 153.

[69] Dana, Journal, August 10, 1848, in Dana Papers; Adams, Diary, August 10,
1848, December 9, 1851, in Adams Papers.

[70] Chase to McLean, August 12, 1848, August 13, 1852, in McLean Papers,
Library of Congress; Weisenburger, *John McLean,* 138; Duberman, *Charles
Francis Adams,* 150; *Reunion of the Free Soilers of 1848 at Downer Landing,
Higham, Mass., Aug. 9, 1877* (Boston, 1877), 24.

delegates offered it unanimously. In portraying the homely virtues of his candidate, the New Yorker gave a picturesque description of Van Buren's pride in his fields of grain, cabbages, and turnips. As he continued, "A tall, gaunt delegate from Ohio shrieked out, 'Damn his cabbages and turnips! What does he say about abolition in the Deestrick of Columby?' " Butler, equal to the occasion, adroitly sidestepped what could have been an embarrassing moment. Although avoiding a direct commitment, he indicated, accurately as it turned out, that Van Buren would accept the platform despite his earlier position on slavery in Washington. With this assurance, the delegates responded enthusiastically.[71]

The members then proceeded to the balloting, with Van Buren and Hale as the only serious contenders. On the first informal ballot most but not all of the Liberty men supported Hale, while all the Barnburners endorsed Van Buren. The balance of power was thus held by the Conscience Whigs, and most of them voted for the former president. With a few Liberty men including Chase and Stanton also supporting him, Van Buren had a clear majority, receiving 244 votes to Hale's 183. Joshua Giddings received 23 and Adams 13. That most Conscience Whigs supported Van Buren is perhaps not as surprising as it first might appear. Few of them had ever been inclined to Hale in the first place, for his reputation was far too limited. As Sumner explained before the convention, Hale was a hopeless coalition leader who should be withdrawn. More important, with McLean not in the race, and there being no other prominent Whig to consider, in the words of Adams, "There is no alternative but Mr. Van Buren." Dana later complained, "Of all the prominent Whig statesmen, there was not one willing to put himself upon our Convention, and abide the issue of our cause. . . ." The Liberty leaders who went with Van Buren did so because of the prearranged bargain with the Barnburners, although they did so against the wishes of most of their party's delegates. The opportunistic Stanton tried to rationalize his desertion to Hale by explaining: "I voted for Mr. Van Buren because I believed he was

[71] Dyer, *Great Senators,* 99-102; Dana, Journal, August 10, 1848, in Dana Papers; Adams, Diary, August 10, 1848, in Adams Papers; Dyer, *Phonographic Report,* 32; *National Era,* September 7, 1848; Stanton, *Random Recollections,* 164.

the only candidate who could be regarded as sure of carrying a single
state, & was the best man to knock to pieces the main prop of Slavery,
the *Northern Democratic Party.* . . ."[72]

When the vote was announced, the Liberty leader, Joshua Leavitt,
conceded Hale's defeat and moved that the convention make the nomination of Van Buren unanimous. With an emotion-choked voice,
Leavitt asserted: "The Liberty party is not dead, but translated."
Samuel Lewis, Liberty leader from Ohio, seconded the motion, and it
was carried amid great uproar. George Julian of Indiana observed that
as Leavitt spoke, "There was not a dry eye in the convention." Julian,
like other Whigs and Liberty men, had formerly been a political enemy
of Van Buren. Not realizing that a deal had been arranged, Julian felt
that the platform more than compensated for the candidate.[73]

With Liberty and Barnburner factions already satisfied, the next
step was to complete the arrangement by nominating a Conscience
Whig for vice-president. Stanton and others rather hypocritically suggested Hale, but the Whigs quickly pressed their claims. Since Van
Buren was an eastern Democrat, many assumed that the second position would go to a western Whig. The general understanding was that
Ohio, the leading western state, would decide and the convention
would acquiesce. The Ohio men, however, in an unexplained action,
surprised the delegates by passing over their own section and supporting Charles Francis Adams instead. Adams at first declined the choice,
saying that the candidate was to be a western man. The Ohio delegates convinced him, however, that the agreement required only that
the choice should be made by the western delegates. The convention
then nominated Adams by acclamation. Part of the reason for the
delegates' interest in Adams was their desire to pay tribute to the
memory of John Quincy Adams and at the same time add the politically powerful name of Adams to the ticket. Adams indirectly encouraged this feeling by wearing a black band in his white hat in

[72] Gardiner, *The Great Issue,* 140-41; Dana, Journal, August 10, 1848, in Dana
Papers; Donald, *Charles Sumner,* 165; Adams, Diary, August 10, 1848, in Adams
Papers; Dana, *Speeches in Stirring Times,* 157; Stanton to Hale, August 20, 1848,
in Hale Papers.
[73] Gardiner, *The Great Issue,* 140-41; Smith, *The Liberty and Free Soil Parties,*
141-42; Julian, *Political Recollections,* 59-60; Leavitt to Hale, August 22, 1848, in
Hale Papers; Sewell, *John P. Hale,* 102-3.

mourning for his father.[74] The decision was thus not a complete surprise to Adams, who had earlier heard rumors that his name was being considered. Although he did nothing directly to encourage his own chances, neither did he act to discourage such support. Earlier he had noted that "The present candidate for the second office will probably be the ultimate leader of the movement." On the balloting for president, he had withheld his vote from Van Buren because of "the rumor respecting myself as a candidate for the Vice Presidency and the indisposition to anything like an appearance of a bargain." In his eyes the nomination was valuable because "it places me somewhat near the level of my fathers." To others in the party it was valuable because it could effectively balance the ticket and appeal to anti-extension Whig factions as well as adding an element of respectability and stern conscience to the movement.[75]

In sharp contrast to the behind-the-scenes maneuvering which characterized the nominations and the adoption of the platform was the idealism and the sincere enthusiasm of the mass meeting in the tent in the city park.[76] Both events were highly symbolic of the Free Soil movement, which effectively combined political realism with a dedicated anti-extension spirit. At the mass meeting some forty-three speakers attacked the South and the major parties with abandon, and the gathering joined in political songs. A family of singers was performing when someone shouted that the delegates had made their choice. On demands for the name of the candidate, the speaker replied, "Martin Van Buren." Pandemonium followed. Hats, banners, and handker-

[74] Adams, who was not present at the delegates' convention, noted in his diary, "Mr. Giddings was also nominated and immediately withdrawn by the Ohio delegation." There is no definitive evidence as to why the Ohio delegates supported Adams rather than Giddings or some other westerner. See Adams, Diary, August 10, 1848, in Adams Papers; Dana, Journal, August 10, 1848, in Dana Papers; Stanton to Hale, August 20, 1848, in Hale Papers; Duberman, *Charles Francis Adams,* 151.

[75] Adams, Diary, August 10, 1848, Adams to J. C. Vaughan, July 7, 1848, Adams to E. S. Hamlin, July 12, 1848, in Adams Papers; Dana, Journal, August 10, 1848, in Dana Papers; Samuel Shapiro, *Richard Henry Dana, Jr., 1815-1882* (East Lansing, 1961), 37; Duberman, *Charles Francis Adams,* 150-51; Brauer, *Cotton Versus Conscience,* 242-43.

[76] For a different interpretation of these events at the Buffalo convention which stresses the idealism of the movement but fails to note sufficiently the behind-the-scenes manipulation, see Rayback, *Free Soil,* 223-30.

chiefs were waved, as cheer followed cheer and the throng shouted its support for "Van Buren and Free Soil."[77] The Free Soil party thus embarked on its short career after an exciting convention.

Men like Julian would later note that there had been no convention equal to this one in Buffalo with regard to seriousness and idealism as well as enthusiasm. Yet those who stopped to weigh the facts realized that this new party, which would emphasize the crusading moralism of its slogan "Free Soil, Free Speech, Free Labor, Free Men" had its dubious and discreditable side also. Joshua Leavitt had noted before the convention that Van Buren had been made the candidate of New York Democrats more "to avenge his old quarrel with the Hunkers than for his sympathy with the cause" of free soil. Critics at that time and since could charge that the Barnburners had tricked the Free Soilers into supplying the guise of reform for their own political revenge on Cass and Polk and for their selfish desire to regain control of the New York Democratic party after the election. As Van Buren told Dix, "A part of what we gain on the State ticket we will lose on the national, but that is a matter of much less importance."[78] The idealism and high moral purpose of the Liberty party was still very much present in the Free Soil party, but the leaders had responded to the need for compromise and political accommodation in order to give the movement a broader appeal and a better chance for success. While the throng of twenty thousand listened to empassioned antislavery speeches in the big tent and responded with the moral fervor of a religious revival, a small group working behind the scenes had determined that the party's direction would be dictated more by political considerations than it would be by idealism. Yet the party would need both its moralistic foundation and its political expediency and realism in the difficult months ahead. The Buffalo convention represented a peak in free soil enthusiasm and spirit, as dedication and opportunism combined to produce a highly meaningful political challenge.

[77] Dyer, Phonographic Account; Hubbell, "Free Soil Convention," 159; "Official Proceedings of the National Free Soil Convention," 3-4; Arthur M. Schlesinger, Jr., The Age of Jackson (Boston, 1945), 466.
[78] Julian, Political Recollections, 59-60; Leavitt to Giddings, July 6, 1848, in Giddings Papers; Stewart Mitchell, Horatio Seymour of New York (Cambridge, 1938), 110-11; Martin Van Buren to Dix, October 2, 1848, in Dix Papers.

4

The Free Soilers:
Politics and Principles

During the summer of 1848 a group of extremely dissimilar men with a variety of motives combined to create a new political party which, unlike the parties it sought to unseat, stressed ideology. The cause which had brought them together, the prevention of the extension of slavery, was one which they themselves had raised during the last four years.[1] In addition they attracted some with their positions on other issues such as slavery in the District of Columbia, internal improvements, homestead, and the tariff. Although failing to win passage of their prime issue, the Wilmot Proviso, they did force Democrats and Whigs to take notice of the Proviso, the subject the two parties wanted most to avoid.

In addition to their anti-extension ideology there were some very real and practical political and racial factors which were equally important in motivating men to join the Free Soil party. Some sought to use the movement for the sake of expediency to regain influence in their old state and national parties. They thus had no real thought of maintaining the third party after the election. Some sought to punish their old parties for their refusal to respond to their demands in the past. And almost all wanted to make sure that the stress on the Wilmot Proviso included the concept that the territories must be kept free for white settlers only. This constant theme of racism which pervaded all of Free Soil ideology allowed the party to win many adherents in a

[1] See Martin Duberman, "The Northern Response to Slavery," in Duberman (ed.), *The Antislavery Vanguard: New Essays on the Abolitionists* (Princeton, 1965), 395-402; Morrison, *The Wilmot Proviso Controversy*, 52-74.

northern society which believed black men to be inferior to whites and which supported discriminatory laws to prevent the equality of the races.

Yet for every northern voter who joined the Free Soilers in 1848, there were more than five who did not. Many of the latter sympathized with the Wilmot Proviso but let themselves be persuaded by the rationalization that the Democrats or Whigs could accomplish anti-extension goals more effectively than a new party. They accepted the argument that third parties traditionally had no chance and that a vote for Free Soil was a wasted vote or that it would actually help the other major party win the election. Thus despite the refusal of the two-party system to come to grips with the issue of free soil many still professed to believe that it would. In addition, others remained loyal Democrats or Whigs because of political expediency, while an even larger number had no interest in free soil or feared the effect third-party agitation might have on national unity.[2]

With these varied reactions to the Free Soil appeal it becomes necessary to analyze more fully what factors may have motivated men to make the decisions they did. One approach to such a study is to look at several important political leaders who represent the many factions and analyze the various motives and interests involved in their decisions. By looking at their backgrounds, at where they stood on the key issues of anti-extension and race and how political considerations affected each, one can better understand the picture of free soil motivation. In this study, John A. Dix and Preston King represent the Barnburners who became Free Soilers; Gamaliel Bailey, the Liberty men; Richard Henry Dana and John G. Palfrey, the Conscience Whigs. Those with some interest in anti-extensionism but who did not join are represented by Hannibal Hamlin among the Democrats and Abraham Lincoln among the Whigs. In all cases the men chosen were not the most prominent of their factions, for prominence often made a figure rather atypical. Yet all of those to be described were important leaders and were in many ways representative of other leaders in their group. While it is impossible to generalize from the actions and thoughts of these seven men and apply the findings to all who were affected by the Free

[2] For a discussion of why many politicians refused to become Free Soilers, see Glyndon Van Deusen, *The Jacksonian Era, 1828-1848* (New York, 1959), 259-63.

Soil appeal, a better understanding of why the Free Soil party had the degree of success it did can be achieved. Such a study also reveals more fully the blending of the ideal and the practical in the movement and points out many of the divergent facets of the Free Soil ideology. The philosophy and actions of two key New York leaders in the 1848 campaign, John Adams Dix and Preston King, reveal a sharp contrast in Barnburner motivation and politics. At the same time there is a surprising similarity of thinking on many key issues by the two men which permitted a certain unity of purpose within the Barnburner faction. Dix, a long time Jacksonian Democrat and supporter of Martin Van Buren and his Albany Regency in the 1820s and 1830s, was among the more cautious of the Barnburners as that faction moved toward its break with the Hunkers during the Polk administration. A highly partisan Democrat, Dix had been elected by the New York legislature to fill the unexpired Senate term of Silas Wright when the latter was elected governor in 1844. Dix's choice came after a bitter struggle in the legislature with the Hunker faction, which had wanted one of its own number chosen. The animosity of the normally gentle Dix toward the Hunkers was seen almost immediately as the new senator reacted with anger at Polk's patronage policy, regarding it as unwarranted favoritism by the president. His partisan feelings toward the Hunkers caused him to look toward an open break as early as 1846: "The only course now is to carry out the controversy, which is in progress, to its true result — a separation of the sound from the unsound elements of the democratic party."[3] Dix regarded the Barnburners as the "sound element" of the party, for he was firmly opposed to leaving the party.

While Dix was thus strongly motivated by political considerations his attitude toward the anti-extension movement was one of cautious moderation and revealed little concern for the moral issue of slavery. In Senate debates on the Wilmot Proviso he did speak in favor of the measure but with great restraint and he privately expressed concern over Preston King's tactics in its behalf. Although he voted for the Proviso, he wrote to a New York colleague, "I now desire, if not too

[3] The only complete study of Dix is by Martin Lichterman, "John Adams Dix, 1798-1879" (Ph.D. dissertation, Columbia University, 1952); See also Morgan Dix, *Memoirs of John Adams Dix* (New York, 1883), I, 202; Smith Van Buren to Martin Van Buren, March 3, 1845, in Van Buren Papers; Dix to Martin Van Buren, March 27, 1846, in Van Buren Papers.

late to substitute *non-slave-holding-states* for *free states,* wherever the
latter expression occurs. You know the extreme sensitiveness of the
South, and I, therefore, prefer to take the form of expression most
acceptable to them." Even Martin Van Buren urged Dix to take a
stronger anti-extension stand, noting that his speeches in the Senate
had fallen "short in spirit of the prevailing sentiment." Dix could not
agree with the Buffalo endorsement of abolition of slavery in Washington, D.C., for he felt that Congress must refrain from such action
until the surrounding states of Maryland and Virginia had abolished
slavery.[4] Thus Dix would find that his sentiments were out of tune
with many in the new party.

Why then did Dix become a Free Soiler and even agree to be the
party's candidate for governor of New York in 1848? Surely it was a
very hesitant decision taken with little enthusiasm or conviction. Despite his feeling toward the Hunkers he had opposed the calling of the
Barnburner meeting at Herkimer in October, 1847. He took little part
in the events leading to the bolting of the Barnburners at Baltimore
and opposed a third party at the time of the Utica convention in June
of 1848. Still desiring to remain a Democrat, he preferred that the
Barnburners not participate at all in the campaign, allowing Taylor
to defeat Cass. In that way Cass and the southern Democrats would
be punished for their actions and the Barnburners could then return
to the party on their own terms. Such a policy, Dix said, would make
the Barnburners "at the end of the next term of four years be the
rallying point of the democracy of the Union." When King suggested
Dix permit his friends to nominate him at Utica, the mild-mannered
senator refused.[5] Yet as the summer wore on he joined the Free Soilers
because he felt he had little choice. Most of his Barnburner colleagues
had joined and were putting pressure on him to help them crush Cass.
Had anyone other than a Barnburner led the Buffalo ticket, Dix would
surely have remained inactive, but it was difficult to refuse to support
his long-time political leader, Martin Van Buren. Concerning his nomination for governor, he told Van Buren that he would have declined

[4] Dix to Flagg, November 9, 1846, March 5, 1847, in Flagg Papers; Van Buren
to Dix, July 14, 1848, Dix to Benton, September 9, 1848, in Dix Papers.
[5] Flagg to Martin Van Buren, June 19, 1848, in Van Buren Papers; Dix to
Flagg, June 5, 1848, in Flagg Papers, Columbia University; Dix to Butler, June
20, 1848, in Butler Papers.

to run had he been consulted ahead of time. The nomination of a former Liberty member, Seth M. Gates, for lieutenant governor added to his unhappiness as a candidate.[6] Political considerations and personal loyalty to Van Buren rather than anti-extension conviction were clearly the major factors in the decision of the reluctant Senator Dix to become a Free Soiler.

Preston King, however, was anything but a reluctant Free Soiler, for aggressiveness and firmness rather than caution were the chief characteristics of the amiable New Yorker from the upstate town of St. Lawrence. A faithful Van Buren Democrat, the short, chubby King was a protegé of Silas Wright, having served as a law student in Wright's office. In his first term in Congress he had helped lead the fight against the joint resolution annexing Texas, noting that without slavery, "I would take Texas tonight." He was one of several northern Democrats to initiate the Wilmot Proviso in the House of Representatives in 1846 and worked successfully to unite northern congressmen against extension. Although not an abolitionist, unlike Dix he was a firm advocate of confining slavery within the southern states. Yet King was motivated by political factors as well as a consistent dedication to anti-extension principle. Desiring to reorient the Democratic party away from its southern leanings, he had been an active backer of Silas Wright for the party's presidential nomination in 1848. Angered by the Hunker role in Wright's defeat for reelection as governor and feeling that it had contributed to Wright's death, King was ready to lead the Barnburner revolt. He had demanded that the state party pass "a resolution on the question of freedom — direct and full, no mealy mouthed affair." When the Hunkers blocked such a move he helped to organize the Herkimer meeting, calling it "a spontaneous movement of democracy" and reporting enthusiastically, "I am on the way with my musket."[7] At the Baltimore convention he publicly spoke for both the legitimacy of the Barnburners as Democrats and their defense of the Wilmot Proviso; but when the convention rejected

[6] John A. Dix to Martin Van Buren, October 7, 1848, in Van Buren Papers; Martin Van Buren to Dix, October 2, 1848, in Dix Papers; Lichterman, "John Adams Dix," 218-25; Dix, *Memoirs of John Adams Dix*, I, 238-39.

[7] King to Flagg, December 21, 1844, January 11, 1845, September 9, October 8, 15, 1847, in Flagg Papers, New York Public Library; Muller, "Preston King," 364-417; *Congressional Globe*, 29th Cong., 2nd Sess., 96.

their demand for sole representation, King was among the first to call for an independent third-party movement. Unsuccessful in persuading Dix to accept the nomination of the Utica convention, he enthusiastically agreed with the choice of Van Buren. Throughout the spring of 1848, King's leadership was a moving force behind the Barnburner drive. As Gideon Welles observed, to Preston King "more than any other man may be ascribed the merit of boldly meeting the arrogant and imperious slaveholding oligarchy and organizing the party which eventually overthrew them."[8]

When the new party formed at Buffalo, King was again in the lead showing a willingness to attack the moral evil of slavery extension and to go much further in terms of free soil conviction than many Barnburners. Before the convention he sought to ease Whig fears about Van Buren by publicly announcing support for abolition in Washington, a position which no other prominent Barnburner had yet taken. As one of the chief organizers at the convention, he worked closely with Chase in drafting a strong platform which included the commitment to abolish slavery in the capital. King was an active participant in the bargain which assured Van Buren's nomination, for he knew that his faction would accept no other candidate. At the same time he was firm enough in his own free soil conviction that he would have supported the ticket even if a Barnburner had not led it. In the ensuing campaign, he was suggested as a candidate for governor, but the party decided against him fearing that his anti-extension views were too pronounced to appeal to voters across the state. Instead, the Free Soilers chose the more moderate Dix, who Van Buren felt would make the best showing, and King became the party's nominee for Congress from the St. Lawrence district. He was the only third-party candidate from New York to win a seat in the new House.[9]

During the campaign, King's actions showed that he, like Dix, was motivated in part by partisanship and a desire for revenge on the Democratic party. But while Dix hesitated on the Wilmot Proviso,

---

[8] *National Era*, June 1, 1848; Flagg to Martin Van Buren, June 19, 1848, in Van Buren Papers; Muller, "Preston King," 420-40; Welles is quoted in Schlesinger, *The Age of Jackson*, 430.

[9] King to John Cochran, *et al.*, July 13, 1848, in New York *Evening Post*, July 19, 1848; Martin Van Buren to Dix, October 2, 1848, in Dix Papers; Muller, "Preston King," 443-58.

King's every action showed that he, more than any other Barnburner leader, had a sincere desire to keep slavery out of the territories.

Although Dix and King differed greatly in their motives and their degree of commitment to both the Wilmot Proviso and the new party, they were in essential agreement on the issue of race. Both wanted slavery kept out of the territories in order to preserve the land for free white settlers only. Both agreed with David Wilmot who explained that he did not introduce the Proviso out of sympathy for the slave: "I have no squeamish sensitiveness upon the subject of slavery, nor morbid sympathy for the slave. I plead the cause and the rights of white freemen." Indicating his total disdain for black men, Wilmot continued: "I would preserve for free white labor a fair country, a rich inheritance, where the sons of toil, of my own race and color, can live without the disgrace which association with Negro slavery brings upon free labor."[10] Dix explained to the Senate that North America was destined to be populated by the white race and the extension of slavery would only diffuse the inferior black race and prolong its unhappy existence. By confining slaves to the South, they "will not be reproduced; and in a few generations the process of extinction is performed. Nor," said Dix, was this the "work of inhumanity or wrong," but rather "the slow but certain process of nature" which brought this inevitable result. The territories, he said, must be reserved for "the multiplication of the white race . . . the highest order of intellectual and physical endowments."[11]

While differing with the Barnburners on many issues, King shared the racist views of Dix and the others of his faction. For him the moral issue might involve slaves but rarely the rights of free blacks. Throughout his speeches ran the theme that the introduction of slaves into the territories meant that free white labor would not be able to compete on an equal footing. When reintroducing the Proviso in 1847, he argued, "If slavery is not excluded by law the presence of the slave will exclude the laboring white man." At the Herkimer convention Wilmot and King accepted the phrase "white man's Proviso" as an accurate description of the measure, and the Utica address called for preserv-

[10] *Congressional Globe*, 29th Cong., 2nd Sess., Appendix, 317-18.
[11] *Ibid.*, 30th Cong., 1st Sess., Appendix, 866ff; Dix to Thomas Hart Benton, September 9, 1848, in Dix Papers; Gardiner, *The Great Issue*, 161-63.

ing western lands "for the Caucasian race."[12] This hypocritical attitude
of the Barnburners was recognized by their Hunker opponents. As
William L. Marcy later put it: "Preston King is not in truth a democrat, he is in action an abolitionist and would break up the Union for
the sake of a few runaway negros. Yet neither he or John Van Buren
care for Negros. They are both playing an unpatriotic political game."
King's attitude accurately reflected the feelings of his constituents, for
when New York voters overwhelmingly rejected black suffrage in 1846,
King's own county of St. Lawrence, which later gave the Free Soilers
a substantial margin, voted by a ratio of more than two to one to deny
blacks the right to vote. Thus when the Buffalo platform called for
keeping the territories free "for the hearty pioneers of our land," it
was clear that King and Dix and most Free Soil voters agreed that
these pioneers should include no black men.[13]

The faction of the Free Soil party most dedicated to the Free Soil
cause and the one which remained most faithful to it after the excitement of 1848 had died down was the Liberty group. Long in the field
of anti-extension politics before the Barnburners and Conscience Whigs
became concerned, they were often eager to go beyond the sometimes
modest demands of their new allies and more willing to stress the moral
issues involved. Yet at the same time they shared a surprising number
of concepts, attitudes, and prejudices with them. While it is impossible
to choose a typical representative of this faction, of those Liberty men
who became Free Soilers in 1848, Gamaliel Bailey stands out as one
of the most important spokesmen. Born in New Jersey in 1807, Bailey
attended Jefferson Medical College in Philadelphia and became a
practicing physician in Cincinnati in the 1830s. He was won over to
the antislavery cause by the debates at Lane Seminary and their appeals to morality, and by 1835 he was a secretary of the Ohio Anti-
Slavery Society. In 1838, he replaced James G. Birney as editor of the
Cincinnati paper, *The Philanthropist,* and held that position until
1847. When the Liberty party was formed, he was quickly won over
to the political approach and used his paper to spread the Liberty

---

[12] *Congressional Globe,* 29th Cong., 2nd Sess., Appendix, 317-18; "The Herkimer Convention," 14; Gardiner, *The Great Issue,* 134.
[13] Thomas M. Marshall (ed.), "Diary and Memoranda of William L. Marcy,
1849-1851," *American Historical Review,* XXIV (1919), 451; *Whig Almanac,
1847,* 43; Porter and Johnson (comps.), *National Party Platforms,* 13-14.

cause. In 1844, he was an active backer of Birney's candidacy and attacked anti-extensionist Whigs and Democrats for their failure to join the third party.[14]

Bailey's residency in Cincinnati brought him into close contact with Salmon P. Chase, with whose ideas he was usually in close agreement. The two men were the leaders of the Cincinnati group which worked to broaden the Liberty party's appeal after 1844 and sought coalition with anti-extension factions of the Democratic and Whig parties. With the help of Chase and Lewis Tappan, Bailey moved to Washington, D.C., and began the *National Era,* which quickly established itself as the leading and most popular Liberty paper in the country. He used its columns to forward the Chase approach and, following the Liberty nomination of John P. Hale in October, 1847, continued to advocate a broader union of all opposed to the extension of slavery.[15]

Bailey's decision to join the Free Soilers was a natural one for he had never been among those Liberty men who demanded interference with slavery in the southern states. As he indicated as early as 1842, the only place the Liberty party should attack slavery was in the District of Columbia and the territories. During the 1848 campaign he noted that although he was morally opposed to slavery everywhere, the Constitution did not "confer on the General Government any power to abolish the slavery of the States." Summing up the position later taken by the Buffalo platform, he argued that the containment of slavery in the southern states "is the real object of the Federal Government." While he preferred Hale for the nomination he was among those who urged the senator to let the Buffalo convention make its decision regardless of earlier nominations. His only reservation concerning Van Buren was the latter's original unwillingness to support an attack on slavery in the capital. Following the convention he became one of Van Buren's staunchest defenders, urging his readers to

---

[14] There is no published biography of Bailey. See Joel Goldfarb, "The Life of Gamaliel Bailey, Prior to the Founding of the *National Era;* The Orientation of a Practical Abolitionist" (Ph.D. dissertation, University of California at Los Angeles, 1958) ; Filler, *The Crusade Against Slavery,* 78; Stewart, *Joshua Giddings,* 96.

[15] Rayback, *Free Soil,* 104-6; *National Era,* January 7, May 27, September 2, 1847. Tappan organized a fund raising drive to support Bailey's paper until it was self-sufficient. See Wyatt-Brown, *Lewis Tappan,* 279.

forget about his past record: "It is folly to talk to us of the conduct of this man in 1836-40. You say it was subservient to slavery — grant it — what is his course *now?* ... You stone Van Buren for his sins committed twelve years ago, though *you* yourself now fall far below the well-doing to which he has since attained!"[16]

Unlike Salmon P. Chase, who was motivated by a combination of anti-extension conviction and opportunism, Bailey was perhaps more typical of the Liberty faction in his unselfish advocacy of anti-extensionism as the most practical way to attack the moral evil of slavery everywhere. With his constant stress on the moral righteousness of the cause, he remained dedicated to the Liberty goals throughout his life. When he saw that these goals could be more effectively advocated with a broader movement, he gladly became a Free Soiler. In defending Bailey against charges by Liberty Leaguers that he was too cautious in not attacking slavery in the South, Tappan explained: "Dr. Bailey is never ultra. . . ." Unlike Dix and King and other Barnburners, he had no ulterior political motive in mind. Much more firmly committed to anti-extensionism on moral grounds, he was willing to go beyond most Barnburners to expand the attack on slavery to include Washington. Yet the efficient editor consistently rejected the abolitionist approach to slavery in the South and strove to convince his readers of the wisdom of the Free Soil appeal. To the moralistic Bailey, the nomination of Van Buren and Adams "shows that a crisis has come, in which minor questions are to be merged, old animosities forgotten, in the common Sentiment of devotion to Freedom and opposition to Slavery."[17]

At the same time Bailey shared many of the convictions of the Liberty faction on the issue of race. His philosophy, while much more advanced than the Barnburners in terms of opposition to discriminatory laws, nevertheless accepted the widely held view of the inferiority of blacks. Bailey endorsed the plank in the Liberty platform of 1847 which resolved "that the laws in the several states designed to oppress and degrade particular classes of individuals are indefensible." In attacking John A. Dix's Senate speech which demanded that blacks be

16 Rayback, *Free Soil,* 104; *National Era,* July 6, August 3, 24, 1848.
17 Tappan is quoted in Wyatt-Brown, *Lewis Tappan,* 279; *National Era,* August 24, 1848.

excluded from the territories, Bailey berated him for his "expediency and appeal to race," and charged that the address lacked a "sense of Justice." Strongly opposed to the views of Dix, King, and other Barn-burners, he endorsed the sentiments of his contributing editor John Greenleaf Whittier who defended the right of blacks to enter the territories as free men: "Have they then no claim to an equal partici-pation in the blessings which have grown out of the National inde-pendence for which they fought? Is it just . . . to convert them by political disfranchisement and social oppression into enemies?"[18]

While Bailey opposed legal distinctions between the races and at-tacked state laws which excluded free blacks, he also explained that he laid "no claim to being one of the 'peculiar friends' or champions of the free people of color." They were "entitled to justice and kind considerations," but he explained that they "are not quite so intelli-gent or agreeable as their white brethren." In another fundamental disagreement with most abolitionists, Bailey expressed the wish that blacks would voluntarily emigrate to Africa or some part of the United States not inhabited by whites. He agreed with Chase's sentiments: "I have always looked forward to the separation of the races."[19] Both Bailey and Chase were far more willing than most Free Soilers to resist discriminatory laws but neither could free himself completely from the racism of northern white society.

The Conscience Whig role in the Free Soil movement is more diffi-cult to evaluate than that of either the Barnburners or Liberty men. While most Barnburners were moved more by political considerations than free soil principles and most Liberty leaders more by a moral opposition to the extension of slavery than any other factor, the Con-science Whigs present an example of the close interworkings of politi-cal expediency and high moral principle. As young members of the Massachusetts aristocracy with little connection with manufacturing, they sought to gain control of the state Whig party from the textile manufacturers. Seizing on the issue of the extension of slavery they hoped to use it to displace the Cotton Whigs. Yet they were also moved

[18] *National Era,* November 4, 1847, July 20, 1848, February 24, 1848, July 22, 1847.
[19] *Ibid.,* April 19, 1849, November 28, 1850, May 27, 1852; Chase to Frederick Douglass, May 4, 1850, in Chase Papers, Historical Society of Pennsylvania.

by a sense of their own moral righteousness and a belief in the basic evil of human bondage.[20] The experiences in this movement of John Gorham Palfrey and Richard Henry Dana reveal this dual motivation as well as a great contrast with Barnburner and Liberty leaders. They also show that the Conscience men were not always in complete agreement among themselves as to tactics and political philosophy.

Palfrey was somewhat of an exception as a Conscience Whig in that he was older than most, being fifty-two at the time of the campaign of 1848. Yet in many other ways he was quite typical. He was the son of a seaman who eventually became the owner of a sugar plantation in Louisiana. After graduation from the Harvard Divinity School young Palfrey became the minister of a Unitarian church in Boston. During the 1830s he was first a professor and then dean of the Divinity School. After 1840 he became increasingly interested in politics, editing a Whig review, the *North American,* before entering entering the state legislature. He first came to grips with the slavery issue when his father died in 1843 leaving part of his estate, including twenty slaves, to Palfrey. He soon made the personal decision to free these bondsmen and bring them to Boston at his own expense. Although he did not support the abolitionists' contention that the federal government had the authority to interfere with southern slavery, he nevertheless became convinced of the self-serving intentions of the "Slave Power." By 1844, he was ready to join in the campaign to resist the annexation of Texas.[21]

Still a loyal Whig, Palfrey soon joined with Adams and Sumner in the anti-Texas movement. When the three agreed to meet with Massachusetts abolitionists, the split with the Cotton faction developed. Palfrey and the others were unwilling to go beyond anti-extensionism and embrace abolitionism, and they were thus uncomfortable in the presence of abolitionists. Yet their informal association with them continued, and the Whig schism widened. As the extension issue shifted to the Mexican War territories, Palfrey attempted to get the state party to adopt a resolution to support only those candidates who displayed an "uncompromising opposition to the extension of Slavery." The rejection of this resolution revealed to him that "some more distinctness was given to the separating line between patriotism and servility, between

---

[20] See Brauer, *Cotton Versus Conscience,* 1-29.
[21] For a perceptive account of Palfrey's career, see Gatell, *John Gorham Palfrey.*

Conscience and Cotton." Adherence to the Wilmot Proviso had become the test of a man's sincerity and morality in Palfrey's mind. This he proved again when as a Whig congressman from Massachusetts he withheld his vote in Robert Winthrop's effort to become speaker of the House and brought down upon himself the wrath of the Cotton Whigs. As he later explained it, "I could not without a sacrifice of my own integrity help to entrust him with that power. He was no representative of the principles which had been solemnly affirmed by the Whigs who sent me to Congress."[22]

Feeling that his political influence would remain insignificant as a Whig, Palfrey joined the Conscience men in challenging the Cotton Whigs while at the same time using the extension issue to express his genuine moral revulsion and hatred of slavery. He could possibly have gone further in Whig politics had he been willing to remain loyal to the Cotton faction. Yet Palfrey broke with them over the Wilmot Proviso and over his vote for speaker, and while he was more reluctant than some Conscience Whigs to unite with the Barnburners, he agreed to join the Free Soil movement following the nomination of Zachary Taylor. His biographer persuasively argues that a partial explanation for his decision was his attempt "to bolster his self-esteem" after several personal failures. "What better way to uphold his principles, in contrast to conservative Boston's alleged commercial and political capitulation to Southern domination, than to champion the highest principle — human freedom?"[23] Yet his reluctance to join with the former Democrats in the Barnburner movement revealed how far apart the two groups were in motivation. Palfrey could not help but feel that the Barnburners were not as sincere in their support of the Wilmot Proviso as he and his Conscience colleagues were.

Richard Henry Dana was born in 1815 into a once-prominent Massachusetts family which had lost its influence with the rise of the banker and manufacturer groups. Yet his upbringing in Cambridge was that of a gentleman. His only escape from family tradition came at the age of nineteen when he took two years out from his Harvard education and became an ordinary seaman. The result of his voyage

[22] Boston *Whig*, October 2, 1847; John Gorham Palfrey, *Letter to a Friend* (Cambridge, 1850), 12; Gatell, *John Gorham Palfrey*, 122-48.
[23] Gatell, *John Gorham Palfrey*, 134.

was his famous book, *Two Years before the Mast*, although back in
Boston he immediately finished his education and settled down as a
somewhat typical Whig lawyer. His interest in politics and the anti-
extension issue came later than most Conscience Whigs, for he took
no part until 1847. An unhappy home life, a rather unsuccessful law
practice, a growing awareness that the Whigs of Boston had not approached him for his services, and a general frustration finally brought
him to public life. Like many gentlemen of Boston he was not especially
interested in reform at first but rather hoped for the restoration of older
virtues of Federalist days. His reaction to having attended an abolitionist meeting in Boston is revealing: "Garrison ... is a fanatic by
constitution, and hater of everything established and traditional, and
an infidel and socialist. . . . All the other speakers were a nest of ignor-
ant, fanatical, heated, narrow-minded men."[24]

The Free Soil movement provided the type of crusade which would
take Dana's mind off his own troubles because it was more "respectable" than abolitionism. Unlike abolitionism, the Wilmot Proviso principle was one he could embrace for it sought "only a restoration of the
old doctrine of the Northwest Ordinance." Dana was in fact "a Free
Soiler by inheritance," for his grandfather had seconded the original
ordinance in the Articles of Confederation Congress.[25] Yet he soon
became convinced of the moral righteousness of the cause. He justified his bolting the Whig party because that party had ignored "the
only important question," the Wilmot Proviso, "for the sake of party
success." While Dana favored the Free Soil nomination of John Mc-
Lean or some other Whig, and remarked that "It is asking too much
to require Whigs to vote for V. Buren," the nomination of Adams for
vice-president greatly reassured him and gave the movement the proper
respect and dignity. Unaware of the political maneuvering at Buffalo,
even though he was a delegate to the convention, he viewed the Free
Soil movement as a "return to the paths of the revolutionary patriots."[26]

[24] Shapiro, *Richard Henry Dana, Jr.*, 1-31; Dana, Journal, June 1, 1843, in
Dana Papers.
[25] Adams, Diary, January 20, 1848, in Adams Papers; Boston *Daily Whig*, July
11, 1848; Dana to Daniel Lord, January 26, 1854, quoted in Charles Francis
Adams, Jr., *Richard Henry Dana, A Biography* (Boston, 1890), I, 124; Shapiro,
Richard Henry Dana, Jr., 31.
[26] Dana to Edmund Dana, July 21, 1848, Dana to Jared Wilson, July 26, 1848,
in Dana Papers; Adams, Diary, August 10, 1848, in Adams Papers.

His opposition to the extension of slavery was real and based on moral conviction, and like Palfrey he viewed the Free Soil movement as a means of asserting his own moral righteousness and superiority. Both men also saw the movement as a way not only of halting the spread of slavery but of gaining political influence at the expense of their former Whig allies. Yet unlike the Barnburners, the emphasis was always on the Wilmot Proviso rather than political expediency.

Palfrey and Dana were somewhat representative of the Conscience Whigs in their racial attitudes as well, although Dana was more prejudiced against blacks than most. Palfrey, more than Dana, reflected the conflicting tendencies of many in the movement of favoring an end to laws which discriminated because of race but of being unwilling to accept black men as their social and intellectual equals. In this sense he was much like Bailey and many other Liberty leaders. As a member of the Massachusetts legislature, Palfrey had helped in the fight to repeal the ban on interracial marriage in Massachusetts and had spoken in Congress against the suffrage restriction against blacks in the Oregon Territorial bill. Although on another occasion he denied southern claims of racial inferiority, he admitted he had no desire for social relations with black people. His paternalistic approach was a reflection of his own egocentricism, for his ideas on race were clearly threatened by any evidence of black achievement. He had little friendship for blacks and expressed amazement when he discovered that there were three among the recent medical graduates of Kings College and that one, who was "an uncommonly pronounced Negro," had won honors. With such a condescending attitude, Palfrey, not surprisingly, felt all other races inferior; he opposed taking Mexican territories with their "foreign habits, and their nameless Indians and mongrel breeds."[27]

Dana on the other hand, despite his later defense of accused fugitive slaves, showed no interest in the early efforts to repeal discriminatory laws in Massachusetts. Similar in his thinking to most Barnburners, he did not hesitate to speak to segregated audiences. His reaction to

[27] Adams, Diary, January 19, 1842, Palfrey to Adams, July 28, 1848, in Adams Papers; *Congressional Globe*, 30th Cong., 1st Sess., 1019; Palfrey to Mary Ann Palfrey, May 15, June 11, 1856, Palfrey, Journal, May 11, 29, 1856, Palfrey to J. Mann, July 30, 1846, in Palfrey Papers.

his contact with two later prominent free blacks shows his racist thinking: "Two conceited, shallow-pated Negro youths, named [Charles] Remond and [Frederick] Douglass, were among the chief speakers. They seemed to have been entirely spoiled by the notice taken of them, and evidently had but little strength of mind by nature." While he might not have agreed fully with James Russell Lowell's "Biglow Papers" which presented blacks as "long-legged swine" who ruin the territories for the northern white farmer, Dana was clearly convinced of their inferiority. And he was concerned that his endorsement of Free Soil might confuse him in people's minds with those abolitionists who wanted social equality for free blacks.[28] A man who believed that social distinctions should be maintained even among whites, the young aristocratic Dana was certainly not prepared to extend equality to include blacks. For both Dana and Palfrey, then, paternalism and condescension were the rule, and the decision to become Free Soilers never involved a commitment to racial equality. Had it required such a commitment, it is doubtful whether they would have joined the third-party movement.

If the Free Soil party were going to have any significant and permanent effect on the political structure of the country it would have to win the support of many professed Democrats and Whigs who had not been directly affiliated with their party's anti-extension factions but who nevertheless sympathized with the Wilmot Proviso. That the party failed to do so to any real extent should not be surprising given the strength of old party loyalties and the traditional difficulties of any third party. It was unable to convince a significant number that it had a real chance in the election. Many preferred to rationalize that their own party was sufficiently free soil–oriented or that the new party represented a real threat to national unity. Many important Democratic and Whig leaders endorsed the Wilmot Proviso yet refused to support the only party which openly supported the Proviso. Hannibal Hamlin of Maine, a Democrat, and Abraham Lincoln of Illinois, a Whig, were somewhat typical of this reaction. These two men were

28 Shapiro, *Richard Henry Dana, Jr.,* 34; Dana, Journal, June 1, 1843, in Dana Papers; James Russell Lowell, *The Biglow Papers* (Boston, 1848), 26-31; Dana to Daniel Lord, January 26, 1854, quoted in Adams, *Richard Henry Dana,* I, 126.

to become the standard bearers of the Republican party in 1860 on a platform strikingly similar to the Free Soil platform of 1848. Yet in 1848 they were not willing to risk their political careers in an anti-extension movement whose future was so uncertain.

Hannibal Hamlin was born in the tiny Maine village of Paris Hill in 1809, the son of a successful and socially prominent physician.[29] An enthusiastic Jacksonian Democrat, the tall, muscular Hamlin became a member of the state legislature in the 1830s and was elected to Congress in 1843. As an anti-extension Democrat he was denied election to the Senate in 1846 by the proslavery faction of the party, a defeat which would teach him valuable lessons for the future. In the House, Hamlin did make an impression, however, for as a believer in the charge that the Mexican War was a slaveowners' plot to extend their institution, he joined with other anti-extension Democrats in sponsoring the Wilmot Proviso. President Polk had no trouble dismissing Hamlin's "mischievous course" by noting that his motivation was "that I did not appoint some friend of his in Maine, whom he had recommended to some petty office last winter." While this may have been a minor factor in Hamlin's decision, there was no change in his political principles. He sincerely felt that although the federal government could not interfere with slavery in the South, it did have a moral obligation to stop its expansion.[30]

Despite his anti-extension conviction, however, Hamlin refused to join the Free Soil party. A loyal party man, Hamlin took a seat in the state legislature in 1847 and used his position to work for his own election to the United States Senate when the opportunity presented itself early in 1848. As the new Democratic senator, he attended the Baltimore convention and worked for the nomination of a fellow New Englander, Levi Woodbury of New Hampshire, believing him to be "safe" on the slavery question. Although disappointed in Cass's nomination, he nevertheless refused to join the Barnburners in revolt. An early biographer attempted to justify his decision by explaining, without any real evidence, that Hamlin "saw General Cass, and from him

---

[29] The best account of Hamlin's life is the recent biography by H. Draper Hunt, *Hannibal Hamlin of Maine, Lincoln's First Vice-President* (Syracuse, 1969).

[30] Quaife (ed.), *The Diary of James K. Polk*, I, 304-6; Hunt, *Hannibal Hamlin*, 38-41.

obtained a definite statement, that if elected President, he would not
veto a bill prohibiting the extension of slavery into territory then
free."[31] Without question there were more important reasons for Hamlin's decision to remain a Democrat. Although he had backed Van
Buren as president, he now suspected that the New Yorker merely
wanted revenge of Polk and was not sincere in his free soil conviction.
He rationalized that should he become a Free Soiler, the Maine Democratic party, in his absence, would fall into the hands of the Slave
Power. Hamlin thus argued that the best chance for forwarding his
anti-extension principles was to remain in the Democratic party and
work to defeat its proslavery elements. The Barnburners, he felt, had
manipulated the Buffalo convention for their own selfish purposes, and
a new party with that kind of leadership had little chance for permanency. More importantly, as a practical politician he realized that he
owed his seat in the Senate to the Democracy and any chance for reelection depended on continued party loyalty.[32]

A more secure political future was also among the factors which
motivated the ambitious Whig politician from Illinois, Abraham Lincoln, to remain outside of the Free Soil movement. The tall Springfield
lawyer of humble origins clearly saw that his chances for political advancement lay in his remaining a loyal Whig in 1848. He had served
four terms in the Illinois legislature and was elected to the House of
Representatives in 1846 for his only term before returning to his law
practice and state politics. He had not shown much interest in the
Texas issue, feeling that southerners would bring their slaves there
whether or not the United States annexed the region. But following
his election to the House, he opposed the Mexican War and introduced
his famous "Spot Resolutions" to embarass the Polk administration and
show the war to be unnecessary and unconstitutional. He agreed with
Hamlin that the war was a slaveowners' plot and consistently voted for
the Wilmot Proviso, believing that if confined to the South, slavery
would gradually die out. Horace Greeley recalled Lincoln in Congress
in 1848 as "one of the most moderate, though firm opponents of slavery

[31] Charles Eugene Hamlin, *The Life and Times of Hannibal Hamlin* (Cambridge, 1899), 180-81.
[32] *Ibid.;* Hunt, *Hannibal Hamlin,* 46-47.

extension." The fact remains, however, that the Illinois congressman was not especially sensitive to the extension question as he would be a decade later, and he never spoke on it during his term in Washington. On the other hand, although he felt that Congress had no power over slavery in the South, he was opposed to the extension of slavery and did introduce an abolition bill in the House for the District of Columbia.[33] But his endorsement of free soil principles was not wholehearted enough in 1848 to make him willing to risk Whig unity by joining the third party.

Long before the nominating conventions, Lincoln had decided that his favorite, Henry Clay, could not be his party's choice for president and he therefore decided to back Zachary Taylor. He was a delegate to the Whig convention and following Taylor's nomination he exclaimed, "We shall have a most overwhelming glorious triumph." He explained his position fully when asked to deliver several campaign addresses in Massachusetts where the Conscience Whig appeal was expected to endanger Taylor's chances. In a manner similar to Hamlin's defense of Cass, Lincoln explained that he "did not know that General Taylor had professed that he would *not* veto the Wilmot Proviso, but *believed* that he would not. . . . As the constitutionality of the Wilmot Proviso had never been disputed, it was therefore acquiesced in by the people and consequently Taylor was bound not to veto it." In attacking Van Buren and the Free Soilers he claimed that their position on the territories was the same as the Whigs. He charged: "If their platform held any other [principle], it was in such a general way that it was like the pair of pantaloons the Yankee peddler offered for sale, 'large enough for any man, small enough for any boy.' " He condemned the Free Soilers, saying they indirectly helped Cass, who was less likely to promote freedom in the territories than Taylor. Part of Lincoln's decision to remain a Whig was due to Martin Van Buren's past "with all his Locofocoism," but his own partisan appeals indicate

---

[33] *Congressional Globe,* 30th Cong., 1st Sess., 64, Appendix, 93-95, 2nd Sess., 212; Roy P. Basler (ed.), *The Collected Works of Abraham Lincoln* (New Brunswick, N.J., 1953), II, 20-22; Filler, *The Crusade Against Slavery,* 219; Horace Greeley, *Recollections of a Busy Life* (New York, 1868), 226; Harlan H. Horner, *Lincoln and Greeley* (Urbana, Ill., 1953), 46-47, 53, 69.

that he was a party man first and an anti-extensionist second.[34] Although he would not hold public office again until elected president in 1860, a promising future in the Whig party more than any other factor kept Lincoln loyal in 1848.

Although members of opposite parties in 1848, the future Republican president and vice-president held similar views on race, views which conformed to those of the overwhelming majority of their constituents. As an early advocate of the Wilmot Proviso, Hamlin agreed with his anti-extension colleagues in the House that one of the purposes of the Proviso was to preserve the land for whites only. Government must "advance the true interests of our Caucasian race. . . . We will stand in defence of freedom of our soil as right in principle and beneficial to free white labor in all parts of our common country." His racist philosophy and belief in black inferiority was revealed as he explained his support of the Proviso principle: "I would resist the introduction of that institution [slavery] in justice to a superior race of men — men who are capable of a higher state of social and political refinement."[35] Thus he agreed fully with the Barnburners whose major purpose in advocating the Wilmot Proviso was to protect white labor from the competition and "contamination" of black slave labor.

Lincoln agreed with Hamlin on the territorial issue, for in a speech he made several years later in regard to the Kansas-Nebraska territory he noted: "The whole nation is interested that the best use shall be made of these territories. We want them for the homes of free white people. This they cannot be, to any considerable extent, if slavery shall be planted within them." His views in 1848 were the same. An advocate of colonization, he opposed extending blacks equal rights and

34 Basler (ed.), *Works of Lincoln*, II, 1-11; William H. Herndon and Jesse W. Weik, *Abraham Lincoln: The Story of a Great Life* (New York, 1892), I, 283-87; Richard H. Luthin, "Abraham Lincoln and the Massachusetts Whigs in 1848," *New England Quarterly*, XIV (1941), 624-32. The term "locofoco" referred originally to insurgent members of the New York Democratic party who struggled with conservative Tammany Hall Democrats for control of the party in the 1830s. They received their name when, in 1835, the organization Democrats turned out the lights at a party meeting to prevent the opposition from seizing power. The insurgents retaliated by lighting the new friction matches popularly known as locofocos. The term was later used to refer to any Democrats who endorsed economic equality and limitations on monopolies. See Van Deusen, *The Jacksonian Era*, 95; Schlesinger, *The Age of Jackson*, 191-92.
35 Quoted in Hunt, *Hannibal Hamlin*, 49-50.

during the 1840 campaign had attacked Van Buren for "his votes in the New York convention of 1821 in allowing Free Negroes the right of suffrage. . . ." Throughout the period Lincoln also opposed extending the rights of citizenship to blacks in Illinois, for as he explained in his debates with Stephen A. Douglas, "I am not, nor ever have been in favor of bringing about in any way the social and political equality of the white and black races. . . ." He continued by admitting his racism: "There is a physical difference between the white and black races which I believe will forever forbid the two races living together on terms of social and political equality. . . . I as much as any other man am in favor of having the superior position assigned to the white race."[36] Because so few Free Soilers would have disagreed with Hamlin and Lincoln on race, the two men could make their decision to remain aloof from the movement on other grounds.

The Free Soil position on race was in fact little different from that of the Democrats and Whigs. On the other hand, its third-party predecessor, the Liberty party, had on several occasions included the rights of free blacks in its statement of principles. Its 1844 platform had called for "the restoration of equality of rights among men," and urged Liberty men to oppose "any inequality of rights and privileges" based on color. In 1847, the party attacked state laws "designed to oppress and degrade particular classes of individuals."[37] Despite their own concepts of black inferiority, some Liberty men and Conscience Whigs in the Free Soil movement of 1848 probably would have been willing to go this far again in the Buffalo platform. Yet the records and the personal descriptions of the convention indicate no discussion or pressure to include any commitment to racial equality. Dana, Adams, and other Conscience Whigs present were completely silent on the issue and Gamaliel Bailey, although not present in Buffalo, never used the columns of his *National Era* during the campaign to comment on the issue or urge an end to discrimination. Thus by their silence they readily endorsed this omission from the Free Soil platform. This silence

[36] Basler, *Works of Lincoln*, I, 210, II, 268, III, 179; Paul M. Angle (ed.), *Created Equal? The Complete Lincoln-Douglas Debates of 1858* (Chicago, 1958), 235.
[37] Porter and Johnson (comps.), *National Party Platforms*, 4-8; *National Era*, November 4, 1847.

was further proof of the racist views of the members and especially the Barnburners who were most in control. In order to broaden its appeal to northern white voters, the members fully accepted the notion that the party must divorce itself from the ideal of racial equality. For Barnburners like Preston King and John A. Dix, it was easy to rationalize this omission and agree with Walt Whitman who argued that it was simply "a question between the grand body of white work-ingmen and the millions of white mechanics, farmers and operatives of our country, with their interests on one side — and the interests of a few thousand rich, 'polished,' and aristocratic owners of slaves at the South, on the other side."[38] The Free Soilers' opposition to the exten-sion of slavery relied as much on a desire to assure all white men equal opportunity as it did on their feeling that slavery was a moral evil. For most, support of the Wilmot Proviso then included virtually no willingness to extend this equality to blacks.

With all three parties in the election of 1848 in fundamental agree-ment on the issue of race, the primary appeal of the Free Soil party was its wholehearted advocacy of the Wilmot Proviso. At a time when Democrats and Whigs attempted to straddle the fence or evade the issue entirely, the new party made some inroads with its anti-extension platform. While unable to convince most voters that it provided the only sure guarantee against the extension of slavery or that the issue was an important enough one to warrant changing parties, the Free Soil party nevertheless won the active backing of many divergent groups. Barnburners like John A. Dix and Preston King joined out of a combination of anti-extension conviction and political expediency while Liberty leaders like Gamaliel Bailey saw the movement as the only practical way to attack the moral evil of slavery everywhere. For Conscience Whigs like John G. Palfrey and Richard Henry Dana their own moral position as well as dedication to the principle that the fed-eral government must divorce itself completely from slavery led them to join the Free Soilers. Such a diversity of motivation and background was the source of constant conflict within the movement and would

[38] Brooklyn *Eagle*, September 1, 1848, quoted in Walt Whitman, *Gathering of the Forces*, ed. Cleveland Rodgers and John Black (New York, 1920), I, 208; Eric Foner, "Racial Attitudes of the New York Free Soilers," *New York History*, XLVI (1965), 311-29.

make it difficult to obtain Free Soil unity in the future. With this in mind, many northern politicians like Hannibal Hamlin and Abraham Lincoln rationalized that a new untried party was not the best way to prevent the extension of slavery or to forward their own political careers. Their sentiments, strengthened by the inconsistencies and weaknesses of the Free Soil party, proved that the North was not yet ready in 1848 for a purely sectional party, even one which included no commitment to racial equality.

5

The Free Soil Campaign:
Motivations, Issues,
and Results

Even as the Free Soilers were meeting in Buffalo, Congress continued
to wrestle with and to attempt to evade the critical issue of slavery in
the territories. By 1848, the agitation of two decades was beginning to
have an effect, as northern anxiety over the extension of slavery gradually increased. With the acquisition of vast new territories from Mexico, Congress faced the necessity of determining whether slavery should
be restricted or not. The lawmakers soon revealed, however, that they
were not yet ready to face the question squarely. Unwilling to consider
the proposals of either pro- or anti-extensionists, they appeared incapable of coming to grips with the crisis. The Wilmot Proviso was
the answer of the Free Soil party for all new territories, but there was
little chance that such a solution could receive either Senate approval
or President Polk's signature. After weeks of debate little of real
substance was resolved. Although agreeing to an Oregon territorial
bill with the restriction against slavery included, Congress simply postponed any solution for the more critical territories of California and
New Mexico.[1] The extension of slavery was too explosive an issue to

[1] Quaife (ed.), *The Diary of James K. Polk*, IV, 25-96. See also the debates
in the *Congressional Globe*, 30th Cong., 1st Sess.; Morrison, *The Wilmot Proviso
Controversy*, 165-66. The Oregon bill also denied suffrage to blacks. Except for
John G. Palfrey, the Free Soil men in Congress made little effort to provide for
black suffrage, again revealing the lack of commitment to the end of racial dis-
crimination. See *Congressional Globe*, 30th Cong., 1st Sess., 1019; Eugene H.
Berwanger, *The Frontier Against Slavery: Western Anti-Negro Prejudice and the
Slavery Extension Controversy* (Urbana, Ill., 1967), 81-83.

settle during a presidential campaign. Despite Free Soil efforts to the contrary, the Democrats and Whigs would do their best to avoid the question during the ensuing months.

As a new organization, the Free Soilers faced countless other problems in their efforts to force the established parties to settle the extension issue. They had to convince many Democratic and Whig leaders and voters who opposed the extension of slavery that the Free Soil party provided the best means to achieve passage of the Wilmot Proviso. They had to prove that a vote for Free Soil would not be a wasted vote. Van Buren and Adams had little party organization with which to support a national campaign. Except in New York and Massachusetts, where the Barnburners and Conscience Whigs brought already functioning groups with them, the new party had little from which to build. Most of the other northern states had small Liberty party groups already operating but, except for Ohio, none on a large enough scale to offer much positive assistance. In some cases the Liberty name and organization may actually have hurt the cause because of its identification in the popular mind with abolitionism. With its stress on national rather than local issues, the new party had to organize with little local base to work with and do it quickly after the August convention. With less than three months between the Buffalo convention and election day, the Free Soilers were at an obvious disadvantage against the major parties which had been in existence for years and often had permanent and smoothly functioning local organizations.

These handicaps were made even more difficult in that Van Buren, true to the time-honored custom, did no campaigning himself, except to write an occasional letter. Even then his letters did not always fully satisfy his supporters. Following the pattern he had maintained during his long years as a politician, he continued to straddle important issues. For example, in his letter accepting the nomination, Van Buren stressed the right of Congress to prohibit slavery in the territories. At the same time he explained that although the reasons he held in 1837 for opposing abolition in the District of Columbia no longer existed, he would still refuse to take a definite stand on the issue. He did promise, however, that should Congress pass a bill ending slavery in the capital, "I should not if President, think it within my line of duty, to arrest its passage by the exercise of the veto power."[2] Although most Free Soilers would have preferred a more positive statement from their candidate, they were forced to accept Van Buren's evasive assurance. At the same time, they tried to say as little as possible about the District of Columbia issue during the campaign.

When the campaign of 1848 opened, the Free Soil party still had to overcome the doubts held by some of its own assumed supporters before it could make a successful appeal to the general northern voting public. There were doubts especially over Van Buren's candidacy. For the most part those who had led the movement for the Buffalo convention were already sufficiently committed to the third party, both politically and ideologically, that they were willing to accept the candidate even if he were not their first choice. On the other hand, those who had hesitated before Buffalo continued to find excuses, some real and some mere rationalizations, to justify their unwillingness to participate. Because of Van Buren's candidacy, anti-extension Democrats were typically enthusiastic, while Whig and Liberty elements were not so easily convinced. As the campaign progressed, however, many of those with reservations agreed to support the movement. The *National Era* expressed the views of most Liberty men when it observed that it was time to stop worrying about Van Buren's past record and to start concentrating on his present position: "Mr. Van Buren was subservient to the Slave Power in 1836, you say — well, he is not, like Gen. Cass, a vassal of it, or like Gen. Taylor, its embodiment in 1848. On the contrary, he is its open, direct antagonist." Salmon P. Chase optimistically reported that Whigs and Liberty men of Ohio's Western Reserve were coming to Van Buren's support despite lingering doubts about his attitude on slavery in the District of Columbia. Late in August, 1848, John P. Hale, true to his earlier pledge, officially withdrew as the Liberty candidate and urged a "hearty, energetic, and unanimous support of Messrs. Van Buren and Adams, as the most consistent course for the enlightened friends of liberty to pursue."[3] Having firmly committed themselves to Van Buren, men like Chase, Hale, and

[2] Martin Van Buren to Butler, White, and Chase, August 22, 1848, Martin Van Buren to Louis Lapham, October 16, 1848, in Van Buren Papers.

[3] *National Era,* August 24, 31, 1848; Chase to Martin Van Buren, August 21, 1848, in Van Buren Papers; Hale to Lewis, August 28, 1848, quoted in the *National Era,* September 7, 1848.

Bailey were eager to convince others that the Buffalo delegates had chosen wisely.

Not surprisingly, the tiny abolition element of the old Liberty party which had not accepted Hale's Liberty nomination had mixed feelings about Van Buren as well. As a result, most of them continued in their separate movement, the Liberty League. Gerrit Smith persisted as the candidate of the League and would draw 2,600 votes in November, but even he advised any who were not prepared to support an unqualified abolitionist to vote for Van Buren. Others like James G. Birney refused to associate with the Free Soilers, and doubts about the new party lingered in many minds. From the point of view of the Liberty League, a party which acknowledged the constitutionality of slavery in the states and called only for containment rather than abolition did not go far enough to merit its support. James Russell Lowell's "Hosea Biglow" could not hide his disappointment over Van Buren:

> I used to vote fer Martin, but I swan I'm clean disgusted —
> He aint the man that I can say is fittin' to be trusted,
> He aint half antislav'ry 'nough, nor I aint sure, ez some be,
> He'd go in for abolishin' the Deestrick o' Columby.

Yet Lowell also wrote in the third-party's defense and expressed the views of many abolitionists: "It should always be remembered that the Free Soil party is not an abolition party in any sense of the word. Yet perhaps it will be wiser for us to be thankful for what they are than to reproach them for what they are not."[4]

The Conscience Whigs also retained many of their misgivings, although having already seceded from the Whig party, they had little choice but to support Van Buren. Adams and other Conscience Whigs waged a fairly enthusiastic campaign for the New Yorker by which they hoped to wrest control of the state away from the Whigs. Although they found Van Buren's candidacy an embarrassment and had reservations about his leadership, many, like Sumner, called on voters

[4] Gerrit Smith to Judge Nye, July 27, 1848, in Smith Papers, Syracuse University, quoted in Harlow, *Gerrit Smith*, 187; Fladeland, *James G. Birney*, 266; Lowell, *The Biglow Papers*, 131; *National Anti-Slavery Standard* (New York), August 10, 1848. For a revealing discussion of the thinking of the Liberty League leaders and other abolitionists on the problem of whom to support in 1848 see Kraditor, *Means and Ends in American Abolitionism*, 178-89.

to forget the past record of the candidates and think only of their present positions. Adams explained that despite the personal prejudices against Van Buren in Massachusetts, there had been real progress by the new party. He noted in his diary: "Mr. Van Buren is a mixed character. In early life right, in middle life swayed by his ambition and his associations, he seems towards the close of his career to be again falling into the right channel."[5] Dana defended Van Buren's "disinterestedness and magnanimity" in accepting the nomination and observed that Van Buren faced "the terrible ordeal of a Presidential campaign, without the slightest hope of success."[6] On the other hand, most Conscience men labored to avoid mentioning Van Buren's name in their campaigning and stressed instead the issue of free soil. The overall approach of the anti-extension Whigs was to appeal to principles instead of men. The reason was clear. Whigs would support Van Buren less readily than almost any other possible Free Soil candidate.

Some anti-extension Whigs associated with the Conscience men did refuse to join the Free Soil party. One of the prime examples was Horace Mann, whom the voters had chosen to complete the congressional term of John Quincy Adams.[7] The Conscience Whigs expected much from Mann because of his known opposition to slavery and support of the Wilmot Proviso. No amount of persuasion by Sumner, Wilson, and others, however, could convince Mann that his duties as a representative and politician were more important than his position as secretary of the Massachusetts Board of Education, which he said prevented him from becoming involved in the campaign. His independent stand did him no harm personally because he received both the Free Soil and Whig nomination for Congress in the fall and won reelection. Mann's decision was more political than anything else, for in addition to his lack of enthusiasm for Van Buren, he realized that

[5] *Works of Charles Sumner*, II, 141; Adams to Butler, White, and Chase, August 22, 1848, in Van Buren Papers; Adams to Ezekiel Bacon, September 25, 1848, Adams to Seth M. Gates, October 1, 1848, Adams, Diary, September 6, 1848, in Adams Papers.

[6] Dana, *Speeches in Stirring Times*, 155; Gatell, *John Gorham Palfrey*, 175-76.

[7] Adams had been eager to replace his father in Congress, but his break with the Whigs had already gone too far. Whigs received suggestions of his nomination with derision. See Adams, Diary, March 15, 1848, in Adams Papers; Pierce, *Charles Sumner*, III, 182-83.

his support of Free Soil would prevent the Whigs from endorsing him for Congress. The result of Mann's neutral position, however, was to lose what would have been a valuable voice in behalf of Van Buren and Adams.[8]

The reaction to the anti-extension challenge among politicians not sympathetic to the Free Soilers contained few surprises. Those Democrats who remained loyal and refused to secede knew, however, that their chances for victory had been gravely weakened by the Free Soilers. The danger was apparent that Van Buren would carry many more Democrats than Whigs into the new party. New York's Hunkers were especially alarmed because they realized that the Whig party of New York could now place itself more firmly in power. Even worse, a strong showing by the Barnburners in the fall elections might jeopardize Hunker dominance over the state Democratic party should their opponents attempt to regain control. Their immediate reaction was to demand that President Polk remove from office all Barnburners whom he had appointed. In July, Polk brought the matter before his cabinet. As he recorded, "they all agreed that the Barnburners who had bolted from the regular nominations . . . deserved to be removed." But because of the approaching election, the consensus was that it would be "highly inexpedient" to make the removals at that time. Finally, in September, Polk gave in to the Hunker pressure and removed the prominent Barnburner and close Van Buren adviser, Benjamin F. Butler, from his post as Attorney of the United States in New York. The president reasoned that Butler had abandoned the Democratic party and "is endeavoring to divide the country into geographical parties."[9]

Polk refrained from wholesale removals, however, fearing that he would produce a group of Free Soil martyrs. William Marcy soon decided that even Butler's dismissal had been a blunder after all, because

[8] E. I. F. Williams, *Horace Mann, Educational Statesman* (New York, 1937), 300; Gatell, "Bolt of the Conscience Whigs," 39; Wilson to Mann, March 17, July 10, 1848, Sumner to Mann, July 2, 1848, Mann to Sumner, June 28, 1848, E. Everett to Mann, September 19, 1848, in Mann Papers, Massachusetts Historical Society.

[9] Quaife (ed.), *The Diary of James K. Polk,* IV, 11-12, 114-15; Marcy to Wetmore, April 25, July 9, 1848, in Marcy Papers; Spencer, *William L. Marcy,* 180-81.

it might have the effect of bringing more support to Van Buren. On the other hand, the threat of removal helped to prevent some of the more timid anti-extension Democrats from openly endorsing Free Soil. One of the reasons for Marcus Morton's failure to become more active in the Free Soil party was his alleged fear that he would lose his post as Collector of the Port of Boston. But in Morton's case, as with many others like him who lacked free soil conviction, there were other equally important political factors involved in his decision. His political rivals, the Conscience Whigs, dominated Free Soil leadership in Massachusetts, and the highly partisan Morton was never able to overcome past political animosities. He later attempted to rationalize his hesitancy by referring to Adams as the "greatest Iceberg in the Northern Hemisphere."[10]

The reaction of other key Democrats to a movement led by one of the most prominent Jacksonian Democrats became an important factor in the election. For the most part, party loyalty proved much stronger than devotion to Martin Van Buren or to Free Soil. Even an appeal to the wishes of Andrew Jackson had little effect. Distorting Jackson's thoughts, Francis Blair, who had been a close adviser of Jackson and a member of his Kitchen Cabinet, published a letter the general had written shortly before his death in 1845, in which he expressed the hope that justice would be done and Van Buren returned to the presidency: "I cannot hope to be alive and witness the acclamation with which the people of the United States will call Mr. Van Buren to the Presidency at the expiration of Mr. Polk's term. . . ." That Jackson surely had in mind Van Buren's election as a loyal Democrat did not prevent Blair from adding his own interpretation. Apparently Blair himself was not convinced either, for he announced later that although "my heart is with Mr. Van Buren and his principles," he would nevertheless vote for Cass out of party loyalty.[11] The same was true of most other important Democratic leaders outside of New York, such as Thomas Hart Benton. Although the Missourian favored the Wilmot

---

[10] Marcy to Wetmore, September 8, 1848, in Marcy Papers; Morton to Nicholas Fillinghart, September 20, 1848, Morton to John Van Buren, October 4, 1852, Morton to Flagg, December 6, 1852, in Morton Papers; Duberman, *Charles Francis Adams*, 153.

[11] Jackson to Blair, January 24, 1845, in Blair-Lee Papers, Princeton University; William E Smith, *The Francis Preston Blair Family in Politics* (New York, 1933), I, 239-40; Rayback, *Free Soil*, 297n.

Proviso, he was not willing to risk an established position in the Democratic party to defend it. A few Democrats like Gideon Welles seceded out of loyalty to Van Buren, but they were the exceptions rather than the rule. George Bancroft, Polk's minister to London and an old friend of Van Buren, wrote: "I supported Van Buren while he was true to himself, but I cannot support him now."[12]

In the Midwest most of the prominent Democrats refused to bolt and instead helped to secure the support of the mass of their party's voters for the Cass ticket. The leading anti-extension Democrat of Illinois, Congressman John Wentworth, was typical of most midwestern Democrats in ignoring the enthusiastic Free Soil appeal and instead taking the more practical, partisan point of view. Wentworth saw the election as one between Cass and Taylor only, with there being no choice but to vote for the Democrat. He also had his own political future to worry about, for he realized that his chances for reelection to the House were better as a Democrat than as a Free Soiler. As he explained somewhat insincerely to his Democratic colleagues, he "never had any idea of bolting the Presidential ticket." At the same time, however, as an ardent supporter of the Wilmot Proviso, he did no active campaigning for Cass.[13] When forced to talk of the territorial question, Wentworth, like many other Democrats, argued that Cass's popular sovereignty doctrine would secure free soil without congressional action, thus making the third party unnecessary. He and Hannibal Hamlin even made the claim that Cass would not veto the Wilmot Proviso, Cass's own earlier statement to the contrary notwithstanding.[14] Cass's calculated silence on the issue following his nomination per-

---

[12] Benton, *Thirty Years View*, II, 723; Smith, *Thomas Hart Benton*, 239; Nevins, *Ordeal of the Union*, I, 211-12; Blair to Martin Van Buren, June 26, 1848, in Van Buren Papers; Welles to A. E. Burr, June 25, 1848, in Welles Papers; Bancroft to Prescott, quoted in Russel B. Nye, *George Bancroft, Brahmin Rebel* (New York, 1944), 177; Bancroft to Samuel Hooper, October 20, 1848, in Bancroft Papers, Massachusetts Historical Society.

[13] Holt, "Party Politics in Ohio," 298-300; Schlesinger, *The Age of Jackson*, 468; Bean, "Party Transformations in Massachusetts," 29; *Weekly Chicago Democrat*, August 22, September 5, 12, 1848; Fehrenbacher, *"Long John" Wentworth*, 83-85.

[14] Washington *Daily Union*, August 12, 1848; Cleveland *Daily Plain Dealer*, June 7, 1848. Congressman John Wentworth's *Weekly Chicago Democrat* asserted that Cass "would never veto a bill having a free clause in it." See Bessie Louise Pierce, *A History of Chicago* (New York and London, 1937), I, 398-99; Hamlin, *Hannibal Hamlin*, 180-81.

mitted northern Democrats to distort his views in this way for campaign purposes.

Similar factors affected the reaction of loyal and partisan Whigs to the Free Soil movement. Some, like the Whig boss of New York, Thurlow Weed, were not alarmed by the challenge, for they felt it would hurt the Democrats the more. Weed threw himself vigorously into the campaign and strove to widen the Democratic schism. Henry Clay, resentful over his own rejection, retired to his home in Kentucky and took no part in the campaign. Others with stronger anti-extension convictions were placed in a serious dilemma because of their mixed feelings over Taylor's candidacy. William H. Seward supported Taylor despite his dislike for Fillmore and the effect that the ticket might have on the voters of the North. He stated in Boston that slavery "can and must be abolished, and you and I can and must do it," but he continued, the Free Soil party would not be able to accomplish it. Perhaps hoping that he might influence Taylor's actions as President, he argued that only the Whig party could effectively take the lead in the anti-extension movement.[15]

The offer of a Whig congressional nomination was the decisive factor in Horace Greeley's decision to remain a Whig. Before his party's convention, Greeley's major interest had been to block Taylor's nomination. To this end, he had been willing to support Clay, Corwin, or McLean. His reaction to the convention was his famous remark that it had been a "slaughterhouse of Whig principles," and to anyone devoted to those principles, Taylor's nomination seemed "impossible." Throughout the summer of 1848, Greeley's New York *Tribune* pursued a course of neutrality between the Free Soilers and the Whigs. He continually warned that he might vote for Van Buren and gave the third party high praise and generous coverage in his columns. He observed that because of the sincerity of the Free Soilers they would receive "the votes of nearly all who regard resistance to slavery extension as the paramount public duty of the day. . . ."[16] Finally in late

[15] Albany *Evening Atlas*, June 23, August 11, 14, 1848; Glyndon Van Deusen, *Thurlow Weed, Wizard of the Lobby* (Boston, 1947), 161-62; Van Deusen, *The Jacksonian Era*, 256; Glyndon Van Deusen, *William Henry Seward* (New York, 1967), 109-10.

[16] New York *Daily Tribune*, June 10, 14, 26, August 12, 1848; Van Deusen, *Horace Greeley*, 121-23.

September, with party lines tightening, Greeley brought the *Tribune* around to a very sour endorsement of Taylor. Such a course was necessary to defeat the Democrats and "that pot-bellied, mutton-headed, cucumber Cass." He announced that this step indicated "no new conviction unless it be that of the impossibility of defeating General Cass otherwise than by supporting Gen. Taylor." His decision had clearly been made only after weeks of inner turmoil over the morality of supporting a slaveholder for president. He later rationalized his action by explaining that the Free Soil party's refusal to support a high tariff was the decisive factor in his decision.[17] But as with Horace Mann, even though neither man was a professional politician, the knowledge that political advancement was more readily available through the Whig party, provided the most important incentive to remain loyal.

Early in the campaign the Free Soilers had reason to believe that Daniel Webster might endorse their movement and thus persuade many New England Whigs to do the same. They printed his Senate anti-extension speeches on the Oregon question in Free Soil campaign tracts. Dana felt that "one speech from Webster at Faneuil Hall would put an end to the Boston Taylor faction forever," and a Free Soil campaign song expressed the hope that Webster might still join the movement:

> Our Webster's styled a Taylor man,
> Now this I hold but humming
> For to bring up the army's van,
> Great Daniel's surely coming.[18]

Webster, however, had long since decided to remain a Whig because of his influential position in that party and the apparent poor chances of the third party. He had written to his son in June: "These northern proceedings can come to nothing useful to you or to me. The men are

[17] New York *Daily Tribune*, September 22, 29, 1848; Nevins, *Ordeal of the Union*, I, 209; Schlesinger, *The Age of Jackson*, 468; Greeley, *Recollections of a Busy Life*, 211-15.
[18] Gardiner, *The Great Issue*, 169-73; Dana to R. H. Dana, July 11, 1848, in Dana Papers; *Free Soil Songs for the People* (Boston, 1848), 25; Henry Wilson implied several years later that Webster would have accepted the Buffalo nomination. Wilson to L. V. Bell, quoted in the Boston *Commonwealth*, July 14, 1852.

all low in their objects." In August, he wrote that he could not support the Buffalo nomination because he had no confidence in Van
Buren, his old political enemy. He rationalized that free soil was a
distinctively Whig doctrine. Finally on September 1, the great orator
reluctantly endorsed Taylor. The nomination, he said, was "not fit
to be made," but Taylor was the least objectionable candidate. Significantly, he noted, "We can do no good by holding out. We shall
only isolate ourselves."[19] Long associated with professional party politics, Webster apparently experienced little of the inner turmoil of the
political amateur Horace Greeley in making his decision.

An important factor in the Whig campaign against the Free Soilers,
especially in Massachusetts, was the candidacy of Charles Francis
Adams. Because the Whigs expected Adams to draw off a significant
number of normally Whig votes, perhaps enough to endanger their
control of the state, they did everything possible to discredit his candidacy. They ridiculed his rather austere and forbidding character and
attacked him for having deserted the party of his father. At the Whig
state convention Rufus Choate kindled a delighted response from his
audience by referring to John Quincy Adams as "the last of the
Adamses."[20] Whigs cleverly pointed out in a campaign pamphlet that
Adams was running on a ticket with a man he had formerly condemned. In 1844, Adams had written a vehement denunciation of
Van Buren's slavery record. There was no answer to this reminder
other than that a man's past should not be held against him. In continuing their attack on the Van Buren–Adams ticket, the Whig pamphlet observed: "To the astonishment of all we are called to witness
the UNION OF THE HOUSES OF LINDENWALD AND BRAINTREE — a mar-

---

[19] Webster to Fletcher Webster, June 19, 1848, quoted in C. H. Van Tyne (ed.),
Letters of Daniel Webster (New York, 1902), 369; Webster to E. R. Hoar, August
23, 1848, quoted in Hoar, *Autobiography of Seventy Years*, I, 149-50; Julian,
Political Recollections, 63; Boston *Daily Republican*, September 4, 1848; Nevins,
Ordeal of the Union, I, 210; Richard Current, *Daniel Webster and the Rise of
National Conservatism* (Boston, 1955), 154-56.

[20] Adams revealed his own martyr complex when he retorted: "It has been the
fate of three generations of our race to stand as the guardians of Liberty in the
Commonwealth against the competing principles of a moneyed combination."
Adams, Diary, September 14, 1848, in Adams Papers; Adams, *Charles Francis
Adams*, 94; Duberman, *Charles Francis Adams*, 154-55.

riage extraordinary between all that is superlative and rampant in modern Democracy and all that is cold, selfish, austere and vinegar-like in the remains of the American aristocracy dying out and tapering off in the third generation." The Whigs charged that Adams was associating with one of his father's enemies, and they reminded the voters that the senior Adams had once denounced Van Buren for "fawning servility" to the South and "profound dissimulation and duplicity."[21]

Despite their surface confidence, however, Whigs in both Massachusetts and Ohio were plainly worried about defections to the Free Soil party and the loss of much of their young and dynamic blood. So serious was the challenge that the party in both states called in Whig speakers from outside areas to help rally their remaining elements. In Massachusetts, both Lincoln and Seward were asked to campaign and both defended the Whig party as the best hope of anti-extension advocates. At Worcester, Lincoln charged that "the self-named 'Free Soil' party was far behind the Whigs" in regard to the Wilmot Proviso.[22] In Ohio the importance of the Free Soil vote became clear when the Whig candidate for governor, Seabury Ford, refused to take sides in the presidential race in hopes of retaining the anti-extension vote as well as that of the regular Whigs. The Whigs were naturally embarrassed by Ford's silence and, fearing a crushing defeat, they persuaded Seward to campaign in the strongly anti-extensionist Western Reserve. In Cleveland, Seward gave a vigorous defense of Taylor and the Whig position, but found things "infinitely worse" on the Reserve than he had expected. Even Horace Greeley wrote a long address to the "Free Soil Men of Ohio" in which he appealed for support of Taylor as the best way to realize their goals. The Whigs, knowing that Van Buren was a bitter pill to accept in a predominantly Whig area, tried unsuccessfully to wean Joseph Root away from the new party by offering him their nomination for Congress if he would simply refrain from

[21] *The Charles F. Adams Platform, or a Looking Glass for the Worthies of the Buffalo Convention* (1848), 1-7; Adams, Diary, September 6, 1848, Adams to Charles Allen, October 19, 1848, in Adams Papers; Duberman, *Charles Francis Adams*, 153.

[22] Herndon and Weik, *Abraham Lincoln*, I, 283-87; Luthin, "Abraham Lincoln and the Massachusetts Whigs in 1848," 624-32; Van Deusen, *William H. Seward*, 109-10.

attacking Taylor. Unlike Greeley and Horace Mann, however, Root
remained true to his principles by maintaining his attack on the Whigs
and accepting a Free Soil congressional nomination.[23]

One of the most effective weapons used by the Ohio Whigs against
the Free Soil appeal was Taylor's pledge not to use the veto. This
meant that if the opponents of slavery extension elected Taylor and a
Whig Congress, the interests of the North would be secure. This idea
was developed most fully by two men whom the Free Soilers had
earlier counted on for support. Horace Greeley used it in his appeal
to Ohio Whigs. So did Thomas Corwin, the Whig senator who had
earlier been considered by the Conscience Whigs as a prospective candidate because of his speech attacking the Mexican War. Now Corwin
was actively defending the man who had led the war effort and was
seeing no inconsistency in it. Anti-extensionism had never been one
of his interests while a strong Union and Whig unity remained his
primary goals. He campaigned throughout the state and had to answer
many charges, including one that Taylor used bloodhounds to catch
his runaway slaves. He replied weakly that the dogs were used only in
tracking slaves. The apparent turnabout in Corwin's position was most
difficult to explain, especially to Free Soilers on the Reserve, although
Chase later admitted that Corwin's campaign had hurt the Free Soilers
in Ohio.[24]

Not all Ohio Whigs were as willing as Corwin to defend their candidate and attack the Free Soilers publicly. Judge John McLean was
one who decided that silence was the best policy. Having rejected an
active role in the Free Soil party, he saw little to be gained by endorsing Van Buren. Instead, he came close to allying himself with the
Whigs when he published a letter to a Whig committee announcing

[23] Holt, "Party Politics in Ohio," 305-6; Elisha Whittlesey to Oran Follett,
October 11, 1848, William H. Seward to Follett, November 9, 1848, in Hamlin
(ed.), "Selections from the Follett Papers," XI, 30-31, 32-33; George E. Baker
(ed.), *The Works of William H. Seward* (Boston, 1886), III, 291-302; Price, "The
Election of 1848 in Ohio," 297.

[24] Holt, "Party Politics in Ohio," 306-7; Cleveland *Daily Plain Dealer,* July 8,
1848; Corwin to John G. Whittier, August 21, 1848, in Corwin Papers; W. F.
Giddings to Chase, September 20, 1848, in Chase Papers, Library of Congress;
Chase to Sumner, November 27, 1848, in Bourne (ed.), "Chase Correspondence,"
142-43; Graebner, "Thomas Corwin and the Election of 1848," 176-79.

his refusal of the Free Soil nomination. He preferred to bide his time in hopes of a Whig nomination at a later date.[25]

Most prominent Whigs throughout the North followed the lead of Seward and Corwin by putting loyalty to the party first and endorsing the Whig nomination. Benjamin Wade of Ohio and Thaddeus Stevens of Pennsylvania, later to be ardent anti-extension Republicans, supported Taylor. William Pitt Fessenden of Maine gave serious consideration to crossing over to the Free Soil party before rejecting the idea. He had nothing but contempt for scheming northern politicians like Thurlow Weed whose selfish aims, he felt, had forced Taylor on the party. But despite his unhappiness he followed the wishes of his party. He observed: "The principle of the free soil movement had my sympathy and respect. But I cannot see that it will lead to any practical result other than the election of General Cass. . . ."[26] Had a Whig led the Free Soil party, Fessenden and others like him might have been more willing to stress principle.

While many northern Democrats and Whigs concerned themselves with party loyalty and various justifications of their own parties as advocates of the Wilmot Proviso, the free black community of the North also wrestled with the question of whether or not to endorse the Free Soil party. Unlike their white counterparts in the Democratic and Whig parties, however, their concern was the lack of real commitment of the new party to racial justice and equality. This had not been an obvious issue when the Liberty party had had the antislavery field to itself. In 1840, although many blacks accepted the Garrisonian view and opposed political activity of any kind, the *Colored American,* edited by Samuel Cornish, which was somewhat indicative of black thinking, endorsed James G. Birney and the Liberty party. At the National Convention of Colored Citizens in 1843, the Presbyterian minister Henry Highland Garnet persuaded the delegates again to

[25] McLean to Charles Morse, October 26, 1848, in McLean Papers, Library of Congress; *Ohio State Journal* (Columbus), August 21, 1848.

[26] Hans L. Trefousse, *Benjamin Franklin Wade: Radical Republican from Ohio* (New York, 1963), 57; Richard N. Current, *Old Thad Stevens: A Story of Ambition* (Madison, 1942), 82; Fessenden to William Fessenden, July 17, 1848, in "Miscellaneous Collection of Maine Historical Society," quoted in Charles A. Jellison, *Fessenden of Maine, Civil War Senator* (Syracuse, 1962), 56.

endorse the Liberty party. This support was reported to the Liberty convention of 1843 by Garnet and other blacks, including the orator Samuel Ringgold Ward. Impressed by their support, the delegates resolved: "We cordially welcome our colored fellow citizens to fraternity with us in the Liberty party, . . ." and they pledged themselves to "the restoration of equality among all men." The delegates did not specify the forms of inequality they wished to eliminate, and some blacks no doubt realized that there was still a vast gulf between the egalitarian rhetoric of the Liberty men and their oftentimes paternalistic actions. Nevertheless, Garnet and other black leaders did campaign for the Liberty party in the 1844 election.[27]

Although Liberty party members frequently spoke against political and social discrimination, such was not the case with most Free Soilers. Nevertheless, many blacks were attracted to the new party because it promised to keep slavery within its current bounds. By informing Americans of the evils of slavery it could perhaps best dramatize the antislavery movement. On the other hand, the Free Soilers were definitely not abolitionists; they conceded that Congress had no power over slavery in the South. On the state level and in Congress, Free Soilers frequently supported discriminatory legislation. Blacks were well aware of the fact that the party had not called for equal rights and privileges for all men in their platform as the Liberty party had done. They knew that, since more than ninety percent of the northern black population lived in states which completely or practically excluded them from the right to vote, the Free Soil party was not likely to make an appeal for their support.[28] The new party had thus seemingly abandoned the most important black goals, the abolition of slavery everywhere and the end of racial discrimination.

Several black abolitionists, including Douglass, Ward, Garnet, Charles Remond, and Henry Bibb, attended the Free Soil convention in Buffalo. The convention recognized and accepted them but failed

[27] *The Colored American* (New York), May 23, 1840; Benjamin Quarles, *Black Abolitionists* (New York, 1969), 183-85; W. M. Brewer, "Henry Highland Garnet," *Journal of Negro History*, XIII (1928), 44-47; Wesley, "The Participation of Negroes," 44; Porter and Johnson (comps.), *National Party Platforms*, 4-8.
[28] In 1848 all of the New England states except Connecticut provided for black suffrage. However, blacks could not vote in any other state in the nation except New York where they had to meet special residence and property requirements. See Leon Litwack, *North of Slavery: The Negro in the Free States, 1790-1860* (Chicago, 1961), 75-92.

to put this recognition into any concrete action. Douglass was invited to speak, but he said only a few words and wished the party well. One delegate later recalled that the Barnburners had not wanted Douglass to be recognized at the convention because "they didn't want a 'nigger' to talk to them." While Douglass was at least paternalistically tolerated by the white delegates, other blacks were not, for at least one delegate complained about their presence.[29] Such a complaint was probably typical of the attitude it reflected. Given the racist views of most of the delegates, it is not surprising that the party never considered an attack on northern discrimination.

Douglass never made his position completely clear on the candidates of 1848. Significantly there is no record of Free Soilers seeking out Douglass's support, for the party had no interest in attracting the small black vote. Yet in his paper, the *North Star,* Douglass said that although the new party was not all he could ask or wish, it was "a noble step in the right direction." Apparently flattered by the willingness of the Buffalo convention to let him speak and impressed by the proceedings, his initial response was one of enthusiasm. Later in the campaign he began to have second thoughts. In late August, he urged his readers to vote for Gerrit Smith and the Liberty League because of its endorsement of black rights; but by mid-September he was recommending a vote for Van Buren and Adams because they had more of a chance for success. He warned, however, that blacks should not regard the party as "the real anti-slavery movement of the country." Ward, a minister and editor, insisted that Gerrit Smith deserved black support for only he was openly opposed to slavery and all that it meant. The Free Soil platform failed to reassure Ward, and he implied that an equal rights plank had been intentionally left out in order not to conflict with the "words, deeds and character of the leading men of the Free Soil party." In his view, the Barnburners were "as ready to rob black men of their rights now as ever they were. . . ."[30]

---

[29] *Reunion of the Free Soilers of 1848,* 43; Dyer, *Phonographic Report,* 4, 21; Price, "The Election of 1848 in Ohio," 249.

[30] *North Star* (Rochester), August 11, 25, September 10, 22, November 24, 1848; Dyer, *Phonographic Report,* 21; Frederick Douglass, *Life and Times of Frederick Douglass Written by Himself* (Boston, 1892), 275-78; Benjamin Quarles, *Frederick Douglass* (Washington, 1948), 143-46; Wesley, "The Participation of Negroes," 53; Foner, "Racial Attitudes of the New York Free Soilers," 320-21; Quarles, *Black Abolitionists,* 185-86.

Few New York blacks had reason to endorse the Free Soil party, since the Barnburners had done little to forward their interests. In 1846, the Democrats worked to prevent any change in the almost prohibitive requirement which forced a black to own two hundred fifty dollars worth of property to qualify for suffrage. It was a requirement that Martin Van Buren had helped to establish in 1821. In Ward's words, "Mr. Dix and Mr. Butler we know to be approvers and fosterers of the bitterest prejudices against us." While philanthropist Gerrit Smith had set aside 120,000 acres of New York land for blacks in 1846 with one of his purposes being the increase of black voters, many Barnburners had voted against changing the suffrage restriction at the recent New York constitutional convention. During the campaign Douglass charged that Van Buren and nine-tenths of the Barnburners opposed equal voting rights for blacks, and Ward chastised the Free Soilers for not demanding an end to the discriminatory Preemption Act of 1841. Nor was Ward convinced of Van Buren's sincerity on abolition in the District of Columbia.[31] Certainly the past record of Van Buren and other party leaders on the race issue provided little reason for Douglass, Ward, and other blacks to be optimistic.

In early September, 1848, a small group of black leaders met in convention in Cleveland to formulate their political views and expectations. In so doing they quickly revealed their ambivalent feelings toward the Free Soilers. The members chose Douglass president of the convention, and they accepted his *North Star* as their official newspaper. The immediate issue was whether or not to endorse the Free Soil party. In one resolution they refused to approve any political party which was not committed to equal rights and privileges for all. There was great discussion over whether this would eliminate the Free Soil party, but it was the general understanding that it did not. The convention rejected a resolution recommending black support of Free Soil candidates, but it did recognize the claim of the Buffalo convention "as calculated to increase the interest now felt in behalf of the downtrodden and oppressed of this land." Many of the members supported a resolution which explained "that while we heartily engage

[31] Litwack, *North of Slavery*, 81-89; Dixon Ryan Fox, "The Negro Vote in Old New York," *Political Science Quarterly*, XXXII (1917), 253-67; *North Star*, September 1, 1848.

in recommending to our people the Free Soil movement, and the support of the Buffalo convention, nevertheless we claim and are determined to maintain the higher standard and more liberal views which have heretofore characterized us abolitionists." While this was later modified somewhat, it was clear that the members were anything but enthusiastic in their support of the Free Soilers.[32]

As a rule the free black community was not willing to commit itself firmly to the new party in 1848, although it did recognize that the party might have some value. Most blacks accepted Douglass's warning that if we "stand off and act the part of fault finders — pick flaws in the Free Soil platform," we will "play into the hands of our enemies." After the election, however, Douglass lamented his earlier qualified support: "What has the Free Soil movement done?" It had "promised much and performed little" and even worse it had "swallowed up the Liberty party press and weakened its once powerful testimony against slavery." He now admitted that "the cry of Free Men was raised, not for the extension of liberty to the black man, but for the protection of the Liberty of the white." Anti-extensionism was not enough for Douglass, for "to denounce it [slavery] in California, to oppose its introduction in New Mexico, and give it constitutional and political sanction in New Orleans, is worse than inconsistent, and can only end in a revelation of folly and hypocrisy without advancing the cause of freedom at all."[33]

Despite Douglass's disillusionment, the election of 1848 helped to intensify and focus attention on the many partisan and sectional disputes of the past four years. The Free Soil party was one important result of these conflicts, and it now sought to bring to the fore the question the major parties wished most to avoid, the extension of slavery. The Free Soil party was the only one to endorse the Wilmot Proviso. Martin Van Buren made it clear in his letter of acceptance, and the platform stated forthrightly, that it was not only the right but the duty of Congress to stop the spread of slavery. Lewis Cass, on the other hand, wanted to let the inhabitants of the territories decide for

[32] Howard H. Bell, "The National Negro Convention, 1848," *The Ohio Historical Quarterly*, LXVII (1958), 357-68; Wesley, "The Participation of Negroes," 53.
[33] *North Star*, August 18, 1848, March 25, January 12, 1849.

themselves at a deliberately unspecified time in the territorial process. His was a middle-of-the-road approach, which he hoped would have strong appeal to the great mass of the voters, both North and South, who had no burning conviction, pro or con, on the subject of slavery extension. Although the Democrats took no stand in their platform and Cass said little about it during the campaign, he had endorsed popular sovereignty long before the nomination. Zachary Taylor and the Whig platform said nothing on the issue, but because the general was a slaveholder, many Americans assumed, incorrectly as it turned out, that he favored the expansion of slavery. Many Democrats and Whigs believed with President Polk that the issue was a mere abstraction. Slavery, they felt, would not expand into the West, and the agitation would have no other result except to endanger the Union.[34] It was this attitude that the Free Soilers would have to overcome if they expected to increase their influence.

Nevertheless the Proviso was politically popular throughout the North, for during the course of the Polk administration it had come to express accurately the feelings of many northerners. It became their answer to every southern demand which carried sectional importance. The North had long felt abused and neglected because southern influence, symbolized by slavery, seemed to them to dominate national affairs. The Wilmot Proviso was perhaps the means to right the balance between North and South. Many northerners had a real fear that slavery would expand to the new territories if not checked. If these territories were opened to a slaveholding hierarchy on equal terms with free labor, the North reasoned that free labor could not compete. The Free Soil party hoped to appeal to the large segment of northern feeling that had become convinced that slavery should not be given an opportunity to gain new footholds at the expense of northern settlers.

To a much smaller number in the North, who were more concerned with the basic wrong of slavery in the South as well as the territories, the Wilmot Proviso was the most convenient way to raise the moral issue. The Constitution indirectly protected slavery in the states, and thus most northerners could not easily oppose it there. But in the territories the question was unsettled, and antislavery men saw their chance to bring the whole issue to a head. Some believed that by not

---

[34] Quaife, *Non-Intervention*, 36-59.

allowing slavery to expand, it would be placed on the road to ultimate extinction. A direct assault on slavery itself might endanger the Union and be taken by the South as an attack on private property, while an indirect attack through the Wilmot Proviso was less likely to produce these results.

To many northerners the extension of slavery had more meaning and was more of an immediate threat than the existence of the institution in the southern states. Although some could argue that the territories in question were not particularly suited to slave labor, most came to believe that the issue was one of tremendous importance. An increasing number of northerners saw the Proviso as a means to stave off subjugation of their section by the South because, in their view, free and slave labor were incompatible. What they wanted was not abolition in the South but rather the localization of slavery there. For in that way not only would northern white farmers be spared the competition of a slave economy, they would also avoid any contact with black men at all.[35] Thus the Wilmot Proviso had the advantage of answering the needs of several diverse northern groups: politicians who wished to end southern domination of national affairs, or who had other purely political motives; men who feared what slavery would do to the opportunities of free white settlers in the territories; and men who wished to raise the moral issue of slavery everywhere without unduly risking national harmony. In the past these groups had often overlapped but frequently had come in conflict with each other. The deep unrest in northern feeling now could at last find a political voice in the Free Soil party. The Wilmot Proviso enabled the party to place its political program in terms of right and wrong. It could carry all of the sincere and noble purposes of the Liberty party but could also appeal to northern racism as well as the political and material interests of the North and West now in sharp conflict with the South.

As a result of the Proviso's great appeal, Democrats and Whigs soon realized that it was a liability to present their candidates as being opposed. Both parties preferred to ignore the issue entirely, but the Free Soil agitation made this impossible. Northern Democrats had

---

[35] For a revealing analysis of the appeal of anti-extensionism see Duberman, "The Northern Response to Slavery," 395-402 and Morrison, *The Wilmot Proviso Controversy,* 52-74.

the more difficult time convincing voters that Cass did not oppose the Proviso but some made the effort. After his letter of December, 1847, endorsing popular sovereignty, Cass wisely remained silent on the whole subject, realizing that a clear-cut statement either supporting or opposing the sentiments of the letter would have meant the loss of many votes. Consequently, many northern Democrats allowed politicians to convince them that Cass had changed his mind or that popular sovereignty was really a free soil doctrine. This task was made easier for northern Whigs because of Taylor's writings. Although they did not claim that their candidate supported the Proviso, they instead assured the voters that Taylor would not veto it if Congress passed it. One Wisconsin newspaper noted, "he has given the word of a brave soldier and an honest man that he will not interfere with the action of Congress. Surely this is all we can expect from a Southern President."[36] Thus it was easier to portray Taylor than Cass in the North as being opposed to the spread of slavery and in the South as being proslavery. This would be an important factor in the outcome of the election.

Because of the Free Soil challenge, one of the major problems facing the Democrats, and to a lesser extent the Whigs, was how to maintain party loyalty in the South while keeping northern voters happy. With the Free Soilers forcing northern Democrats to equivocate or take a stronger anti-extension stand than they would have liked to, southern Democrats showed signs of discontent. As a rule, southern Whigs did not rebel, for their presidential candidate was a southern slaveholder who was believed to represent southern interests. But within the southern Democracy William L. Yancey and John C. Calhoun emphasized the free soil implications in Cass's popular sovereignty position and demanded a firmer guarantee of southern rights in the territories. As the election approached Calhoun advised his followers "to conduct the canvass with moderation," and he himself did no campaigning. With the Free Soilers maintaining their relentless attack in the North, Democrats labored to convince southerners that Cass would best protect southern interests while Whigs claimed the same for Taylor.[37]

[36] *Wisconsin Argus* (Madison), August 29, 1848; Milwaukee *Sentinel and Gazette*, July 13, 1848.
[37] Charles M. Wiltse, *John C. Calhoun, Sectionalist, 1840-1850* (Indianapolis and New York, 1951), 359-73; John W. DuBose, *The Life and Times of William Lowndes Yancey* (Birmingham, 1892), 224; Morrison, *The Wilmot Proviso Con-*

Throughout the North, on the other hand, the Free Soil campaign placed Whigs and Democrats on the defensive. They attempted to counter the third-party challenge by arguing that it merely duplicated their own positions. Again the Whigs had the advantage because they were often willing to endorse the Wilmot Proviso while Democrats usually were not. Whigs denied the new party's right to exist because, they said, free soil had always been a part of their creed. Webster argued: "I think we are as good free soil men as they are." The Walworth County (Wisconsin) Whig convention resolved that "the Free Soil Party has stolen the Whig thunder and hopes to ride into office on Whig principles."[38]

The Free Soilers realized that Democratic and Whig efforts to present themselves as anti-extensionists were having some success. They therefore labored continuously throughout the campaign to convince the voters that the two major parties were southern-dominated and controlled and that a victory for either would mean the continued subordination of northern interests. In Massachusetts, where the Whigs were the dominant party, Charles Sumner charged that the nomination of General Taylor was brought about by an "unholy conspiracy between the cotton planters and fleshmongers of Louisiana and Mississippi and the cotton spinners and traffickers of New England — the lords of the lash and the lords of the loom." Gamaliel Bailey's *National Era* summed up the major Free Soil campaign desire: "Suppose the mists which the arts of politicians have raised to obscure the positions of Generals Taylor and Cass could be this hour dispelled, and the People could see them in their true light as the pledged guardians of the Slave Interest and the opponents of the policy of Slavery Restriction, we do not believe that either of them could carry a single free state."[39] Bailey never got his wish, for Democrats and Whigs largely

troversy, 158-63, 169-70; Avery Craven, *The Growth of Southern Nationalism*, Vol. VI of *A History of the South* (Baton Rouge, 1953), 49.

[38] Boston *Post*, September 6, 1848; Julian, *Political Recollections*, 63; Boston *Advertiser*, September 14, 1848; Milwaukee *Sentinel and Gazette*, October 12, 20, 1848. For an example of Whig arguments that a vote for Van Buren was a vote for Cass, see Seward speech, October 5, 1848, quoted in Baker (ed.), *Works of William H. Seward*, III, 303-5.

[39] Appleton to Sumner, August 17, September 4, 1848, Sumner to Appleton, August 21, 1848, in Sumner Papers; Sumner to Appleton, August 31, 1848, in Appleton Papers; Boston *Daily Republican*, October 24, 1848; *National Era*, October 12, 1848.

succeeded in representing one position in the North and the reverse in the South. Consequently the campaign never achieved the potential significance that the Free Soil challenge represented, and the London *Times* could dismiss the contest as one of "ficticious partisanship."[40] As Whigs and Democrats distorted their own views and those of their opponents, it became difficult to distinguish one party from the other. Yet most voters concluded that they were confronted with a meaningful decision in choosing between Cass and Taylor — a decision that the Free Soilers seemed powerless to change.

As far as the Free Soilers were concerned, the only issue of major importance was the Wilmot Proviso. Nevertheless, the party had learned from the example of the Liberty party that a one-idea party had little appeal to the average voter. Fully aware that there were other issues causing public concern, the Free Soilers, through their platform, opportunistically took the positions most likely to appeal to a wide number of people while alienating the fewest. In doing so, they again revealed their ability to combine politics and principle to their own advantage.

Second only to the extension of slavery as a campaign issue, especially to midwesterners, was the expenditure of federal funds for internal improvements. Consequently, the Free Soilers tried to capitalize politically on this situation by taking up the midwesterners' cause. Traditionally, the Whig party had also favored federal aid while the Democrats opposed it on the constitutional grounds that most of these projects were local in nature and therefore not a function of the national government.[41] Both the Jackson and Van Buren administrations had spent a bare minimum on improvements, and in 1846, President Polk vetoed the first of three such bills. Midwestern Democrats already angry with the administration over Oregon, patronage, and extension policies were thus given further cause for unrest. When Whigs in the region took the lead in the protests by calling a rivers and harbors convention to meet in Chicago in July, 1847, they were joined by many Democrats and Liberty men, most of whom were soon to become Free Soilers. Most prominent politicians including Martin Van

---

[40] London *Times*, n.d., quoted in Van Deusen, *The Jacksonian Era*, 259.
[41] This partisan division is best revealed in the voting records of the two parties in Congress. See Joel Silbey, *The Shrine of Party: Congressional Voting Behavior, 1841-1852* (Pittsburgh, 1967), 36-39, 75-76, 87-88, 116-18.

Buren were well aware of the political implications of the convention and rushed to recognize its legitimacy whether they agreed with its purpose or not. Lewis Cass, however, made the politically unwise decision to remain noncommittal.[42]

The Democratic platform of 1848 further embittered midwesterners by opposing any broad program of federal improvements, and with Cass's pledge to support the platform, many voters assumed that he would continue Polk's policy. His evasive reply to the rivers and harbors convention became a burning campaign issue, with his Whig and Free Soil opponents charging that the Michigan senator was deserting his section. With no southern voters to worry about, the Free Soilers quickly seized on the opportunity and, recognizing the legitimacy of federal aid for river and harbor improvements, noted in their platform "that it is the duty of Congress, in the exercise of its constitutional powers," to provide for them. Van Buren hedged somewhat in his acceptance of this plank, but nevertheless modified his earlier opposition enough to satisfy improvements advocates. The overall effect of the issue was to cost the Democrats substantial support in the Great Lakes area. Some Democrats, already interested in the Wilmot Proviso and alienated by President Polk, found the issue of internal improvements the deciding factor in turning them toward the Free Soil party. This was especially true in the southeastern counties of Wisconsin, areas where Democratic anti-extension views were strongest.[43] Thus the opportunistic Free Soilers, in recognizing the economic needs of the Midwest, were quick to seize on the political potential to embarrass their Democratic opponents.

[42] Robert Fergus, "Chicago River and Harbor Convention: An Account of its Origin and Proceedings," *Fergus Historical Series,* No. 18 (Chicago, 1882), 14-15, 75-76. Cass's reply to an invitation to attend the convention was curt and to the point: "Circumstances, however, will put it out of my power to be present at that time." He had voted for several internal improvements bills in the Senate, but because he needed southern support for the Democratic nomination he dared not endorse the convention. The delegates naturally took his reply to signify his opposition to their objectives. Albert Cole, "The Barnburner Element in the Republican Party" (M.A. thesis, University of Wisconsin, 1951), 20-27; Fehrenbacher, *"Long John" Wentworth,* 76-77; Woodford, *Lewis Cass,* 267. See also Mentor L. Williams, "The Chicago River and Harbor Convention, 1847," *Mississippi Valley Historical Review,* XXXV (1949), 607-26.

[43] Porter and Johnson (comps.), *National Party Platforms,* 14; Gardiner, *The Great Issue,* 148-49; Smith, *The Liberty and Free Soil Parties,* 122-23, 146.

Another issue causing some interest was the tariff. Because they found themselves appealing to Democrats and Whigs who held opposite viewpoints on the tariff, the Free Soilers attempted with some success to straddle the issue. Although they went somewhat beyond the Democratic position of a tariff for revenue only, they refused to endorse the Whig position of a protective tariff. In his letter of acceptance, Van Buren spoke only of a revenue tariff, and this did not please Conscience Whig elements already upset by what they felt was a Barnburner domination of the party. The issue remained subordinate to more pressing matters, however, and probably did the Free Soilers little harm.[44]

Unlike the tariff, the homestead issue was one which the Free Soilers were able to use to their own political advantage, especially in their effort to win the support of workingmen away from the Democratic party. The idea of giving small amounts of the public domain to actual settlers and preventing it from falling into the hands of land monopolists and speculators was not a new one in 1848. It had been championed by a group known as the National Reform Association, led by George Henry Evans, which successfully appealed to labor leaders for support. Interest in the issue increased as the campaign of 1848 opened, and in June the Industrial Congress, at its annual meeting, announced its support for Gerrit Smith and the Liberty League because it had supported its land demands. But the Barnburners also made an appeal for labor support, and in a letter in July, Van Buren indicated he was sympathetic to the free land movement. At Buffalo, the party included a homestead plank calling for "the free grant to actual settlers" and during the campaign the Free Soilers made some headway in winning the support of workingmen's newspapers representing the skilled crafts.[45] Again politics and principle combined as the Free Soilers expressed their sincere concern for the land issue in order to seek the votes of many who might not otherwise be interested in their movement.

In addition to the homestead idea in their appeal for the support of workingmen, the Free Soilers used the fear of slave labor in the terri-

---

[44] Smith, *The Liberty and Free Soil Parties*, 147; Porter and Johnson, *National Party Platforms*, 13-14; Gardiner, *The Great Issue*, 149.

[45] Rayback, *Free Soil*, 220-22; David Bryant to Gerrit Smith, June 12, 1848, in *Calendar of the Gerrit Smith Papers;* Van Buren to A. E. Bovay, July 20, 1848, quoted in Albany *Evening Atlas*, July 26, 1848; Porter and Johnson (comps.), *National Party Platforms*, 13-14.

tories and hatred of black men in general to win support. Third-party orators made constant references to the need for the Wilmot Proviso to assure that western lands would be preserved for free white labor. John Van Buren spoke frequently to urban laboring groups and emphasized the degrading influence of slavery upon free labor.[46] This effort to win the support of northern white labor reinforced the Free Soil willingness to omit any mention of ending racial discrimination in the North. Generally, northern laborers, especially those who were not members of craft unions, had been apathetic and even opposed to the anti-extension movement. Before the formation of the Free Soil party, antislavery groups had not been greatly interested in the needs of laboring men. In addition, the indifference and even hostility of unskilled workers was due in part to their dislike and fear of the free blacks who lived among them and posed employment competition. This was especially true of Irish and German immigrants. German workers in Wisconsin, for instance, voted more than three to one against black suffrage in 1847. The Free Soil party thus realized the growing importance of the labor vote and made its open and direct appeal for support, noting that a vote for Van Buren would "elevate and dignify labor." Labor suspicion of the third party continued to be significant, however, and most workers remained in the Democratic party where they felt their interests were better served.[47]

In their appeals to northern workers and in their use of the extension, homestead, and internal improvements issues, the Free Soil movement held little attraction for the average southern voter. Yet in the border states, where slavery did not dominate the economy to the extent that it did in the Gulf states and where the voters had much in common with voters in the North, there was minor interest in the third party. Maryland, Virginia, and Kentucky sent delegates to the Buffalo convention and following the convention small Free Soil gatherings

---

[46] Joseph Rayback, "The American Workingman and the Antislavery Crusade," *Journal of Economic History*, III (1943), 152-63.

[47] Williston H. Lofton, "Abolition and Labor," *Journal of Negro History*, XXXII (1948), 261-73; Florence Elizabeth Baker, "A Brief History of the Elective Franchise in Wisconsin," *Proceedings of the State Historical Society of Wisconsin, 1893* (Madison, 1894), 121. See also Leslie Fishel, "Wisconsin and Negro Suffrage," *Wisconsin Magazine of History*, LXVI (1963), 180-96; Albany *Evening Atlas*, November 7, 1848.

met in Maryland, Delaware, North Carolina, Kentucky, and Missouri.
Former governor Thomas of Maryland and former senator Haywood
of North Carolina endorsed Van Buren.[48] This limited support adds
further proof to the thesis that the South was not as single-minded on
the slave issue as many have assumed. Probably the greatest amount of
slave state interest in Free Soil was in Missouri. Although most of the
Missouri press opposed the Wilmot Proviso or regarded it as an abstraction, Francis P. Blair's son Frank actively campaigned for Van
Buren and even started an anti-extension campaign newspaper. The
paper, the *Missouri Barnburner,* commenced publication in St. Louis
in September but despite bold editorials by Blair, failed after several
issues because of lack of funds. Blair defended Van Buren and argued
that the Free Soilers had as much right to agitate as the Revolutionary
leaders of 1776. He also helped organize a Free Soil rally in St. Louis
in September. The movement soon collapsed, however, and an attempt
to organize a Free Soil electoral ticket failed.[49]

Kentucky had an anti-extension movement, but the traditional suspicion of northern agitation there prevented any cooperation with the
Free Soilers in 1848. Only in Virginia did the party manage to organize an electoral ticket and get on the ballot. Van Buren received nine
votes in Virginia, and when some Free Soilers raised the cry of fraud,
a Virginian is said to have answered: "Yes Fraud! And we're still
looking for that son-of-a-bitch who voted nine times."[50]

For both northern and southern voters the only issue of major significance was that of slavery in the territories. And with the Democrats
and Whigs remaining so evasive on the subject, the campaign frequently degenerated into personal abuse and ridicule of the individual
candidates. None of the contenders was exempt. Free Soilers gleefully
quoted Taylor as having said he had "little time or inclination to in-
vestigate the great issues or subjects of discussion." They called atten-

[48] Wilson, *The Slave Power,* II, 159; Alexander, *Martin Van Buren,* 404, 406;
Kenneth M. Stampp, "Opposition to Slavery in the Upper South, 1808-1860"
(M.A. thesis, University of Wisconsin, 1937), 88, 109.
[49] Benjamin Merkel, *The Antislavery Controversy in Missouri, 1819-1865*
(St. Louis, 1942), 13-14 (dissertation abstract); Smith, *The Blair Family,* I, 240.
[50] Henry F. Watson to Martin Van Buren, August 17, 1848, in Van Buren
Papers; David Smiley, "Cassius M. Clay and John G. Fee: A Study in Southern
Anti-Slavery Thought," *Journal of Negro History,* XLII (1957), 201-13; Stanwood,
A History of the Presidency, 243.

tion to his lack of education and political inexperience, and most important, they denounced him as a trafficker in human flesh. Nor did they hesitate to ridicule Cass, calling him a Michigan doughface interested only in surrendering to southern demands in order to obtain the presidency.[51]

Yet Martin Van Buren and the Free Soilers were the victims of more abuse than either Taylor or Cass. No term was too harsh to apply to Van Buren, "the traitor and the hypocrite, the Judas Iscariot of the nineteenth century." Critics charged he was putting personal ambition and revenge above his country's welfare. When not trying to show they were just as devoted to the Wilmot Proviso as the Free Soilers, Democrats and Whigs inconsistently argued that their opponents were dangerous abolitionists. One midwestern newspaper charged that the party included men who were "destitute of fixed principles who have betrayed every party they ever belonged to." The Free Soil answer was to turn attention away from what they had been in the past and instead emphasize that they were the party of the future. The Southport *Telegraph* (Kenosha) expressed this viewpoint best: "We are not abolitionists, democrats, or whigs; we are free soilers."[52]

Of the three parties, the Free Soilers displayed by far the most enthusiasm in what turned out to be a fairly lackluster campaign. With the exception of a short tour through the East in June by General Cass, none of the candidates for president did any personal campaigning, preferring to follow tradition and let others speak for them. And in this task the new party, despite its late start and lack of established local organization, was the only one that appeared to believe what it was saying. Probably the party's most effective orator and the hardest worker during the campaign was John Van Buren. Recognizing his value to the cause, the Buffalo delegates had unanimously passed a resolution inviting him "to stump the United States generally." "Prince John" responded by making at least thirty major addresses in a two-month period, speaking in New York, New England, Pennsylvania, and Ohio. Contemporary accounts agreed that he was one of the

[51] *Wisconsin Barnburner* (Milwaukee), September 1, 1848; *Wisconsin Freeman* (Milwaukee), October 10, 1848.

[52] Smith, *The Liberty and Free Soil Parties,* 148; *Wisconsin Argus,* October 10, 1848; Southport *Telegraph,* October 6, 1848.

greatest stump speakers of his generation. Years later the New York *Times* noted that he won in this campaign "a more brilliant reputation than has ever been won in a single political campaign by any other man." His popularity and effectiveness were due to his platform personality, for he had an almost hypnotic power over his audiences as he savagely ripped into the southern "slavery conspiracy" and the compromising of the Whig and Democratic parties.[53] Despite his overriding interest in using the movement for Barnburner political purposes, he was able to persuade many with his eloquent appeal to principle.

To back up young Van Buren and other third-party orators, Free Soil newspapers sprang up all over the North, the most important being Bailey's *National Era* and the Boston *Republican* which Henry Wilson organized to replace the defunct *Daily Whig*. Walt Whitman, after being dismissed from the Brooklyn *Eagle* for supporting Free Soil, began a short-lived paper of his own, the *Weekly Freeman*.[54] In addition to the many Free Soil papers initiated during the campaign, countless Democratic, Whig, and Liberty dailies and weeklies endorsed the Van Buren ticket. Probably the most influential of these were the two Barnburner dailies, the Albany *Evening Atlas* and the New York *Evening Post*.

In their great enthusiasm and eagerness, the Free Soilers lived and enjoyed the contest to the fullest. In their campaign songs they displayed a spontaneous fervor last seen in the Whig campaign of 1840:

> Come, ye hardy sons of toil,
> And cast your ballots for Free soil;
> He who'd vote for Zacky Taylor
> Needs a keeper or a jailor.
> And he who still for Cass can be,
> He is a Cass without the C;
> The man on whom we love to look,
> Is Martin Van Buren from Kinderhook.[55]

---

[53] Dyer, *Phonographic Report*, 27-28; New York *Tribune*, August 11, 1848; New York *Times*, October 17, 1866; Alexander, *A Political History of New York*, II, 128-30; John Bigelow, *Retrospections of an Active Life* (New York, 1909), I, 87; Ferree, "The New York Democracy," 221; Schlesinger, *The Age of Jackson*, 467.

[54] Loubert, "Henry Wilson," 75-77; Gay Wilson Allen, *The Solitary Singer: A Critical Biography of Walt Whitman* (New York, 1955), 90-103.

[55] *Free Soil Songs for the People*, 21-22.

Throughout most of the campaign, most Free Soilers maintained an unrealistic optimism which sustained them temporarily but only made the results harder to accept. Rarely in Free Soil writings, including private correspondence, were there predictions for anything less than victory in 1848. The *National Era* expressed continual optimism and noted that northerners were turning to the cause by the thousands. Enthusiasm was greatest during and immediately following the Buffalo convention. Adams noted in his diary: "I do not imagine that any event of the age in which I live will lead to consequences more important." Despite the unpopularity of Van Buren among Conscience Whigs, both Adams and Sumner predicted he would carry Massachusetts. Of all the Free Soilers, Sumner was by far the most exuberant and optimistic. He wrote to Chase that "the whole country seems to be arousing at last."[56]

Later in the campaign, however, Adams, in a more realistic mood, admitted, "Enough is visible to me to satisfy me that the people of the Free States are not yet roused so fully as they should be to the necessity of sustaining their principles." More experienced politicians like Van Buren made no predictions of victory, and Adams expressed one of the major Free Soil problems when he observed: "Party connexions still retain much of their force."[57]

The enthusiasm of the Free Soil party in the presidential race frequently carried over into congressional, state, and local elections. Here again, however, the lack of an established party organization was a severe handicap, probably even greater than in the contest for president. Not only did Whigs and Democrats have well established state and local organizations in most areas, but they usually had greater financial resources. Yet as political realists, the Free Soilers were often able to take advantage of Democratic and Whig weaknesses and seize on issues which could attract significant numbers of votes. In other cases a stricter adherence to principle sometimes resulted in defeat at the polls. Nevertheless, taking into account that the party did not even exist until August, 1848, it did achieve moderate success. In areas

[56] *National Era,* August 31, 1848; Adams, Diary, August 11, 1848, in Adams Papers; Sumner to Chase, July 7, 1848, in Chase Papers, Library of Congress; Sumner to Giddings, September 3, 1848, in Giddings Papers.

[57] Adams, Diary, October 13, 1848, Adams to Seth Gates, October 1, 1848, in Adams Papers.

where one of the major parties was relatively weak, the Free Soilers frequently entered into coalitions, and in a few cases Free Soil candidates replaced either Democrats or Whigs in two-way races. In some instances Free Soilers won because men who were already congressmen with established reputations joined the new party and brought their supporters with them.

In Massachusetts, Free Soil candidates for Congress were not always willing to make the necessary political compromises to secure election. Horace Mann, however, was an exception, for he received the nominations of both Whig and Free Soil parties for Congress and was elected in the district formerly served by John Quincy Adams. As already noted, Mann refused to endorse Van Buren and often sounded more like a Whig than a Free Soiler. Charles Sumner ran against Robert Winthrop for the latter's seat in Congress in a campaign based primarily on national issues. Sumner did not expect to do well in the normally Whig district, and Winthrop was an easy winner. In fact Sumner did little better than the Liberty candidate had done in the race for the same seat in 1846. Relative to the Winthrop showing in 1846, Sumner actually lost ground slightly. His pronounced anti-extension ideas thus had little appeal in a district where the voters preferred to stay with the proven Cotton Whig leadership of Winthrop.[58]

Massachusetts law required that to be elected to Congress a candidate had to receive an absolute majority, and with three candidates competing, several runoffs in which all the candidates participated, were frequently necessary. The district including Worcester elected Free Soiler Charles Allen, Samuel Adams's grandson, over Whig Charles Hudson and a Democratic opponent in the first runoff in January, 1849. A result was not so easily reached in the fourth district in which former Whig John G. Palfrey ran for reelection. Shortly after the Buffalo convention, the Whigs had expelled him from the party, even though Palfrey was far from enthusiastic in his support of Van Buren. Although Palfrey had hoped to receive both Free Soil and Whig nominations he found himself in a three-way race. He received a plurality in the November election but not a majority. In the second try, Conscience leaders including Adams urged him to

---

[58] Williams, *Horace Mann,* 300; Donald, *Charles Sumner,* 169; Sumner to Giddings, November 10, 1848, in Giddings Papers.

accept a Democratic coalition, but the stubbornly principled Palfrey argued that no political office was worth the contamination of working with "Loco Foco dough-face leaders." In the second election he came within forty-three votes of victory. More runoffs followed with no result as Palfrey continued to spurn Democratic support, and when the Thirty-First Congress opened in December, 1849, there was no representative from the fourth district. Finally in 1851, after thirteen unsuccessful tries in the district, the legislature agreed to a plurality law. Palfrey, having antagonized numerous Free Soilers because of his stubbornness, lost on the fourteenth vote. New England would thus have only two fully committed Free Soilers in the new Congress. In addition to Allen of Massachusetts, Amos Tuck won reelection in New Hampshire with the backing of Free Soil and Whig voters.[59]

Two former Democratic congressmen responsible for much of the anti-extension agitation in Congress, Preston King and David Wilmot, won reelection with Free Soil support. King won without difficulty in the upstate New York district which included St. Lawrence. The Whigs attacked King's early inconsistent record on sectional issues while the Democrats called him an abolitionist. King was the only Free Soiler to win in the state, the congressional delegation of which included thirty-two Whigs and only one Democrat. The third party, drawing heavily on Democratic strength, was largely responsible for this result.[60] Wilmot won reelection from Pennsylvania's twelfth district by effectively combining local and national issues. Nominally he remained a Democrat despite there being another Democrat in the race pledged to Cass. Wilmot, in explaining his strategy, said that no state except New York was ready for a third party because the two major parties were still too powerful: "In Penna. apparently but little interest is taken in the question of slavery extension, out of my own district." The reality of local Pennsylvania politics meant that running on a standard ticket was necessary for success. Yet after winning reelection in the October race, Wilmot could safely extend his campaign-

---

[59] Gatell, *John G. Palfrey*, 173-200; Adams to Palfrey, December 25, 1848, in Adams Papers; Palfrey manuscript autobiography, Palfrey Papers, 215; Estes Howe to Palfrey, September 13, 1849 and E. Rockwood Hoar to Palfrey, May 27, 1851, in Palfrey Papers; Sewell, *John P. Hale*, 142-43; Charles R. Corning, *Amos Tuck* (Exeter, N.H., 1902), 50-51.

[60] Muller, "Preston King," 454-58.

ing for Van Buren and Free Soil, speaking twenty-five times, mostly
in New York state.[61]

In the Midwest, Free Soilers won election to Congress in several
key races. In Ohio's Western Reserve, Joshua Giddings, who had long
resisted the Liberty party, now officially left the Whigs to join the
Free Soilers. Giddings, unlike Wilmot, represented a locale where anti-
extension sentiment was strong enough to permit him to switch parties
and maintain a reasonable chance of success. Despite his lack of enthusiasm for Van Buren, he now argued that in supporting Free Soil
he was being consistent with his former position, for the Whigs had
abandoned their principles by nominating Taylor. The Whigs did not
bother to nominate anyone to oppose the popular Giddings and instead
combined with the Democrats in their efforts to unseat him. Their
strategy failed, however, as Giddings swept the district by more than
3,000 votes. Following similar strategy, Joseph Root won election on
a Free Soil ticket in the same area of Ohio after rejecting Whig support.[62] Both men won largely with the assistance of former Whigs in
a state where Whigs were more inclined toward the Wilmot Proviso
than Democrats.

In Indiana another former Whig won election to Congress in a
contest held in 1849. George Julian broke with his party to support
Van Buren and later viewed this campaign as the greatest crusade of
his long political career. Unlike John G. Palfrey, he was not above
working with the Democrats if it increased his chances for victory.
Taking advantage of the Democrats' weakness, Julian sought out and
won their endorsement in this usually Whig district. Julian was the
winner by 153 votes, and Whigs lamented that the victory of the "free
dirters" would bring disaster to Indiana. During the campaign, Julian
recalled that he was "subjected to a torrent of billingsgate which ri-
valed the fish market." He was called an "amalgamationist, a woolly-
head, and apostle of disunion." It was the standing Whig joke that he
carried in his pocket a lock of the hair of Frederick Douglass to revive
his strength when he grew faint and that his usual audience consisted

---

[61] Going, *David Wilmot*, 277, 310, 317; Wilmot to Chase, May 29, 1848, in
Chase Papers, Historical Society of Pennsylvania.
[62] Stewart, *Joshua R. Giddings*, 158-59.

of "eleven men, three boys and a Negro."[63] In strongly Free Soil southeastern Wisconsin, former Liberty party member Charles Durkee successfully combined the Wilmot Proviso and internal improvements issues to unseat the Democratic incumbent in a close three-way race.[64] Thus whenever the Free Soilers were willing and able to enter the rough game of politics by exploiting issues of local significance or by taking advantage of a major party's weakness, their chances for success improved greatly.

Free Soil candidates also ran in congressional races in many other northern districts with encouraging results considering their handicaps. Because of the many contests in which coalitions participated, it is difficult to say how many bona fide Free Soilers were elected. In the Thirty-First Congress there would be at least eight Free Soilers, including Allen, Tuck, King, Wilmot, Giddings, Root, Julian, and Durkee. In addition there were four representatives who were elected with the aid of Free Soil coalitions, who sometimes voted with the Free Soilers. They included Horace Mann, Walter Booth of Connecticut, William Sprague of Michigan, and John W. Howe of Pennsylvania.[65] As a result the party could usually depend on from eight to twelve votes.

Although the Free Soilers were primarily interested in national issues, they did enter into numerous state and local contests. Nowhere was the party powerful enough to win control of a state government, although numerous Free Soilers won seats in state legislatures. In New York, the Barnburners persuaded Senator John A. Dix to run for governor in what he considered a hopeless campaign. Their interest here was in large part due to their desire to regain control of the

[63] Grace Julian Clarke, *George W. Julian* (Indianapolis, 1923), 78-79, 86; Julian, *Political Recollections*, 59-67; Patrick W. Riddleberger, *George Washington Julian, Radical Republican: A Study in Nineteenth Century Politics and Reform*, vol. XLV of *Indiana Historical Collection* (Indianapolis, 1966), 45-50; H. S. Finch to Julian, December 2, 1848, in Julian Papers, Indiana State Library; Samuel Parker to Caleb Smith, July 2, 7, August 10, 1849, David Halloway to Smith, August 8, 1849, in Caleb Smith Papers, Library of Congress.
[64] Theodore C. Smith, "The Free Soil Party in Wisconsin," *Proceedings of the State Historical Society of Wisconsin, 1893* (Madison, 1894), 118.
[65] Julian, *Political Recollections*, 72-73. Joseph Rayback also lists three Ohioans — Campbell, Hunter, and Crowell — as Free Soilers; however, because they rarely cooperated with the third party they should be considered Whigs instead. See Rayback, *Free Soil*, 280n.

Democratic party after the election. Should they win the governorship and control the legislature the Hunkers could be forced into a subordinate role. Although Dix thought his chances of election slim, Van Buren optimistically told him that he could "begin with safety to cast about for the subjects of your first message" as governor. But with two candidates splitting the normally Democratic vote, the Whigs took advantage of this schism and swept to an easy victory. Dix did gain more votes than his Hunker opponent and ran slightly ahead of Van Buren in New York, but this was small consolation to a man whose heart was never with the Free Soil movement or to the Barnburners who had sought to unseat the Hunkers from Democratic control.[66]

The Free Soilers also played a prominent role in state elections in two other states with strong anti-extension feelings. In Massachusetts the Conscience Whig element which dominated the leadership of the new party hoped to use the election results to force their old party to accept their anti-extension goals and thus reenter the party on their own terms. The Free Soilers nominated Stephen C. Phillips, a former Whig, for governor, and John Mills, a former Democrat, for lieutenant governor, and made a concentrated effort to topple the well-established power of the Boston Whig machine. They fell far short of their goal, however. Governor G. N. Briggs was easily reelected although Phillips did substantially better than the Democratic candidate, Caleb Cushing, who was sympathetic with the South's position on slavery.[67] The results meant that the Conscience Whigs, having failed to displace their Cotton Whig opponents, now had little choice but to continue as an independent party.

In Ohio, the Whig candidate for governor, Seabury Ford, made a direct appeal for Free Soil support and was able to win a close election only because the third party refrained from making a separate nomination. Ford refused to endorse General Taylor, and under heavy third-party pressure, announced his support of the Free Soil drive to repeal Ohio's Black Laws. Yet Ford defeated Democrat John B.

[66] Martin Van Buren to Dix, October 2, 1848, in Dix Papers; Dix to Martin Van Buren, October 7, 1848, in Van Buren Papers; Albany *Evening Atlas,* September 29, 1848; Lichterman, "John Adams Dix," 218-25; Dix, *Memoirs of John Adams Dix,* I, 238-39.
[67] Darling, *Political Changes in Massachusetts,* 354; Duberman, *Charles Francis Adams,* 155-56.

Weller by only 345 votes out of almost 300,000 cast and was not able to win the support of as many Democrats as he had expected. Nevertheless, the Free Soilers had helped to elect a governor who would be sympathetic to their cause.[68]

In most other northern states the Free Soil showing in state and local elections was disappointing, as Democratic and Whig anti-extensionists stressed political reality over principle and refused to join a party whose chances for success were poor. In Maine, for example, neither the Democrat Hannibal Hamlin nor the Whig William Pitt Fessenden, both staunch supporters of the Wilmot Proviso, was willing to endorse the new party. Both distrusted Van Buren's motives and neither was willing to stake his political future with a new and untested party. Because of this kind of attitude, the Maine Free Soil organization remained weak with leadership falling to relatively unknown politicians. With only one significant newspaper in support, the Portland *Inquirer,* organization and communication was ineffective. Samuel Fessenden, a Portland lawyer, ran on the third-party ticket for governor but received only about fifteen percent of the vote, despite the fact that campaign speakers in the state had included Sumner, Hale, and John Van Buren.[69]

In Connecticut there was an active Free Soil campaign led by the young Van Buren Democrat, Gideon Welles, and former senator John Niles. But the Free Soilers scarcely affected the hold of the regular parties on the state.[70] Of much more significance was the third-party activity in Vermont. Here Free Soil interest grew from a strong Liberty nucleus and received an important boost when the anti-extension Whig, former governor William Slade, announced his support of Van Buren. The movement drew support from both major parties but harmed the

[68] Weisenburger, *The Passing of the Frontier,* 467; Chase to Ford, July, 1848, in Bourne (ed.), "Chase Correspondence," 138-39; Holt, "Party Politics in Ohio," 310; Price, "The Election of 1848 in Ohio," 189; Smith, *The Liberty and Free Soil Parties,* 152-53.

[69] Louis Clinton Hatch, *Maine, A History* (New York, 1919), II, 340-44; Hamlin, *Hannibal Hamlin,* 180-81; Edward O. Shriver, "Antislavery: The Free Soil and Free Democratic Parties in Maine, 1848-1853," *New England Quarterly,* XLII (March, 1969), 82-88.

[70] Cole, "The Barnburner Element," 14; Welles to John Niles, September 5, 1848, Niles to Welles, October 8, November 12, 1848, A. E. Burr to Welles, October 18, 1848, in Welles Papers.

Democrats more. At first the Democrats were amused by the party, and one newspaper ridiculed it as "the free-soil, free-speech, free-labor, free-anything-else-you-can-catch-a-stray-vote-party." Numerous papers endorsed Free Soil, however, and in the state election in September, the third-party candidate for governor, Oscar Shafter, outpolled his Democratic opponent. With the Conscience Whig bolt kept to a minimum, however, the Whigs continued their domination of Vermont.[71]

David Wilmot's residence in Pennsylvania gave his state an importance in the third party out of proportion to actual Free Soil strength. A state Free Soil convention did assemble in Reading and formed an electoral ticket, but the movement was not strong enough to nominate separate candidates for state elections.[72] Why a heavily populated state such as Pennsylvania should show so little interest in Free Soil while its immediate neighbors to the North and West provided much of the leadership and support of the movement is difficult to understand. A partial explanation is that Pennsylvania was more concerned with issues of local significance like the tariff than it was with the extension of slavery. In addition, many leading Whigs of the state endorsed the Wilmot Proviso, thus taking away some of the interest in a separate anti-extension party. With the exception of Wilmot, no leader of any significance from either major party joined the new party, and there was little Liberty support on which to build. Without such direction few voters showed any interest.

In the Midwest, three states, Illinois, Iowa and Indiana, held summer elections for state offices; hence the Free Soil party did not have sufficient time to organize and present separate candidates. Equally significant, the phrase "free soil" was not as distinctive in some midwestern areas as it was in other parts of the North because it was claimed by the candidates of the major parties as well as by the Van Buren followers. In Illinois most of the Free Soil support was drawn from the Democratic stronghold in the northeastern part of the state, and only the refusal of the most prominent anti-extension Democrat, John Wentworth, to renounce his party prevented the defections from

[71] David M. Ludlum, *Social Ferment in Vermont, 1791-1850* (New York, 1939), 190-97; *Vermont Patriot,* August 31, 1848, quoted in *ibid.,* 197.
[72] Henry R. Mueller, *The Whig Party in Pennsylvania* (New York, 1922), 151-56; Sister M. Theophane Geary, *A History of Third Parties in Pennsylvania, 1840-1860* (Washington, 1938), 135-38.

being much larger.[73] Michigan held state elections in November, and a movement began for a Whig–Free Soil coalition. Because of the great popularity of Lewis Cass in his native state, most Democrats remained loyal, while the opposition formed limited combinations in an attempt to destroy his control of the state. The Whigs and Free Soilers combined in the second district to elect their candidate to Congress, and several other coalitions succeeded.[74] In Wisconsin, by the November election, the Free Soilers were better organized than those of any other midwestern state. In addition to electing Charles Durkee to Congress, they became the second party in the state legislature.[75] Thus, throughout the North the Free Soil showing in state elections was mixed at best. Nowhere did the members have time to organize thoroughly, and in some states this situation was made worse because elections were held much in advance of the November vote for president. For the most part, prominent Whigs and Democrats placed party over principle and resisted the temptation to bolt their parties. The Free Soilers rarely came to grips with local issues and thus frequently they could not offer a meaningful choice to the voters. Yet only by emphasizing local issues at the expense of the Wilmot Proviso could this result have been changed.

The results of the presidential election surprised few people. With the Free Soil vote kept to a minimum, the effect of Van Buren's appeal on the electoral vote was such that had no third party existed Zachary Taylor would still have been the winner. Again the nation preferred a military hero with few opinions to a rather unattractive established politician like Cass. The Democrats had antagonized many northerners and had not won the confidence of the South. With the whole nation voting on the same day for the first time, the vote was light: 2,878,023 ballots were cast out of a population of 23,000,000. Taylor won with an electoral vote of 163 to Cass's 127; Van Buren failed to carry a single state. Of the popular vote, Taylor received 1,360,099, Cass

---

[73] Smith, *The Liberty and Free Soil Parties,* 155-59; Pease, *The Frontier State, 1818-1848,* 336; Cole, *The Era of the Civil War,* 60-61.

[74] Floyd B. Streeter, *Political Parties in Michigan: An Historical Study of Political Issues and Parties in Michigan from the Admission of the State to the Civil War* (Lansing, 1918), 99-100.

[75] Cole, "The Barnburner Element," 32-39; Smith, "The Free Soil Party in Wisconsin," 117-18.

Table 1.   1848 Presidential Election Returns

State	Popular Vote			Van Buren's Percentage	Electors	
	Taylor	Cass	Van Buren		Taylor	Cass
Alabama	30,482	31,363				9
Arkansas	7,588	9,300				3
Connecticut	30,314	27,046	5,005	8.02	6	
Delaware	6,421	5,898	80	.64	3	
Florida	3,116	1,847			3	
Georgia	47,544	44,802			10	
Illinois	53,047	56,300	15,774	12.58		9
Indiana	69,907	74,745	8,100	5.30		12
Iowa	11,084	12,093	1,126	4.63		4
Kentucky	67,141	49,720			12	
Louisiana	18,217	15,370			6	
Maine	35,125	39,880	12,096	13.85		9
Maryland	37,702	34,528	125	.17	8	
Massachusetts	61,070	36,281	38,058	28.35	12	
Michigan	23,940	30,687	10,389	15.98		5
Mississippi	25,922	26,537				6
Missouri	32,671	40,077				7
New Hampshire	14,781	27,763	7,560	15.09		6
New Jersey	40,015	36,901	829	1.07	7	
New York	218,603	114,318	120,510	26.43	36	
North Carolina	43,550	34,869			11	
Ohio	138,360	154,775	35,354	10.76		23
Pennsylvania	185,513	171,176	11,263	3.06	26	
Rhode Island	6,779	3,646	730	6.54	4	
South Carolina	(*)					9
Tennessee	64,705	58,419			13	
Texas	4,509	10,668				4
Vermont	23,122	10,948	13,837	28.88	6	
Virginia	45,124	46,586	9	.01		17
Wisconsin	13,747	15,001	10,418	26.60		4
TOTALS	1,360,099	1,220,544	291,263	10.13	163	127

Sources: Stanwood, *A History of the Presidency*, 243; Svend Petersen, *A Statistical History of the American Presidential Elections* (New York, 1963), 29-30.
* Electors appointed by the legislature.

1,220,544 and Van Buren 291,263.[76] The Whigs carried all of the doubtful states in the traditionally Democratic South and won 52 percent of the votes in slaveholding areas. The efforts of Calhoun and

[76] The Liberty League candidate, Gerrit Smith, polled 2,646 votes, of which all but 101 were concentrated in New York. See Burnham, *Presidential Ballots*, 900, 932, 933.

Yancey apparently convinced many southerners that Cass, with his ambiguous territorial position, was no more to be trusted than Van Buren. Cass carried seven slave states and all of the Midwest, while Taylor won eight slave states and the important northern states of New York, Pennsylvania, and Massachusetts.[77] The difference between Cass's total and Taylor's was 140,000 — less than half of Van Buren's vote. The Free Soiler outpolled Cass in New York, Vermont, and Massachusetts. In Ohio, where most of the Free Soil vote had formerly been Whig, Van Buren prevented a Taylor victory. On the other hand, Van Buren carried mostly Democratic votes in New York and helped prevent a Cass victory there.[78]

Van Buren's showing was somewhat disappointing after the many predictions of success for him. He received only about 10 percent of the total vote cast in the country at large and had failed to arouse the expected widespread interest in the free states where his percentage of the popular vote was a little more than fourteen. Some Free Soilers blamed Van Buren for the poor showing and said Hale or McLean would have secured a firmer hold on the moral sentiment of the country. Sumner lamented that McLean could have swept Massachusetts easily. One westerner noted that "many strong Free Soilers would not support the ticket" because of a "dislike of the man and of the managers."[79]

Nevertheless, there had been an almost fivefold increase in the third-party vote since 1844, and most Free Soilers were far from discouraged. Sumner believed there was "high cause for satisfaction" because "we have found a large number of men through all the Free States who are willing to leave parties and join in a new alliance of prin-

[77] The discussion which follows will concentrate on the North and specifically on the Free Soil vote. For a revealing analysis of the election returns in both North and South from the perspective of all three parties see Rayback, *Free Soil*, 279-87.
[78] It is highly probable that Taylor would have carried New York without Van Buren's candidacy. The Free Soil and Democratic parties together polled a majority of only 16,225. Of the 120,510 votes that Van Buren gained in New York, he probably received support from at least 8,113 former Whigs which would mean that he did not prevent a Cass victory. See Stanwood, *A History of the Presidency*, 243; Fred J. Guetter and Albert E. McKinley, *Statistical Tables Relating to the Economic Growth of the United States* (Philadelphia, 1924), 5; Burnham, *Presidential Ballots*, 32-40; Thomas H. McKee, *The National Conventions and Platforms of All Political Parties, 1789-1900* (Baltimore, 1900), 70.
[79] Smith, *The Liberty and Free Soil Parties*, 160; Sumner to Giddings, November 10, 1848, in Giddings Papers.

The Free Soilers

ciple." Even Martin Van Buren professed to be encouraged by the
results. He had surely never expected victory in 1848, and he wrote
to Blair that, "Everything was accomplished by the Free Soil movement that the most sanguine friend could hope for and much more
than there was good reason to expect."[80] Free Soilers throughout the
country looked to the future with high hopes, feeling that a good start
had already been made.

The Whigs mostly ignored the Free Soilers in their celebrations over
Taylor's victory and their return to power. Democrats, in casting
about for an explanation for their defeat, naturally singled out the
Free Soil party rather than admitting that their platform was ambiguous and their candidate unattractive. They renewed their charges that
revenge had been Van Buren's motive and one Hunker imagined the
Free Soil leader boasting, "It was I that killed your Cass and made
your Taylor president! Yes, Gentlemen I did it and have thus settled
my account with the illustrious nominee and treacherous wire-pullers
of the Baltimore convention!"[81]

Although the Free Soil party did not change the outcome of the
election it played a very significant role and was indicative of things
to come. As a third party, it carried numerous counties throughout the
North; it took three in New England, eight in the Middle Atlantic
states, and twenty-one in the Midwest.[82] It had demonstrated that the
hold of the Democrats and Whigs on the voters was weakening and
that it was possible to arouse the people on the issue of slavery. A more
successful sectional party might soon be possible. For this reason, it is
important to locate the source of the Free Soil voting strength. Which
of the two parties did it affect more significantly? An analysis of the
voting returns of 1848 throughout the North reveals that more Democrats voted for Van Buren than Whigs, although in several states the
Whig party was the bigger loser.[83]

Hunkers and Free Soilers divided the normal Democratic vote in
New York where the overwhelming majority of the third-party voters

[80] Sumner to Chase, November 16, 1848, in Chase Papers, Library of Congress;
Van Buren to Blair, December 11, 1848, in Blair Papers.
[81] Milwaukee *Sentinel and Gazette,* November 23, 1848; G. A. Worth to
William Marcy, November 12, 1848, in Marcy Papers.
[82] Burnham, *Presidential Ballots,* 36-37.
[83] See Rayback, *Free Soil,* 299-301.

had been Democrats before the election. This is hardly surprising considering the hold that Martin Van Buren had on a large faction of the Democratic party. The total vote in New York was down seven percent from 1844, a larger drop than in the rest of the nation. This was partly an indication that anti-extension Whigs would not vote for either a slaveowner or their archenemy Van Buren. The Barnburners led the movement in New York, although they did not exclude Whigs and Liberty men. The counties the party carried in 1848 had previously been Democratic, and enough Democratic votes were drawn away elsewhere to give the Whig candidates most of the remaining counties. Although no county in New York can be regarded as typical, the example of Essex County is indicative of what happened in the state as a whole, with the Whig vote remaining fairly constant and the Free Soilers gaining substantially from Democratic strength:

	1844	*1848*
Democratic	1,998	1,002
Whig	2,612	2,629
Third Party	143	1,126

Taylor carried hitherto strongly Democratic sections of upper New York state. Equally revealing in 1852, with most of the Barnburners back in the Democratic party, the Free Soil vote was approximately one-fifth what it had been in 1848.[84]

The source of the anti-extension vote in Massachusetts is not so easily determined. On the surface it would appear that because the Conscience Whig faction provided most of the leadership of the Free Soil party, the Whigs would have lost more substantially. But a careful study of the voting figures has revealed that just the reverse was probably the case.[85] Comparing the gubernatorial votes of 1847 and 1848 shows that in 1847, the Whig vote was 51 percent, Democratic 37 percent, and Liberty 12 percent. In 1848, the Whig vote was 49½ percent, Democratic 21½ percent, and Free Soil 29 percent. A comparison of the 1844 and 1848 presidential vote indicated in 1844:

[84] Stanwood, *A History of the Presidency*, 243, 257; Burnham, *Presidential Ballots*, 36-37, 636; *Whig Almanac* (1848), 53, (1853), 50; Albany *Argus*, November 22, 1848.
[85] Bean, "Party Transformations in Massachusetts," 32-35.

Whig 51 percent, Democratic 40 percent, and Liberty 9 percent. In 1848, the Whig vote was 45 percent, Democratic 27 percent, and Free Soil 28 percent. A county-by-county study also backs up these findings. Taking Middlesex County as somewhat representative for the entire state, the results show:

	1844	*1848*
Democratic	9,124	6,820
Whig	9,581	9,854
Third Party	1,718	5,964

The figures thus indicate that more Free Soilers had been Democrats than had been Whigs. This despite the Adams, Palfrey, Sumner leadership of the party. Apparently Van Buren's candidacy had a positive effect on Massachusetts Democrats which was stronger than their dislike of Adams. Similarly, it kept many anti-extension Whigs from joining the movement. Marcus Morton later complained that although the Whigs made up a minority of the Free Soil party, they held a majority of the offices. Finally, the formation of a Free Soil–Democratic coalition after 1848 adds further weight to the evidence.[86]

The Free Soilers drew more heavily from the Democrats in two other important anti-extension New England states. In Vermont, Van Buren received 29 percent of the total vote, his best showing in the entire country. Here the Democratic vote declined from $37\frac{1}{2}$ percent in 1844 to 23 percent in 1848 while the Whig vote fell only from $54\frac{1}{2}$ percent to 48 percent. As in other states of the East, the Van Buren candidacy prevented many Whigs from joining the anti-extension party. Windham County shows what happened throughout Vermont:

	1844	*1848*
Democratic	1,703	608
Whig	2,642	2,648
Third Party	385	1,443

In Maine, the Whigs won 40 percent of the vote in both 1844 and 1848 while the Democratic vote declined from 53 percent to 46 per-

[86] Morton to B. V. French, November 22, 1850, in Morton Papers; See also Darling, *Political Changes in Massachusetts*, 355-58n; *Whig Almanac* (1848), 52, (1850), 55; Burnham, *Presidential Ballots*, 512.

cent. In New Hampshire, which voted strongly for Cass, Taylor was the bigger loser to Van Buren. Hillsborough County is a good example of what occurred throughout the state:

	1844	*1848*
Democratic	4,583	4,773
Whig	3,124	2,799
Third Party	675	1,257

In Rhode Island, Connecticut, and New Jersey, the Free Soil vote was too small to be indicative of any clear trend. In Pennsylvania, the disappointingly small Free Soil strength lay in the areas which had hitherto been Democratic, much of it in counties bordering on New York and Ohio. Wilmot's role was a key factor in persuading Democrats to change parties.[87]

In the Midwest, the source of the Free Soil vote was more evenly divided, although the Whigs probably lost somewhat more heavily than the Democrats. In terms of Free Soil leadership and total vote, Ohio was the most important state in the region. The third party vote in Ohio of 35,000 was a big disappointment, however, and amounted to only 11 percent of the total, less than the northern average. As expected, most of the Free Soil support was in the former Whig stronghold of the Western Reserve. Six Reserve counties went to the third party, with Giddings's home county of Ashtabula delivering 55 percent. But because the Reserve had been a Whig area, Van Buren's candidacy made the total less than it might have been otherwise. The Cleveland *True Democrat* observed: "In no portion of the Union were prejudices so strong against Martin Van Buren. . . . John P. Hale, Judge McLean, or any other man would have received at least 10,000 more votes on the Reserve than were cast for Martin Van Buren." In addition, the campaigning of Senator Corwin convinced many Whigs that Taylor would not veto the Wilmot Proviso. Nevertheless, the Whigs suffered heavily at the hands of the new party and probably lost the state because of it. A comparison of the 1844 and 1848 presidential vote indicates for 1844: Democratic 49 percent, Whig 48 percent, and Liberty

[87] Stanwood, *A History of the Presidency,* 223, 243; Burnham, *Presidential Ballots,* 37-38, 816; Ludlum, *Social Ferment in Vermont,* 197-98.

3 percent. For 1848: Democratic 47 percent, Whig 42 percent, and Free Soil 11 percent. Typical of what happened to the Whigs on the Western Rerserve were the results in Cuyahoga County (Cleveland):[88]

	1844	*1848*
Democratic	2,388	2,368
Whig	3,331	1,776
Third Party	312	2,594

In Indiana, Van Buren received only 5 percent of the total vote. Democrats and Whigs lost substantially the same although a large Whig Quaker element in eastern Indiana supported Van Buren. In Illinois, the figures show conclusively that the third party attracted mostly Democratic votes. The northeastern area of the state, which normally voted Democratic, provided nearly all of the Free Soil strength. The statistics reveal that in 1844 the Democrats received 53½ percent, the Whigs 43 percent and Liberty 3½ percent. In 1848, the Democratic vote was 45 percent, the Whigs 43 percent and Free Soil 12 percent. Cook County (Chicago) shows the drawing power of the Free Soil party in a normally Democratic area:

	1844	*1848*
Democratic	2,027	1,622
Whig	1,119	1,708
Third Party	317	2,120

In Michigan, on the other hand, Free Soil drew more heavily from the Whigs than the Democrats as seen in the example of Jackson County:

	1844	*1848*
Democratic	1,389	1,547
Whig	1,302	969
Third Party	475	1,070

[88] Stanwood, *A History of the Presidency,* 223, 243; Cleveland *True Democrat,* November 14, 1848; Price, "The Election of 1848 in Ohio," 297-309; Chase to Sumner, November 27, 1848, in Bourne (ed.), "Chase Correspondence," 142-45; Smith, *The Liberty and Free Soil Parties,* 155-56; Burnham, *Presidential Ballots,* 38, 680.

The popularity of Lewis Cass in his home state helps to explain why fewer Democrats than Whigs bolted in 1848.[89]

In Wisconsin, the Van Buren party had a good deal to show for its efforts, winning more than one-quarter of the total vote. Free Soil voting strength concentrated in the normally Democratic southeastern counties of the state. Van Buren outpolled his rivals in six Wisconsin counties, four in this area. In the normally Whig southwestern part of the state, the Free Soilers made a poor showing. This further substantiates the evidence that Van Buren's vote was drawn from Democratic ranks even though Cass still managed to win the state. In both Wisconsin and Illinois the Free Soilers won many former Democratic votes because they stressed internal improvements as well as the Wilmot Proviso. In Iowa, the Free Soilers attracted most of their small total from the Whig party.[90] Thus, although more former Democrats than Whigs throughout the North voted for Van Buren, the figures indicate that there was no general rule as to the source of the Free Soil vote. In the Middle Atlantic and New England states Van Buren drew most heavily from his own former party. In the Midwest the situation was less clear with the Free Soil vote closely divided between Whig and Democratic antecedents.

The results of the election of 1848 are not easily summarized. Because both Democratic and Whig parties presented themselves as supporters of the Wilmot Proviso in many northern areas, the Free Soil percentage of the total vote did not indicate the full strength of the anti-extension movement. This was true even though Van Buren appealed to some who were not truly dedicated to Free Soil. On the other hand, the major parties' dodging of the issues disgusted many voters

---

[89] Stanwood, *A History of the Presidency,* 223, 243; Cole, "The Barnburner Element," 38-39; Ameda R. King, "The Last Years of the Whig Party in Illinois, 1847-1856," *Transactions of the Illinois State Historical Society,* XXXII (1925), 123-24; Smith, *The Liberty and Free Soil Parties,* 156. W. Dean Burnham contends that Illinois would have been in the Whig column had it not been for the Free Soil challenge. Burnham's county by county analysis of the returns, however, indicates that the majority of the Free Soil voters were former Democrats. See Burnham, *Presidential Ballots,* 38, 368-90, 522.

[90] James R. Donoghue, *How Wisconsin Voted, 1848-1954* (Madison, 1956), 32; Cole, "The Barnburner Element," 33-34; Smith, *The Liberty and Free Soil Parties,* 156-57; Smith, "The Free Soil Party in Wisconsin," 118-19.

who simply stayed away from the polls. The total vote was scarcely larger than that of 1844 even though four new states had entered the Union and the population had grown substantially.[91] The campaign was characterized by apathy in many areas despite the intense enthusiasm with which the new party had been launched. Yet anti-extension sentiment had greatly increased, and the old issues over which parties had fought for years were declining in importance. The organization and the hold of the Whig and Democratic parties on the voters were still strong, but they were clearly weakening.[92]

The major parties had worked hard to stress party loyalty and issues other than slavery in order to draw attention away from the Free Soil party, and this appeal had succeeded in many cases. The results showed that most northern voters were not yet ready for a purely sectional party. Some were not sufficiently moved by the extension issue to leave their old parties, while others feared the disruptive influence the Free Soilers might have on national unity. Important political leaders who opposed the extension of slavery, such as Webster, Seward, Corwin, Greeley, Benton, and Wentworth, had nevertheless rejected the third-party appeal. Many refused to leave their party because of the traditional hopelessness of third-party movements, but nevertheless, in less than three months the Free Soil party had galvanized public opinion on the slavery issue to an impressive extent. The distinction between Democrat and Whig had, to many voters, become nominal, and the new party offered the only choice. In the 1840s both the Democratic and Whig parties were consciously nonsectional in character and hence the two-party system had not allowed room for a party which stressed sectional issues. The significance of the appeal of the Free Soil party in 1848 lay in part in the fact that it was a sectional, ideological party at a time when the major parties had appeal in all sections and studiously avoided ideology.[93] The political situation had entered a period of

[91] Stanwood, A History of the Presidency, 242.

[92] For a revealing analysis of the continuing importance of traditional party loyalties in the face of deepening sectionalism, see Silbey, The Shrine of Party, especially, 102-3.

[93] The nonsectional character of the two-party system and its avoidance of divisive issues in the 1840s is best described in Richard P. McCormick, The Second American Party System: Party Formation in the Jacksonian Era (Chapel Hill, N.C., 1966).

change, and the Free Soil campaign had increased the chances for the organization of parties along purely sectional lines. Equally important, the anti-extension campaign waged by the Free Soilers had aroused the North sufficiently so that the further spread of slavery would be much more difficult if not impossible in the future.

Yet the election also had the result of disillusioning many Free Soilers as to the practicality of a third-party movement, for they realized that their efforts had brought few immediate and tangible results. Although the Free Soilers stressed ideology and sincerely believed in the anti-extension cause, they were also politicians hungry for office and political power. Consequently, it would be increasingly difficult to sustain the high peak of enthusiasm that had been attained during the campaign of 1848. Whether the Free Soil party could hold the initiative and maintain its momentum and its independence remained to be seen, for the temptation to forget the Wilmot Proviso and reenter the two-party system would be great indeed.

6

Coalition and the Decline of
Free Soil Principles

With the election over, Free Soil leaders stopped to consider the future of their movement. The party had successfully focused attention on the slavery question and had helped intensify sectional conflict in 1848. Free Soilers such as Chase, Giddings, and Bailey must have asked themselves how they could best continue their agitation and maintain anti-extension interest; should they attempt to preserve their independence from the major parties or should they, by forming coalitions, seek to bring Democrats and Whigs to their point of view? They realized that one of the glaring weaknesses of the party during the campaign had been the lack of an established organization. Support had grown spontaneously with the enthusiasm of electioneering, but there had been no central coordination or direction and little local organization. Now there would be little to sustain the movement unless someone seized the initiative and acted quickly.

In their Buffalo platform, the Free Soilers had pledged to "fight on and fight ever, until a triumphant victory shall reward our exertions." After the election the Free Soil press was almost unanimous in its endorsement of this promise. The Cleveland *True Democrat* remarked: "The campaign of 1848 is now ended, but not so the mission of our party. . . . This day begins the campaign of 1852." Many of the more ardent anti-extensionists agreed with these sentiments and wanted to keep the new party alive as a going concern between elections. Gamaliel Bailey noted the practical problem of establishing a party organization and keeping the public aroused: "We must pre-occupy the public mind and establish a machinery of agitation." Many Free Soilers felt that the original Liberty party policy of political independence was still the best policy. Joshua Giddings spoke for many when he argued that the group must resist the efforts "to get our members back into the old parties."[1]

Not all Free Soilers were concerned with the third party's independence; some were already thinking of regaining their positions of influence in their old parties. Martin Van Buren believed that the chances were good for Thomas Hart Benton to reorganize the northern Democracy on a free soil basis for the next election. Van Buren clearly had little interest in continuing his support of the Free Soil party as a separate organization. He had always viewed the movement more as a means to reorient the national Democratic party and to regain control of the New York Democracy than as an end in itself. Even some with more commitment to the Wilmot Proviso favored coalition as a means of winning others to their point of view as well as increasing their own political power. Charles Sumner, for example, argued that the Free Soilers must join with northern Democrats and organize "a grand Northern opposition."[2]

The events of 1849 to 1851 would reveal that the Free Soilers were sharply divided between the Sumner and Giddings approaches. For the most part, however, they took the path which seemed to promise the most immediate results and agreed on coalition. Because there was no national organization, the process of combination was accomplished on a statewide basis, with the individual situation determining which of the two parties the Free Soilers chose to merge with. Often they cooperated with the second party of a state in an effort to drive the leading party from power. More often than not they combined with the Democratic party, the original home of a majority of the Free Soilers. In the process, the Free Soil party almost became defunct in several states, and bargain and compromise characterized its activity throughout the North. Only the small band of Free Soilers in Congress main-

[1] Porter and Johnson (comps.), *National Party Platforms*, 13-14; Cleveland *True Democrat*, quoted in *National Era*, November 23, 1848; Bailey to Adams, November 1, 1848, in Adams Papers; Giddings to Thomas Bolton, November 14, 1848, in Giddings Papers.

[2] Smith, *The Blair Family*, I, 243; Sumner to Giddings, November 10, 1848, in Giddings Papers.

tained its political independence and commitment to principle. On the
state level Free Soilers were too often willing to sacrifice their earlier
devotion to the anti-extension cause in an effort to obtain office. As
northerners and southerners argued the need for compromise on sectional issues, the result for the Free Soil party was near disaster. Members fell away, and the party struggled on with sharply reduced numbers, fighting for its very survival.

The future of a strong and independent third-party movement would
depend greatly on the firm resolve of its dominant element, the Barnburners of New York, who had controlled the leadership and decision-
making process in 1848 and had furnished more than one-third of the
total vote. Nevertheless, although they professed their devotion to Free
Soil, by the end of 1849 they had formed a shaky coalition with the
Hunker faction at the expense of their anti-extension principles.[3] In
their search for renewed political influence they sought again the security of the two-party system, seeming almost to wish the death of the
third party. Their desertion, reinforced by Martin Van Buren's withdrawal from politics, would be the most important factor in reducing
the Free Soil party to a tiny reflection of what it had been in 1848.

The primary factor leading to Democratic reunion in New York was
the common desire of the two factions for the spoils of office. In the
election of 1848 the Whigs had swept into power in a devastating rout.
The makeup of the 1849 legislature and congressional delegation reveals the completeness of the Whig victory:

	Assemblymen	Senators	Congressmen
Whig	108	23	32
Free Soil	13	7	1
Democratic	7	2	1

This, even though the combined Democratic–Free Soil vote in the
state had exceeded the Whig total by a small margin. No one needed
further proof to show that continued separation meant continued Whig
victories and subsequent loss of patronage. One Hunker, on noting the

[3] The most complete accounts of the New York reunion are found in Donovan,
The Barnburners, 112-15; Spencer, *William L. Marcy,* 187-90; Alexander, *A
Political History of New York,* II, 148-55; Ferree, "The New York Democracy,"
244-99.

initial unwillingness of the two factions to compromise, argued that "we must have Whig domination til such feelings change." The first concrete result of the division after the election was the loss to the Whigs of the Senate seat of John A. Dix. The legislature overwhelmingly elected William H. Seward over Dix and a Hunker opponent. The Whigs, led by Seward and Thurlow Weed, naturally had worked to perpetuate the Democratic division and would continue to try to convince both groups that coalition was not to their best interests.[4]

The dispute between the Barnburners and Hunkers dated back long before the presidential campaign and hence was not easily resolved. Neither faction could agree within its own ranks how best to achieve unity, although no one denied it was desirable in some form. Significantly, of the many Barnburners who had advocated bolting the Democratic party in 1848, none of the leaders now favored the continued separate identity of the Free Soil party in New York. Yet most did insist that if they were to cooperate with the Hunkers it would have to be on a free soil basis. Benjamin Butler felt that the Utica platform of June, 1848 "must be made the COMMON RALLYING GROUND." John A. Dix, smarting from the loss of his Senate seat, claimed that agreement on principle with the Hunkers was the primary consideration; but for a man like Dix who had never been fully committed to the third-party concept, yielding to Hunker principles would be acceptable if such an agreement would bring a return to political power. That reunion was inevitable in some form was apparent when such a determined anti-extensionist as Preston King began to talk of possible cooperation with the Hunkers, although King argued that a separate organization must be maintained at least temporarily.[5]

For several reasons the Hunkers had even more misgivings about reunion than the Barnburners. They had received fewer votes in 1848 and in any fair division of power could expect to receive less from a co-

[4] Albany *Evening Atlas*, November-December, 1848; Ferree, "The New York Democracy," 250; J. W. Tamblin to Marcy, May 28, 1849, in Marcy Papers; Van Deusen, *Thurlow Weed*, 165.

[5] Butler to Benton, June 2, 1849, in Charles Benton Papers; Dix to Martin Van Buren, June 9, 1849, Henry S. Randall to Martin Van Buren, December 18, 1848, in Van Buren Papers; King to Sumner, December 25, 1848, in Sumner Papers. See also John Van Buren to Giddings, December 12, 1848, in Giddings-Julian Papers.

alition. Union would probably mean the destruction of one or the other of the local organizations, and many Hunkers feared they would lose more in this respect. As a result they would demand stringent guarantees in order to protect their position before agreeing to coalition. Equally important, many New York voters supported a congressional prohibition on the further extension of slavery, but for the Hunkers to yield to the Barnburner demand and endorse the Wilmot Proviso would mean repudiating their former position. William L. Marcy, the leading Hunker advocate of reunion, explained the dilemma of his faction: "The barnburners will not bug [*sic*] from their platform and many of our friends think it is a good enough place to stand on, if they could get thru in some decent way. . . . We cannot be sustained in Gel. Cass's position that Congress has no right to act on the subject."[6]

Hunker leaders thought they saw a way out of their dilemma if the Barnburners could be persuaded to omit any mention of the slavery question in a common platform. Yet the leading Hunker newspaper, the Albany *Argus,* charged that the Barnburners were attempting to dictate the terms of reunion by insisting on the inclusion of their anti-extension views as a basis for reunion. Lewis Cass explained the primary Hunker misgiving when he wrote to Marcy: "I am afraid from what I hear that the barnburners will insist on an unconditional surrender. . . . If they could agree to come together without making this question the Shibboleth of party . . . all would be well."[7]

The pressures for reunion, however, were becoming too great to resist. Few voters understood the need or wisdom of two competing factions. Most could see little distinction between the slavery expansion positions of each since both were essentially opposed to slavery in the territories. Consequently, the more moderate leaders of both factions gradually came to understand that their division was not popular and would cost votes. Most of them agreed with Marcy that the masses were "sincerely desirous of union," and they realized that Democratic reunions in several other states had already resulted in Whig defeats. Since union was the only apparent means available to regain control of the state, negotiations began in the spring of 1849. A few Barnburners like Preston King feared that such cooperation "might negotiate away

[6] Marcy to Gen. P. M. Wetmore, July 23, 1849, in Marcy Papers.
[7] Albany *Argus,* November 25, 1848; Lewis Cass to Marcy, July 23, 1849, in Marcy Papers; Ferree, "The New York Democracy," 245.

our principles." But his was a minority view. The Free Soilers made the first move when they issued a conciliatory statement saying they would welcome discussions for harmony. After initial opposition led by the Albany *Argus*, the Hunker Central Committee responded by publishing an invitation calling for the two groups to hold simultaneous August conventions in Rome, N.Y. These meetings would be "for the purpose of consultation, and devising means of union and if it shall be deemed expedient, to meet in joint convention, and suggest the names of a union ticket for state offices."[8]

John Van Buren and Charles S. Benton wrote the reply for the Barnburners accepting the invitation but suggesting that, since the people of New York had endorsed the Free Soil doctrine, this must be recognized as the basis for union. The Hunker reply contended that the Wilmot Proviso meant a "needless agitation of a dangerous irritating sectional question." It pointed out that settlers opposed to slavery were in the majority in California and other newly opened territories and that there was therefore no need for congressional action. Yet despite the apparent unwillingness of either side to compromise, plans for the Rome conventions proceeded. Barnburner leaders and newspapers, including the Albany *Evening Atlas* and the New York *Evening Post*, supported the reunion efforts. Martin Van Buren, always willing to place party before principle, endorsed the steps toward the union of the Democratic party and rationalized that it would be "upon the well understood principles of its illustrious founder" (Jefferson). Many Hunker leaders and papers, however, led by the Albany *Argus*, continued to express doubt and opposition. So did some Free Soilers outside New York. The *National Era* worried lest the Barnburners be tricked by "scheming politicians, more anxious for office than principle." The paper feared that Liberty and Whig elements of the third party would be forgotten in the proposed union.[9]

[8] Marcy to Wetmore, May 11, 31, 1849, in Marcy Papers; James B. Jewett to Benton, May 24, 1849, King to Benton, June 11, 1849, in Charles Benton Papers; Albany *Evening Atlas*, April 9, May 21, 26, 1849; Albany *Argus*, June 23, 1849.

[9] Benton to John Pruyn, July 3, 1849, quoted in Albany *Evening Atlas*, July 3, 1849; Pruyn to Benton, July 4, 1849, in Charles Benton Papers; *Proceedings of the Democratic and Free Democratic Convention, Rome, Aug. 15-17, 1849* (Rome, N.Y., 1849), 4-5; Ferree, "The New York Democracy," 260-66; Martin Van Buren to George C. Clyde, August 11, 1849, in Van Buren Papers; *National Era*, July 12, 19, 1849.

In Rome, the Barnburners immediately adopted resolutions endorsing the Wilmot Proviso and appointed a negotiating committee headed by Preston King to demand Hunker adherence to their resolutions. Meanwhile the Hunkers, led by William Marcy, sought to avoid all discussion of slavery. In their resolutions they conceded very little: "We are opposed to the extension of slavery to the free territory of the United States; but we do not regard the slavery question in any form of its agitation, or any opinion in relation thereto as a test of political faith or as a rule of party action." With neither side willing to compromise, the conventions adjourned without having reached agreement.[10]

Despite the stalemate at the Rome meetings it was clear that both groups were still moving in the direction of compromise. In the case of the Hunkers such a movement was over the strong opposition of many who opposed reunion and who adhered to the Cass argument that Congress had no power over slavery in the territories. On the other hand, William Marcy led a group which argued that Congress did have the power and believed that coalition with the Barnburners was possible.[11] Marcy had altered his earlier opposition in a switch which ultimately made reunion possible. He did so because he, like the Barnburners, believed a united Democratic party was the only way back to political power. He now argued that the voters of both factions demanded it: "There has been from the first agitation of the union question a general movement in most of the counties coming from the lower stratum for a union. It was too general and too strong to be combatted or neglected."[12]

Immediately after the Rome conventions, each group stiffened its terms in an effort to obtain the maximum benefit from the compromise

[10] Spencer, *William L. Marcy*, 187; *Proceedings of the Democratic and Free Democratic Conventions;* New York *Herald* and Albany *Evening Atlas*, August 16-25, 1849.

[11] There were now two distinct Hunker factions. Those who adhered to the national Democratic platform and the Cass position were called the Hards and those who were said to have softened their opposition to the Wilmot Proviso gained the name Softs. See *New York Hards and Softs: Which is the True Democracy?* (New York, 1856), 17; Marcy to Wetmore, August 24, September 11, 1849, in Marcy Papers; Spencer, *William L. Marcy*, 187-88.

[12] For Marcy's new attitude see Samuel Beardsley to Marcy, August 27, 30, 1849, in Marcy Papers. Alexander argues that Horatio Seymour persuaded Marcy to change his position. See Alexander, *A Political History of New York*, II, 149.

which each knew had to come. John A. Dix noted that the Barn-burners could not abandon their insistence on the Wilmot Proviso, while Marcy again pointed out the Hunker dilemma, observing that they "can go no further in the path of concession than their convention at Rome has gone without stepping on to that of the free soil organization." But efforts for unity remained very much alive, and immediately further calls for mass conventions went out.[13]

Meeting in Syracuse in September, the Hunkers nominated a full slate of candidates for the fall election but also took an important step leading toward a reconciliation of the warring factions. Over significant opposition the convention resolved its willingness to withdraw its candidates for four of the eight state offices and support "acknowledged Democrats" whom the Barnburners might choose at their convention. Although Marcy had not been an official delegate, he had an important role in getting the members to agree to the offer. Over the opposition of those who insisted that the Barnburners must abandon completely their advocacy of the Wilmot Proviso, the convention adopted Marcy's resolution "that opinions upon slavery should not be made a test nor a persistence in antislavery agitation deemed a heresy."[14] Nevertheless, for the Barnburners to accept would mean abandoning their 1848 platform.

The Barnburner convention, meeting several days later in Utica, revealed a great division over what to do with the Hunker proposal. Yet the desire to reenter the Democratic party was irresistible, and led by John Van Buren and Preston King, the members finally voted to accept the joint-ticket arrangement and nominate candidates for four of the offices. In an effort to get around their dilemma and to avoid an appearance of abandoning principle, they rejected the Hunker conditions which did not require endorsing the Wilmot Proviso and instead endorsed the Free Soil stand which did require such an endorsement. Finally a joint convention met in Syracuse on September 14, to formalize the union ticket. Because they could postpone a solu-

[13] Dix to Benton, August 14, 1849, in Charles Benton Papers; Marcy to H. H. Coats, August 29, 1849, in Marcy Papers; Albany *Evening Atlas*, August 24, 1849.
[14] New York *Herald*, September 6-9, 1849; Spencer, *William L. Marcy*, 188; *New York Hards and Softs*, 17. See also Marcy to Campbell, September 19, 1849, in Marcy Papers.

tion no longer, the members passed a compromise resolution on the territorial issue which might permit the Barnburners to save face: "That it [Congress] possesses in our opinion full power over the subject in the territories. . . . But as the constitutional power is questioned, we are willing to tolerate the free exercise of individual opinions upon the question among members of the Democratic family. . . ."[15]

By accepting this resolution the Barnburners had affirmed their abandonment of the independent Free Soil party. Believing that their political futures were secure only in the two-party system, they had agreed to reenter the Democratic party of New York without guarantees that that party would fight for the Wilmot Proviso. The Barnburners themselves professed to be well satisfied and claimed that, since the party had gone on record against extension, they had gotten the better part of the arrangement. Few were willing to admit that free soil principle had been sacrificed. Even their firmest advocate of the Wilmot Proviso, Preston King, could rationalize his position by announcing that he supported the joint ticket because both groups "approximated each other so nearly" that there was "hope of seeing the important State of New York united upon the right side in the great contest for human freedom." John Van Buren was more candid when he admitted to a friend that the spoils of office had been the overriding factor: "We are asked to compromise our principles. The day of compromise is passed; but in regard to candidates for State offices, we are still a commercial people."[16]

Both sides claimed to be well pleased by the agreement although some Hunkers were less than enthusiastic. Marcy accepted the compromise resolution because he felt that it expressed what the great majority of the party believed. A few Barnburners admitted their misgivings but sometimes for the wrong reasons. Azariah C. Flagg observed privately that "the failure to unite on principles at Rome and the junction of men at Utica has a bad aspect to the faithful of other states." But he was unhappy less because principle had been sacrificed than because the coalition might appear too contrived to

[15] Albany *Evening Atlas*, September 13, 14, 19, 1849; New York *Herald*, September 16, 17, 1849; Spencer, *William L. Marcy*, 188-90; Ferree, "The New York Democracy," 285-88.

[16] New York *Herald*, September 15, 16, 1849; Albany *Evening Atlas*, September 14, 1849; *National Era*, September 24, 1849; Stanton, *Random Recollections*, 82.

merit voter support. Flagg noted in a letter that many "will be disgusted with a patched up ticket, which they will regard as a mere arrangement for the spoils." On the other hand, John Bigelow's New York *Evening Post* felt that despite John Van Buren's pressure to rally the Barnburners around the joint ticket, the Free Soil movement had been compromised. The Whigs were vehement in their denunciation of the reunion. Horace Greeley noted in the New York *Tribune* that it was a complete Free Soil surrender and that "New York Hunkerism refuses to concede one iota of principle to the Barnburners." According to Greeley, it was easier for the Barnburners to forget their principles than to receive no spoils.[17]

Free Soilers outside of the state had many more reservations about the union than did the Barnburners. The *National Era* maintained a brave front when it professed to believe that the Barnburners had preserved anti-extension integrity: "While we deny the wisdom of the policy pursued by the Radical Democrats, we are unwilling to believe that they adopted it in disregard of their principles. They are in concert, but they are politicians and do as politicians do." Even Salmon P. Chase, a staunch advocate of coalition with the Democrats, expressed his disapproval of their acceptance of union after the Hunkers had rejected their platform. That such a man as Chase could question the Barnburner strategy revealed both hypocrisy on his part and the extent to which the New Yorkers had in fact sacrificed their free soil principles. But most others were at least willing to suspend judgment until the coalition had shown more clearly the course it would take.[18]

The reunited Democratic party of New York faced numerous problems during the campaign and met with only limited success. The union was severely strained at times and broke down on several occasions although never completely. Most serious was the bolt led by a group of New York City Hunkers allegedly under the urging of the

[17] Dickinson to Marcy, September 23, 1849, Marcy to Campbell, September 19, 1849, in Marcy Papers; A. C. Flagg to Benton, September 27, 1849, in Charles Benton Papers; New York *Evening Post,* October 23, 1849; New York *Tribune,* September 17, 1849.

[18] *National Era,* September 27, 1849; Bailey to Sumner, September 23, 1849, in Sumner Papers; Sumner to Chase, September 18, 25, 1849, in Chase Papers, Library of Congress; Chase to Sumner, September 15, 19, 1849, in Bourne (ed.), "Chase Correspondence," 183-88.

Whigs. Statewide returns gave the Democrats a small majority of the total vote although they won only four of the eight state contests and the Whigs won a small majority in the state legislature. The Barnburners elected only one of their candidates and the Hunkers three, indicating that Hunker defections may have been significant.[19] Yet the party had come close to achieving its goal of political control of New York, and the lesson was clear to the Barnburners that the chances for a more complete victory were much better as Democrats than as Free Soilers.

More important for the anti-extension movement, a strong voice in the independent party had succumbed to the scramble for immediate power and had reentered the two-party system. The Barnburners were merely one of several state groups to form an agreement with one of the old parties. But because they represented the largest and most significant part of the movement of 1848, their action was decisive. It could not be seen in 1849 that their return to the Democratic party would be permanent, but the Hunkers had actually conceded very little. Should other Free Soilers be willing to accept such terms, there would be little to sustain a third party. The Barnburners could claim with some validity that the Hunkers had approached the Free Soil position and as a result there was no further need for the third party. But the Hunkers had not bound themselves to anything. Much of the invaluable third-party spirit and leadership of 1848 had been lost in the reunion of the New York Democrats.

Long before the Barnburners of New York returned to the Democratic fold, Ohio Free Soilers had also grappled with the problem of coalition. The issue was complicated by the fact that the two leading Free Soilers of the state, Salmon P. Chase and Joshua Giddings, were divided themselves, with Chase favoring coalition with the Democrats and Giddings an independent third party. In the end Chase got most of what he wanted including his own election to the Senate and the modification of Ohio's discriminatory Black Laws.[20] In the process, however, the party seriously compromised its position. It also set a

[19] Albany *Evening Atlas,* November 6, 7, 13, 23, 1849; Marcy to Wetmore, November 13, 1849, in Marcy Papers; Donovan, *The Barnburners,* 116.

[20] The most complete accounts of the political events in Ohio are found in Smith, *The Liberty and Free Soil Parties,* 162-82, and Holt, "Party Politics in Ohio," 332-83.

dangerous precedent which, if followed by Free Soilers in other states, could mean the end of the entire third-party movement.

The state election results of 1848 placed the Ohio Free Soilers in an extremely good position to use their influence for a positive effect. Holding the balance of power in the legislature, they would play a key role in Ohio politics and could possibly enhance their own position.[21] Unfortunately for the party's future, its members could not agree among themselves how best to act, and the result was a long, drawn out power struggle within the party. With Democrats and Whigs typically being closely divided, the Whigs in early 1848 had pushed an apportionment law through the legislature designed to insure Whig control of the next legislature as well as the election of a Whig to the Senate. In an obvious gerrymander, they devised the law so as to divide Chase's Hamilton County into two districts in the hopes of winning one in this normally Democratic area. Democrats, however, questioned the law's constitutionality and refused to honor it in the election of 1848. The result was that each newly created district sent two sets of representatives to Columbus.[22] The issue became crucial because the outcome would determine which party controlled the legislature. And with the Free Soilers holding the balance of power, they in fact were in a position to determine the outcome and elect one of their own members to the Senate.

In the struggle which followed, the Free Soilers displayed an alarming lack of unity, reflecting the opposing strategies of Chase and Giddings. Each man wanted to be chosen for the Senate, but Chase's overriding ambition drove him to seek it at the expense of the third party. Giddings, on the other hand, sought to maintain Free Soil unity and independence and was unwilling to use the party to bargain for his own election. Of the eight Free Soilers in the Ohio Assembly, Chase influenced two, Norton Townshend and John F. Morse, to vote with the Democrats on the Hamilton County issue and on other mea-

---

[21] In the Ohio House there were thirty-two Democrats, thirty Whigs and eight Free Soilers. There were seventeen Democratic senators, fourteen Whigs, and three Free Soilers. Smith, *The Liberty and Free Soil Parties,* 162-63.

[22] Holt, "Party Politics in Ohio," 320-24; Weisenburger, *The Passing of the Frontier,* 470-71; Smith, *The Liberty and Free Soil Parties,* 163. On the question of the law's constitutionality, see Hale to Chase, March 2, 1849, in Chase Papers, Library of Congress.

sures in organizing the House. The rest, having Whig backgrounds and
having been elected with the help of Whig votes, were inclined toward
their former party. Townshend and Morse agreed with the Democrats
on other important state issues including banking and currency while
the others favored the Whig position.[23] Much more important in determining whether the Free Soilers supported the Democrats or the
Whigs, however, was the fact that Townshend and Morse supported
Chase for the Senate seat and the rest favored Giddings. Since the
third-party men could not agree among themselves, the Democrats
negotiated with them concerning Chase's election and the Whigs did
the same concerning Giddings.[24] Former party allegiances and political
ambition combined to produce an unfortunate inability of Ohio Free
Soilers to unite on a common policy.

Chase himself was an active participant in the bargaining. He appeared in Columbus at the strategic times and took advantage of his
many Democratic contacts in the legislature. He did little to hide his
desire to be senator, writing to his close confidant, Stanley Matthews,
that the Democrats in the legislature would probably prefer those Free
Soilers "supposed to be democratic in sentiment." He admitted that he
would be highly gratified to be elected to the Senate, because he felt
he understood "the history, principles and practical workings of the
Free Soil movement as thoroughly as most men."[25] Chase's Democratic
leanings had been noticeable for several years, and by 1849 he believed
that the best hope for anti-extensionism lay in Free Soil union with
the Democrats. He hoped to use the situation in the legislature as the
means to bring about the desired coalition. Albert Riddle, an ex-Whig
Free Soiler who directed the Giddings campaign in the legislature,
wrote that Chase had favored the Democrats "to an almost dangerous
extent." When the Ohio Free Soilers held a convention in Columbus

[23] *Ohio Standard* (Columbus), December 9, 1848; *Ohio State Journal*, January
3, 1849; Weisenburger, *The Passing of the Frontier*, 471; Holt, "Party Politics in
Ohio," 332-36.
    [24] Weisenburger, *The Passing of the Frontier*, 471; Holt, "Party Politics in
Ohio," 336-37.
    [25] Chase to Stanley Matthews, December 23, 1848, in "Some Letters of Salmon
P. Chase, 1848-1865," *American Historical Review*, XXXIV (1929), 536-37;
Chase to Nichols, November 9, 1848, in Bourne (ed.), "Chase Correspondence,"
140-41; Chase to Mrs. Chase, December 20, 25, 1848, in Chase Papers, Library
of Congress.

in December, 1848, the Chase faction had dominated. Chase himself wrote the platform which endorsed many Democratic positions on economic issues not related to slavery. This had naturally pleased the Democrats and furthered talk of their support of Chase for senator.[26]

While Case worked for his own election, those Free Soilers who had originally been Whigs continued to push Giddings's candidacy and to seek a working agreement with their former party. Giddings himself, remaining in Washington for the congressional session, was not personally involved in these maneuverings and actually chastised one Free Soiler who had tried to make a deal with the Whigs to secure his election. At the same time, he confided to his friend Riddle that he would be as grateful for an election to the Senate as for any "earthly exaltation." He indicated in his diary that he would have mixed feelings about leaving the House where his influence was substantial, but "the moral effect of my election would be great, and on that account I feel a desire to succeed to that office."[27] Had Giddings actively sought the post as Chase did his chances might have improved, but to him coalition with either major party meant a compromise of free soil principles. He realized that both the Democratic and the Whig parties had powerful southern wings to consider and therefore could never adopt a strong anti-extension stand. The idealistic Giddings possessed an inflexible certainty of the worthiness of his approach and thus reflected the dismay of many Ohio Free Soilers over Chase's devious but nonetheless pragmatic actions.

Of the two, Chase was probably the logical choice for the Senate. Giddings was already in Congress, and his election would mean resigning his seat in the House. Chase had been the organizer of the Free Soil movement in Ohio and would add an additional anti-extension voice in Congress. Nevertheless, his actions and those of his supporters made him vulnerable to charges of a political bargain. He

[26] Riddle to Giddings, January 15, February 21, 1849, Chase to Giddings, April 4, 23, 1849, in Giddings Papers; Chase to Mrs. Chase, December 30, 1848, Stanley Matthews to Chase, January 11, 20, 1849, in Chase Papers, Library of Congress; Cleveland *True Democrat*, January 4, 1849.

[27] Giddings to Riddle, November 11, 1848, Riddle to Giddings, November 18, December 22, 1848, in Giddings Papers. See also Giddings's diary for his reactions to the senatorial election, January 23, 1849, *ibid.;* Stewart, *Joshua Giddings,* 173-76.

professed to be interested only in free soil, writing to Morse: "Every-thing but sacrifice of principle, for the cause, and nothing for men except as instruments of the cause." In the same letter, however, he called for his own election to the Senate by noting the need of someone "acceptable to the old Liberty men and Democratic Free Soilers."[28]

In the bargain finally pushed through the legislature by the Demo-crats, Townshend and Morse agreed to vote in favor of seating all of the Democrats from Hamilton County, thus giving the Democrats enough power to organize the House. They also agreed to work for the repeal of the Whig apportionment law which had raised the Hamilton County issue. In return for their votes the Democrats agreed to the election of Chase and revision of the Black Laws. The arrange-ment was completed with the election of two Democrats as judges. Predictably, Whigs throughout the state vehemently denounced Town-shend, Morse, and especially Chase for "selling out to the loco focos in the legislature." On the other hand, despite his own disappointment, Giddings now sought to calm the angry emotions of his own Free Soil supporters and continued to work for party unity.[29]

The one point that Ohio Free Soilers could agree on was that sup-port for the modification of Ohio's Black Laws would be required of whichever party with which they cooperated. The state's discrimina-tory code was among the harshest in the North, and even those Free Soilers with little interest in the rights of blacks saw the need for some change. During the state campaign of 1848 the party platform had called for repeal of the laws. At the same time, however, it noted the Free Soil opposition to a large permanent black population in Ohio, explaining, "We desire a homogeneous population for our state." De-spite this sentiment the Free Soilers did work to carry out their cam-paign pledge in the 1849 legislature. Fearful that the Democrats would not keep their promise, they demanded and received a written pledge that they would support revision. They felt that since Democratic strength was concentrated in the southern part of the state where anti-

---

[28] Chase to Morse, January 10, 1849, Matthews to Chase, January 20, 1849, T. Noble to Chase, February 24, 1849, in Chase Papers, Library of Congress.

[29] Smith, *The Liberty and Free Soil Parties*, 167; Holt, "Party Politics in Ohio," 360-62; John Teesdale to McLean, February 22, 1849, in McLean Papers, Library of Congress; Albert J. Riddle, "The Election of S. P. Chase to the Senate, Feb-ruary, 1849," *The Republic*, IV (1875), 179; Stewart, *Joshua Giddings*, 174-75.

black resentment was strongest, the Democrats would not have agreed had not it been a necessary part of the bargain. Chase and his supporters now feared that Whigs would oppose the Free Soil–sponsored bill because of the nature of the arrangement and because of resentment over his election to the Senate.[30]

These fears proved to be unfounded, although the change in the laws was not as complete as Chase would have liked. His bill, which was introduced by Morse, would have repealed many of the laws making distinctions on the basis of race, but it was amended in the Senate to deny blacks the right to sit on juries or secure poorhouse relief. Under the new law blacks could now enter Ohio without restriction; they could testify against whites; and they were to be provided separate schools. But many rights were still denied them, rights which for the most part Chase and the Free Soilers had not demanded. Blacks were still not considered legal residents of the state nor could they vote or hold office. These disabilities plus the denial of racially integrated schools showed that racism still prevailed. And it was clear that despite the large majorities with which the bill passed both houses, many were strongly opposed to revision and voted for it only because of party pressure to carry out the bargain. As the Cleveland *True Democrat* noted, Democrats had favored the bill not because of principle but "by contract."[31] Although Free Soil agitation had won some reforms it was only a beginning, and these were possible only because of political maneuvering and not because of any change of heart by the white majority. Yet given the powerful bargaining position held by the Free Soilers in the Ohio legislature in 1849 the fact that they

[30] A. G. Riddle, "Recollections of the Forty-Seventh General Assembly of Ohio, 1848-49," *Magazine of Western History*, VI (1887), 350; N. S. Townshend, "The Forty-Seventh General Assembly of Ohio — Comments Upon Mr. Riddle's Paper," *Magazine of Western History*, VI (1887), 625-26; *Ohio Statesman*, December 30, 1848; Stanley Matthews to Chase, January 26, 1849, in Chase Papers, Library of Congress; Morse to Chase, January 24, 1849, in Chase Papers, Historical Society of Pennsylvania.

[31] Holt, "Party Politics in Ohio," 367, 380; Frank U. Quillin, *The Color Line in Ohio: A History of Race Prejudice in a Typical Northern State* (Ann Arbor, 1913), 38-40; J. Reuben Scheeler, "The Struggle of the Negro in Ohio for Freedom," *Journal of Negro History*, XXXI (1946), 221-22; Charles T. Hickok, *The Negro in Ohio, 1802-1870* (Cleveland, 1896), 47; Eric Foner, "Politics and Prejudices: The Free Soil Party AND the Negro, 1849-1852," *Journal of Negro History*, L (1965), 240-42; *National Era*, February 22, 1849; Cleveland *True Democrat*, March 26, 1850.

did not demand greater reform of the laws indicates that their own commitment to racial equality was far from complete.

The bargain completed in 1849 reflected little credit on the Free Soil party of Ohio. Although each of the major parties was capable of offering various "deals" for their support, the Free Soilers were unable to transform this potential into the formation of a powerful anti-extension party. Chase and his followers seemed most concerned with ending the third party's existence through Democratic coalition, a process which he knew would strengthen his hand in Ohio politics. Yet Chase also honestly felt that the cause of anti-extensionism could be furthered if the Free Soilers controlled one of the major parties rather than remaining independent. The Whigs, having been the immediate losers, were vehement in their reaction against Chase. Their feelings were expressed by the *Ohio State Journal:* "Every act of his was subsidiary to *his own ambition.* He talked of the interests of Free Soil, he *meant* HIS OWN. He harangued on the benefits of electing a Free Soil Senator — he intended that none but himself should be that Senator." Nor could the ex-Whig Free Soilers reconcile themselves to the selection of Chase. As Albert Riddle said, "I would not regard the election of Mr. Chase as a thing to be seriously depricated [*sic*] if it was not to be effected by the means that will be employed to accomplish it."[32]

Other Free Soilers like Sumner of Massachusetts admitted they were confused on seeing party members split between Giddings and Chase. But unlike some of his friends, Giddings showed no trace of bitterness toward his rival or toward Townshend and Morse. In a letter to Sumner, he successfully hid his unhappiness as he noted: "I could not disguise the fact that his election would carry conviction to the doubting portion of the community that our cause was rapidly advancing, and that in the end he might do more in that body than I could." Nonetheless, neither Giddings nor most other Free Soilers looked upon Chase's course in early 1849 as an honorable one. Two great Free Soil goals had been achieved: the modification of Ohio's Black Laws and the election of a Free Soil senator. Probably some kind of bargain was inevitable, but Chase's self-righteousness and his overeagerness for

[32] *Ohio State Journal,* April 19, 1849; A. G. Riddle to Giddings, February 21, 1849, in Giddings Papers.

the office helped to divide the Free Soil party.[33] He had confused his own ambition with the good of the anti-extension movement. In the process he had laid himself and other Free Soilers open to charges that the party was simply a temporary means for political gain to be given up at the most expedient time.

The apparent good feelings between Chase and Giddings reflected no basic agreement as to the future course of Ohio Free Soilers. Chase continued to support a permanent fusion with the Democratic party, feeling that the Democrats could be brought around to an anti-extension position without the Free Soilers compromising themselves. In June of 1849, he wrote: "I am a Democrat unreservedly. Investigation and reflection satisfied me long since that the leading measures and maxims of the Democracy were right." He felt that the Democrats were "tired of the alliance with slavery" and ready to agree to Free Soil terms on sectional issues. In anticipation of such a union, he had dropped the name Free Soil and referred to the movement as the Free Democracy. He optimistically believed that the defeat of Cass in 1848 had broken the last link binding Democrats "to the slave powers."[34]

Even though Chase temporarily achieved victory through cooperation with the Democrats in 1849, he only partially succeeded in his efforts to create a permanent coalition with that party. In a state where most Free Soil support centered in the Western Reserve and was Whig in origin, there was not likely to be much enthusiasm for the Democratic views of Chase, a Cincinnatian. Instead, many Free Soilers were more interested in unity within their own party than in union with the Democrats. Personal ambition and practical politics had motivated Chase to try to overcome the original loyalties of most of the members of the third party, but it was a difficult task even

[33] Sumner to Chase, February 27, 1849, in Chase Papers, Library of Congress; Giddings to Sumner, February, 1849, quoted in Julian, *Joshua Giddings*, 268. See also Chase to Giddings, March 6, 1849, in Giddings Papers; Chase to John F. Morse, March 14, 1849, quoted in Jacob W. Schuckers, *The Life and Public Services of Salmon Portland Chase* (New York, 1874), 95-96.

[34] Chase to George Reber, June 19, 1849, Chase to Sumner, November 27, 1848, in Bourne (ed.), "Chase Correspondence," 178-79; Chase to Asa G. Dimmock, August 6, 1849, quoted in Warden, *Salmon P. Chase*, 333-34. The name Free Democracy was first mentioned at the Buffalo convention of 1848, but it was seldom used during the campaign of that year. By 1849 it appeared more frequently and by 1850 it was used more often than the name Free Soil. See Smith, *The Liberty and Free Soil Parties*, 178-79.

for a politician of Chase's ability. At a Western Reserve convention of Free Soilers in May, 1849, the members pledged themselves to support "the great principle of Human Freedom" and to ignore insignificant questions such as the Hamilton County issue on which Chase staked his hopes for permanent Democratic coalition.[35] Giddings had arranged the meeting in an effort to create a Free Soil display of unity and to overcome past differences. Both he and Townshend delivered speeches calling for a restoration of the mutual confidence of all Free Soilers, and the delegates agreed to a national convention to meet in July for the same purpose.[36] Chase's absence from the meeting, however, indicated that such unity would be difficult to achieve.

The July convention which Giddings arranged to hold in Cleveland to celebrate the passage of the Northwest Ordinance of 1787 proved to be somewhat of a disappointment. A large audience heard addresses by Giddings and John Van Buren, among others, and then reaffirmed the principles of the Buffalo convention. Representatives of the five states where the ordinance had banned slavery were invited. Even Chase agreed to attend, and temporarily, unity prevailed. But Giddings's intention of preserving Free Soil independence and avoiding coalition could not be achieved. With Barnburner-Hunker union becoming a reality in New York, the most prominent wing of the Free Soil party was leading the way toward coalition, and Chase was eager for Ohio to be included. He rationalized that such progress had been made in the national Democratic party that there was no need for an independent third-party movement.[37] In the prevailing atmosphere of compromise and personal ambition, there was little room for Giddings's idealism.

[35] Chase had written to Giddings: "Such harmony resulting in a triumph of the Democrats and Free Democrats in the state election, would strengthen infinitely, your position in the House and my position in the Senate, and give complete ascendency to our principles and measures in the state. This harmonious cooperation cannot be had, I apprehend, without a definition of its position by the Free Democracy on the Hamilton County question, and therefore I say that it does not seem to me desirable to avoid it." Chase to Giddings, April 4, 1849, in Giddings Papers.

[36] *National Era*, May 17, 1849; Smith, *The Liberty and Free Soil Parties*, 177-78; Stewart, *Joshua Giddings*, 177-78.

[37] *National Era*, August 2, 1849; Chase to Butler, July 26, 1849, in Bourne (ed.), "Chase Correspondence," 161; Holt, "Party Politics in Ohio," 376-77; Chase to John G. Breslin, July 30, 1849, quoted in Schuckers, *Salmon P. Chase*, 101-3; Smith, *The Liberty and Free Soil Parties*, 177-78.

Chase was unable before the election to work out the complete union with the Democrats that he desired, however. Democrats rejected his demand that they accept anti-extension principles, and Free Soilers refused his request that they embrace the apportionment issue. Therefore leaders in each Ohio district were left to form a coalition if they desired. Surprisingly, agreements were most frequent in northern Ohio, including the Western Reserve, because the Democrats there were often willing to accept the Free Soil position. The coalitions helped the Democrats retain power, but the Free Soilers elected independently four members in the Senate and six in the House. Again the party held the balance of power in both houses, although as an independent party it received only about forty percent of its 1848 total. Giddings was far from happy with the results and told Sumner that Chase's campaign methods "came near ruining us in this state."[38] Only in the Western Reserve had the Free Soilers retained a degree of permanency, and this was due largely to Giddings's influence.

The results of a year's Free Soil agitation in Ohio did not bode well for the future of the party as a separate movement. The united, enthusiastic and independent Free Soil party of 1848 had lost its drive and had become divided and dependent on others. The personal ambitions and Democratic leanings of Salmon P. Chase and his followers had led many Free Soilers into a highly unsatisfactory coalition with Ohio Democrats. Only the Whig background of many of its members and the dedicated leadership of Joshua Giddings prevented a complete loss of identity. With New York and Ohio leading the way back into the Democratic party there seemed little left to sustain a separate third-party movement.

The year 1849 was disastrous for the Free Soil party of Wisconsin. Unlike its counterparts in New York and Ohio, it lacked strong capable leaders, making it even less able to resist an unfavorable coalition with the Democrats. After the election of 1848 the Wisconsin party was in a relatively strong position. It had won more than twenty-five percent of the vote, had taken one of the three congressional seats and held the balance of power in the lower house of the legislature.

[38] Cleveland *Daily Plain Dealer,* October 24, 1849; *Ohio State Journal,* October 16, 1849; Giddings to Sumner, October 29, 1849, in Sumner Papers; Holt, "Party Politics in Ohio," 383; Stewart, *Joshua Giddings,* 179.

It needed skillful leadership to remain together once the initial enthusiasm had worn off, however, and in 1849 this was not forthcoming. A large proportion of the Free Soil vote and leadership in Wisconsin had been Democratic in origin, and the temptation was strong to coalesce with that party in the hope of gaining office. Because of this unfortunate tendency the Democrats were able to outmaneuver the Free Soilers completely, bringing most of them into the Democratic party on Democratic terms. A few of the more committed Free Soilers resisted the temptation to desert the party and struggled on during the ensuing three years under the old Liberty leadership. But they did so only with greatly reduced influence.[39]

In the senatorial election of 1849 the Wisconsin Free Soilers quickly demonstrated that they did not know how to use their newly won power. Although the Democrats held a small plurality over the Whigs and Free Soilers, a Whig–Free Soil coalition on the basis of the Wilmot Proviso could probably have defeated Isaac P. Walker, the Democratic candidate. Anti-extensionists discussed such a union but partisanship prevented them from agreeing on a candidate. The Democratic origin of most of the Free Soil leaders was the major reason that the two groups could not get together. As a result the Free Soilers missed their first chance to use their potential power. Walker won an easy victory over the separate Free Soil and Whig candidates in an election in which two Free Soilers voted for the Democrat.[40]

Part of the Free Soil difficulty was that both major parties in Wisconsin presented themselves as anti-extensionists. During the 1848 campaign, third-party members had found that they were not the only ones to endorse the Wilmot Proviso. Nevertheless, at that time the enthusiasm of a national campaign had pushed them to great success. By 1849, this impetus was gone and many voters, instinctively opposed to third-party politics anyway, were inclined to return to the two-party system. In most cases this meant rejoining the Democratic party. With local questions again prominent, the Free Soil party would suffer because of its overemphasis on national issues. Since all three parties

[39] The most complete accounts of the Wisconsin Free Soil party are found in Smith, "The Free Soil Party in Wisconsin," 119-32 and Smith, *The Liberty and Free Soil Parties*, 208-14.

[40] Smith, *The Liberty and Free Soil Parties*, 208; Smith, "The Free Soil Party in Wisconsin," 119-20.

basically agreed on the Wilmot Proviso and since the Free Soilers made the mistake of playing down state issues, many could no longer see the need of a third party. Nor did the party have the organizational and financial base of the two major parties to sustain it as voter interest lagged.

These difficulties became apparent at a Free Soil state convention which met in Madison in January, 1849. The delegates reaffirmed Free Soil principles but also endorsed other measures such as free trade, thus appealing to the Democrats. The delegates then expressed their willingness to cooperate and even to unite with any party that would agree with their platform. Obviously uncomfortable outside of the two-party system, most of the members appeared overly eager to get back into their original party. Following their none-too-subtle appeal for a Democratic coalition, Moses M. Strong, a Democrat, appeared at their convention and advocated union with the Democrats. To most Free Soilers the trend was a happy one, and the Oshkosh *True Democrat* observed: "We have a strong love for the Democratic party, and after having left it we look with yearning anxiety to see it assume a position that will warrant our return to its support."[41] The party thus ignored the feelings of the Whig and Liberty elements as it rushed headlong into a marriage with the Democrats.

Late in January the Wisconsin legislature voted almost unanimously to direct its senators and representatives in Washington to support the application of "the antislavery clause of the Ordinance of 1787 to all new territory" (i.e., the Wilmot Proviso) and the abolition of slavery in Washington, D.C.[42] This action seemed additional proof that the major parties of the state were thoroughly anti-extensionist in outlook. Hence many Wisconsinites had further reason to believe that there was no need for a Free Soil party. The movement for coalition grew, and in late March, Free Soil and Democratic members of the legislature met in conference where they agreed on the Buffalo platform as a

[41] Madison *Express,* January 16, 1849; Oshkosh *True Democrat,* February 23, 1849; Smith, "The Free Soil Party in Wisconsin," 120-22.

[42] Senator Walker immediately disobeyed these instructions by introducing a bill providing for territorial organization without the anti-extension clause. The legislature then overwhelmingly approved a resolution demanding his resignation. See Smith, *The Liberty and Free Soil Parties,* 209. See below, 190.

basis for union. They then recommended that the parties abandon their separate organizations and unite.[43]

Although the suggested terms of coalition appeared to be very favorable to the Free Soilers, the state committees of the two parties temporarily continued to function, and the union was not immediately formalized. At this point, even some of the former Liberty members were encouraged. Sherman Booth expressed his approval at the expected terms of coalition and told Salmon P. Chase: "I will urge the union on right principles." Free Soilers then invited the Democrats to call a union convention, but the lack of response gave them their first indication that the Democrats were having second thoughts. Finally, in June, Free Soil fears were verified when the state Democratic committee repudiated the vote of its members in the legislature and refused to agree to formal coalition. According to the committee, formal reconciliation was unnecessary, and union on equal terms would be unfair, since the Democrats were more numerous. Instead, the party would accept the return of individual Free Soilers on Democratic terms rather than the coalition of the two organizations.[44]

The Free Soilers, now in a dilemma of their own making, were badly divided as to the best course to follow. The Liberty element wished the party to act alone so as to keep its independence. As the Kenosha *Telegraph* expressed it, "We are cooly told that we went off without reason and the most we can ask is the privilege of coming back unquestioned. We see but one course for the Free Democrats to pursue. Hold their convention, make their nominations, and elect their ticket if they can." Many of the ex-Whig Free Soilers had already been driven out, and Liberty men such as Booth, bitter because of the Democratic snub, refused the Democratic terms.[45]

Most of the Democratic element of the party reluctantly accepted, however. They were willing to reconcile themselves to the idea that the third party had served its purpose. In 1848 their consciences had forced them to repudiate Cass and the Democratic platform, but having done that they could now return with their consciences purged and without

[43] Milwaukee *Daily Wisconsin*, April 11, 1849; Smith, "The Free Soil Party in Wisconsin," 125.

[44] Sherman Booth to Chase, April 5, 1849, in Chase Papers, Library of Congress; Smith, *The Liberty and Free Soil Parties*, 210-11.

[45] Kenosha *Telegraph*, July 6, 1849.

losing face to a state party which endorsed their anti-extension views. That it was highly unlikely that the national Democratic party with its southern wing would support such a position did not stop them, for they seemed almost to wish the death of the Free Soil party in their rush to return to the two-party system. Third-party politics had become increasingly uncomfortable to these men who instinctively opposed remaining outside of the political mainstream. In the Democratic convention to nominate candidates for the fall election, no Free Soilers were chosen, but the party did adopt an anti-extension platform. The Democratic trap worked perfectly. The third party had offered to unite with any party agreeing to its principles, and this the Democrats had done. The Free Soilers themselves, however, could find no place for their organization in the union and were permitted to join only as individuals.[46]

Some Free Soilers then made an attempt to preserve their independence by holding their own "union" convention, but only about forty attended. Even this small group could not agree on a common strategy although most felt that some kind of coalition was still desirable. When this proved impossible those few unwilling to rejoin the Democratic party chose a Free Soil slate for state offices headed by Warren Chase for governor.[47] Those who supported Chase were mostly members of the Liberty faction who had long since broken with the major parties. They were men who felt that commitment to the anti-extension cause was more important than political considerations. But their ticket had no chance, for not only would the bulk who had been Democrats support their old party, most Whig Free Soilers had long since deserted also.

Thus as the election approached the third party was a sorry sight. Torn by dissension, with its platform imitated by the major parties, the Free Soil party of 1849 was reduced to little more than the Liberty element of 1847 and early 1848. Most voters looked on the members as simply a faction of the Democratic party which had failed to live up to its promises after the Democrats had met its terms for union. By a lack of foresight and leadership, most Free Soilers had allowed themselves to be absorbed. Having made little effort to counter the

[46] Smith, "The Free Soil Party in Wisconsin," 127-28.
[47] Smith, *The Liberty and Free Soil Parties,* 212-13.

Democratic demands, they had almost willingly given up their own organization in their desire to reenter the two-party system. With most of the Free Soil votes of 1848 going to the Democrats, Chase received only 3,700 votes out of 41,000 cast. Nor would the party be able to regain any of its lost support in 1850, for in that year the Free Soilers struggled on in this reduced form under the old Liberty leadership.[48] After having made such an auspicious start in 1848, the Wisconsin Free Soil party had declined rapidly in a few short months, a truly disheartening development for the future prospects of the entire anti-extension movement. It had made little effort to win either a permanent place in the party system of Wisconsin or significant concessions from the major parties.

The year 1849 marked a general trend toward Free Soil coalition with the Democratic party throughout the North, highlighted by the Barnburner-Hunker reunion in New York. In many areas the Free Soilers waged a losing battle to maintain their strong independent movement. Once local Democrats and Whigs no longer had to speak for national candidates and platforms which had been either silent on the slave extension issue or had endorsed the southern position, they could assume firmer ground. With the national campaign over, the Democrats of the North could take a more vigorous position than the Whigs because they were now the party out of power and no longer had to defend the policies of an unpopular president. In addition, because a large proportion of the Free Soil vote of 1848 had originally been Democratic, coalition on an anti-extension basis became a reasonable possibility.

Throughout the North, Free Soil organizations, reflecting the influence of the New York Barnburners, made limited moves toward coalition which cost them much of their identity. Massachusetts, moved hesitatingly toward Democratic coalition, slowed by the highly influential Conscience Whig element in the party.[49] In Vermont and Connecticut, Free Soilers and Democrats agreed to resolutions providing for coalition in one form or another, while in Maine, although no formal coalition occurred, many Free Soilers returned to the Democratic

[48] Milwaukee *Sentinel and Gazette,* September 17, 1849; *Whig Almanac* (1850), 61; Smith, "The Free Soil Party in Wisconsin," 129-32.
[49] See Chapter Eight.

party on an individual basis. In Pennsylvania where Free Soilers had stirred little interest in 1848, the movement remained dormant in 1849 and acquiesced in most Democratic nominations.[50] In the Midwest a similar pattern again revealed the Barnburner influence and the strong anti-extension stand taken by northern Democrats. By the end of 1849 the Free Soil party as an independent organization in Indiana had ceased to exist. In Illinois, although anti-extension sentiment was strong in many parts of the state, the Free Soil organization quietly disintegrated in 1849.[51] Only in Michigan did the Free Soilers join forces with the Whigs, and this was because the strong influence of Lewis Cass prevented any Democratic endorsement of the Wilmot Proviso. But the result was essentially the same — the loss of Free Soil identity and the return of most anti-extensionists to their old parties.[52]

Defections were quietly but quickly reducing the Free Soil party to a small body of dedicated crusaders similar to those who had led the Liberty party. The events of 1849 had revealed that most Free Soilers were determined to return to the two-party system even though in some cases it meant a sacrifice of their anti-extension principle as well as the loss of their political independence. The security of the two party system with its potential patronage and political power were more important and realistic to most than dedication to their cause of 1848. In New York, the Barnburner leadership was almost unanimous in its efforts to form a coalition with the Democrats even though the Wilmot Proviso was sacrificed in the process. In Ohio, Chase's direction led many into Democratic union, although the equally strong leadership of Giddings preserved many with Whig backgrounds in the independent movement. In Wisconsin, Free Soil leadership which might have prevented coalition was lacking. In all three states only the Giddings faction seemed to want the third party to continue. Free Soilers in

[50] John A. Dix to Benton, August 14, 1849, in Charles Benton Papers; *National Era*, May 3, June 7, 14, 1849; I. Toucey to Marcy, April 18, 1849, in Marcy Papers; Albany *Evening Atlas*, June 5, 1849; Boston *Courier*, June 9, 30, September 21, 1849; Br. J. Robert Lane, *A Political History of Connecticut During the Civil War* (Washington, 1941), 8-9; Hatch, *Maine*, II, 346; Geary, *Third Parties in Pennsylvania*, 141.

[51] Smith, *The Liberty and Free Soil Parties*, 187-97; Cole, *The Era of the Civil War*, 61-62.

[52] Streeter, *Political Parties in Michigan*, 107-16; Smith, *The Liberty and Free Soil Parties*, 198-208.

other northern states were also willing to join their New York, Ohio, and Wisconsin colleagues in rationalizing away the need for a separate organization by arguing that the Democrats and Whigs had agreed to their anti-extension terms. Yet the events of 1850 would prove this was no more than a rationalization, for the spirit of compromise so evident among Free Soilers in 1849 was about to prevail in Washington as well. The Wilmot Proviso would be a victim of this spirit in Congress just as the independent third party had been the victim in many states.

Given the campaign of the Free Soilers in 1848, the passage of the Compromise of 1850 should have stiffened their desire to retain their independence. Instead it had the reverse effect. The Omnibus measures which became law only after a nine-month struggle in Congress did authorize California to enter the Union as a free state and did abolish the slave trade in the District of Columbia. But the Compromise did not abolish slavery in the District. Even worse from a Free Soil perspective, it included a Fugitive Slave Act which protected slaveholders in their efforts to capture alleged fugitives and enormously increased the powers of the federal government to assist them in this process. The law also provided for stringent penalties for anyone assisting a fugitive and thus went against everything Free Soil advocates claimed to stand for. In relation to the rest of the Mexican War territories the Compromise dealt a serious defeat to the Wilmot Proviso by organizing Utah and New Mexico territories without reference to slavery.[53] Thus the major plank of the Buffalo platform had been rejected leaving the issue of extension up to the residents of those territories. Although the Free Soilers in Congress had fought valiantly against what they considered to be the proslavery aspects of the Compromise,[54] many third-party men now seemed more willing than ever to forget their campaign of 1848 and return to the two-party system.

The Free Soil party reached its lowest point in 1850 and 1851 as Whigs and Democrats worked successfully to convince the voters of the finality of the Compromise. True, the Fugitive Slave Law provoked numerous disputes. Furthermore, in June, 1851, *Uncle Tom's Cabin*

[53] *The Public Statutes at Large and Treaties of the United States of America* (Boston, 1845-1963), IX, 446-58, 462-65, 467-68.
[54] See Chapter Seven.

began appearing in serial form in the *National Era*.[55] Portraying slavery in a highly unfavorable light, Mrs. Stowe's book was soon being read by thousands of Americans. Within a year it had become the most effective piece of antislavery literature ever published. Yet the Free Soil party remained in semi-inactivity during this period, as the nation tried to keep the slavery issue out of politics. Members continued to drift away from the third party, with many agreeing to absorption by the Democrats. In their desire to return to the security of the two-party system many of the less committed preferred to accept the rationalization that the issue had been settled. Nowhere did Free Soilers show the vitality and enthusiasm of 1848, as politicians everywhere argued that there was no need for further agitation.

Barnburner activity in 1850 and 1851 appeared to foretell the complete end of the independent third-party movement throughout the North. In New York, Free Democrats, as they now called themselves, agreed to meet with the Hunkers in the fall of 1850 in an attempt to weld the groups into a more united Democratic party than had been possible in the reunion of 1849. Such an event now seemed highly likely, for during the congressional debates, John Van Buren and most other Barnburners had completely given up the idea of maintaining a separate organization. As pressure for passage of the Compromise increased, they tacitly abandoned the Wilmot Proviso, realizing that Congress would never consider it in relation to Utah and New Mexico territories. While not approving of parts of the settlement, by midsummer the Barnburners began to think its passage inevitable.[56] They had insisted on the Wilmot Proviso in 1849 as the basis of reunion, but they were now convinced that party unity came before anti-extension principle. Having already begun their retreat in 1849, the passage of the Compromise gave them one more excuse to continue it in 1850. They professed to believe there was now no further need for agitation, realizing full well that Democratic unity was the surest means of a return to political power in New York. In this respect they

[55] The novel was published in the *National Era*, from June 5, 1851 to April 1, 1852.
[56] Dix to Flagg, July 16, 1850, in Flagg Papers, Columbia University; Albany *Argus*, August 5, 1850; Blair to Martin Van Buren, October 14, 1850, in Van Buren Papers.

were no different from Free Soilers in other states, but their earlier dominance in the movement gave their actions a greater significance. A joint Democratic convention met in Syracuse in September, 1850, to nominate candidates for governor and other state offices, for by this time the Barnburners as a distinct group had virtually disappeared. After nominating Horatio Seymour for governor, the convention resolved, with only twenty dissenting votes, its full support of the Compromise of 1850. The Proviso resolutions which had figured in every platform since 1847 were quietly dropped. The attitude in New York was perhaps best expressed by former Liberty member Henry B. Stanton who had long since abandoned his earlier approach and had joined the Barnburners in their search for office. He wrote to Chase: "The Buffalo party served its temporary purpose and is rapidly becoming extinct. In my sober judgment the day for 'third parties' on the slavery question is gone."[57] To Stanton and the Barnburners it was easy to rationalize that the Compromise had closed the issue.

A few voices could still be heard protesting the abandonment of free soil. The *National Era* denounced the New York developments: "And among the principal agents in this apostate movement, we find leading Barnburners, who not long since grew hoarse in declaiming against slavery. A more shameless profligate abandonment of principle is not on record." Such sentiments, however, were clearly in the minority. John A. Dix later admitted that the Barnburners had reentered the Democratic party on Hunker terms. He noted that in 1848 the Barnburner policy had been "Harmony is a good thing, but honesty is better," but in 1850 their acceptance of a Compromise platform indicated that the reverse was true.[58]

The Whigs of New York quickly seized on this opportunity and, by endorsing William H. Seward's opposition to the Compromise, became the more vehement anti-extension party in New York in 1850. In an extremely close contest they elected Washington Hunt governor, de-

[57] Albany *Argus*, September 23, 1850; *New York Hards and Softs*, 25; New York *Evening Post*, September 14, 16, 1850; King to Flagg, August 26, 1850, in Flagg Papers, Columbia University; Stanton to Chase, September 23, 1850, in Chase Papers, Library of Congress. For Stanton's career see Filler, *The Crusade against Slavery*, 189.

[58] *National Era*, September 19, October 3, 18, 1850; Dix to Benton, October 24, 1853, in Charles Benton Papers.

feating Seymour, and they maintained control over both houses of the legislature. With Preston King again a Democrat and ready to re-enter the Democratic congressional caucus in 1851, Democrats and Whigs each won seventeen seats in Congress. In early 1851, the legis-lature elected Hamilton Fish to the Senate over his Democratic oppo-nent, John A. Dix. Except for a small remnant of former Liberty members, the New York Free Soil party virtually ceased to exist. The Whigs, without any cooperation from former third-party members, temporarily filled the free soil vacuum.[59]

In 1851, opposition to the Fugitive Slave Law kept interest in sec-tional issues alive in New York, but it was confined to the two major parties. This interest was in part motivated by political considerations. Having endorsed the Compromise of 1850, some of the former Free Soilers began to have second thoughts. John Van Buren led the attack on the fugitive law and called for open defiance of it. He also sought to prevent the state party from endorsing it and worked unsuccess-fully for a state law which would have made federal enforcement more difficult. But there was no interest in a third-party movement on his part. One of the prime instigators of the Free Soil revolt in 1848, young Van Buren now clearly reflected the feelings of his father in his desire to stay within the two-party system. In this regard, political opportunism more than principle was the rule, for Van Buren and others sought to use the fugitive slave issue to help gain control of the state Democratic party and the state itself. For Van Buren and most other Barnburners, party control was their major concern. They real-ized that opposition to the Fugitive Slave Law was popular in New York and might help them to attain their goal. As they had before the 1848 convention, they hoped to dominate the delegation to the 1852 national convention and thus take control away from those Hun-kers who refused to cooperate.[60] But the lesson of 1848 would make them very wary about bolting again should they not get their way.

[59] Muller, "Preston King," 510; New York *Evening Post*, November 7, 1850, February 4, 1851; Philip S. Foner, *Business and Slavery: The New York Mer-chants and the Irrepressible Conflict* (Chapel Hill, N.C., 1941), 38-50.

[60] John Van Buren to Sumner, June 5, 1851, in Sumner Papers; Albany *Eve-ning Atlas*, April 14, June 6, 1851; John Van Buren to Martin Van Buren, March 4, 1851, in Van Buren Papers.

For the Van Buren group, the New York convention was only a partial success as it accepted the finality of the Compromise but did avoid a direct endorsement of the Fugitive Slave Law. Although the bickering and struggle for power continued, harmony among New York Democrats was maintained at least on the surface, and independent action remained out of the question. "It does not seem to me," Preston King said, "that a separate organization is either practicable or desirable." According to King, who was typical of most Barnburners, the Buffalo organization was broken and beyond recall. To Marcy, the only choices open to the Barnburners were either to remain in the Democratic party or "to become a component part of a sectional party which could never be a national party."[61] Most Barnburners agreed.

The Free Soilers of Ohio displayed some of the same weaknesses and labored under the same handicaps as their associates in New York but, due to the influence of Joshua Giddings, they were able to prevent the dissolution of their movement and even enjoy a moderate revival in 1851.[62] Although the party was much smaller in 1850 and 1851 than in 1848, the Free Soilers maintained a degree of independence and were thus in a position to play a leading role in the resurgence of the party in 1852. Throughout 1850, however, the Ohio party remained in the weakened position that had resulted from its struggles of 1849. With support for the Compromise widespread, it experienced a further loss of members as voters could see little need for third-party agitation. In their desire to reenter the two-party system, many Free Soilers were willing to accept the Democratic and Whig claim that the Compromise was a final settlement. Because of this attitude and because of his own personal ambition, Salmon P. Chase redoubled his efforts to unite his "Free Democracy" with the regular Democrats of the state. His efforts were futile, however, and he further weakened the third party in the process. The Democrats

[61] New York *Herald*, September 10-15, 1851; Marshall (ed.), "Diary and Memoranda of William L. Marcy," 453; King to Blair, February 26, 1852, in Blair Papers.

[62] The best accounts of Ohio Free Soil activity in 1850 and 1851 are found in Weisenburger, *The Passing of the Frontier*, 474-79; Eugene H. Roseboom, *The Civil War Era, 1850-1873*, vol. IV of *The History of the State of Ohio*, Carl Wittke (ed.) (Columbus, 1944), 256-65; Smith, *The Liberty and Free Soil Parties*, 184-87, 235-42.

nominated an anti-extensionist for governor in 1850 and, refusing to endorse the Compromise, let each district define its own position. With Giddings's wing of the party centered in the Western Reserve still consistently opposing Democratic coalition, the Free Soilers selected an old Liberty party leader, the Rev. Edward Smith, for governor and strongly condemned the congressional settlement. The Whigs of Ohio were embarrassed by President Fillmore's endorsement of the Compromise and attempted to avoid discussion of the issue, leaving the Free Soil party as the only one to take a definite stand. The party did not benefit from this situation, however, because Chase resisted the wishes of his party and continued to look for Democratic union. When this failed, he announced he would remain neutral, while the party's leading newspaper, the Cleveland *True Democrat,* was less than enthusiastic about Smith. Free Soil meetings were poorly attended and displayed little of the enthusiasm of 1848. As a result, few were surprised when Smith's showing was only about one-third of the party's total of two years earlier. Giddings was the lone Free Soiler from Ohio returned to Congress.[63]

Another indication of the third party's declining state was the minimal role it played in the state constitutional convention of 1850-51. Only in the Western Reserve did Free Soilers run as independent candidates for the position of delegate and only three of their number were elected. The convention, which lasted almost a year, concerned itself with many aspects of Ohio politics not directly of interest to the third party. But it also considered several racially discriminatory provisions, and no progress was made in removing the remaining black codes. Before the document was submitted to the voters, the delegates voted overwhelmingly to exclude blacks from the militia, to deny them the right to vote, and to forbid them to enter schools with whites. Although Giddings's Ashtabula *Sentinel* attacked this "outrage on a valuable class of people," few other voices, Free Soil or otherwise, were raised in opposition.[64] In fact, the few Free Soilers at the convention

---

[63] Chase to E. S. Hamlin, February 20, April 16, 1850, Hamlin to Chase, May 23, July 1, 1850, B. B. Chapman to Chase, March 6, 1850, in Chase Papers, Library of Congress; Cleveland *True Democrat,* July-September, 1850; Roseboom, *The Civil War Era,* 256-59; Smith, *The Liberty and Free Soil Parties,* 185-87.

[64] Quillin, *The Color Line in Ohio,* 75-87; Roseboom, *The Civil War Era,* 129; Ashtabula *Sentinel,* April 26, 1851, quoted in Stewart, *Joshua Giddings,* 199.

had offered little organized resistance to these measures and had little impact on either the proceedings or the final document.

The year 1851 marked a slight resurgence of Free Soil strength in Ohio. Despite its poor showing in the 1850 state election, it did manage to win enough seats in the legislature to retain its balance of power. It was thus in a position to influence the election of a senator as it had done in 1849. Chase naturally hoped for a Free Soil colleague to join him in Washington and even held out the prospect of election to Giddings if he would only cooperate with the Democrats more closely. If Giddings could be persuaded, the major obstacle in the way of Chase's desired coalition would be removed. But Giddings was unwilling to sacrifice his free soil principles or his political independence. When the two parties were unable to agree on anyone else, Free Soil–Whig agreement for a coalition remained the only possibility. Such a prospect alarmed Chase, who wrote privately that it would gravely endanger his plans for a national Free Soil–Democratic fusion. In the early balloting of the state legislature Free Soilers remained loyal to Giddings. Finally, with a deadlock developing, Free Soilers and Whigs combined to elect an anti-extension Whig, Judge Benjamin Wade, the only prominent candidate on whom they could agree. Over Chase's opposition, Wade received Free Soil support because of his vehement opposition to the Fugitive Slave Law. His election to the Senate was a personal defeat for Chase, however, and indicated to him that union with the Democrats had become only a remote possibility in Ohio.[65]

The election of Wade did not mean greater influence for the independent Free Soil party or even increased opposition to the Compromise. In fact, declining Free Soil strength throughout the country in 1851 indicated that the Compromise was still acceptable to most. But Ohioans of all parties had many reservations, and neither Whigs nor Democrats were willing to endorse the finality of the Compromise. Neither were they willing to attack the settlement openly and directly, however. They apparently feared the potential divisiveness of the issue

[65] Chase to E. S. Hamlin, December 9, 1850, in Chase Papers, Library of Congress; Chase to Giddings, October 22, 1850, Giddings to Addison Giddings, December 16, 1850, in Giddings Papers; Chase to Sutliff, January 16, 1851, in Bourne (ed.), "Chase Correspondence," 230-32; *Ohio State Journal*, March 17, 1851; Trefousse, *Benjamin Wade*, 67.

too much to make a major issue of it.[66] Yet the Free Soilers recognized the unpopularity of the Compromise in Ohio and, under Giddings's leadership, prepared for an active campaign for the governorship. Once again the Western Reserve led the way, firmly rejecting Chase's efforts to turn the movement into a Democratic coalition. At a convention at Ravenna attended by two thousand, the delegates reaffirmed their independence and condemned the Compromise and the Fugitive Slave Law. At the state convention, with Giddings presiding, a united party gave its gubernatorial nomination to Samuel Lewis, one of the original and most dedicated Liberty party leaders. The unity was genuine as the delegates adopted uncompromising free soil resolutions. Largely because of Giddings's leadership the third party had been turned away from all thoughts of coalition toward a strong independent stand, and Free Soil prospects appeared promising for the first time since 1848.[67]

Not surprisingly, Salmon P. Chase could find no place in the revived Free Soil party. With his efforts for coalition now thoroughly frustrated through Giddings's efforts, his future in Ohio politics dictated that he become a Democrat. Stung by this reversal of fortunes, he announced in August that he would support the Democratic candidate, Judge Reuben Wood, against Samuel Lewis. Emphasizing the record of the Democrats of Ohio, he professed to believe that the Democratic party throughout the North was becoming an antislavery party. By his support of Wood he indicated that his own political future was more secure as a Democrat, "whenever it involve[d] no sacrifice of his principles," than as a Free Soiler.[68] But he had to ignore

[66] The Whig state convention of 1851 resolved that since the Compromise measures, including the Fugitive Slave Law, were not party matters, each Whig was at liberty to hold his own opinions respecting them. The Democrats in their state convention in August did not refer to the Compromise, but reaffirmed the slavery resolutions of their convention of 1848. These resolutions condemned slavery "as an evil, unfavorable to the full development of the spirit and practical benefits of free institutions." The party continued, however, that each state had a right "to regulate its own internal affairs." For proceedings of the Whig convention, see *National Era,* August 28, 1851; for those of the Democratic convention, *National Era,* August 14, 21, 28, 1851.

[67] Roseboom, *The Civil War Era,* 263-64; Smith, *The Liberty and Free Soil Parties,* 237-38; *National Era,* July 10, August 7, 28, 1851; Stewart, *Joshua Giddings,* 200-202.

[68] *National Era,* September 11, 1851; Cleveland *True Democrat,* September 8, 11, 1851.

the strong Compromise sentiment in his new party choice in other parts of the nation, a sentiment much stronger among Democrats than Whigs.

Free Soilers throughout the state were shocked by Chase's desertion and were naturally harsh in their criticisms. But they did not let it dampen their revived enthusiasm. Chase's defection no doubt cost the party some support in the gubernatorial race, but it increased its total vote over 1850 by three thousand and carried the Reserve. The Democratic sweep of the state, however, meant that the Free Soilers no longer held the balance of power in the legislature that they had enjoyed so long. Nevertheless, Chase's bolt did not seriously hurt the Free Soil party in Ohio. The great majority, under the leadership of men like Giddings and Lewis, no longer hampered by the compromising of Chase, continued and even began to make plans for the national campaign of 1852.[69]

Although third-party efforts revived in Ohio, the trend throughout most of the rest of the North followed the example of the Barnburners of New York. In the East, except in Massachusetts, Free Soil activity was almost as minimal as in New York. In Pennsylvania, David Wilmot withdrew from his race for reelection to Congress when Democrats refused to support him. In Maine, independent action remained out of the question also as the Free Soilers combined with anti-extension Democrats to reelect Hannibal Hamlin to the Senate.[70] In the Midwest, outside of Ohio, Free Soil activity was minimal in 1850 and 1851. In both Michigan and Illinois most Free Soilers returned to their former parties.[71] In Indiana the party lost its one voice in Congress as George Julian was defeated by a Whig who received significant Democratic support.[72] There as in Wisconsin the Free Soilers were left to

[69] *Ohio State Journal*, November 20, 1851; Roseboom, *The Civil War Era*, 264-65; Stewart, *Joshua Giddings*, 203.
[70] Going, *David Wilmot*, 430; James T. DuBois and Gertrude S. Mathews, *Galusha A. Grow, Father of the Homestead Law* (Boston, 1917), 66-69; Mueller, *The Whig Party in Pennsylvania*, 175; Geary, *Third Parties in Pennsylvania*, 148-50; Hatch, *Maine*, II, 353; Hamlin, *Hannibal Hamlin*, 238-49.
[71] Streeter, *Political Parties in Michigan*, 116-38; John S. Wright, "The Background and Formation of the Republican Party in Illinois, 1846-1860" (Ph.D. dissertation, University of Chicago, 1947), 69-70; Smith, *The Liberty and Free Soil Parties*, 193-97, 204-8, 231.
[72] Julian, *Political Recollections*, 117-18; Riddleberger, *George W. Julian*, 78-83; Smith, *The Liberty and Free Soil Parties*, 233-34.

return to their old parties as individuals. Surprisingly, the party did retain its seat in Congress in Wisconsin. Realizing the futility of their surrender to the Democrats in 1849, they now cooperated with the Whigs to reelect Charles Durkee. Yet the party remained extremely weak elsewhere in the state and the members declined to nominate a candidate for governor in 1851.[73]

With the exception of Ohio and Massachusetts, the Free Soil party had fallen on lean times in 1850 and 1851. Especially in the East there appeared to be little future for the movement as men returned by the thousands to their former parties. Continuing the trend begun in 1849, former Free Soilers increased their efforts for political position through the two-party system. Unhappy in a party which had brought them few immediate and tangible results, many forgot their 1848 platform pledge to continue independently. Instead they rationalized that if the voters were convinced that the settlement made by Congress in 1850 was a final solution there was indeed little need for a third party. The majority favored the Chase approach over that of Giddings. Yet in Congress, Giddings and the small group of Free Soilers had acted out of a much different conviction in their dedicated efforts to prevent the Compromise from becoming law.

[73] Smith, "The Free Soil Party in Wisconsin," 133-35.

7

The Free Soilers Resist
Compromise in Congress

The closing months of the Polk administration witnessed an increase in sectional animosities. As the Thirtieth Congress met for its second session in December, 1848, members were preoccupied with questions dealing with the expansion of slavery. State legislatures in both North and South were flooding the Capital with inflammatory resolutions, and feelings were becoming dangerously heated.[1] The Free Soilers had helped create this atmosphere in their campaign of 1848 through their advocacy of the Wilmot Proviso and by appealing above practical politics to the nation's moral conscience. They had helped to arouse anti-extension feelings through their agitation both in and out of Congress. As Congress convened, there appeared to be little prospect that a spirit of compromise could even temporarily reassert itself, for the members of Congress were in anything but a conciliatory mood. Southerners declared that they would resist to the end passage of the Wilmot Proviso or any interference with slavery in the District of Columbia. In increasing numbers northern legislatures began endorsing the Proviso and advocating the discontinuation of the slave trade in Washington. The situation gave both the Free Soilers and southerners in Congress an excellent opportunity to present their views and make the nation aware of the dangerous implications of the crisis.[2]

The Free Soilers in the House, under the leadership of the veteran Joshua Giddings, had met before the session opened to plan their

[1] Nevins, *Ordeal of the Union*, I, 219-21.
[2] See *Niles' Register*, January 24, 31, 1849.

strategy on how best to present their position. Less than a week after the session began, John G. Palfrey, Free Soiler from Massachusetts, attempted to introduce a bill in the House repealing all legislation protecting slavery in the District of Columbia. The House denied him permission to do so by a vote of 82 to 69. Joseph Root of Ohio then reintroduced the Wilmot Proviso by asking that the House instruct the Committee on Territories to introduce a bill organizing California and New Mexico as territories prohibiting slavery. The measure was initially passed with solid northern support but then rejected as some of the less-committed northern congressmen changed their votes in an effort to avoid antagonizing southerners. In January, the Free Soil offensive continued as Giddings proposed a bill to restrict and gradually abolish slavery in Washington, and Daniel Gott, a Whig from New York, offered a bill to abolish the slave trade in the capital. These men were all vehement in their attacks on slavery and its consequences. Gott called the slave trade "contrary to natural justice and the fundamental principles of our political system" as well as "a serious hindrance to the progress of republican liberty among the nations of the earth."[3]

Although the Free Soilers were too small in number to continue their well-planned attack, their proposals and those of other anti-extensionists greatly alarmed the South. Claiming to see new evidence of northern aggression and a grave threat to the Union itself, southerners reacted immediately. In the wake of the Free Soil assault, eighty southern members of Congress met in caucus and agreed to leave their seats should Congress pass the Wilmot Proviso or abolish the slave trade in the District of Columbia. They also appointed a committee to prepare a statement explaining their position. The result was Calhoun's "Address of the Southern Delegates in Congress to their Constituents" attacking the "unconstitutional Northern invasion of Southern rights" and appealing for southern resistance and unity.[4] Next, southerners and their northern allies attempted to put their words into legislative action. Senator Isaac P. Walker of Wisconsin introduced a bill extending the

[3] *Congressional Globe*, 30th Cong., 2nd Sess., Appendix, 38-39, 55-56, 83-84; Craven, *The Coming of the Civil War*, 241-42; Nevins, *Ordeal of the Union*, I, 222; Stewart, *Joshua Giddings*, 167-68.
[4] Cralle (ed.), *The Works of John C. Calhoun*, VI, 290-313; Nevins, *Ordeal of the Union*, I, 225; Craven, *The Coming of the Civil War*, 242-43.

Constitution and the laws of the United States over the territories acquired from Mexico, thus abrogating Mexican laws including those prohibiting slavery. Walker's action in effect would have extended popular sovereignty to these territories. It was in violation of his instructions from the Wisconsin legislature, which immediately censured him and demanded his resignation.[5] His proposal ran counter to the feelings of the great majority of Wisconsin voters and was further proof to the Free Soilers that the major parties were not to be trusted on matters relating to slavery. The Walker bill passed the Senate, but in the House the Free Soilers led the opposition, with Giddings and others using obstructionist tactics to prevent approval. They knew that if they could succeed here, in the next Congress there would be more Free Soilers to aid them in their efforts. Finally anti-extensionists of all parties combined to defeat the measure on the last day of the session.[6]

President Polk was determined to resist any sectional disturbance by either North or South as long as he was in office. He had written: "The agitation of the slavery question is mischievous and wicked and proceeds from no patriotic motive by its authors." He thus firmly put himself on record against the sentiments of Calhoun's address and appeal for southern unity. On his last day in office he went to the Capitol determined to veto any last minute measure embodying the Wilmot Proviso. No veto was necessary, however, for Congress remained bitterly deadlocked and adjourned without decisive action.[7] Congress thus failed to provide any government for the California and New Mexico territories or to deal with slavery and the slave trade in the District of Columbia. Ardent southerners, and anti-extensionists under Free Soil leadership, had combined to produce a sectional crisis with which a new Congress and president would have to contend.

Before the Thirty-first Congress convened in December, 1849, events

[5] Walker had won his seat in the Senate in 1849 when the Free Soilers and Whigs in the Wisconsin legislature had failed to unite to prevent the choice of a Democrat. See above, 172. The censure and demand for his resignation passed the Wisconsin legislature by votes of 10 to 6 in the Senate and 42 to 9 in the House with some Democrats joining with the Whigs and Free Soilers to support the resolution. See Smith, *The Liberty and Free Soil Parties*, 209.

[6] *Congressional Globe*, 30th Cong., 2nd Sess., 695-98; Giddings, Diary, March 3, 4, 1849, in Giddings Papers; Stewart, *Joshua Giddings*, 172.

[7] Giddings, Diary, March 3, 1849, in Giddings Papers; Quaife (ed.), *The Diary of James K. Polk*, IV, 249-51, 285-89, 362-72.

outside of Washington made a settlement between North and South even more urgent. The discovery of gold in California in 1848 brought 80,000 people to the region by the end of the following year. Congress could no longer postpone giving California territorial organization. In 1849, agitation over fugitive slaves and the status of slavery in the nation's capital increased. Yet despite the urgency, the new House was temporarily unable to organize and elect a speaker, so bitter were sectional animosities.[8] For this immediate crisis concerning the speaker, the Free Soil party was largely responsible.

The exact Free Soil strength in the House of Representatives of the Thirty-first Congress is difficult to determine, although it may safely be estimated at twelve. More important, it is certain that the third party held the balance of power. Those clearly aligned with the new party included Preston King of New York, David Wilmot of Pennsylvania, Charles Allen of Massachusetts, Amos Tuck of New Hampshire, Joshua Giddings and Joseph Root of Ohio, George Julian of Indiana and Charles Durkee of Wisconsin. Several others, including Walter Booth of Connecticut, Horace Mann of Massachusetts, William Sprague of Michigan, and John W. Howe of Pennsylvania, were classified at the time as Free Soilers and could be counted on to vote with the party on many issues.[9] If either Democrats or Whigs were to elect a speaker, they would have to obtain some Free Soil support, for the makeup of the House included 111 Democrats, 107 Whigs, and 12 Free Soilers. Yet as the contest opened all three parties had candidates: the Democrats, Howell Cobb of Georgia; the Whigs, Robert Winthrop of Massachusetts; and the Free Soilers, David Wilmot. As the balloting

---

[8] Craven, *The Coming of the Civil War*, 246-47; Nevins, *Ordeal of the Union*, I, 229-51; Holman Hamilton, *Prologue to Conflict: The Crisis and Compromise of 1850* (Lexington, Ky., 1964), 37-42.

[9] The confusion over the number of Free Soilers in Congress occurred because several men were elected with the help of a Free Soil coalition with one of the major parties. As a result, some sources list them as Free Soilers and others as Whigs or Democrats. In addition to Mann, Booth, Sprague, and Howe, who were elected by coalitions, the *Congressional Globe* lists William Hunter of Ohio as a Free Soiler. However, despite the fact that Hunter did receive some Free Soil support in winning election, he worked more closely with the Whigs than with the third party throughout the session. See *Congressional Globe*, 31st Cong., 1st Sess., 1-15; See also *Biographical Directory of the American Congress, 1774-1961* (Washington, 1961).

proceeded, party lines held firm, and the Free Soilers prevented a decision.[10]

As the deadlock continued through December, the government could do little business. With the House unable to organize, the Senate marked time, and President Taylor had to hold back his annual message. In the initial balloting most of the Free Soilers voted for Wilmot with his total varying from six to nine. None of the men who were clearly aligned with the third-party voted for Winthrop or Cobb. As the voting continued Cobb's total fell and the leading Democrat became William J. Brown of Indiana. Finally on the fortieth ballot Brown's total reached 112 votes, two short of the necessary majority, and he appeared on the verge of election. On that ballot, Giddings and five other Free Soilers surprisingly had thrown their support to Brown, thus joining with northern and southern Democrats.[11]

When the voting pattern was apparent, southern congressmen naturally became suspicious, and Representatives Thomas H. Bayly of Virginia and Edward Stanly of North Carolina charged that rumors "which this morning had been in whispers through this Hall," indicated that "something improper had taken place between the Democratic party and the Free Soilers. . . ." On pressing their claims they discovered that some of the Free Soilers had reached a private agreement with Brown and that Wilmot and King had obtained the following pledge from him: "Should I be elected Speaker of the House of Representatives I will constitute the committees on the District of Columbia, on the territories, and on the Judiciary in such a manner as shall be satisfactory to yourself and your friends." Practical politics had dictated that the Free Soilers support a man who might indirectly aid their cause even if he did not fully endorse their principles. Southerners finally forced Brown to read to the House the letter he had written to Wilmot. Following the reading bedlam broke loose in the House as members traded insults and threats. As recorded in the *Congressional Globe:* "Indescribable confusion followed — threats, violent gesticulations, calls to order, and demands for adjournment were mingled together. The House was like a heaving billow." Immediately

[10] *National Era,* December 6, 13, 1849; *Congressional Globe,* 31st Cong., 1st Sess., 1-15.
[11] *Congressional Globe,* 31st Cong., 1st Sess., 16-22.

Brown withdrew from the race, and the Free Soilers found themselves under attack from all sides.[12]

Both Brown and Wilmot defended their understanding as a completely honorable one, and there is little doubt that their action was an accepted practice by members of both major parties. Although Brown did indicate that he had "always opposed the extension of slavery," all the Free Soilers had asked of him was a guarantee that the men chosen for the key committees be "impartial and unprejudiced upon the question of slavery," not that Free Soilers necessarily be included. Wilmot explained that what he had sought were simply men "who would not stifle the expression of the sentiments of the people of the North." He and others pointed out that there were indeed precedents for such guarantees and that southerners themselves in past instances had written to northern candidates for the speakership concerning the slavery issue "distinctly making a satisfactory answer a *sine qua non* to their vote."[13] But southeners professed to be horrified at what they hypocritically labeled a corrupt bargain and refused to admit that there was nothing unique in the arrangement. Thus when the dispised Free Soilers followed typical major party political practices it was not to be tolerated if it meant including Wilmot Proviso advocates on the key committees.

Yet the Free Soilers themselves had not been united in their support of Brown, for Julian, Root, and Tuck had refused to vote for him, thus preventing his election. In this instance the party displayed a disturbing lack of unity and was unable to match the discipline of the older parties. Free Soil opposition to Brown was in large part because the members did not fully trust him on the sectional issues. Although Brown indicated that he would not oppose the passage of the Wilmot Proviso, he also called it "unnecessary and useless" and indicated that he preferred to let the people of the territories decide the issue. Julian, who knew of Brown's career from firsthand experiences in Indiana politics, contended that Brown really sympathized with the South, which would have controlled him as speaker. He argued that a few committee posts would

[12] *Ibid.*, 20-22, 26-27.
[13] Washington *Union*, December 12, 1849, quoted in Going, *David Wilmot*, 360-64; *Congressional Globe*, 31st Cong., 1st Sess., 20-22.

not be worth the price.[14] None of the three Free Soilers who withheld support for Brown had Democratic backgrounds as did many of those who supported him. Hence a stubborn adherence to strict free soil principle along with their own previous political leanings prevented their support of a man who might have aided their cause. The other Free Soilers refrained from criticizing these dissidents, but most felt that support of Brown would have been the wiser course. Adams argued that Free Soil support of Brown was justified because "they had sufficient assurances that their opinions would be respected" by him. Bailey's *National Era* also viewed the Free Soil course as completely honorable.[15]

Having failed to gain their objective, the Free Soilers exposed themselves to further criticism by permitting the election of a southern Democrat. Following the Brown episode, the House voted twenty more times before agreeing to a plurality rule proposed by the Whigs. The Free Soilers naturally opposed such a solution to the deadlock knowing that it would destroy their bargaining power. Both Giddings and Root tried to block the plurality motion, which passed 113 to 106. All of the Free Soilers opposed the plurality motion except Mann and Sprague, both of whom had been elected with Free Soil–Whig coalitions. On the sixty-third ballot Howell Cobb of Georgia defeated Robert Winthrop 102 to 99 with most of the Free Soilers voting for Wilmot.[16] Significantly, Mann, Sprague, and Tuck, all of whom had refused to support Brown, voted for Winthrop. But the rest of the party by its action had willfully prevented the election of a northern Whig who, although not opposed to slavery, would probably have been preferable to a southerner. In casting their votes for Wilmot they could be accused of the same kind of impracticality for which they had often criticized abolitionists in the past. Yet a Free Soil decision to support Winthrop, the

[14] *Congressional Globe*, 31st Cong., 1st Sess., 21; Going, *David Wilmot*, 362-63; Julian, *Political Recollections*, 75-76; Julian, *Joshua Giddings*, 273. Later in the year Brown voted for every one of the Compromise measures, including the Fugitive Slave Law and the rejection of the Wilmot Proviso in Utah and New Mexico. See Hamilton, *Prologue to Conflict*, 195.

[15] Adams, Diary, December 11, 1849 in Adams Papers; *National Era*, December 20, 1849. See also Chase to Hamlin, December 30, 1849, in Chase Papers, Library of Congress.

[16] *Congressional Globe*, 31st Cong., 1st Sess., 63-66.

bitter enemy of the Conscience Whigs, would have been equally difficult and clearly inconsistent with their principles. Winthrop's record in
Congress, including his support of the Mexican War and his role in
the election of the speaker two years earlier, was hardly one to instill
confidence among Free Soilers.[17] Adherence to the Wilmot Proviso thus
gave the Free Soilers little choice but to support their own candidate.

Northern Whigs now subjected the Free Soilers to the worst possible
abuse for their role in Cobb's election, for they had assumed when they
proposed the plurality rule that the third-party members would acquiesce and support Winthrop. The Whigs had not bothered to seek
an assurance of this beforehand, however. Horace Greeley called the
Free Soil act one of gross ingratitude as well as a stupid betrayal of
their own cause. The *National Era* turned the blame on the Whigs for
suggesting the plurality rule, which they knew might elect Cobb, and
Adams observed that "the punishment of the treacherous and faithless
Whigs is no greater than they deserve." In defending his own vote,
Amos Tuck argued that the Free Soilers had made a great mistake because Winthrop, "surrounded by Northern influence and lashed by
Northern criticisms would have done better for the cause of freedom
than Cobb. . . ." Horace Mann, who supported Winthrop, was vehement in his opinion of the Free Soilers: "Howell Cobb is Speaker, one
of the fiercest, sternest, strongest, proslavery men in all the South. . . .
And by whom was he allowed to be elevated to this important post? By
the Free Soilers, who, at any time might have prevented it. . . ."[18] Yet
surprisingly, Cobb did give the Free Soilers a limited amount of consideration in committee appointments. Although all but one of the
committees had Democratic chairmen and more than half of these
were from the South, King was placed on the Judiciary Committee,

[17] *Ibid.*, 18, 65-66; Robert C. Winthrop, Jr., *A Memoir of Robert C. Winthrop*
(Boston, 1897), 97-98; Duberman, *Charles Francis Adams*, 164. For Winthrop's
role in the previous Congress, see above, 38-39. In defending the Free Soil position in 1849, Giddings reviewed Winthrop's record as Speaker in the Thirtieth
Congress and showed how he had permitted the southerners to solidify slavery in
the District of Columbia. See *Congressional Globe*, 31st Cong., 1st Sess., Appendix,
35-40.
[18] New York *Tribune*, December 25, 1849; *National Era*, January 3, 1850;
Adams, Diary, December 23, 1849, in Adams Papers; Tuck to Palfrey, January 13,
1850, in Palfrey Papers; Winthrop, *Robert Winthrop*, quotes Horace Mann, 101;
Mann to Sumner, January 9, 1850, in Sumner Papers.

Giddings on the all-important Committee on Territories, and Charles
Allen on the Committee on the District of Columbia.[19] Significantly,
the Free Soilers had not received even this much recognition when
Winthrop was speaker during the previous Congress.[20]

Certainly the third party had gained little stature or respect from
firm party men in Congress, and the defeat of Winthrop had aggra-
vated the bitter feelings between themselves and northern Whigs. Political considerations were no doubt a factor in the Free Soil decision
not to support Winthrop after many had been willing to support
Brown. Yet their decision was based more on anti-extension principle
than it was on politics, for as unappealing as Winthrop might be to
the Free Soilers, practical politics would have dictated that they support
him rather than permit the election of a southerner. Unlike many Free
Soilers on the state level who seemed almost to wish the death of the
Free Soil organization through their coalition efforts, the men in Congress were committed to maintaining their independence as the best
way to achieve their goals. As Adams told Giddings in praising the Free
Soil stand in the House: "There is no further help to be found in the
indirect aid to be given to us by either Whigs or democrats. We must
go back once more to our independent and insulated position."[21] Yet
as Congress finally turned to the pressing business at hand, third party
influence was declining as the mood of compromise gradually triumphed over free soil principle.

In their desire for compromise, Whigs and Democrats showed only
contempt for the bloc of Free Soilers in Congress, for they regarded
their ideas as dangerous to the political status quo and potentially detri-
mental to any peaceful settlement between the sections. In an effort to
lessen Free Soilers' influence, Democratic and Whig leaders often gave

[19] The committee assignments made by Cobb of Free Soilers in the Thirty-first
Congress included: Claims, Root, Wilmot; Post Office and Post Roads, Durkee;
District of Columbia, Allen; Judiciary, King; Public Expenditures, Booth; Indian
Affairs, Sprague; Territories, Giddings; Revolutionary War Pensions, Tuck; Roads
and Canals, Howe; Revisal and Unfinished Business, Julian; Library of Congress,
Mann. See *Congressional Globe,* 31st Cong., 1st Sess., 88-89.

[20] In the Thirtieth Congress, Winthrop had placed Giddings on the Committee
on Indian Affairs and John G. Palfrey on the Committee on Agriculture, positions
from which neither man could forward the cause of anti-extension. See *Congressional Globe,* 30th Cong., 1st Sess., 19-20.

[21] Adams to Giddings, January 27, 1850, in Giddings Papers.

them undesirable committee assignments. With the exception of Giddings, King, and Allen, third-party members were placed on committees which had little relation to sectional issues. Nor were they given a voice in the distribution of patronage. Chase, for example, had expected to be invited to the Democratic caucus because he had been elected "exclusively by Democratic and free democratic votes," but was disappointed when he was ignored. The Free Soil representatives and senators were ostracized by the complacent Washington society which preferred to ignore them when it could or dismiss them as extremists and fanatics when it was forced to take notice. As a result, the third-party outcasts were driven together for both political and social reasons. Gamaliel Bailey's home and Giddings's boarding house became their refuge where they gathered regularly to discuss their problems and plans.[22] Most important, they mapped the strategy that they would use in the congressional debates of 1850 on how best to argue their position regarding the territories and the District of Columbia as well as how best to block those proposals favoring the South.

When the House of Representatives had finally organized, President Taylor was able to present his views to Congress on the issues dividing the country. In his message he recommended the admission of California as a state with its antislavery constitution and implied that he wished New Mexico to enter the same way. He even hinted that he would not oppose the Wilmot Proviso if it were written into a territorial bill applying to the rest of the Mexican War territories. The president had apparently endorsed the political views of Senator Seward and the Free Soilers, and southerners again began to talk of disunion should their interests be further threatened. The situation was becoming more and more ominous each day when Henry Clay rose in the Senate to offer the compromise he hoped would preserve the Union. The most important features of Clay's Omnibus Bill provided for the admission of California as a free state, the organization of the rest of the Mexican War territory on a popular sovereignty basis, the abolishment of the slave trade in Washington, the assumption of the Texas

[22] *Congressional Globe,* 31st Cong., 1st Sess., 45; Chase to E. S. Hamlin, December 17, 1849, in Bourne (ed.), "Chase Correspondence," 189-92; Clarke, *George W. Julian,* 89-90; Stewart, *Joshua Giddings,* 167, 181.

debt by the United States and a new and more stringent fugitive slave law.[23]

Clay's resolutions touched off one of the most famous debates in the history of the Senate. Before it was over nearly everyone had spoken, but the Free Soil demands as well as those of the most inflexible southerners were ignored as the voices of compromise triumphed. Following Clay's defense of his plan, Calhoun, Seward, and Webster gave the most important addresses. The two Free Soilers in the Senate, John P. Hale and Salmon P. Chase, participated actively in the debate but with little success. Hale presented a long eloquent attack on the views of both Calhoun, who had called for southern resistance to the Compromise, and Webster, who had called for northern adherence to it. In closing, Hale made another strong plea for the principle of the Wilmot Proviso by asking Congress not to "extend the boundaries of slavery, or retard the progress of human freedom or improvement." Both Hale and Chase traced the historical policy of slave restriction by Congress beginning with the Northwest Ordinance of 1787 which had received the support of the southern states.[24] But neither the goodhumored Hale nor the pompous Chase was convincing enough to change any votes as the Senate seemed determined to compromise the sectional differences.

The Senate maintained the initiative in the Compromise debates, but passage would be more difficult in the northern-dominated House. Here the Free Soilers again took an active part in the debates. Even before Henry Clay introduced his proposals, Joseph Root had offered a resolution to apply the Wilmot Proviso to all Mexican War territories. The proposal was pigeon-holed for six weeks before it was defeated, for while the House waited for the Senate to act it refused to take any final action of its own. Nevertheless, the Free Soilers waged a constant but futile campaign to force action on issues involving slavery. Wilmot presented nearly fifty petitions, many of them designed to stop the expansion of slavery. He also joined with King to try to get the California bill with its antislavery constitution out of the Committee of the

---

[23] Richardson, *Messages and Papers of the Presidents,* V, 9-24; *Congressional Globe,* 31st Cong., 1st Sess., 244-47; Hamilton, *Zachary Taylor,* 256-59; Craven, *The Coming of the Civil War,* 249-51; Nevins, *Ordeal of the Union,* I, 256-66.

[24] The debates are in the *Congressional Globe,* 31st Cong., 1st Sess. For the Hale and Chase speeches see Appendix, 468-80, 1054-65. See also Adams Jewett to Chase, January 20, 1850, in Chase Papers, Library of Congress.

Whole for a decision. Giddings and Thaddeus Stevens proposed the end of Washington's slave trade while George W. Julian attacked the South and argued that its defense of slavery constituted a grave threat to freedom of speech and civil liberties in general.[25] But the House refused to move on any of the third-party proposals until the Senate finished its debates, for most of the members were not interested in upsetting the chances for a settlement. In neither house were the Free Soilers any match for the oratorical giants who dominated the Senate debates, but more important, their ideas were simply not in harmony with the prevailing compromise sentiment.

Occasionally, the Free Soilers themselves were castigated by members of Congress because they held to their principles and rejected compromise. In attacking the Wilmot Proviso, Robert Winthrop, already angry with the Free Soilers for their role in the speaker contest, presented a bitter tirade against the third party: "Never in the history of our country, never since the existence of political parties anywhere, has there been a party which under the pretext of philanthropy, has so reveled and luxuriated in malice, hatred and uncharitableness, in vituperation, calumny and slander as this 'reviled Free Soil Sect.' " Tensions increased even more as the *National Era* responded to Winthrop sarcastically, "With what proud emotions his great heart must have swelled at being sustained by some 220 Representatives, not to speak of divers Senators, in his brave onslaught against a few members who are feared and hated because they dare to say what they think, and do what they say."[26]

Throughout the debates, Free Soilers in and out of Congress steadfastly maintained their opposition to Clay's plan, showing a degree of perserverance and dedication to the cause rarely seen in the coalition efforts on the state level. At a Massachusetts Free Soil convention in February, Adams warned against the Clay compromise because it meant the surrender of the Wilmot Proviso. He firmly believed that the proposed compromise betrayed "the great principles of the coun-

[25] *Congressional Globe*, 31st Cong., 1st Sess., 91, Appendix, 511ff, 573-79, 1443ff; Stewart, *Joshua Giddings*, 185; Sumner to Julian, June 1, 1850, in Giddings-Julian Papers.

[26] R. C. Winthrop, "Speech of Hon. R. C. Winthrop of Mass.," February 21, 1850; *National Era*, February 28, 1850; Sewell, *John P. Hale*, 129-31.

try." Free Soilers were most vehement in their reaction to Webster's Seventh of March speech which in essence defended Clay's proposals. In this reaction they had the support of Massachusetts public opinion and many leading politicians of the state. Webster had abandoned his earlier support of the Wilmot Proviso and now argued that nature had already made slavery impossible in the Western territories. Even Robert Winthrop, along with many other Whigs, joined in demonstrating Webster's desertion from his earlier position. Horace Greeley pointed out the senator's inconsistency and argued that slavery was indeed possible wherever the South wanted to make an issue of it.[27]

In the midst of the congressional debate, the *National Era* suggested holding a "National Convention of Freemen" to rally the North against the spirit of surrender evident in Webster's speech and to bring pressure to bear against "the time-serving politicians, Presidential aspirants, greedy spoilsmen and crafty demagogues" who supported its sentiment. But Webster was also strongly defended in many areas of the country, and his speech had a positive effect in putting Americans, both North and South, in a conciliatory mood. For example, New York City merchants, already alarmed over the possibility of losing their southern trade, endorsed the Clay resolutions despite the outspoken opposition of William H. Seward.[28] Finally, death removed two of the greatest obstacles to a settlement, John C. Calhoun and Zachary Taylor, and made Millard Fillmore president. Senator Stephen A. Douglas of Illinois then assumed leadership and divided Clay's Omnibus bill into separate proposals. Each measure eventually passed Congress with the support of different blocs and received the new President's signature.[29] The Free Soilers in Congress consistently supported the antislavery sections of the Compromise, including the admission of California and the ban on Washington slave trade, while they opposed those parts favoring the South, notably the Fugitive Slave Law. They also opposed the bills organizing Utah and New Mexico territories, for these repre-

[27] Adams, *Diary*, February 27, March 8, 1850, in Adams Papers; Williams, *Horace Mann*, 301-2; Pierce, *Charles Sumner*, 204; New York *Tribune*, March 9, 1850; Nevins, *Ordeal of the Union*, I, 292-93; *National Era*, March 14, 1850.
[28] *National Era*, April 4, 1850; Foner, *Business and Slavery*, 38; Bayard Tuckerman (ed.), *The Diary of Philip Hone, 1828-1851* (New York, 1889), II, 370-75.
[29] For an account and record of the voting in Congress see Hamilton, *Prologue to Conflict*, 133-65, 191-92, 195-200; Silbey, *The Shrine of Party*, 107-17, 189-200.

sented a rejection of the Wilmot Proviso principle in favor of popular sovereignty. In addition they opposed the proposal for the United States to assume the Texas debt. None of the Free Soilers broke ranks in either chamber on any of the proposals.[30] Although some eight other senators and fifty representatives from the North also voted the same way,[31] the Free Soilers were in part responsible for the fact that there was even this much northern unity on issues involving slavery.

Even before the death of the president, most Free Soilers had begun to realize that despite their earlier feelings, Taylor was perhaps their lone hope in protecting anti-extension principles. His first message to Congress, although opposing congressional debates on slavery, had called for the admission of California and perhaps New Mexico as free states without agreeing to any southern demands. Throughout the debates he had maintained this position in the face of growing sentiment for compromise. Despite their many attacks on Taylor during the presidential campaign, the Free Soilers had come to respect him by 1850. Julian, who had earlier labeled him "an old outrageously ugly, uncultivated, uninformed man and sure enough a *mere* military chieftain," now lauded his rugged honesty and firmness with which he had opposed the dictates of the South. Even the *National Era* indirectly praised him for attempting to maintain freedom in California and New Mexico, while John P. Hale noted that his loss was "a very great and serious public calamity."[32] With Taylor gone, the Compromise could be passed.

Adams summed up the typical reaction of the Free Soilers to the enactment of the Compromise when he told Julian: "The consummation of the inequities of the most disgraceful session of Congress is now reached." Adams called for northerners of all parties to issue a joint address attacking the outcome. "If this cannot be done," he wrote, "then our Free Soil band have a duty to perform." Julian, speaking for all of the Free Soilers in Congress, vehemently attacked the settlement and criticized those northern congressmen who had abandoned

[30] See Appendix D for the Free Soil voting records on the Compromise proposals.
[31] See Hamilton, *Prologue to Conflict*, 191-200.
[32] Julian to Isaac Julian, January 25, 1850, in Giddings-Julian Papers; Clarke, *George W. Julian*, 102-3; *National Era*, July 18, 1850; John P. Hale to Mrs. Hale, July 10, 1850, in Hale Papers.

the Wilmot Proviso. He warned that the Fugitive Slave Law would convert every northerner "into a constable and jailkeeper for slave-holders."[33]

In contrast to Free Soil feelings, the immediate reaction of a majority of Americans both North and South to the Compromise was a sigh of relief that a settlement had been reached. Thoroughly frightened by the increase of sectional animosity before 1850, many preferred to regard the agreement as the final solution to the issues dividing North and South. In the next session of Congress all appeared to be in harmony as former enemies suddenly became friends. Some northern states even rescinded their earlier endorsement of the now-rejected Wilmot Proviso. Those who stopped to think may have realized that the Compromise, rather than a final settlement, was simply a postponement of any permanent solution. But most were so eager to bring an end to sectional tensions that they were unwilling to consider the dangers ahead. The issues dividing the nation before 1850 were still unresolved, but many forgot this as they rushed to praise the Compromise and denounce any further agitation by either section as unnecessary. This atmosphere inevitably produced a further loss of prestige for the Free Soil party.[34]

Even some third-party men endorsed the settlement. In the most flagrant example of the abandonment of Free Soil principle, fewer than half of the Barnburner delegates opposed the resolution at the New York Democratic convention "that we congratulate the country upon the recent settlement by Congress."[35] Their eagerness to reenter the Democratic party seemed to know no bounds. As more and more Americans spoke of the finality of the Compromise, the less dedicated Free Soilers saw little need for a third party. By late 1850, the name Free Soil was almost forgotten, and the small independent movement that still existed now called itself the Free Democratic party. To many, the rejection of the Wilmot Proviso had made the term "free soil" obsolete: "Free Democratic" was a broader name which could represent positions on other issues. In addition, the trend toward union with the

[33] Adams to Julian, September 14, 1850, in Giddings-Julian Papers; *Congressional Globe*, 31st Cong., 1st Sess., 1965.
[34] Nevins, *Ordeal of the Union*, I, 346-50; Smith, *The Liberty and Free Soil Parties*, 226-32; Webster to Fillmore, November 24, 1850, in Everett Papers.
[35] New York *Evening Post*, September 14, 16, 1850.

Democratic party appeared irresistible and the new name could be used toward this end.[36] Bailey's call for a "National Convention of Freemen" to oppose the Compromise went unheeded, for few saw any need for independent action. Chase used this atmosphere to push even harder for a coalition with the Democrats. The Barnburners of New York prepared for a more permanent reunion with their old party on the basis of the recent congressional settlement. Even Wilmot and King shunned associating with the other third-party men in Congress in their strategy sessions, so intent were the two Barnburners in regaining recognition as Democrats from other congressmen. Seth Gates, former Liberty party leader and Free Soil candidate for lieutenant governor in 1848, wrote of the general rejoicing over the Compromise and the disappearance of the Barnburners as a political factor in New York. Seward's opposition to the Compromise was unpopular even with many northern Whigs, while groups of Free Democrats in all parts of the North forgot their Buffalo platform.[37]

Not all of the Free Democrats surrendered their principles so easily. Some felt that the Compromise with its hated Fugitive Slave Law was a southern victory. Chase wrote to Sumner that "the slaveholders have succeeded beyond their wildest hopes twelve months ago." Even those who accepted the Compromise could not endorse the Fugitive Slave Law. The law was applied *ex post facto* and denied to alleged escaped slaves the right of trial by jury. In a further violation of the Constitution the law denied the accused the right to confront witnesses as well as his right of habeas corpus. It offered financial advantages to federal commissioners who would decide cases in favor of masters instead of accused fugitives. Federal marshals were to make great efforts to recover fugitives, and any person aiding in the escape of a slave was liable to a fine of one thousand dollars or six months in jail. The law then was clearly designed to protect slaveholders rather than the per-

---

[36] The Barnburners of New York and the Chase faction of Ohio were most responsible for the frequent substitution of the term Free Democratic for Free Soil. This became especially apparent in 1849 as each group worked for a coalition with the Democrats. See for example, John Van Buren to Giddings, May 26, 1849, in Giddings-Julian Papers; Chase to Asa G. Dimmock, August 6, 1849, quoted in Warden, *Salmon P. Chase*, 333-34.

[37] *National Era*, April 4, 1850; Smith, *The Liberty and Free Soil Parties*, 226-27; Gates to Giddings, November 16, 1850, in Giddings Papers; Stewart, *Joshua Giddings*, 195.

sonal liberty of blacks in the free states. Considering these terms, it was
not surprising that it helped to prevent the Compromise from becoming the final settlement that President Fillmore and leaders of both
major parties desired.[38]

Joshua Giddings led the attack on the Fugitive Slave Law in the
second session of the Thirty-first Congress and predicted the impossibility of enforcing the law: "Let the President . . . use the bayonet,
the sword and the cannon. . . . Let him drench our land of freedom in
blood; but he will never make us obey that law." Giddings, Julian,
Hale, and others successfully labored to keep the fugitive issue open
for debate through various parliamentary devices at a time when Congress would have preferred to deal with less explosive questions. In
a manner reminiscent of the efforts of Giddings and John Quincy
Adams to get around the gag rule a decade earlier, Free Democrats
seized on numerous fugitive slave incidents to bring the issue before
Congress. As expected, many newspapers castigated the Free Democrats for their attacks on the Compromise, thus only drawing further
attention to their cause.[39] In Massachusetts, soon to be the scene of
open defiance to the new law, Charles Sumner set the tone in his violent attack on Fillmore for signing the bill: "Into the immortal cata-
logue of national crimes it has now passed, drawing by inexorable necessity, its authors also, and chiefly him, who, as President of the United
States, set his name to the Bill. . . ." Sumner attempted to create a
mood whereby the law could not be enforced. Although not directly
calling for violence, he said, "I CANNOT BELIEVE — THAT THIS BILL
WILL BE EXECUTED HERE. . . . the public conscience will not allow a
man who has trodden our streets as a freeman to be dragged away as
a slave." Even John Van Buren called on northern states to pass laws
to make the act unenforceable and argued that it should be disobeyed
in order to prove its unconstitutionality.[40]

Throughout the North, open disobedience of the Fugitive Slave

[38] Chase to Sumner, September 8, 1850, in Bourne (ed.), "Chase Correspondence," 219-20; *Congressional Globe,* 31st Cong., 1st Sess., Appendix, 1447-91.

[39] *Congressional Globe,* 31st Cong., 2nd Sess., 15, Appendix, 253-54; Stewart,
Joshua Giddings, 196-97.

[40] Pierce, *Charles Sumner,* 228; *The Works of Charles Sumner,* II, 405-10;
Albany *Evening Atlas,* April 14, 1851; John Van Buren to Sumner, June 5, 1851,
in Sumner Papers.

Law, led by antislavery elements including Free Democrats, for a time threatened the truce between North and South. There were numerous cases in which northern mobs prevented or tried to prevent the return of a fugitive to slavery. In Christiana, Pennsylvania, a mob killed a southerner attempting to retrieve his slave. In New York and Massachusetts mobs aided the escape of several fugitives. Vigilance committees in many northern cities, including whites and free blacks, abolitionists and anti-extensionists, attempted to prevent the act's enforcement. Richard Henry Dana took up the cause of the fugitive in Massachusetts courts with some success. Various northern states passed new personal liberty laws nullifying parts of the act while others debated similar bills.[41] Nevertheless, after the initial excitement died down, many northerners appeared ready to acquiesce in the law if not to endorse it openly. Temporarily at least, the Compromise was surviving its first test as the pleas of antislavery leaders went unheeded.[42]

Acceptance of the Compromise of 1850 if not the Fugitive Slave Law was the rule for Free Democrats in many parts of the North. Between 1849 and 1851 in states from New England to Wisconsin there were coalitions formed which seemed to foretell the end of an independent third-party movement. Many of these were formed at the expense of the principles which the party had advocated in 1848. Yet in Congress, the Free Democrats had, with few exceptions, maintained their unity and had refused to accept compromise as embodied in the settlement of 1850.

Part of the explanation for this apparent inconsistency is that in Congress the Free Democrats came face to face with the national issues which had inspired their movement in the first place. It was here that the territorial and District of Columbia questions were constantly debated. The defeat of the Wilmot Proviso and the passage of the Fugitive Slave Law could not be accepted complacently and in

[41] Wayland Fuller Dunaway, *A History of Pennsylvania* (New York, 1935), 477-78; Lawrence Lader, *The Bold Brahmins; New England's War Against Slavery: 1831-1863* (New York, 1961), 137-39; Fladeland, *James G. Birney*, 279; D. Burwell to John Van Buren, January 4, 1851, in Van Buren Papers; John Van Buren to Sumner, April 7, 1851, in Sumner Papers; Shapiro, *Richard Henry Dana*, 55-62.

[42] For the general northern reaction to the Fugitive Slave Law, see Stanley W. Campbell, *The Slave Catchers: Enforcement of the Fugitive Slave Law, 1850-1860* (Chapel Hill, N.C., 1970), 49-79.

many cases only gave the members greater resolve to resist. Stronger leadership and commitment among third-party men in Congress also accounted for the greater unity and independence than was evident in most state organizations. On the state level, with state and local issues taking precedence and with slavery issues seemingly not of as immediate importance, there appeared to be more to be gained by coalition. Having already begun the process of returning to their old parties in 1849 the Compromise settlement served to reaffirm that decision. Motivated by a desire for office and patronage before 1850, it was easy to rationalize that the Compromise ended any further need for an independent party. Thus with a few notable exceptions such as Giddings in Ohio, the most practical thing to do seemed to be to forget the Free Soil organization and return to the two-party system.

In Washington where many of the same Free Soilers held seats in Congress, however, the decision was the opposite. Some, such as King, Wilmot, and Chase, scurried to get back into the Democratic party, but most, driven by a greater devotion to the cause and a greater commitment to an independent third party than those on the state level, refused to give up their identity or their principles. Should such an approach be maintained in the key state of Massachusetts, the future for the party in the election of 1852 would not be quite as bleak as many had predicted.

8

The Massachusetts Coalition

The Free Soil party of Massachusetts had made a better showing in 1848 than all but the most confident had dared hope for. Gaining close to 29 percent of the vote, the party had replaced the Democrats as the state's second party in both state and national elections. Although the Whigs had won a complete victory in Massachusetts, they could maintain control only as long as the Democrats and Free Soilers remained divided. To most observers the prospect for a continuation of this division appeared strong, since so much of the Free Soil leadership had originally been Whig. But an important and growing group of men led by Henry Wilson fully understood the practical political value of a Democratic coalition. These men had great popular support, and they gradually convinced the party of the wisdom of such a union. Once formed, the coalition temporarily gained control of the state and in 1851 elected Charles Sumner to the Senate. Throughout the struggle the Conscience Whig element opposed cooperation with the Democrats and almost prevented it.[1] The results in Massachusetts showed both the positive and negative effect of coalition. On the one hand, union with a major party brought increased influence in the

---

[1] Throughout this chapter the name Free Soil will be used rather than Free Democratic because most of the events described took place prior to the name change. For the most part members of the party in Massachusetts used the name Free Soil until 1851 or 1852. The most complete accounts of the Massachusetts coalition are found in Ernest A. McKay, "Henry Wilson and the Coalition of 1851," *New England Quarterly*, XXXVI (1963), 338-57, and Martin B. Duberman, "Behind the Scenes as the Massachusetts 'Coalition' of 1851 Divides the Spoils," *Essex Institute Historical Collections*, XCIX (1963), 152-60.

form of important political office as well as the forcing of a stronger anti-extension position on some of the leaders of the majority party in question. On the other hand, it meant some sacrifice of free soil principle, although not as much as in New York and Ohio, as well as the weakening of a strong independent third-party movement which had served as a stern voice of conscience to the major parties. Coalition also resulted in increased bitterness among disagreeing anti-extension leaders themselves.

The potential value of Free Soil cooperation with Massachusetts Democrats was obvious. There was the real possibility of placing a Free Soiler in the Senate following the example of the election of Chase in Ohio and Hale in New Hampshire. In addition, the electoral laws of Massachusetts were designed to perpetuate the Whigs in power and only through coalition could they be displaced. Candidates for state office needed an absolute majority to be elected, and a joint ballot of the legislature decided in cases in which no candidate met the requirement. In most elections, Boston and other Whig strongholds sent their full quotas to the legislature while many other towns frequently failed to elect. The legislature would then declare the Whigs the winner, thus continuing that party in power. Only if the Democrats and Free Soilers could agree on joint candidates could they hope to end the Whig stranglehold on the legislature.[2]

Because it was the majority party and because of past bitterness, the Whig party offered little possibility of return for the Free Soilers. As a result, many anti-extensionists began to turn to the Democrats, for they viewed continued independence as impractical. As Charles Sumner explained it: "If I must vote for a Whig or a Democrat, let me vote for the Democrat because in that way we secure the *balance of power.*" Many third-party leaders such as Wilson, E. L. Keyes, and Francis Bird did have much in common with Democrats on secondary issues but still needed agreement on the basic question of free soil principle before union could be achieved. As early as 1849, they began to talk of antimonopoly and anticorporation reforms and other issues of interest to the Democrats. On these problems these Free Soilers were basi-

[2] McKay, "Wilson and the Coalition," 338-39; R. H. Dana, Jr., to E. Dana, December 2, 1849, in Dana Papers; Duberman, "The Massachusetts 'Coalition,' " 152.

cally closer to Massachusetts Democrats such as Nathaniel Banks, Robert Rantoul, and George Boutwell than they were to Conscience men like Adams and Dana who usually agreed with the Whigs on economic matters.[3]

The chances for a coalition looked promising, for as Sumner had written immediately after the election of 1848: "As I view it, the Democratic party is not merely defeated; it is entirely broken into pieces. It cannot organize anew except on the Free Soil platform." Feeling that the Democrats would thus be susceptible to coalition, Sumner expressed the dominant view of the Free Soilers in favoring at least limited cooperation with them. Sumner was correct in his surmise, for in 1849, the Democrats of Massachusetts were prepared to take the anti-extension ground he had predicted. With an eye toward a coalition, they stated their opposition to the expansion of slavery and argued that Congress had no power to establish it in the territories. This was a significant concession for men who had so recently supported Lewis Cass. They also adopted a resolution looking to the time when "all who think alike on the abuses of our state legislature" should unite on state reforms.[4] With the example of Free Soil–Democratic coalitions in other states, the prospects improved for cooperation in Massachusetts. Thus the majority in each party were willing to make overtures to the other party for essentially the same reasons. Out of power and with little influence as long as the Whigs controlled the legislature, each was ready to approach the other's position in significant areas of policy. Many Free Soilers agreed with the Democratic position on state reform issues while many Democrats accepted the Free Soil position on the extension of slavery. Each felt it could maintain its principle in the area which meant most to it and at the same time gain political power in the process.

There were, however, important minority elements in both parties opposed to coalition. Some Democrats would be unwilling to cooperate with former enemies and go against their national party's platform.

---

[3] Boston *Advertiser*, September 14, 1849; Bean, "Party Transformations in Massachusetts," 34-35; Sumner to Palfrey, October 15, 1850, in Palfrey Papers.

[4] Sumner to George Sumner, November 15, 1848, quoted in Pierce, *Charles Sumner*, III, 185; Boston *Post*, September 19, 1849.

Much of the Conscience Whig faction, led by Adams, Palfrey, and Dana could never be comfortable working with Democrats, for their own social and economic outlook precluded it. Seeing the trend toward coalition, in February, 1849, Adams had helped prevent the introduction of questions not related to slavery into the state Free Soil platform, for he feared that any cooperation with the Democrats would mean the subordination of free soil issues to secondary "loco foco" issues. With an eye on the New York proceedings of 1849, he noted, "The Democracy as such could never come to us. The danger of our courting it would be that we might be ultimately compelled to struggle for our own liberty."[5] Adams's efforts to maintain third-party independence would be an uphill battle, however, for more than twice as many Democrats as Whigs had joined the Free Soil movement in 1848,[6] and this group was thus predisposed to some kind of an agreement.

The principle figure in the events which led to eventual coalition was the Massachusetts shoe manufacturer Henry Wilson. Nicknamed the "Natick Cobbler," Wilson had been one of the original members of the Conscience Whigs but lacked the social background and the elitest outlook which had made a break with the Whigs difficult for some. Wilson came from an obscure family and was largely self-educated. As a result he was somewhat more resourceful than many of his more comfortable Conscience colleagues. He was also a highly practical politician interested more in power than in consistency of principle. As a Whig member of the legislature in the early 1840s he had helped lead the fight against the annexation of Texas. He had worked for the formation of an organization of abolitionists and anti-extension Whigs and Democrats to petition Congress to resist southern demands over Texas. In 1848, as a delegate to the national Whig convention he had defied the party when it chose Zachary Taylor and had helped organize the movement for the Buffalo convention. A close associate of Adams until after the 1848 election, Wilson would soon break with him over the issue of Democratic coalition. Despite his own business interests, which he gave up in 1847 to devote full time to politics, he supported reforms aiding Massachusetts workers and others not of the higher income group. Although he had more in common

---

[5] Adams, Diary, September 8, 18, November 24, 1849, in Adams Papers.
[6] Rayback, *Free Soil,* 300.

with the Democrats than Adams did, more important as a motivating factor for the "Natick Cobbler" was his desire for political power. The political situation now gave him the opportunity he needed. In recognition of his resourceful leadership and hard work during the campaign of 1848 he was made chairman of the state Free Soil party in 1849. He also became sole owner of the party's chief newspaper, the Boston *Republican,* and hence was in a good position to arrange the union he desired.[7]

A lack of preparation and organization along with continued partisan bitterness prevented the complete coalition that Wilson desired in 1849, and instead there was only limited cooperation. Given the opposition, he felt that a single Democratic–Free Soil slate and a common platform were not necessary immediately. If the two parties could agree on candidates to oppose Whigs in some legislative districts, this would be a big step. Surprisingly, even Adams gave his reluctant support to the creation of joint tickets with the Democrats on the town and county level, arrangements which required no commitments from either side. Adams's action was due in part to his desire to aid Palfrey in his continuing bid to win the necessary majority for election to Congress. Nevertheless, the coalition did poorly, and the Free Soil vote fell off. In the contest for governor, the anti-extension party fell to third place. Adams feared that union had caused many to question the consistency and integrity of the Free Soilers. Realizing that the joint-ticket arrangement was the first step toward the coalition he opposed, he later regretted his limited support and would be unwilling to cooperate with the Democrats again.[8]

Although the first hesitating move toward a Democratic–Free Soil coalition in Massachusetts had been taken, there remained many obstacles. At the Free Soil convention before the election of 1849, Sumner had emphasized the issues which separated his group from the major parties on the national level. Adams, running for the state senate, blamed his defeat on Democrats who opposed him. John G. Palfrey,

[7] For Wilson's early career see Brauer, *Cotton Versus Conscience.* See also Loubert, "Henry Wilson," 40-80. Wilson's own work, *History of the Rise and Fall of the Slave Power,* I-II, also gives many insights into the author's motivations.

[8] Duberman, *Charles Francis Adams,* 162; Boston *Advertiser,* November, 1849; Wilson, *The Slave Power,* I, 339; Adams, Diary, November 12, 13, 1849, in Adams Papers.

continually resisting offers of coalition, failed reelection to Congress. Some of the Conscience Whigs were also personally jealous of Henry Wilson, the architect of the proposed coalition. Having risen from obscurity to a position of influence through skillful maneuvering, he was regarded with distrust by many of those who were more elitist. Dana, for example, attacked him and other "low-bred" politicians who were attempting to "democratize our party."[9]

The Compromise debates of the following year, and especially Daniel Webster's speech in support of the Omnibus bill, helped to prepare the ground for closer cooperation between Massachusetts Democrats and Free Soilers. Early in 1850 the Whig party of the state had appeared ready to assume a free soil position. In a message to the legislature, Whig Governor G. N. Briggs advocated congressional prohibition of slavery in the territories and abolition of slavery in the District of Columbia. Webster's famous Seventh of March speech ended any further speculation over the Whig position, however. Rising in the Senate, he defended Clay's Compromise resolutions including the fugitive slave provisions. Whatever the effect of the speech elsewhere, in Massachusetts it further dampened any possibility of the return of the Free Soilers to the Whig party. Opposition to the Compromise of 1850 was as strong in Massachusetts as in any other state.[10] Adams called Webster "a profligate adventurer from another state who has done much to corrupt the hearts of the young." Realizing that Massachusetts Whigs were not in complete agreement with Webster, Adams concluded that an attack on the Compromise would further divide them and perhaps bring the revenge that he sought. Webster's action would not make the Adams group willing to work with the Democrats, however. On the other hand, Henry Wilson, in search of an issue after the Whigs had earlier assumed Free Soil ground, now had what he needed. The Whig legislature of 1850 also

9 *Sumner, Works,* II, 282-321; Pierce, *Charles Sumner,* III, 188; Adams, Diary, November 3, 10, 12, 13, 1849, in Adams Papers; Duberman, *Charles Francis Adams,* 161; Donald, *Charles Sumner,* 182; Dana, Journal, October 7, November 8, 9, 1849, quoted in Adams, *Richard Henry Dana,* I, 171-72; Shapiro, *Richard Henry Dana,* 56.
10 Bean, "Party Transformations in Massachusetts," 41-42; *Congressional Globe,* 31st Cong., 1st Sess., Appendix, 269-76; Donald, *Charles Sumner,* 185; Wilson, *The Slave Power,* II, 257-58.

turned down all demands for local reforms and thus further antagonized the other parties. When Webster demanded acceptance of the Compromise as a test of party loyalty, a Democratic–Free Soil coalition became even more likely despite the many obstacles still in its way.[11]

In the spring of 1850 the Whig-dominated legislature rejected Henry Wilson's resolution calling upon Webster to vote against the pending Compromise measures. Wilson then seized on the issue and declared himself willing "to cooperate with any body of men to drive the dominant party from power, and to send to the Senate a statesman who would fitly represent the cherished and distinguishing opinions of the Commonwealth." Although the Whigs refused to make the finality of the Compromise a campaign issue, Webster's influence remained great. With Fillmore now president, Webster became secretary of state, and Governor Briggs appointed the Conscience group's archenemy Robert C. Winthrop to Webster's place in the Senate. The Free Soilers realized more than ever that little could be expected from the Whigs as an anti-extension party. Concerning Winthrop's appointment, Adams observed sarcastically: "Such are the performances of a Governor pledged to the Wilmot Proviso."[12]

As interest in a Democratic–Free Soil alliance increased, an alarming difference of opinion became more apparent within the third party. Henry Wilson, representing the view of the majority of the rank and file of the party, much of it of Democratic origin, bent every effort to perfect the union. Yet resistance continued from Adams and Palfrey who, although in a minority, represented the Conscience Whig leadership which had controlled the party organization through the 1848 election. At an informal meeting of the Free Soil state committee in early August, 1850, Adams obtained a postponement of any formal decision, although he realized that a majority opposed his views. At stake in the fall election were not only the governorship and control

[11] Adams, Diary, March 8, April 8, 1850, April 3, 1851, in Adams Papers; Loubert, "Henry Wilson," 91; Wilson, *The Slave Power,* II, 257-58; Boston *Post,* May 10, 1850; Bean, "Party Transformations in Massachusetts," 39-40; Webster to Fillmore, quoted in Van Tyne (ed.), *Letters of Daniel Webster,* 432.

[12] Wilson, *The Slave Power,* II, 341; Boston *Atlas,* October 2, 1850; Adams, Diary, July 28, 1850, in Adams Papers.

of the state legislature but also the United States senatorship. There were already suggestions that if the Free Soilers would support Democrat George Boutwell for governor, Democrats would endorse a Free Soiler for the Senate. Charles Sumner was the most frequently mentioned possibility. From the start, Adams felt that such a deal with the Democrats was not worth the price: "To join with them . . . merely for the sake of the bait of a Senator's place to one of us strikes me as a renunciation of all moral character which will ultimately lead to our annihilation as a party." Richard Henry Dana agreed with Adams that they should concern themselves with "a sense of justice and national honor" and oppose union with a party whose national organization had consistently rejected the Free Soil program. The Wilson faction clearly disagreed.[18] As the dispute within the party developed it became clear that the same desire for political power at the expense of third-party identity which was at work in other northern states would control the actions of the majority of Massachusetts Free Soilers. Again the differences between free soil principles and practical politics were about to cause serious problems.

In the fall of 1850 Wilson moved to gain complete control of the Free Soil party, and in the process the schism within his party deepened. Wilson first called a meeting of the Free Soil state committee but omitted inviting Adams. This tactic apparently backfired, for at the meeting, after Wilson attacked Adams and Palfrey for their views and virtually read them out of the party, those present reacted by further postponing any decision on a Democratic coalition. The old Conscience Whig leadership, although declining in influence, was still dominant enough on the state committee to block the manipulations of Henry Wilson. At the next meeting Adams was included, and he along with Palfrey, Dana, and others, successfully frustrated Wilson's plans. The committee prohibited the central organization from taking any official action toward combination, and Wilson, lacking party sanction, was therefore reduced to individual negotiations with the Democrats. During the campaign many local Free Soil groups did unite with the Democrats, and Wilson continued to work behind the scenes to lay

18 Adams, Diary, August 10, 1850, in Adams Papers; Adams, *Richard Henry Dana*, I, 169; Wilson, *The Slave Power*, II, 341; Elias Nason and Thomas Russell, *The Life and Public Services of Henry Wilson* (Boston, 1876), 93.

the groundwork for complete coalition at a later date. Thus although Wilson did not yet control the Free Soil state committee, he was gradually replacing Adams as the acknowledged third-party leader and more and more members were becoming persuaded of the benefits of coalition. Wilson's emphasis on party machinery over principle was gaining him support. He furthered these efforts by establishing a special campaign newspaper, the *Free Soiler,* which advocated the proposed alliance in order to win a Senate seat for the party.[14]

As the campaign unfolded, the tactics of Wilson and the Democrats became apparent. Forbidden to unite formally, they would run separate candidates for governor and combine on candidates for the legislature wherever possible. In the legislature the two parties, having won control from the Whigs, would then elect the Democrat as governor and a Free Soiler as senator. As Francis W. Bird explained it, "Our paramount object is to advance the cause of freedom by breaking down a proslavery organization and electing a U.S. Senator; their paramount object is to accomplish sundry reforms in state policy." The Free Soilers chose Stephen C. Phillips to run for governor, but it was generally understood that if the decision went to the legislature they would support Democrat George Boutwell. Throughout the campaign this arrangement was strongly rumored, but the Free Soilers made no official mention of coalition, knowing that it was not popular with some voters. Instead, they devoted their efforts to an issue which would win more votes, attacking Webster's support of the Fugitive Slave Law and his repudiation of the Wilmot Proviso.[15]

Free Soil interest in coalition centered around winning the Senate seat for Charles Sumner. Because of his Whig background Sumner at first wrote to Wilson: "I should be unwilling to be a party to any such bargain." His support of the Whig party, however, had never been strong and by the late 1840s he had become more sympathetic to the Democratic attacks on economic injustices allegedly perpetrated by the Whigs. More important, however, Sumner also was fully aware that through Democratic coalition he could realize his growing ambition for

[14] Adams, Diary, August 27, 31, September 5, 10, 1850, in Adams Papers; Wilson, *The Slave Power,* II, 342-43; McKay, "Wilson and the Coalition," 344-46.
[15] *Free Soiler,* quoted in Boston *Commonwealth,* January 14, 1851; Boston *Post,* September 19, 1850; Wilson, *The Slave Power,* II, 344.

political office. Later, as his name was mentioned more frequently, he told Charles Allen that there was great value to be gained in influencing the choice of senator. Through his speeches he sounded more and more like a candidate, for he now expressed a guarded willingness to cooperate with the Democrats.[16] The prospect of personal gain and the opportunity to advocate his free soil beliefs in the Senate had overcome the opposition to coalition that he had initially shared with the Adams faction.

These circumstances made the role of Charles Francis Adams even more difficult. Not wishing to anger Sumner, Adams was hesitant to sacrifice a close personal friendship for Free Soil principle and identity. Yet he feared that Sumner's course might commit the party "too irrecoverably to the democratic connexion. On this point I think Sumner has manifested some want of character." Adams felt that Sumner's course had encouraged "some who have far worse motives." He could not understand how the character of Free Soil coalitions in other states had failed to persuade Sumner of his error: "He has never manifested the same opinion of Chase's operations in Ohio which I have held. . . ." Consultation in Washington with Ohio Free Soilers convinced Adams that the Ohio party "has never recovered from the blow. And just such a result do I fear in Massachusetts."[17]

Adams's feelings on Sumner's role were also part of a more complex dilemma created by his own interest in the Senate seat. He had received feelers from the Whigs suggesting Free Soil support of Whig state candidates in return for Whig support of Adams for the Senate. Highly flattered by the idea, he nevertheless insisted that the Whigs show some positive evidence of their support of Free Soil principles before any negotiations proceeded. Concerning the suggested exchange of Boutwell for Sumner he noted in his diary: "This makes still greater caution necessary on my part to avoid the malice of my opponents who will seek to attribute to private feelings of disappointment my opposition to this trade."[18] That he would even contemplate, however briefly, a trade of a similar nature with the Whigs for his own election indicates

[16] Sumner to Wilson, September 9, 1850, Sumner to Charles Allen, October 15, 1850, quoted in Pierce, *Charles Sumner*, III, 223, 218-19; *Sumner, Works*, II, 405-11; Donald, *Charles Sumner,* 179-80, 187-88.

[17] Adams, Diary, October 12, November 16, December 11, 1850, in Adams Papers.

[18] *Ibid.,* October 3, December 21, 1850, February 6, 1851.

that, like Sumner, his devotion to Free Soil principle and identity was modified by personal ambition. Although Adams insisted on stringent free soil terms in his negotiations with the Whigs, terms which would eventually help to prevent the completion of such a bargain, he was still willing to discuss what he must have realized could lead to the same kind of results he attacked in Ohio.

At the same time the much more promising discussions for Free Soil–Democratic coalition continued with the results of the state election of 1850 being almost ideal from the Wilson-Sumner point of view. Although the Whig candidate Briggs led for governor, he did not have the required absolute majority. The legislature which would decide would be composed of more Democrats and Free Soilers than Whigs in both houses.[19] Henry Wilson could now expect to see his hopes fulfilled. Even Charles Francis Adams expressed joy that the Whigs were no longer in control and that "the domination of Daniel Webster has been demolished." As plans developed for consummating the bargain, the Whigs predictably expressed self-righteous outrage.[20] Their command over Massachusetts politics was about to end but not without a struggle and heavy damage to the shaky Free Soil–Democratic coalition.

As the legislature prepared to convene, the Free Soil opponents of coalition continued to express doubts about Wilson's plans. Gamaliel Bailey, disillusioned by the New York proceedings, inquired of Sumner: "Will not the rascally Hunker Democrats try to cheat you?" Dana had little hope for the future of an independent party but argued that the coalition should be resisted because "it is a mere trade." Even though Sumner refused to make any pledges to the Democrats as to what his course would be in the Senate, Adams felt that the alliance was "but the beginning of the end" for the Free Soil party.[21] John G.

[19] Bean, "Party Transformations in Massachusetts," 59-61. In the Senate there were 11 Free Soilers, 10 Democrats, and 11 Whigs, while in the House there were 113 Free Soilers, 107 Democrats, and 176 Whigs. Boston *Commonwealth,* January 30, 1851.

[20] Adams, Diary, November 12, 1850, in Adams Papers; Boston *Advertiser,* January 7, 18, 1851; Donald, *Charles Sumner,* 190.

[21] Bailey to Sumner, November 27, 1850, in Sumner Papers; Dana to Edwin Dana, October 27, 1850, in Dana Papers; Adams, Diary, December 11, 1850, January 5, 7, 1851, Adams to Sumner, December 10, 1850, Sumner to Adams, December 16, 1850, January 2, 1851, in Adams Papers.

Palfrey wrote a public letter to the Free Soilers in the legislature urging them to stand fast for Stephen C. Phillips for governor because the price for a Free Soil senator was too great to pay. He argued that Boutwell as governor would be the state representative of the national "proslavery" party and that with him chosen, Democrats might renege on their pledge to support Sumner.[22] Although Wilson continued to push for coalition in the legislature, the differences in his own party were now more evident than ever. In a futile effort to reconcile Adams to the arrangement, Wilson even offered him a place on the governor's council. Adams indignantly rejected the idea and was highly insulted at the suggestion that he advise a Democratic governor.[23]

Nevertheless, most Free Soilers remained committed to the proposed alliance, and soon after the general election the Wilson faction of the party conferred with the Democrats in the legislature on the division of spoils. Committees of the two parties met in joint session and agreed formally that they would elect Sumner to be senator, while Boutwell, the Democrat, would receive the governorship. The Democrats would also receive a greater share of the remaining state offices. The Democratic caucus accepted Sumner with only six dissenting voices, and those six agreed not to participate when the full legislature voted. When the legislature met, the coalition secured Henry Wilson's election as president of the Senate and Democrat Nathaniel P. Banks as speaker of the House.[24] Even though they outnumbered the Democrats in the legislature, the Free Soilers were willing to surrender the choicer state posts in return for the six-year Senate seat. The Free Soil Boston *Commonwealth* observed accurately that its party's aims were national while the Democrats were more concerned with state affairs. For both groups, however, practical politics took precedence over principle, for the Democratic party had refused to repudiate the Compromise of

    [22] John G. Palfrey, "To the Free Soil Members of the General Court of Massachusetts for the Year 1851," 1-4; Duberman, "The Massachusetts 'Coalition,' " 155; Wilson, *The Slave Power,* II, 347; Wilson to Palfrey, May 19, 1851, in Palfrey Papers.
    [23] Adams, Diary, January 8, 1851, in Adams Papers.
    [24] The arrangement also included the awarding to the Democrats of the remaining six weeks in the term of the other Massachusetts senator in Washington. Duberman, "The Massachusetts 'Coalition,' " 157; McKay, "Wilson and the Coalition," 349-50.

1850 and the Free Soilers had given no guarantee to support the Democrats on state issues.[25]

By mid-January, the coalition had completed the arrangement with the major exception of the last part, the long-term Senate seat. Unfortunately, in the process of electing Boutwell governor, the Free Soilers needlessly antagonized Stephen C. Phillips, their own gubernatorial candidate, and demonstrated their political immaturity. The law provided that the House would nominate two candidates for final decision by the Senate. Instead of submitting the name of Briggs, the leading candidate, along with that of Boutwell, the Free Soilers helped nominate Phillips. He was infuriated since his party now would have to abandon him publicly in order to vote for Boutwell. He regarded the negotiations as "unprincipled and corrupt. I consider that it involves the overthrow of the Free Soil party, and, to a great extent, the abandonment of its cause." He told Sumner he regretted that his election "must be so dearly purchased." For a basically practical-minded group, the Free Soilers were displaying a surprising amount of political insensitivity. Adams felt that there had never been "a more reckless disregard of the feelings and usefulness of the public men of a party than had been exhibited in this instance." Sumner realized the injustice and favored breaking the coalition to support Phillips in the final vote, but most party members thought it was too late to change. They rejected Palfrey's suggestion that they were not bound to support Boutwell, realizing that refusal at this point would mean sacrificing a Free Soil seat in the Senate.[26]

Signs of additional trouble appeared when Governor Boutwell delivered his initial message to the legislature. In it he announced support of the Compromise of 1850 and refused to endorse resistance to the Fugitive Slave Act. Yet, so cautious were the Free Soilers about offending their new allies that they let the statement pass without public

[25] Adams Diary, January 7, 1851, in Adams Papers; Boston *Commonwealth*, January 6, 30, February 18, 1851. The Boston *Republican* had ceased publication in 1850 and was replaced by the *Commonwealth* at the start of 1851. Both papers were under Wilson's leadership.

[26] McKay, "Wilson and the Coalition," 350; Phillips to Sumner, January 7, 1851, in Sumner Papers; Adams, Diary, January 9, 10, 12, 1851, in Adams Papers; Palfrey, "To the Free Soil Members," 1-4.

protest. Wilson's Boston *Commonwealth* observed that the Free Soilers had "made up their minds to this and can afford it." But they soon began to realize that the Democrats in the legislature had them at their mercy following Boutwell's election. As Adams noted, "We are in the jaws of the monster without a bit of protection from his bite but his own magnanimity."[27]

A few Democrats then moved to take advantage of the situation and block Sumner's election. In late January, the Senate endorsed Sumner, but to be elected he had to receive an absolute majority of each house voting separately. On the first House ballot he failed to obtain the necessary majority, receiving 186 votes to 167 for Winthrop. Thirty scattered votes were cast, mostly by Democrats who refused to abide by their party's decision. The leader of these dissidents was a former Democratic candidate for governor, Caleb Cushing, who had opposed the coalition from the start. According to Wilson, the Democratic caucus had pledged the party to support any Free Soil candidate acceptable to a two-thirds vote of the members. Although the caucus had approved Sumner by a vote of 65 to 6, Cushing claimed he was not pledged in any way. He said no Democratic caucus could bind the minority unless it sustained "Democratic principles." He disapproved of Sumner as a "one idead [*sic*] agitator." Cushing's stand was in the face of the fact that more than 60 percent of the Democrats in the legislature had taken part in the caucus decision and more than 90 percent of those voting had agreed to Sumner. As in the case of the Free Soilers then the decision to support a coalition was not one imposed on the party membership by the leadership but rather it reflected the wishes of the majority.[28]

For a time it appeared that Cushing might succeed in blocking Sumner's election, for a growing number of Democrats seemed intent on refusing to honor their party's pledge. The Boston *Post,* a Democratic paper, claimed that the coalition had been formed for state purposes only and had no reference to the Senate race. According to the *Post,* to elect Sumner with Democratic votes would be treason to the national

---

[27] Bean, "Party Transformations in Massachusetts," 65; Boston *Commonwealth,* January 20, 1851; Adams, Diary, January 11, 1851, in Adams Papers.

[28] Wilson, *The Slave Power,* II, 348; Claude M. Fuess, *The Life of Caleb Cushing* (New York, 1923), II, 98-103; Boston *Commonwealth,* February 18, 1851; Boston *Post,* February 7, 1851.

Democracy. The New York *Tribune* charged that to elevate "that agitator" to the Senate would be an action not soon forgiven by national Democratic leaders. Marcus Morton, who had cautiously supported Van Buren in 1848 and had helped form the coalition, now tried to convince Democratic legislators that they were not bound to Sumner. Governor Boutwell might have broken the developing stalemate, but not wishing to antagonize members of his own party, he preferred a noncommittal hands-off policy. He announced that the decision was up to the legislature.[29]

The Whigs of Massachusetts naturally did everything in their power to prevent Sumner's election. Men like Robert C. Winthrop found the choice of Sumner thoroughly repugnant. Some felt that Sumner as a senator would work to upset the national equilibrium that Webster and Clay had sought to maintain. Congressman Samuel Eliot wrote to Amos A. Lawrence from Washington: "For heaven's sake keep him home! You can hardly imagine the disgust and loathing with which such men as Sumner, Hale of New Hampshire, Giddings and that set are looked upon by honest men here." Lawrence, Nathan Appleton, and other Whigs labored hard to defeat Sumner. The Whig state committee even began contacting the major manufacturing companies for contributions to be used against him, and made arrangements for men "good and true" to hunt up Whigs and *"carry them to the ballot box"* to defeat Sumner.[30] President Fillmore's quick and drastic action to quell opposition to the Fugitive Slave Act in Boston was regarded by Free Soilers as primarily aimed at Sumner's candidacy for the Senate.[31]

These bitter partisan attacks on Sumner and the Whig and Democratic intrigues to defeat him placed the Free Soilers on the defensive,

[29] Boston *Post,* January 20, 1851; New York *Tribune,* January 13, 1851; Morton to B. V. French, November 22, 1850, Morton to F. Robinson, November 22, 1850, in Morton Papers; McKay, "Wilson and the Coalition," 354-55; Adams, *Richard Henry Dana,* I, 176.

[30] Winthrop, *A Memoir of Robert C. Winthrop,* 145; Samuel Eliot to Amos A. Lawrence, January 23, 1851, John E. Tyler to Lawrence, February 11, 1851, in Lawrence Papers, Massachusetts Historical Society; Winthrop to Appleton, January 17, 1851, in Winthrop Papers; "Address to the People of Massachusetts," (n.d.), 13.

[31] New York *Evening Post,* February 19, 20, 1851. The Free Soilers had no absolute evidence of Fillmore's intentions, although he had ordered the militia, army, and navy to break up the "insurrection" in Massachusetts following the successful escape of the fugitive slave Shadrach (Frederick Jenkins). Richardson, *Messages and Papers of the Presidents,* V, 109-10.

but they quickly fought back. Henry Wilson led the counterattack. He rejected Cushing's suggestion that anyone but Sumner, including Wilson himself, might be acceptable to all Democrats. The harried Wilson also vigorously accused Morton of lobbying against Sumner. Morton denied the charge but could not deny that in January he had sent a public "Letter to the Free Soil and Democratic members of the Legislature of Massachusetts" in which he demonstrated Sumner's unfitness for the Senate. Morton attempted unconvincingly to prove that he had no interest in the Senate race and that his meetings with legislators were purely coincidental.[32]

Despite the persuasive efforts of Democratic Speaker Nathaniel Banks in behalf of the coalition, Cushing and his followers continued to resist Sumner's candidacy. Banks did not favor Sumner but urged Democrats to unite behind him to preserve the useful coalition. Nevertheless, the charges and countercharges continued, and the legislature failed to elect on ballot after ballot. In the increasing tension and bitterness the Wilson-dominated Boston *Commonwealth* stooped to personal attacks on Cushing: "His only sister died on Monday morning and was hurried into the grave by him at half past two P. M. on Tuesday that he might be in his place to vote against Mr. Sumner on Wednesday!" Sumner began to fear that the legislature might be indefinitely stalemated and suggested several times that he resign from the race. He wrote to Wilson: "Abandon me then, whenever you think best without notice or apology. The cause is everything; I am nothing." Given Sumner's own inconsistency on the coalition of having first opposed it and then endorsed it when his own election became a possibility, his statement to Wilson cannot be regarded as a completely sincere one. Although he had remained aloof from the contest in the legislature he nevertheless did everything honorably possible to win the seat in the Senate which he dearly coveted. Nevertheless, Sumner continually rejected Democratic offers to support him in return for his pledge

---

[32] McKay, "Wilson and the Coalition," 354-55; Pierce, *Charles Sumner*, III, 242; Morton to Free Soil and Democratic Members, January 18, 1851, Morton to Sumner, March 12, 1851, in Morton Papers; Morton to Boston *Commonwealth*, March 19, 1851. Morton went to ridiculous extremes to refute Wilson's charges. Most of the legislators, however, refused to support Morton's claims. See Morton to F. Robinson, March 24, 1851, Morton to George Austin, March 27, 1851, in Morton Papers.

to refrain from anti-extension agitation.[33] Through it all, the Free Soilers remained firm, hoping for the eventual break that would elect Sumner.

During the deadlock, the Whigs continued to search for a more acceptable candidate who, as a substitute for Sumner, could win sufficient Free Soil endorsement. It was then that they approached Adams, praising him as "By far the ablest man of the party in this state." The Whig hope was to divide the Free Soilers further, but Adams, despite his own interest in election, published a letter praising Sumner and declaring his election to be most desirable. Both Adams and Palfrey commended Sumner for remaining aloof from the contest and displaying no selfish motives. Palfrey told him: "No one acquainted with your course in this matter can ever say that it has not been the most high and honorable."[34]

The break that Wilson and the Free Soilers were looking for finally came on April 24, when, after almost four months of balloting, Sumner received exactly the required number of votes.[35] Sumner himself was gratified, although he somewhat hypocritically expressed mixed feelings about giving up a life of quiet study. Adams thought that Sumner would do "himself and the country credit." The new senator expressed his thanks to Wilson: "To your ability, energy, determination and fidelity our cause owes its present success. For weal or woe you must take the responsibility of having placed me in the Senate of the United States." The reaction of the Whigs, however, was one of self-righteous outrage. On the day following the final decision some of

[33] Fred Harvey Harrington, *Fighting Politician: Major General N. P. Banks* (Philadelphia, 1948), 11-12; Boston *Commonwealth,* April 24, 1851; Sumner to Giddings, April 3, 1851, in Giddings Papers; Wilson, *The Slave Power,* II, 349; Sumner to John Bigelow, January 21, 1851, quoted in Bigelow, *Retrospections of an Active Life,* I, 106-7; Sumner to Adams, January 7, 1851, Adams, Diary, February 13, 1851, in Adams Papers; Donald, *Charles Sumner,* 196-97.

[34] Adams, Diary, November 19, December 21, 1850, February 6, 11, March 20, 23, April 24, 1851, in Adams Papers; Boston *Atlas,* January 6, 7, 1851; Duberman, "The Massachusetts 'Coalition,' " 157; Donald, *Charles Sumner,* 196-97; Palfrey to Sumner, February 25, 1851, quoted in Pierce, *Charles Sumner,* III, 234.

[35] Because of the secrecy and confusion of the balloting it is impossible to know for sure which legislators switched to make Sumner's election possible. It was widely rumored, however, that a Whig, Nathaniel Borden, and a Democrat, Israel Haynes, made the difference. Fuess, *Caleb Cushing,* II, 104; New York *Tribune,* April 26, 1851; Wilson, *The Slave Power,* II, 349-50; Donald, *Charles Sumner,* 202n.

them appeared on the streets of Boston with wide bands of black crepe on their arms.[36]

Wilson definitely had been the prime force behind the coalition and was therefore most responsible for Sumner's election. Having displaced Adams in the party's leadership he had emerged as the key figure to carry on Free Soil work in Massachusetts. Yet it was no longer an independent third party that he led. Free Soil principle and identity had been sacrificed in order to gain a highly valuable seat in the Senate. In the process, Wilson had exposed the party to charges of political expediency by forming a coalition with a party which continued to endorse the Compromise of 1850. The Democrats of Massachusetts had been equally willing to join a coalition, indicating that many Free Soilers were not really much different from politicians of the major parties. The decision to cooperate in both cases had to be taken over vigorous opposition, with Adams and Palfrey leading the resistance in the Free Soil party and Cushing and Morton in the Democratic. Yet the great majority in both organizations had finally agreed and had sacrificed principle for office. Nor were Henry Wilson and the Free Soilers of Massachusetts unique in their desire ultimately to reenter the two-party system. Such a trend had already become obvious in many other northern areas of Free Soil influence.

Following Sumner's election, the coalition-dominated legislature moved to carry out a series of reforms long demanded by the Democrats. The reforms which were enacted included, among others, the secret ballot, homestead and lien laws, and state regulation of Harvard College. Yet the coalition continued to be divided on issues relating to slavery. Before the election the Free Soilers had pledged that they would not agitate in the legislature on sectional issues, but as the controversy over enforcement of the Fugitive Slave Law increased, some Free Soilers could not be contained. Despite the determined opposition of the Whigs and Democrats, third-party leaders attempted to strengthen the state's personal-liberty law of 1843 to make enforcement of the hated Compromise measure more difficult. No more willing to carry out their part of the bargain than some Democrats had been in

---

[36] Sumner to George Sumner, April 29, 1851, quoted in Pierce, *Charles Sumner,* III, 247; Adams, Diary, April 24, 1851, in Adams Papers; Sumner to Wilson, April 25, 1851, quoted in Nason and Russell, *Henry Wilson,* 93-94; McKay, "Wilson and the Coalition," 357; Boston *Post,* April 25, 1851.

relation to Sumner's election, these Free Soilers were nevertheless being true to principle at least in this instance. Two fugitive-slave cases in Boston in early 1851 provided the specific occasion. The first was that of Shadrach, who escaped to freedom before his trial, and the second that of Thomas Sims, who was finally returned to slavery. In both cases Richard Henry Dana played a prominent role in the legal defense of the fugitives. Dana, along with Sumner, was also responsible for the new personal-liberty bill introduced into the legislature. The proposed law, by giving the accused a trial by jury, would have made enforcement of the national law almost impossible. Democrats and Whigs combined to defeat the bill, however, and to prevent a formal condemnation of the Fugitive Slave Act.[37]

During the debates on the proposed personal-liberty law, the Democrats of Massachusetts revealed that they were sharply divided among themselves on the Compromise measures much in the manner of the Hunkers in New York. This division meant that continued Democratic participation in the Free Soil coalition would be difficult to achieve. The majority, led by Benjamin Hallett and Caleb Cushing, supported the position of the national party, while a minority, led by Robert Rantoul, agreed with the Free Soilers that the Fugitive Slave Law was a flagrant violation of constitutional and moral standards and hence should be resisted. The disagreement over Sumner's election was one early manifestation of the growing Democratic schism, with the Cushing group having led the opposition to Sumner in the legislature. Rantoul and other Democrats like him did not feel strongly enough about extension and other antislavery matters to join the Free Soilers, but the proslavery character of the Fugitive Slave Law was simply too much to endure silently. At the Democratic state convention of 1851, the dispute continued with Governor Boutwell being renominated, but the members dividing over the platform. Finally the Rantoul forces lost control, and the party condemned agitation on the subject of slavery by again endorsing the Compromise measures.[38]

[37] Bean, "Party Transformations in Massachusetts," 89-90; Shapiro, *Richard Henry Dana*, 61-63; Adams, *Richard Henry Dana*, I, 185.
[38] Fuess, *Caleb Cushing*, II, 107-8; Bean, "Party Transformations in Massachusetts," 94-95; Luther Hamilton (ed.), *Memoirs, Speeches and Writings of Robert Rantoul, Jr.* (Boston, 1854), 741; Fred Harvey Harrington, "Nathaniel Prentiss Banks, A Study in Anti-Slavery Politics," *New England Quarterly*, IX (1936), 632n.

With pro-Compromise influences regaining control of the Massachusetts Democratic party, Free Soil opponents of the coalition renewed their opposition to continued cooperation with the Democrats. Frustrated by the Wilson faction again in 1851, some of them, however, simply withdrew from active participation in politics. Adams, Dana, and Palfrey had previously thwarted Wilson's drive for a complete fusion of the two organizations, but the election of Sumner had solidified the coalition. As Wilson's influence increased, Adams tried for a few months to stay completely out of politics, and Dana began to withdraw from public affairs. Adams especially felt that his position was rather hopeless because of the coalition's success and he saw nothing to be gained at this point by further open resistance to it.[39] Yet in acquiescing to Wilson's dominance he was indicating that his own free soil motivation was not strong enough to weather a major setback. Palfrey, still stubbornly refusing to work with the Democrats, found himself without Sumner's and Wilson's support in his own struggle for reelection to Congress and was defeated in the final vote in May, 1851. Sumner and Wilson were rather vindictively repaying Palfrey for his opposition to the coalition and his inactivity in Sumner's election struggle. Palfrey was defeated by only 87 votes out of over 13,000 votes cast, and a valuable Free Soil voice was lost from Congress. Again factionalism and politics within the third party had contributed to a serious setback for the movement. After serving briefly as editor-in-chief of the Free Soil newspaper, the Boston *Commonwealth,* Palfrey lost this position, too, because of his opposition to the coalition.[40]

When the Free Soilers met in convention in September, 1851, the coalition remained foremost and Adams was conspicuous by his absence. Wilson had urged his attendance, but Adams feared that all Wilson wanted from him was financial assistance for a coalition campaign. Adams still suspected the worst of Wilson: "The rise and career of that man is curious. Beginning well, possessed of good ideas rather than solid principles, his connexion with politics has gradually corroded his heart. . . ." The keynote of the convention was continued coopera-

[39] Duberman, *Charles Francis Adams,* 175-76; Shapiro, *Richard Henry Dana,* 63-64.
[40] Adams to Palfrey, May 28, 1851, in Adams Papers; Sumner to Palfrey, May, 1851, Wilson to Palfrey, May 19, 1851, in Palfrey Papers; Gatell, *John G. Palfrey,* 193-202.

tion with the Democrats, but the Democrats' endorsement of the Compromise prevented a complete merger. Again, each party was to nominate for major offices and then cooperate in the legislature. Remaining in power seemed to be the foremost consideration of both Democrats and Free Soilers, and not even the breaking of pledges by both sides the previous year made them more skeptical of the other's trustworthiness. Major obstacles remained, but, having tasted the fruits of victory, the two groups had more interest in cooperation than ever before. Sumner, by now hoping to see the Free Soilers and Democrats merge into a true anti-extension party, was disturbed by the Democratic position: "Nothing but Boutwell's half Hunkerism prevents us from consolidating a permanent party in Massachusetts, not by *coalition* but by *fusion* of all who are truly liberal, humane and democratic."[41]

Both Democrats and Free Soilers nominated candidates for governor with the understanding that the Free Soilers would support Boutwell, if, as expected, the decision should be up to the legislature. Since again the Free Soil candidate would probably be sacrificed, Stephen C. Phillips refused to accept renomination. Wilson and other leaders then persuaded Palfrey to take the hopeless candidacy, and Palfrey accepted, naively thinking it a compliment. At the last minute, however, Wilson decided that the legislature might yet elect a Free Soiler, and still the opportunist, he now sought the nomination for himself. It was too late, however, for the convention had already decided on Palfrey. During the campaign the Free Soilers did the bare minimum of campaigning for their candidate and even the party newspaper, the Boston *Commonwealth,* although endorsing Palfrey, nevertheless refrained from criticizing Boutwell. The Whig candidate, Robert Winthrop, won the largest number of votes but not a majority, with Boutwell second and Palfrey a poor third.[42]

The voters had indirectly sustained the coalition by failing to give

[41] Wilson to Adams, August 26, 1851, Adams, Diary, August 30, September 15, 1851, in Adams Papers; Boston *Commonwealth,* September 23, 1851; Sumner to Bigelow, quoted in Bigelow, *Retrospections of an Active Life,* I, 108.

[42] Gatell, *John G. Palfrey,* 203-4; Adams, Diary, September 22, 1851, in Adams Papers; Boston *Commonwealth,* October 25, 1851; Bean, "Party Transformations in Massachusetts," 110-11; Boston *Advertiser,* September 11, 1851; Nason and Russell, *Henry Wilson,* 98.

Winthrop or the Whigs in the legislature an absolute majority. As a result, when the legislature convened it quickly chose Boutwell as governor, much to the disgust of those Free Soilers who had opposed the coalition. Adams noted that by its desertion of Palfrey, the Free Soil party had "permanently fixed its destination, and taken its luck with a democracy far involved in pro-slavery embraces." He feared "an amalgamation with the democrats irrespective of principles on the slave question." Like Dana, Adams rejoiced that the Whigs were again defeated but wished Palfrey had won "in lieu of that doublefaced trimmer who rejoices in our support." Adams feared that "this democratic connexion has spread disease into the very heart of our friends. . . ."[43]

Yet if the coalition was firmer than before, Adams, Palfrey, and Dana were themselves partially to blame, for they had not taken an active role in opposing it after its initial success. The acknowledged leaders of what was by now a dwindling minority of Free Soil opponents of coalition, they were showing little of the firm resolution of Joshua Giddings's successful resistance to Chase's coalition efforts in Ohio. But the Massachusetts Free Soilers were revealing some of the same unfortunate divisive characteristics so evident in the Ohio third party. With the wide variation in political background of the individual leaders, there was rarely agreement over whether the movement should cooperate with a major party or maintain its independence. Because the nature of the coalition did not fit in with its own Whig background, the Adams faction could argue idealistically that only a compromising of principle would result from a Democratic connection. On the other hand, the more practical Wilson men, strengthened by their own predisposition to the Democratic party, emphasized the rewards in terms of political office available through coalition.

During the winter of 1851-52, a seemingly unrelated event, the visit to the United States of the Hungarian patriot Louis Kossuth, further divided Massachusetts Free Soilers. Congress had expressed sympathy for the Hungarian people whose struggle for liberty had been suppressed with the aid of the Russian army. As an official guest of the United States government, Kossuth hoped for American assistance to

[43] Adams, Diary, September 22, 1851, January 14, 1852, Adams to Sumner, January 1, 1852, in Adams Papers; Dana, Journal, November 16, 26, 1851, in Dana Papers.

the Hungarians. In Massachusetts, many members of the Free Soil–
Democratic coalition favored such assistance, but most of those of the
Conscience Whig tradition opposed it.[44] The usually practical-minded
Henry Wilson inexplicably became the staunchest advocate of American intervention in Hungary. When Lewis Cass cautiously called for
American aid, Wilson was willing to back him for the presidency "if
we must have a Democrat." When Cass later changed his mind, Wilson accused him of having "made a fool of himself." On the other
hand, Charles Sumner, not wanting to divert attention from the free
soil cause, consistently opposed American involvement in a European
affair. In a speech on the Senate floor he appealed to Kossuth: "But
respect our ideas, as we respect yours. Do not seek to reverse our traditional, established policy of peace. . . . Leave us where Washington
points the way."[45] As a result of this difference, relations between
Sumner and Wilson cooled noticeably for a short time. Wilson helped
secure a Massachusetts legislative resolution that the United States
should use all proper means "to restore the exile to his country and his
country to freedom." Upon invitation of the coalition, Kossuth visited
Massachusetts and was received as a hero.[46] Fortunately for the cause
of third-party unity, however, Kossuth was soon forgotten.

Sumner also became involved in a more significant controversy when
he failed to speak up promptly in the Senate on issues related to slavery. As a freshman senator and member of a despised tiny minority
which included in addition only Hale and Chase, he was in a difficult
position, for he was denied significant Senate committee assignments
and privileges. At first he simply bided his time, waiting for a suitable
occasion to speak out. His silence was best explained by an unrealistic
desire to gain experience in the Senate before speaking on the most
important topic of slavery. As he justified it, "I desire by early caution
and reserve, and by strengthening myself on other subjects, to place

[44] Pierce, *Charles Sumner*, III, 266; Boston *Commonwealth*, January 10, 1852;
Congressional Globe, 32nd Cong., 1st Sess., 415, Appendix, 143-45; Adams, Diary,
December 11, 12, 1851, in Adams Papers.

[45] Wilson to Sumner, December 15, 1851, February 17, 1852, in Sumner Papers;
Boston *Commonwealth*, January 10, 1852; *Sumner, Works*, III, 8-9; Sumner to
Bigelow, December 13, 1851, quoted in Bigelow, *Retrospections of an Active Life*,
I, 121-22.

[46] Wilson to Sumner, February 17, 1852, in Sumner Papers; Nason and Russell,
Henry Wilson, 98-101; Boston *Commonwealth*, May 3, 1852.

myself in a position to speak from a vantage-ground when at last I do speak."[47] Sumner's reticence was a case of extremely poor political judgment, however, for it allowed his critics to charge that he was surrendering his principles now that he had obtained office. His silence was naturally most embarrassing to Free Soilers, who continually wrote to urge him to present his views. After months of silence, Wilson wrote in desperation: "Do not for Heaven's sake fail to speak, cost what it may of effort or trouble. I tell you frankly that our people are in a state of disappointment and almost despair. For months they have looked to have you speak." Wilson warned that the Whigs were ridiculing Free Soilers and claiming Sumner was afraid to say anything.[48] Thus Sumner's troubles were only beginning when he won election to the Senate.

As the presidential election approached, Sumner found it increasingly difficult to get permission to address the Senate. He explained to Palfrey, however, that he would not let the session end without speaking. Both Dana and Adams were quick to defend Sumner's course and express their faith in his ability. Both men had long since overcome any hostile feelings against Sumner that they might have held because of his role in the coalition. Adams observed that the approach of the election made the major parties wish to avoid agitation. When the Senate denied him permission to speak on a motion, Adams noted that this would not have happened before the national conventions. The issue became all the more acute because Sumner was distrusted by many Free Soilers in Massachusetts. He had not fully identified himself with either the Wilson group, which continued to labor for coalition, or the Conscience group, which opposed all such efforts. Dana warned him: "You must be prepared for a coldness to which you have never been accustomed."[49]

Sumner finally found the moment to speak after introducing a motion to repeal the Fugitive Slave Act. Near the end of the session,

[47] Sumner to Palfrey, February 11, 1852, in Palfrey Papers; Donald, *Charles Sumner*, 222-23.
[48] F. W. Bird to Sumner, June 3, 1852, Wilson to Sumner, June 29, August 3, 1852, in Sumner Papers.
[49] Sumner to Palfrey, July 2, 1852, in Palfrey Papers; Sumner to Adams, July, 1852, Adams to Sumner, August 1, 1852, in Adams Papers; Dana to Sumner, August 9, 1852, in Sumner Papers.

on August 26, he held the floor for three hours and forty-five minutes. Stressing the antislavery views of the founding fathers, he argued that the federal government had no constitutional right to protect slavery.[50] The speech helped to restore Sumner temporarily to the good graces of Massachusetts Free Soilers, even though on the vote on Sumner's motion, only Hale, Chase, and Wade supported him.[51] As the election approached, both Democrats and Whigs were more intent than ever on avoiding discussion of troublesome sectional issues, and the arguments of men like Sumner were ignored as much as possible.

It was now up to the Free Soil party to convince the voters that the Compromise had not solved the basic issues dividing North and South. Much would depend on the Massachusetts Free Soil party, one of the very few in the country to maintain a degree of its identity between presidential elections. Although it had suffered setbacks and internal divisions, it had gained some benefits from Democratic coalition and had kept its independence at least partially intact. Unlike the Chase faction in Ohio, which advocated abandonment of the Free Soil organization and refused to participate when it did not get its wishes, or the Barnburners of New York, who actually had abandoned the third party, the Massachusetts group had maintained its separate organization. This, however, was due only to pressure from a minority faction within the party, for Wilson, like Chase, desired a complete merger and would have been glad to see the third-party members reenter the two-party system. Clearly the Free Soilers had sacrificed their principles in agreeing to work with Democrats who endorsed the Compromise and had thus set a rather poor example for the national party to follow. With a presidential election approaching, however, there was reason to believe that the positions of the national Whig and Democratic parties would force Free Soilers to reassert their ideals. In this effort the Massachusetts men would provide much of the leadership as the need for separate third-party agitation became more obvious than ever.

[50] *Sumner, Works,* III, 95-106; Wilson to Sumner, September 5, 1852, James Stone to Sumner, August 30, 1852, in Sumner Papers.
[51] Donald, *Charles Sumner,* 237-39.

9

The Free Democrats and
the Election of 1852

In 1852, the third-party members, who now called themselves Free Democrats rather than Free Soilers, participated in their second and final presidential election.[1] In the four years since 1848 the party had declined to a mere fraction of its greatest strength, and several times it had been on the verge of complete collapse. Many factors help explain this decline, including the desire of many to return to the security of the two-party system; the poor grass-roots organization of the third party, which made it difficult to maintain support between national elections; and the lack of importance of the Wilmot Proviso to some of the less dedicated. Yet the interest generated by a presidential election and the continued refusal of the Democrats and Whigs to come to grips with issues related to slavery were sufficient to revive the party somewhat. Although the third party would receive only a little more than half of its 1848 total vote, this was primarily due to the permanent return of the Barnburners to the Democratic party; most Whig and Liberty elements of the Free Soil party remained loyal to the Free Democrats. Yet politicians of both major parties were very successful in persuading the voters that the Compromise of 1850 was the final solution of the slavery question and therefore there was no

---

[1] The name Free Democratic was suggested as early as 1848 and became the official name of the party from 1851 to 1854. The reasons for the change from Free Soil are somewhat elusive especially when it is remembered that many of the Democratic elements of the party had returned to their old organization before the change was made. Because for some the Wilmot Proviso was no longer a relevant issue following the Compromise of 1850, many of the members felt that a

need for a sectional party. This was true despite a vigorous effort by the Free Democratic party to convince the voters of the contrary.

The declining strength of the anti-extension forces after 1848 and the passage of the Compromise of 1850 had combined to force many more dedicated Free Soilers to question the advisability of the third party's approach. Many of the old Liberty leaders felt that the movement should return to the principles and methods maintained before the 1848 campaign. In their view, the Free Soilers had attempted to satisfy too many diverse interests and had sacrificed anti-extension principle in the process. Those who had refused to support Van Buren and had instead endorsed the Liberty League could now claim that subsequent events had borne out their misgivings and apprehensions of that campaign.[2] The Liberty League continued in reduced numbers after 1848 as Gerrit Smith labored valiantly to keep his organization alive. A national Liberty convention which he called for September, 1851, attracted few delegates and accomplished little although some, like Frederick Douglass, remained loyal to him. Douglass explained in his newspaper that the aim of the Free Democratic party was "to denationalize and sectionalize and not to abolish slavery." He supported Smith's views because he could not see how a "less elevated platform can be occupied by those who would radically oppose slavery at the ballot box." Nevertheless, it was clear that the League could not attract the bulk of free soil voters.[3]

broader more inclusive name which could represent other issues besides anti-extensionism would be more appropriate. The Chase faction in Ohio used the name soon after the election of 1848 as a means of identifying itself with the Democrats. In a similar manner the Wilson coalitionists in Massachusetts used the name somewhat later to forward their aims. Both groups were instrumental then in the name change for the national party, although it is surprising that the Whig and Liberty elements, including such leaders as Giddings, Bailey, and Adams, did not resist more than they did. Some did prefer the name Anti-Slavery, but it never received serious consideration and there was never any real debate over the acceptance of the name Free Democratic. See Smith, *The Liberty and Free Soil Parties*, 244; Lewis Tappan to Harriet Beecher Stowe, April 5, 1852, in L. Tappan Papers; Margaret C. McCulloch, *Fearless Advocate of the Right: The Life of Francis Julius LeMoyne, M.D., 1798-1879* (Boston, 1941), 166.

[2] Goodell, *Slavery and Anti-Slavery*, 482-85; A. A. Guthrie to *National Era*, March 4, 1852.

[3] Harlow, *Gerrit Smith*, 187-90; Quarles, *Frederick Douglass*, 146-47; Gerrit Smith to Cassius Clay, August 16, 1851, in Giddings Papers; *Frederick Douglass' Paper*, April 8, 1852, quoted in Wesley, "The Participation of Negroes," 64.

If the Free Democratic movement were to have wide appeal to northern voters, leadership would have to come from those who had endorsed Van Buren in 1848. Emphasis on anti-extension principle, however, would replace much of the questionable political maneuvering and expediency of the Van Buren campaign. In September, 1851, third-party leaders, under the direction of Joshua Giddings, called a national convention in Cleveland "to let the country know that we are not disbanded and do not intend to disband." Giddings told Julian: "We want to embody the entire antislavery force of the United States at the next Presidential election, and we desire to compare views and devise the means of doing it." With Chase supporting the Democrats in 1851, Giddings was in full control of the Ohio party and was the moving force behind the convention. Delegates from most northern states attended, but the convention was dominated by midwesterners, many of whom had once belonged to the Liberty party. Included were Giddings, Samuel Lewis, Julian, Lewis Tappan, and Sherman Booth. The presiding officer was Francis J. LeMoyne, a longtime abolitionist who had refused to support Van Buren in 1848. The delegates adopted firm anti-extension resolutions and appointed a committee to make plans for a national nominating convention to meet in 1852.[4] The year 1851 was the low point in the Free Democratic movement, but the Cleveland convention revealed that it was far from dead. Against the rising chorus endorsing the finality of the Compromise, third party leaders were making plans to keep their agitation before the people.

Not all Free Democrats saw much value in a national meeting a full year before the election. Salmon P. Chase attended only because he feared being left out should the movement assume major significance. Always the manipulator, Chase's heart at this point was really with the Democrats, and he was clearly out of place among these dedicated anti-extensionists. Surprisingly, Massachusetts sent no representatives. Charles Sumner, for example, declined to attend because he was "not aware of any special point, beyond that of general encourage-

4 *National Era*, September 11, October 2, 9, 1851; Giddings to Julian, August 27, 1851, Samuel Lewis to Julian, November, 1851, in Giddings-Julian Papers; Lewis Tappan to Charles Allen, June 17, 1852, in L. Tappan Papers; Julian, *Political Recollections*, 119; McCulloch, *Julius LeMoyne*, 166; William G. W. Lewis, *Biography of Samuel Lewis, First Superintendent of Common Schools for the State of Ohio* (Cincinnati, 1857), 338.

ment, which makes a national convention desirable." Equally important in Sumner's decision was his recent election to the Senate with
the aid of Democratic votes and his desire to see the Massachusetts
coalition become a fusion party. Association with an independent
third party at this time would obviously not further such a cause.[5]

A desire for Democratic fusion was not the only factor which kept
some from participating. Perhaps most surprising was the indecision
expressed by Charles Francis Adams and other Massachusetts leaders
of Whig background. Long the opponent of any Democratic coalition,
Adams now became so discouraged with the third party's prospects
that he talked of endorsing the likely Whig nominee, General Win-
field Scott. In February, 1852, he wrote to Bailey that "no nomination
of candidates *within our own ranks,* can be made with any prospect of
a creditable result." He told Sumner that if the Whigs refrained from
endorsing the Compromise, "my inclination is to declare in Scott's
favor individually, but not collectively as Free Soilers." Adams, whose
Whig background was again asserting itself at the expense of free soil
principle, questioned the value of independent action because the
movement was so divided and could not find a common platform to
stand upon. Yet despite a personal interest in Scott he opposed a formal alliance with the Whigs. He told Bailey it was the duty of the
press to call "our men off from all entangling alliances" and prepare
for the possibility of separate organization. Adams, as well as the
coalitionists Sumner and Wilson, was determined to remain uncom-
mitted until the major parties had nominated and adopted platforms.[6]

No longer a part of the Free Democratic party, the Barnburners
seemed eager to forget 1848 and to pretend that they had never left
the two-party system. They now labored to secure a Democratic candidate acceptable to a wide range of northerners, and in the process
rationalize away, at least in their own minds, the need for a separate

[5] Sumner to Giddings, August 21, September 11, 1851, in Giddings Papers;
Stewart, *Joshua Giddings,* 203-4.

[6] Adams to Bailey, February 2, April 5, 1852, Adams to Sumner, February 5,
June 11, 1852, Adams, Diary, December 12, 1851, March 16, April 23, 1852, in
Adams Papers; Sumner to Wilson, January 10, 1852, in Wilson Papers, Library of
Congress; James Stone to Sumner, June 6, 1852, quoted in Pierce, *Charles Sumner,*
III, 314-15; Sumner to Bigelow, June 28, 1851, quoted in Bigelow, *Retrospections
of an Active Life,* I, 119.

party. Yet despite extensive maneuvering in 1851 and early 1852, they approached the Democratic convention without a candidate, although they remained determined to be loyal Democrats. They had first tried to interest Thomas Hart Benton in running, but in early 1851 he rejected the idea completely. Benton and Blair suggested Levi Woodbury of New Hampshire. Support for Woodbury was growing among Barnburners when he suddenly died in September, 1851. Some proposed Sam Houston, and others suggested General William O. Butler of Kentucky. Houston's name drew little positive response, and when Butler announced his full support of the Compromise, the Barnburners again had to look elsewhere. None of the men they considered in fact were associated with the anti-extension movement in any real way, proving again that the Barnburners were more interested in party influence than they were in free soil principle. On the other hand, despite their unwillingness to operate outside of the Democratic party, the New Yorkers were firmly opposed to the Fugitive Slave Law and desirous of a candidate who would not be a puppet of the South. Yet as the convention approached they had not found their man. As a result, they unenthusiastically agreed to support their Hunker ally since 1849, William Marcy. As if trying to prove their free soil sincerity they announced their determination to hold out against any endorsement of the Compromise.[7]

The Democratic convention, however, quickly revealed them to be inconsistent politicians determined to enjoy the spoils of office. The convention delegates, meeting in Baltimore, struggled through forty-nine ballots before nominating a political unknown, Franklin Pierce of New Hampshire, who was acceptable to both North and South. More important from the point of view of anti-extensionists, the party pledged in its platform complete support of the Compromise measures, including the Fugitive Slave Act, and promised to oppose any renewal of antislavery agitation. The only consolation for the Barnburners was

[7] Blair to Martin Van Buren, January 26, February 25, 1851, Preston King to John Van Buren, February 25, 1851, John Van Buren to Martin Van Buren, March 4, 1851, Thomas Hart Benton to Dix, November 4, 1851, in Van Buren Papers; Smith, *Blair Family*, I, 268; J. D. Baldwin to John N. Niles, September 19, 1851, in Welles Papers; Slidell to Marcy, October 10, 1851, Marcy to Wetmore, September 28, 1851, in Marcy Papers; Roy Franklin Nichols, *The Democratic Machine, 1850-54* (New York, 1923), 79-91.

that the delegates made no outright declaration as to the finality of the Compromise, although the implication was certainly to that effect.[8] Nevertheless, for men eager to remain loyal and to be members of a party in power, the omission of a direct statement was enough. Preston King, a leader in the Barnburner revolt four years earlier, expressed the new attitude: "I disapprove and dissent from the slavery resolutions and shall support the nominations with cheerfulness and cordiality." Although the mission of the third party had not changed, Martin Van Buren and other New Yorkers quickly endorsed the Democratic nominees.[9] Van Buren and the others thus proved again that revenge and party control had been their motives in 1848, and with that accomplished, there was no good reason to hold out again in 1852. Certainly the Democratic party was no more oriented toward northern aims and interests than it had been in 1848, so that the Barnburners could not claim that any of their goals of that year had been achieved.

The *National Era* immediately pointed out the Barnburner inconsistency: "Aye — proclaim war against the Principles of your candidate, and then do all you can for his election, so as to make his Principles operative and controlling." The Barnburner position came as no surprise to the Free Democrats, although some were shocked when John Van Buren endorsed not only the candidates but the entire platform as well.[10] An all important wing of the 1848 movement had firmly renounced its interest in free soil, but the cause would be ultimately strengthened with the loss of those who had joined simply for the sake of expediency.

When the Whigs met in convention in June, 1852, they furnished the final reason most sincere anti-extensionists were looking for to continue their independent movement. Long before the convention many observers felt that the Whigs, torn by dissension, were doomed as a party and were entering their last national campaign because of their failure to offer effective opposition to the Democrats.[11] With

[8] *Proceedings of the Democratic National Convention Held at Baltimore, June, 1852* (Washington, 1852); Porter and Johnson (comps.), *National Party Platforms,* 16-18; Stanwood, *A History of the Presidency,* 248-50.
[9] King to Welles, June 12, 1852, in Welles Papers; New York *Herald,* June 12, 1852; Alexander, *Martin Van Buren,* 411-12.
[10] *National Era,* June 10, 1852.
[11] See for example Van Deusen, *William H. Seward,* 142-44.

more and more southern Whigs drifting out of the party because of alleged northern control, the party seemed eager not to antagonize its southern wing any further by pressing antislavery issues. Many Free Democrats argued that their party should seize on the opportunity to become the true anti-extensionist party. William H. Seward allegedly hoped he could organize a general antislavery party after the final defeat of the Whigs in 1852. At the convention, Seward got his revenge on President Fillmore by helping to engineer his defeat and to secure the nomination of General Scott. Yet the platform deferred to the Compromise spirit and the southern wing of the party by endorsing the Fugitive Slave Law and opposing "all further agitation of the question thus settled as dangerous to our peace."[12]

Neither the northern nor the southern faction of the party was entirely pleased with the outcome. Southern Whigs feared that Seward would dominate Scott as they claimed he had dominated Taylor. On the other hand, Seward, who along with many northerners was disgusted with the platform, wrote: "This wretched platform was contrived to defeat Scott in the nomination or sinke [*sic*] him in the canvass." "We accept the candidate, but split upon the platform," said Horace Greeley in a manner similar to the Barnburners. Having remained loyal to the party in 1848, Whigs like Seward and Greeley were even less inclined to bolt in 1852.[13] Both Whigs and Democrats had avoided an open rupture by adopting almost identical resolutions on the sectional issues and choosing colorless candidates who lacked strong convictions. Politics had again asserted itself over any element of principle in the major parties, and the politicians, as indicated by their platforms and nominations, thought so little of the third-party potential that they no longer looked on it as a challenge worthy of consideration.

---

[12] Adams, Diary, December 11, 1851, in Adams Papers; Rayback, *Millard Fillmore*, 357; Porter and Johnson (comps.), *National Party Platforms*, 20-21; Seward to James B. Taylor, June 26, 1852, quoted in New York *Tribune*, June 29, 1852; Harry J. Carmen and Reinhard Luthin, "The Seward-Fillmore Feud and the Disruption of the Whig Party," *New York History*, XXIV (1943), 348.

[13] Foner, *Business and Slavery*, 85-86; Frederic W. Seward, *Seward at Washington as Senator and Secretary of State: A Memoir of His Life with Selections from his Letters* (New York, 1891), II, 175-78; Nevins, *Ordeal of the Union*, II, 29-32; Stanwood, *A History of the Presidency*, 150-53; Van Deusen, *William H. Seward*, 141-42.

Yet these same platforms and nominations did more than anything else to force the Free Democrats to take action. Of the factions in the 1848 movement, only the Barnburners were willing to endorse a platform which supported the Fugitive Slave Law and opposed further agitation. Adams told Sumner: "I do not well comprehend how any man, either Whig or Democrat, can assent to the platform without at the same time disavowing every particle of practical hostility to slavery." Adams ended his long indecision when he agreed to attend the national Free Democratic convention and to support whichever candidates were nominated. Wilson and Adams were at last in agreement on something when their state party resolved to continue its separate organization. But it was without the enthusiasm which had launched their movement in 1848, for neither had any illusions about the chances for victory. Discouraged that four years of agitation had brought only the negative step of the Compromise, they were more realistic about their chances in 1852. Wilson wrote that they must not support Scott but hoped that their movement might cause his election by drawing votes from Pierce. "That we shall lead a forlorn hope is evident enough," Adams observed, "but we ought to have become used to that service by this time."[14]

As the Free Democrats prepared to meet in convention in Pittsburgh in August, several questions remained to be answered. One involved the nature of the platform to be adopted. Should the third party merely repeat its position of 1848 in the hope of appealing to a broad electorate, or should it go farther in its resolutions and risk the loss of additional support? Unlike most of the delegates, those of the Liberty League element, led by Gerrit Smith and William Goodell and centered in New York, wanted to take more advanced ground in the platform and thus eliminate all who were not completely dedicated to antislavery. Lewis Tappan, for example, protested when all who had endorsed the platform of 1848 were invited to attend, for he felt that the party must take a more extreme position. The adoption of the name Free Democracy rather than Anti-Slavery did not please the

[14] Adams to Sumner, June 23, 1852, Adams to E. Hopkins, June 23, 1852, Adams, Diary, July 1, 1852, in Adams Papers; Pierce, *Charles Sumner*, III, 315; Henry Wilson to Sumner, June 23, 1852, in Sumner Papers.

Liberty League because it was symbolic of too close a conformity to the corrupt two-party system. In general, however, the delegates who assembled in the Masonic Hall in Pittsburgh quickly resolved their differences.[15]

The most frequently mentioned candidates for the nomination, John P. Hale and Salmon P. Chase, reflected the general lack of enthusiasm which characterized many Free Democrats as the convention opened. Neither was eager to head a ticket with so little chance of success, and each urged the other to accept. Interest in Chase was confined to a relatively few delegates, and only their desire for a candidate of some prominence explained their interest in a manipulator of Chase's character. The Ohio senator's position was extremely difficult for he had renounced the third party in the state election of 1851. The national Democratic platform, however, gave him no alternative but to return to the Free Democrats in 1852. He announced that he could not support the "Slavery Platform of Baltimore" but indicated he was still a Democrat: "If we could have an Independent Democratic Rally, thoroughly Democratic in name and fact ... I should support it cheerfully." Even had he desired to head the third party in 1852, Ohio Free Democrats would have rejected him because of his earlier desertion. Adams explained that "the feeling as it respects Mr. Chase is so bitter in Ohio that it will make his nomination impossible."[16] Others, like Chase's fellow-opportunist, Wilson of Massachusetts, continued to hope he would accept a nomination. Chase explained that he would support some other Free Democratic nominee but insisted that without the Barnburners the party could have little effect on the election. That his heart would not be with the third party was clear, yet he still hoped it would be dominated by Democrats rather than former Whigs and Liberty men. Ignoring his own earlier inconsistencies, he even wrote a public letter to Benjamin F. Butler of New York appealing for Barnburner opposition to Pierce and expressing the hope that the New Yorkers would "prefer to act with the INDEPENDENT DEMOCRACY, openly and avowedly on the side of liberty and progress, rather than a

---

[15] *National Era*, July 8, 1852; L. Tappan to Chase, June 23, 1852, L. Tappan to Bailey, June, 1852, in L. Tappan Papers; Lewis, *Samuel Lewis*, 395-97.

[16] Chase to Hamlin, June 28, July 19, 1852, in Chase Papers, Library of Congress; Adams, Diary, August 6, 10, 1852, in Adams Papers.

COMPROMISE DEMOCRACY, intolerant alike of the claims and friends of freedom."[17]

Most Free Democratic leaders favored John P. Hale for the nomination. He had served the anti-extension cause well in the Senate but would have little chance of reelection by the New Hampshire legislature when his term expired in 1853. Early in 1852, conventions in Ohio and Maine had called for his nomination. The lack of a more prominent available politician also helped to place Hale in the lead. Adams, who was unwilling to accept a nomination himself, resolved to support Hale even if the latter resisted. Hale did resist and requested a New Hampshire colleague, George C. Fogg, to explain to the convention his determination not to run. Rumors of Hale's feelings spread before the convention opened, and both Chase and Adams urged him to reconsider.[18] The poor chances of the party having any major effect on the outcome of the election had made all Free Democratic leaders very wary about accepting the nomination. The convention thus faced the dilemma of having no prominent candidate unless Hale changed his mind.

The Free Democratic convention which opened in Pittsburgh on August 11, although highly enthusiastic, was small by the standards of four years earlier. Only about two thousand attended, compared to the approximately twenty thousand at Buffalo. With the Barnburners absent, the convention was dominated by leaders from Massachusetts and Ohio, the two states that had maintained the most active third-party movements. Primary direction fell to Wilson, the president of the convention, and to Adams, Giddings, and Samuel Lewis of Ohio. In attendance were delegates from all the free states plus Delaware, Kentucky, Maryland, and Virginia. For a group which realized that it had virtually no chance of success and little hope of even affecting the outcome, the spirit was remarkable. The national campaign had revived

[17] Wilson to Sumner, July 7, 22, 1852, in Sumner Papers; Estes Howe to Hale, July 7, 1852, Chase to Hale, August 5, 1852, in Hale Papers; Chase to Butler, July 15, 1852, quoted in *National Era*, July 29, 1852; Sewell, *John P. Hale*, 144-46.

[18] Lewis, *Samuel Lewis*, 392, 399; Adams, Diary, August 6, 10, 1852, in Adams Papers; Hale to Fogg, August 4, 1852, Chase to Hale, August 7, 1852, in Hale Papers.

their support of and dedication to the movement; "all those who were with us," Adams noted, "seemed sincerely in the cause."[19]

If the delegates were enthusiastic the potential candidates were not, for both Hale and Chase indicated their lack of desire for a nomination by their absence from the convention. Yet despite Hale's reluctance, there appeared to be no alternative, and the delegates had little choice but to nominate him. Fogg and Wilson tried to persuade Adams to enter the contest, but he flatly refused. Since Chase was unacceptable to so many delegates, Adams urged the leaders to nominate Hale against the latter's wishes. Unwilling to accept a nomination which would bring him little benefit, Adams was quite willing to insist that Hale do what he himself refused to do. At this point, Hale was the strongest candidate the party could offer, and most of the delegates realized it. On the first and only ballot Hale received 192 votes out of the 207 cast, with a scattering of votes for Chase, Adams, and Gerrit Smith.[20] The convention was thus ready to take its chances that Hale could be persuaded to accept what most regarded as a thankless task.

The nomination for vice-president proved more difficult and was accomplished only with some hard feelings. The delegates assumed that the candidate would be a midwesterner in order to provide geographical balance for the ticket. The party was thus ready to follow the standard political procedure although such a balance might not necessarily mean the choice of the most qualified candidate. Before the voting began Samuel Lewis was the only man prominently mentioned. He had played a leading role in Ohio antislavery politics for years and was chairman of the committee that arranged for the Pittsburgh convention. But he was regarded by some as too closely identified with abolitionism, and his nomination would cause a serious division within the Ohio delegation. Having refused to support Lewis for governor in 1851, the Chase faction opposed his candidacy now and, with the cooperation of Henry Wilson, succeeded in blocking it.[21] Chase and Wilson, the men most closely identified with Democratic coalition and

---

[19] *National Era,* August 12, 19, 1852; Adams, Diary, August 11-13, 1852, in Adams Papers; Smith, *The Liberty and Free Soil Parties,* 247-49; Philip Foner, *Frederick Douglass* (New York, 1964), 163; Sewell, *John P. Hale,* 147.

[20] Adams, Diary, August 11, 12, 1852, in Adams Papers; *National Era,* August 19, 26, 1852.

[21] Adams, Diary, August 12, 1852, in Adams Papers.

most strongly motivated by a desire for personal gain rather than to advance the cause of free soil, thus had their way, for only a man of more moderate persuasion could serve their purposes.

Wilson then unexpectedly suggested George W. Julian of Indiana for the vice-presidency, a man that few had considered before the convention. Surprisingly, Julian was chosen on the second ballot. Not everyone was satisfied with this result, for Adams, blaming "the scheming politics of Wilson," felt that great harm was done by the defeat of Lewis. Yet with obvious good will, Lewis wrote to Julian that he was completely satisfied with the outcome, although he implied that he had been eliminated because Chase and his supporters would not support a ticket which included his name.[22] The result produced the only disagreement in an otherwise harmonious convention. The young and vigorous Julian, a former congressman, no doubt did strengthen the ticket.

The strongly worded platform established the Free Democratic party as the only one committed to keeping the slavery issue before the electorate. The resolutions committee consisted of sixteen men, the most prominent being Giddings, Adams, and Gerrit Smith. A significant dispute arose when Smith proposed a plank stating that all laws protecting slavery were illegal. Instead, the convention rejected outright abolitionism and adopted a compromise which termed slavery a sin which "no human enactment can make right." The delegates reaffirmed their 1848 commitment to the Wilmot Proviso by calling for "no more slave States, no slave Territory, no nationalized slavery," and by demanding "the total separation of the General Government from slavery." In other aspects too the platform was more pronounced in its opposition to slavery than that of 1848. With the Barnburners gone, men with more commitment could have their way. The delegates laid heavy stress on the injustice of the Compromise of 1850, labeling it "inconsistent with all the principles and maxims of Democracy and wholly inadequate to the settlement of the questions of which they are claimed to be an adjustment." The Fugitive Slave Law came in for special attack as "repugnant to the Constitution, to the principles of

[22] Julian, *Political Recollections*, 123-28; Lewis, *Samuel Lewis*, 401-2; Lewis to Julian, August 19, 1852, in Giddings-Julian Papers; Clarke, *George Julian*, 131-33; Riddleberger, *George Julian*, 85-86.

the common law, to the spirit of Christianity, and to the sentiments of the civilized world." The party denied the law's "binding force upon the American People" and demanded its immediate repeal.[23]

At the same time the platform followed the example of 1848 and made no demands for the rights of free blacks.[24] In addition to repeating and expanding its 1848 planks favoring internal improvements and a homestead bill, the platform endorsed the cause of the Hungarian patriot Louis Kossuth. In closing, as if anticipating the many charges to come that the party was designed to aid one or the other of the major parties, the members resolved the Free Democratic intention "to defeat them both." Because Democrats and Whigs were "hopelessly corrupt, and utterly unworthy of confidence," the delegates argued that the third-party's purpose was "to take possession of the Federal Government, and administer it for the better protection of the rights and interests of the whole people."[25]

The Free Democratic leaders expressed satisfaction with the results of their convention. "On the whole the effect of the Convention has been to strengthen my confidence in the vigor of the movement," Adams noted. Except in the elimination of Lewis as a vice-presidential candidate, there clearly had been a minimum of the bargaining and behind the scenes maneuvering that had marred the Buffalo proceedings. Julian wrote that the meeting "was one of pure men because all the compromising and trading elements had left to return to old parties."[26] Unfortunately, however, these dedicated reformers would find themselves largely ignored by the major parties as the campaign unfolded, and they were not able to arouse much support for their cause.

Despite their idealism, the Free Democratic campaign began on a note of discord occasioned by the continuing inconsistency of Salmon P. Chase, the slowness of John P. Hale to accept the nomination, and opposition from some Liberty leaders. Chase had not wanted the nomination and in a letter read at the convention, had refused to

23 Adams, Diary, August 11, 12, 1852, in Adams Papers; Porter and Johnson (comps.), *National Party Platforms*, 18-20; Foner, "Politics and Prejudices," 251. See Appendix B for the complete platform.
24 See below, 247-48.
25 *National Era*, August 19, 26, 1852; Porter and Johnson (comps.), *National Party Platforms*, 18-20.
26 Adams, Diary, August 13, 1852, in Adams Papers; Julian, *Political Recollections*, 123.

accept it; but he now hinted that there had been a "conspiracy" against him at Pittsburgh. Although he had earlier urged Hale to run, his immediate reaction to the nomination was unenthusiastic. He agreed to support the platform and ticket "because it is more democratic than the old line" but confided to E. S. Hamlin: "I shall not sink my individuality in this organization, which it seems to me, must be temporary. I propose rather to maintain my position as an Independent Democrat. . . ." Angered by the constant attacks on him by Western Reserve Free Democrats, led by those who knew his opportunism, such as the Cleveland *True Democrat,* Chase seemed incapable of understanding why anyone could question his past inconsistent course. He wrote to Sumner that the "conspiracy" against him would hurt the Hale-Julian ticket. The implication was that the plotting by his opponents had deprived him of a nomination he did not want anyway! The pointless quarrel which served no useful purpose but did hamper the efforts toward unity in Ohio was quieted but not forgotten as the campaign proceeded.[27]

John P. Hale caused the party leaders a great deal of concern before finally accepting the nomination. Numerous Free Democrats wrote urging him to accept. Hale had favored Chase's nomination, and Adams and Sumner sought to assure him that Chase could not have been chosen under the circumstances. "The party with one mind marks out *you* as the leader," Adams told Hale, "and when it does that, your own argument in favor of maintaining the organization must dictate to you that you ought to take your place at the head of it." Walt Whitman, one of the few New Yorkers to maintain an interest in the party, wrote Hale a strong letter urging him to run. Whitman asked him to accept "gracefully and cordially" and then to campaign hard, "but abate not one jot of your fullest radicalism."[28] After a long delay Hale finally wrote to Wilson announcing his acceptance and complete en-

---

[27] *National Era,* August 19, 1852; Chase to Hamlin, August 13, 27, 1852, in Chase Papers, Library of Congress; Chase to Sumner, September 9, 1852, in Sumner Papers; Sewell, *John P. Hale,* 148.

[28] Adams to Hale, August 15, 1852, Adams to Sumner, August 15, 1852, Sumner to Adams, August 25, 1852, in Adams Papers; Wilson to Giddings, August 21, 1852, in Giddings Papers; Whitman to Hale, August 14, 1852, in Hale Papers; Richard H. Sewell, "Walt Whitman, John P. Hale, and the Free Democracy: An Unpublished Letter," *New England Quarterly,* XXXIV (1961), 239-42.

dorsement of the platform. He then quickly followed Whitman's advice by entering enthusiastically into the campaign and speaking in New York and the Midwest.[29]

Although the Free Democrats had taken an advanced position in their opposition to slavery, they had not endorsed the abolitionist view of the Liberty faction headed by Gerrit Smith. Smith and others had attended the Pittsburgh convention and at the time had appeared reconciled to the platform and quite satisfied with the candidates. But Smith's group, still calling itself the Liberty party and smarting from the rejection of its platform suggestions at Pittsburgh, determined to make certain inquiries of Hale and Julian before deciding whether to support the Free Democrats. Specifically they asked whether they believed slavery to be "a naked piracy, around which there can be no possible legal covering — a matchless fraud and crime to which no Constitution, nor Legislature, nor Judiciary can afford the least possible shelter?" Unless the candidates agreed with Smith's argument that slavery could not be legally protected and that Congress must immediately abolish it everywhere, his party would seek other candidates.[30]

Since they firmly disagreed with Smith and felt that Congress should limit itself to preventing the expansion of slavery, Hale and Julian chose to ignore his inquiries rather than to draw attention to their differences. This was the course suggested by Gamaliel Bailey, who noted sarcastically: "The dogma insisted on by Gerrit Smith has no practical value — is merely technical . . . and endorsed only by the few hundred people whom he and Mr. Goodell have been in the habit of assembling in *National* conventions." On receiving no answer from Hale and Julian to the Liberty questions, Smith called a convention which nominated William Goodell for president. Smith wrote the resolutions, which affirmed his antislavery ideas and claimed that "the Free Democracy will fail, as did the Free Soil Party, unless it shall openly and fearlessly aim to identify itself with every political truth." The members confidently expected that Hale would still endorse their views,

[29] Hale to Wilson, September 6, 1852, quoted in *National Era*, September 23, 1852; Hale to Mrs. Hale, September 13, October 2, 12, 15, 17, 24, 1852, in Hale Papers. Julian's acceptance is in Julian to Wilson, August, 1852, in Julian Papers.

[30] Gerrit Smith to Julian, September 2, 1852, in Giddings-Julian Papers; Harlow, *Gerrit Smith*, 191; Quarles, *Frederick Douglass*, 149-50.

but when he persisted in ignoring them, Goodell continued as a candidate.[31]

Smith's Liberty party differed in one other significant area — that of equal rights for the black population of the North. At its Pittsburgh convention the Free Democratic party had omitted any call for an end of racial discrimination in the North, although not before Smith had challenged the wisdom of such a policy. This omission came despite the fact that the Barnburners, who were the most antagonistic to equal rights for blacks, had rejoined the Democrats. It showed quite clearly that the Barnburners had not been alone in their racial attitudes four years earlier. At the Pittsburgh convention, Smith introduced a resolution that the party should seek equal political rights for all persons regardless of sex or race. Even though some delegates privately may have approved of the idea, they argued that it was politically inadvisable to call for equality for free blacks.[32] Such a stand was too extreme even for a party dedicated to the containment of slavery.

On the other hand, the delegates were willing to include in their platform a plank calling for United States recognition of the black nation of Haiti, a matter of obvious racial implications.[33] The apparent contradiction of calling for Haitian recognition while refusing to endorse equality in their own country can only be explained by the fact that Haiti was not an issue causing much interest at the time. The Free Democrats could therefore safely agitate for an end of racial discrimination in a matter of little apparent consequence without losing votes. On the other hand, not only would championing racial equality in the United States cost them support but most of the members simply could not overcome their own racism on a matter which would affect their daily lives.

In defending the platform's omission of black equality, Giddings said he did not wish the party "embarrassed by indefensible positions"

---

[31] Bailey to Julian, September 7, 1852, in Giddings-Julian Papers; Harlow, *Gerrit Smith,* 191. The resolutions of the Liberty party convention are quoted in *Calendar of the Gerrit Smith Papers,* II; Foner, "Politics and Prejudices," 253.

[32] *National Era,* August 19, 1852.

[33] Porter and Johnson (comps.), *National Party Platforms,* 18-20. Haiti went without United States recognition from the time of its independence in 1804 until 1862 when the slave states were out of the Union. See Rayford W. Logan, *Haiti and the Dominican Republic* (New York, 1968), 101-3.

but preferred to let each man decide that issue for himself. Although more open-minded than most, Giddings could still not bring himself to endorse full equality. Adams termed Smith's proposal "not even plausible," and the convention tabled the resolution by a vote of 197 to 14. Only the small Smith group supported it. Thus few of the delegates would challenge the almost universal belief in white supremacy, although it was convenient to explain their inaction in terms of political expediency. Even so dedicated a man as Julian noted his own inability to overcome the "ridiculous and wicked prejudice against color which even most anti-slavery men found it difficult to conquer." Thus the Free Democratic racial ideology had changed little from that of 1848 despite the secession of its most compromising elements, and only a small faction was willing to fight for the rights of the free black community. As a result of this unwillingness, Smith's Liberty platform broke again with the Free Democrats to endorse "its great central principle, that all persons — black and white, male and female — have equal political rights and are equally entitled to the protection and advantages of the Civil Government."[34]

Many in the black community recognized the continued Free Democratic hypocrisy on the issue of race and gave their support to the Liberty party instead. Earlier, however, some, including Frederick Douglass, had expected to campaign for the Free Democrats and had attended the Pittsburgh convention. As a delegate from New York, Douglass was elected secretary and spoke to the delegates, being well received. At Pittsburgh the black delegates met none of the more blatant examples of racism that they had experienced four years earlier at Buffalo. As one observer explained, the white delegates "were far more ready to welcome to their platform the man of sable hue." At the convention Douglass observed that he could support the movement as long as its liberal principles were sustained. Later he told his readers that he was favorably impressed by Hale as "a dreaded foe to slavery" and by Julian as one of "the truest and most disinterested friends of freedom." After the Liberty meeting in September, however, he endorsed Smith's views and supported Goodell for president. Douglass

[34] Adams, Diary, August 11, 12, 1852, Adams to Sumner, August 15, 1852, in Adams Papers; Foner, "Politics and Prejudices," 251-52; Clarke, *George Julian,* 123.

thus recognized the fact that Smith and Goodell had rejected white supremacy, while the great majority of Free Democrats accepted the view of Bailey's *National Era* that an antislavery northerner should not be expected "to admit a black man to his table for the sake of consistency."[35]

As a result of the refusual of Douglass and others of his race to support the Free Democrats, free black allegiance was divided between Hale and the Liberty party. Rallies by blacks in Boston, including as speakers J. C. Beman, William Watkins, and Jermain Loguen, praised the Free Democratic candidates and called on voters to advance the cause of antislavery by supporting the party. The speakers believed, as did many blacks, that as inadequate as the platform and ideals of the Free Democrats might be, they were the only hope their race had in their struggle to end slavery. Many blacks agreed with Douglass's earlier position that "what is morally right is not at all times politically possible." On the other hand, the more militant, including Douglass, argued that since the Free Democrats were unwilling to work to end slavery immediately or to fight for equality they did not deserve the support of blacks.[36] Thus blacks as well as whites in the antislavery movement were divided between the more practical and the more idealistic.

Ignoring the black reaction and the challenge from the Liberty party, the Free Democrats campaigned hard to make an impressive showing against the major parties. One persistent theme ran through all of their rallies: both Whigs and Democrats were controlled by southern interests which had decreed that there should be no further agitation on sectional issues. To the Free Democrats, Pierce and the Democrats were more thoroughly dominated by the South than their Whig opponents. Some third-party men had shown an interest in Scott before the adoption of the Whig platform and, realizing that Seward's influence was still important, hesitated to attack Scott. In addition, Pierce was the strong favorite to win, and there seemed little point in

[35] *Frederick Douglass' Paper*, April 8, August 20, October 15, 1852, quoted in Wesley, "The Participation of Negroes," 64-67; *Reunion of the Free Soilers at Downers Landing*, 43; *National Era*, August 12, 1852; Quarles, *Frederick Douglass*, 147-50.

[36] Quarles, *Black Abolitionists*, 186-87; *Liberator*, December 10, 1852; *Frederick Douglass' Paper*, September 10, 1852.

attacking the underdog. Free Democrats felt that Democratic endorsement of the Compromise was stronger and more sincere than the Whig,
and as a result, they had further reason to concentrate on Pierce.[37]

More important, Free Democratic orators opposed anyone who endorsed the finality of the Compromise and especially the Fugitive Slave
Law. Noting the first anniversary of the rescue of the fugitive Jerry in
Syracuse, Adams called it unfortunate that respectable citizens must
rejoice at the successful resistance to a law. They must continue to
attack those who were responsible for the law: "Theirs is the fault if
we are obliged to rejoice that tyranny in whatever shape it may appear
has been foiled of its prey."[38]

Yet no matter how hard Free Democrats campaigned and tried to
arouse the people against the Compromise, they were met with apathy.
The electorate seemed intent on believing that Congress had achieved
a final settlement of the sectional issues. Tired of the agitation which
had begun with the Texas issue, the country had experienced almost a
decade of continual crisis and seemed eager to believe the politicians'
words concerning the Compromise. The average northerner was eager
to avoid conflict between North and South, and not being committed to
an attack on slavery if it meant upsetting the sectional equilibrium, he
preferred to reject the pleas of the Free Democrats. Giddings argued
that Democrats and Whigs were uniting to keep the truth from the
public eye because debate would endanger the future success of their
organizations. To him, the primary issue was that of human freedom,
and he contended that his party would continue to agitate until the
"great and holy purpose" was accomplished.[39] For the most part, however, the words of Giddings and other Free Democratic orators were
not heard.

When the Free Democrats found the people unwilling to listen to
their attacks on the Compromise, they often turned to other problems.
Shifting somewhat to meet political needs, they thus sometimes ignored

---

[37] Nevins, *Ordeal of the Union*, II, 29-35; Smith, *The Liberty and Free Soil
Parties*, 250-55; William B. Hesseltine, *The Rise and Fall of Third Parties from
Antimasonry to Wallace* (Washington, 1948), 45-46; Boston *Commonwealth*, No-
vember 2, 1852.

[38] Adams to Samuel May, September 30, 1852, in Adams Papers.

[39] *Congressional Globe*, 32nd Cong., 1st Sess., Appendix, 738; Hamilton, *Prologue to Conflict*, 184-85.

what they regarded as the real issue in a desperate search for votes. In the Midwest they stressed the ever-present problem of internal improvements and charged that Pierce as president would continue the policy of James K. Polk in vetoing all bills providing federal assistance. They talked of the homestead issue, again appealing to midwesterners with the demand that land "should be granted in limited quantities, free of cost, to landless settlers." Much of the support that the Free Soilers had received from labor returned to the Democratic party with the Barnburners, but the Free Democrats often spoke of the "Free Labor" pledge in their platform when addressing crowds of workers.[40] Whatever issue they chose, however, they aroused little interest in a rather quiet and listless campaign.

The Free Democratic effort was significant in that Hale and Julian themselves did extensive campaigning in various areas. In 1848 Van Buren had followed custom and had done no campaigning, preferring to rely on his reputation and other speakers. Adams had spoken on a limited scale but only in Massachusetts. In 1852, the party leaders felt that the candidates, lacking established reputations, must go before the people personally to have any effect. Hale spoke in New York before touring parts of the Midwest with Julian. Heavy stress was placed on Wisconsin because of its strong support in 1848. Hale spoke in six Wisconsin cities and Julian in four. Audiences there were large and enthusiastic, and the candidates made a substantial impression. One newspaper caustically contrasted their efforts with the inaction of Pierce and remarked that he was not campaigning because it would be a risk to the Democratic party. Julian displayed great courage by speaking to unfriendly crowds in three Kentucky counties at the invitation of Cassius Clay. In his own state he spoke in Terre Haute shortly after the Free Democratic candidate for governor had been mobbed by a hostile crowd.[41] The party, however, again lacked the local organization

[40] Clinton Fair, "Internal Improvements and Sectional Controversy," (M.A. thesis, University of Wisconsin, 1937), 54; Milwaukee *Daily Sentinel*, July 23, 1852; Madison *Daily Argus and Democrat*, July 26, August 10, 1852; Porter and Johnson (comps.), *National Party Platforms*, 18-20.

[41] Smith, *The Liberty and Free Soil Parties*, 255; Racine *Advocate*, October 6, 1852; *Wisconsin Free Democrat*, October 20, 1852; Kenosha *Telegraph*, October 8, 1852; Clarke, *George Julian*, 133-36; Julian, *Political Recollections*, 126-32; Sewell, *John P. Hale*, 148-49; Riddleberger, *George Julian*, 86-88.

and financial resources so necessary to provide direction to a national campaign, and even the candidates' enthusiasm could not make up for these failures. Four years of declining fortunes, the defection of the Barnburners, and the maneuvering of opportunists like Chase were difficult handicaps to overcome in a three-month campaign.

As the campaign progressed, the third-party members suffered most from the silent treatment given them by both Democrats and Whigs. This had not been their fate in 1848 when they had a prominent candidate and were a distinct threat to effect the election outcome. Now, having long since rejoined the Democrats, the Barnburners especially tried to pretend that the Free Democrats did not exist. Yet the New York *Evening Post,* a leading Free Soil paper in 1848, admitted that it much preferred the third-party platform to the Democratic one. William Cullen Bryant and John Bigelow noted that, as editors of a pragmatic paper, they must support Pierce since Hale had no chance and the Whigs must be defeated. This had not been their view when Van Buren was the Free Soil candidate and they had known that he too had little chance of victory. The editors' views then appeared to the Free Democrats to be an insincere rationalization for not supporting Hale. Bryant admitted privately that "a journal belonging to a large party has infinitely more influence than when it is the organ of a small conclave." Finding they could say little honestly for Pierce, they confined themselves to attacks on Scott while largely ignoring Hale.[42]

The position of the *Evening Post* was typical of most former third-party leaders in New York, for the Democrats in the state as in most of the rest of the nation entered the campaign united as they had not been since 1840. Barnburners and Hunkers alike were intent on enjoying the fruits of their expected victory and would not permit the agitations of the Free Democrats to concern them. Largely ignoring their 1848 revolt, the Barnburners talked only of a Democratic victory. When Salmon P. Chase pleaded with Van Buren to resist the compromise platform of the Democrats and "raise a warning voice against the tendency to reaction in 1852," Van Buren's only response was a letter to a New York City Tammany Hall celebration in which he called for

<hr/>

[42] New York *Evening Post,* June-November, 1852. See especially August 18, September 20, 1852; Margaret Clapp, *Forgotten First Citizen: John Bigelow* (Boston, 1947), 90-95; John Bigelow, *William Cullen Bryant* (Boston, 1890), 105n.

Democratic unity and the election of Pierce. He expressed pleasure that "the disturbing subject of slavery has by the action of both the great parties of the country, been withdrawn from the canvass." In Van Buren's view the party he had led in 1848 was not even worthy of mention. Motivated by considerations unrelated to anti-extension principle, he had entered the Free Soil movement in 1848 for primarily political reasons — reasons which no longer existed in 1852. He later rationalized that in 1852, the Democrats, seeing by experience "the destructive tendency of slavery agitations resolved to avoid them in the future." He even could argue that the election was fought on old and time-honored principles.[43]

Other Barnburners had more difficulty in explaining their support of the Democratic platform, but some nevertheless campaigned for the party much more actively. Preston King had to suppress his "strong repugnance to the miserable slavery resolutions foisted into the platform by the compromisers" before he could speak for Pierce. "If he is a friend of the compromise measures," King rationalized, "he will be found to be equally firm as the enemy of slave propagandism. I believe he will make the Compromise keep the Territories free." John A. Dix delivered at least twenty major addresses endorsing the Democratic nominees.[44]

One of the leading Free Soil campaigners of 1848, John Van Buren, now called for Pierce's election because the country was tired of the sectional agitation. The Compromise should be enforced, for slavery, according to young Van Buren, had ceased to be a political issue. Although many Barnburners did not really believe in the Compromise they had to claim to be satisfied in order to find justification to return to the two-party system and the political influence that it would bring them. Democratic unity and victory were now John Van Buren's only concern: "The covenant of peace on the slavery question entered into at Baltimore I thought wise for the country and indispensable for the democratic party. Northern and Southern democrats differ, utterly

[43] New York *Evening Post*, July 7, 1852; Chase to Martin Van Buren, June 27, 1852, Martin Van Buren to Chase, July 7, 1852, Martin Van Buren to Tammany Society, July 1, 1852, in Van Buren Papers; Van Buren, *Political Parties*, 354-55.

[44] King to Flagg, August 16, September 30, 1852, in Flagg Papers, Columbia University; King to Welles, June 12, July 3, 1852, in Welles Papers; Lichterman, "John A. Dix," 239-40; Dix, *Memoirs of John Adams Dix*, I, 268-69.

differ, on the whole subject of slavery. What then can be done? Why drop the subject, it is the only way to avoid a quarrel."[45] For the Barnburners as for many other Free Soil Democrats, there seemed little reason to hold out against the party they had belonged to so long. Unable to support Lewis Cass in 1848 because of his role in Van Buren's defeat in 1844, they had long since achieved their revenge and had restored themselves to positions of substantial influence in the Democratic party. They had certainly not made that party an anti-extension organization as they had hoped, but they could now expect to influence Franklin Pierce as president.

For similar reasons Marcus Morton led the return of a large group of Massachusetts Free Soilers to the Democratic party in 1852. Morton displayed an extremely short memory by claiming that he had never joined the third party in 1848. He noted that he considered the Free Democratic leaders of Massachusetts to be "the worst Whigs of the state," ignoring the fact that many of these same leaders had cooperated closely with the Democrats since 1848. Desiring renewed influence in his old party, he conveniently forgot the Democratic endorsement of the Compromise and "rejoiced at the nomination of Gen. Pierce because it opened the door to the return of Free Soilers to their proper position in the Democratic party." Not surprisingly, many Free Democrats considered themselves lucky to be rid of the Morton and Van Buren factions and reduced to a more dedicated group.[46]

Since Democrats and Whigs succeeded in preventing discussion of controversial issues, the campaign became hopelessly dull. The major parties confined themselves to comparing personalities and trading insults to prove the qualifications or lack of qualifications of Pierce and Scott. Abuse was the order of the day as the candidates were branded as cowards, drunkards, and bigots. The *National Era* observed: "The coarsest abuse of the candidates of the opposing party, little tales of what General Pierce once did and what General Scott once said, appeals to sectarian prejudice — any claptrap forms the staple of party appeals. The discussion of the great question, the only vital one, is

[45] Alexander, *A Political History of New York*, II, 177-78; John Van Buren to Jeremiah Clemens, February 3, 1854, quoted in New York *Evening Post*, February 11, 1854.

[46] Morton to John Van Buren, February 7, October 4, 1852, Morton to Franklin Pierce, December 6, 1852, in Morton Papers; *National Era*, August 12, October 14, 1852.

Table 2.   1852 PRESIDENTIAL ELECTION RETURNS

State	Popular Vote			Hale's Percentage	Electors	
	Pierce	Scott	Hale		Pierce	Scott
Alabama	26,881	15,038			9	
Arkansas	12,173	7,404			4	
California	40,626	35,407	100	.13	4	
Connecticut	33,249	30,359	3,160	4.73	6	
Delaware	6,318	6,293	62	.49	3	
Florida	4,318	2,875			3	
Georgia	34,705	16,660			10	
Illinois	80,597	64,934	9,966	6.41	11	
Indiana	95,340	80,901	6,929	3.78	13	
Iowa	17,763	15,856	1,604	4.55	4	
Kentucky	53,806	57,068	265	.24		12
Louisiana	18,647	17,255			6	
Maine	41,609	32,543	8,030	9.77	8	
Maryland	40,020	35,066	281	.37	8	
Massachusetts	44,569	52,683	28,023	21.82		13
Michigan	41,842	33,859	7,237	8.73	6	
Mississippi	26,876	17,548			7	
Missouri	38,353	29,984			9	
New Hampshire	29,997	16,147	6,695	12.67	5	
New Jersey	44,305	38,556	350	.32	7	
New York	262,083	234,882	25,329	4.86	35	
North Carolina	39,744	39,058	59	.07	10	
Ohio	169,220	152,526	31,682	8.99	23	
Pennsylvania	198,568	179,174	8,525	2.20	27	
Rhode Island	8,735	7,626	644	3.79	4	
South Carolina	(*)				8	
Tennessee	57,018	58,898				12
Texas	13,552	4,995			4	
Vermont	13,044	22,173	8,621	19.67		5
Virginia	73,858	58,572	291	.22	15	
Wisconsin	33,658	22,240	8,814	13.66	5	
TOTALS	1,601,474	1,386,580	156,667	4.94	254	42

SOURCE: Stanwood, *A History of the Presidency*, 257; Petersen, *A Statistical History*, 32.
* Electors appointed by the legislature.

carefully avoided."[47] Try as they might, Hale and the Free Democrats could not overcome the handicap of being ignored by their opponents.

[47] Roseboom, *The Civil War Era*, 269-71; Roy Franklin Nichols, *Franklin Pierce: Young Hickory of the Granite Hills* (Philadelphia, 1958), 208-10; *National Era*, October 21, 1852.

The outcome of the election of 1852 brought few surprises, with Pierce winning without difficulty in both the popular and electoral votes. In the Democratic sweep, Scott carried only four states — Massachusetts, Vermont, Kentucky, and Tennessee. The Free Democratic vote was slightly more than 150,000 — a little more than half of the party's 1848 total. The third party had received only about 5 percent of the total popular vote, also approximately half of its comparable 1848 figure. The major party effort to play down sectional issues had been at least partially successful although there were still a substantial number of Americans who were not willing to accept the Compromise as the final solution to the nation's problems. The distribution of the vote indicated that the Free Democratic vote did not decline substantially outside of New York where their support dropped from 120,000 to 25,000. In contrast, the Free Democrats of the entire Midwest lost only about 15,000 from their 1848 vote although because the total popular vote there increased significantly, the third-party percentage in some areas was down substantially. In the South the slave states of Delaware, Kentucky, Maryland, Virginia, and North Carolina, all but the latter of which had sent delegates to Pittsburgh, provided close to a thousand votes for the party, a more than four-fold increase over the 1848 results. The southern acceptance of slavery then was clearly not unanimous. Thus despite the overall Free Democratic decline, the results were far from discouraging. As Julian pointed out, much of the vote of 1848 had not come from truly dedicated men but rather from men devoted only to Van Buren. The vote for Hale, however, represented the real strength of the third-party movement. Perhaps a more meaningful comparison showed the Free Democratic vote of 1852 to be more than two and a half times that of the Liberty party in 1844.[48]

Even more significant for the future of the Free Democrats was the fact that the Whig party had been thoroughly crushed, and many people realized immediately it would never recover. With its great leaders Clay and Webster dead, with dissatisfaction strong among its members both North and South, the party had been badly divided over

[48] Stanwood, *A History of the Presidency*, 257; Julian, *Political Recollections*, 132; Roseboom, *The Civil War Era*, 272. The Liberty party candidate, William Goodell, received 1,381 votes, all of them in New York. See Burnham, *Presidential Ballots*, 933.

both its candidate and its platform, and there seemed to be little to support it for the future. The Boston *Commonwealth*, noting the general falling away of its followers, called the election the beginning of the end for the Whigs, although William H. Seward insisted: "No new party will arise, nor will any old one fall." To the Free Democrats, the prospects were indeed promising. "The Democratic party now comes into power on ultra pro-slavery ground. And the Whigs are eliminated," Adams observed. "Of course one great obstacle is removed from us. And we no longer are the third party of the nation."[49] Unknowingly, Adams was in effect forseeing the formation of the Republican party.

In several states the Free Democrats waged an enthusiastic campaign for various state and congressional offices, although in most cases the results were discouraging. In a few areas where they had maintained a separate organization since 1848 the party could enter on an equal footing with Democrats and Whigs, but in too many instances organization had disintegrated after 1848 as the individual members rejoined their old parties. In such cases resurgence efforts were hampered by the lack of an organizational base, although coalition again played a significant role in some third-party successes. In other cases factionalism within the movement cost the party dearly. As in the past, failure to emphasize local issues hurt the Free Democrats, especially with so much of the public intent on believing or rationalizing that sectional issues had been resolved.

In Massachusetts, support of the Compromise by the national Democratic party gravely endangered the future of the coalition. In their state convention Democrats endorsed the national platform without mention of either the Compromise or the coalition. Since they had held the governorship for two years, it was now assumed that it was the turn of the Free Democrats in 1852. This made Democratic cooperation less likely, for influential leaders within the party, including Caleb Cushing, Marcus Morton, and Benjamin Hallett, opposed a continuation of the coalition and claimed that the national party position precluded it.[50]

[49] Boston *Commonwealth*, November 4, 1852; Seward to Sumner, November 9, 1852, in Sumner Papers; Adams, Diary, November 3, 1852, in Adams Papers.
[50] Boston *Post*, September 10, 25, November 25, 1852; Fuess, *Caleb Cushing*, II, 123-25; Harrington, *Nathaniel Banks*, 15-16; Morton to John Van Buren, October 4, 1852, Morton to Azariah Flagg, December 6, 1852, in Morton Papers.

Given the attitude of these men, it is likely that even had it not been the year of a presidential election, they would have found some reason for not supporting a coalition which would put a Free Democrat in the governor's chair. With little to be gained politically from the coalition and with the general mood of acquiescence in the Compromise so widespread, the Free Democrats should not have been surprised that political considerations took precedence with the Democrats.

The mere possibility of the election of a Free Democratic governor nevertheless gave the third-party men an added incentive for an active campaign. Many felt that the logical choice for the office was John G. Palfrey, the sacrificial candidate of a year earlier. Immediately, however, there was opposition from the Wilson faction, interested in nominating Wilson himself and arguing that Palfrey's firm opposition to the coalition made him unacceptable. Adams was thoroughly disgusted by the constant maneuvers of the overly aggressive and ambitious Wilson: "Now that it was supposed possible to get a place, Mr. Palfrey was to be unceremoniously shoved aside.... Our party is now as corrupt as either of the others, if not more corrupt." Although unable to obtain Palfrey's nomination, the Adams faction blocked Wilson and nominated Horace Mann in his place. Mann, after refusing to support Van Buren in 1848, had finally joined the third party in 1850 because of his disgust with Whig policies. Yet he was firmly opposed to Wilson's domination of the party, and his nomination indicated that Wilson's control had not been as great as some had feared.[51] Nevertheless, the Free Democratic convention revealed the party to be more divided than ever.

In spite of Pierce's election, Scott won Massachusetts and the Whigs returned to power in the state by winning an absolute majority of ten in the legislature. Thus the coalition was defeated, the legislature elected John H. Clifford, the Whig candidate, as governor, and there was no occasion to test whether Democrats would have supported Horace Mann. In addition, the Free Democrats had little success in other contests, but Adams among others had no regrets over the coalition's de-

51 Palfrey to Sumner, July 5, 1852, in Sumner Papers; Adams, Diary, September 6, 10-16, 1852, Palfrey to Adams, September 14, 1852, in Adams Papers; Hoar to Palfrey, September 7, 1852, in Palfrey Papers; Dana, Journal, September 15, 1852, in Dana Papers.

feat. Although it meant that Mann and the party would be denied a chance at the governorship, Adams seemed almost relieved because it represented another blow against Wilson and the coalition. Frustrating "The Natick Cobbler" had become to Adams an end in itself regardless of the effect on the third-party movement. He wrote that Wilson and his followers "were depressed at the downfall of their darling edifice." Adams quickly rationalized that the party might now return to pure free soil ground unhampered by the Democrats.[52]

In congressional races, the Free Democrats campaigned actively, but party factionalism again hampered their efforts. Adams, who had refused to be considered for the presidential nomination because it was such a hopeless race, did run for Congress in his father's old district, where he had a real chance for victory. He thus revealed his political ambition and admitted that "no position would be so personally gratifying to my pride." Not surprisingly his race brought further conflict with Wilson. Adams felt that Wilson had tried to prevent his nomination because of his own anger over losing the gubernatorial nomination. When he lost in the runoff by about four hundred votes, Adams blamed his defeat on the apathy of the Wilson wing. Henry Wilson also ran for Congress but with no better luck, losing in a runoff by one hundred votes.[53] Continued third-party infighting had thus contributed to the loss of two highly valuable seats in Congress.

Other problems kept the Free Democratic factions in Massachusetts at odds, for the campaign seemed to bring out all of the long-simmering feuds within the party. The bitterness between the Adams and Wilson factions surrounding the formation of the coalition in 1850 was not easily forgotten. Unable to run for governor in 1852, Palfrey had sought a nomination for Congress. Henry Wilson again used his influence to prevent it, however, and the party chose an avowed coalitionist in Palfrey's district. Adams, suspecting another bargain with the Democrats, was indignant "at this huckstering and trading." The re-

[52] Bean, "Party Transformations in Massachusetts," 134n; Pierce, *Charles Sumner,* III, 318; Adams, Diary, November 18, 23, 24, 27, 1852, in Adams Papers.

[53] Harrington, "Nathaniel Banks," 633-34; Boston *Post,* November 10, December 16, 1852; Pierce, *Charles Sumner,* III, 318; Adams, Diary, September 16, 17, 21, 25, October 19, 21, November 18, 27, December 16, 22, 1852, in Adams Papers; Nason and Russell, *Henry Wilson,* 97.

fusal of Senator Charles Sumner to campaign for the coalition which
had placed him in office caused further trouble and led Wilson to attack
him in the Boston *Commonwealth*.[54] At year's end, not only had the coalition been shattered by the Whig victory, but bickering within the
Free Democratic party threatened the future success of the entire movement. None of the leaders of the party, including Adams, Wilson,
Sumner, and Palfrey, was capable of rising above his personal feuds to
recognize that the squabbles were doing the third-party cause a great
disservice and allowing the Democrats and Whigs to continue to ignore
pressing sectional issues. This constant quarrelling was in large part
responsible for the fact that in the new Congress there would be no
Free Democrats from Massachusetts in the House.

The Free Democratic campaign for congressional and state offices
in other eastern states was characterized by inactivity rather than factionalism. There were third-party candidates for Congress in some districts, but in few places other than Massachusetts did they make a
respectable showing. Pennsylvania, the scene of the party's convention,
continued far down the list in Free Democratic strength as it had in
1848. The party elected no members of the legislature although it held
its small following in Whig counties. David Wilmot, a leader in the
1848 campaign, was no longer active in politics. Following the Barnburner example, he supported Pierce, "not because we believe in him,
but because in our judgment it is the wisest course to prepare for the
conflict which must come upon the extension of slavery in this country." Galusha Grow, who had replaced Wilmot in Congress in 1850 on
an anti-extension platform, now won reelection by pledging himself "to
resist all attempts at renewing, in Congress or out of it, the agitation
on the slavery question, under whatever shape or color the attempt
may be made."[55] Such sentiments were much in keeping with the attitudes of most Pennsylvania voters.

Some of the other eastern states nominated Free Democratic candidates for governor, and in a few cases the results were encouraging.

[54] Adams, Diary, October 22, November 26, 1852, in Adams Papers; Boston
Commonwealth, November 24, 1852; Pierce, *Charles Sumner*, III, 319; Donald,
Charles Sumner, 239-40.
[55] Mueller, *The Whig Party in Pennsylvania*, 199; Geary, *Third Parties in Penn-
sylvania*, 155; Wilmot and Grow are quoted in DuBois and Mathews, *Galusha
Grow*, 93-95.

Many of the state elections were held at different times from the national election, a factor which hurt a party stressing primarily national issues. A direct comparison is not possible, but in Vermont and New Hampshire the third-party candidates for governor each received more votes than John P. Hale. In New York, the Free Democratic nominee for governor, Minthorne Tompkins, won only 20,000 votes out of more than 520,000 cast. With the Barnburners no longer in the movement there were few Free Democratic candidates for Congress from New York. The major surprise there was the election of the Liberty leader Gerrit Smith to Congress from an upstate district. Smith received wide support from free soil elements of all parties and the black community, but, indicative of the lack of interest in sectional issues, he won more because of his endorsement of a Canadian tariff reciprocity proposal than because of his antislavery views.[56]

Third-party results in the Midwest were more encouraging than elsewhere, but even here the vote did not equal that of 1848. The Western Reserve of Ohio continued to show the greatest antislavery interest by electing two Free Democratic congressmen. Using the census of 1850 as justification, the Ohio legislature had tried to eliminate Joshua Giddings by redistricting. Three free soil Reserve counties were taken from his district and two Democratic counties added. Recognizing his own plight, he called for assistance from his supporters who responded with a "Giddings Festival" in Painesville at which Chase and Hale, among others, lavishly praised the candidate. As a result of this open display of support, Giddings won his eighth consecutive term in the House despite an intensive Whig effort to defeat him. The legislature's move backfired completely when the three counties from Giddings's old district combined to elect another Free Democrat, Edward Wade of Cleveland, over Whig and Democratic opponents.[57]

Outside of the Giddings race, which brought an unusual measure of unity to Ohio Free Democrats, the feud between the Chase and West-

---

[56] *Whig Almanac, 1853*, 49-51; Gerrit Smith to Julian, November 18, 1852, in Giddings-Julian Papers; Harlow, *Gerrit Smith*, 312; Quarles, *Frederick Douglass*, 151-52.

[57] Cleveland *True Democrat*, August 18, October 20, 1852; Smith, *The Liberty and Free Soil Parties*, 258-59; *Whig Almanac, 1853*, 57; Stewart, *Joshua Giddings*, 214-16.

ern Reserve factions continued unabated. As in Massachusetts, party members were more intent on attacking the opposing faction than in uniting to forward the third-party cause. The many disputes of the past four years were difficult to forget. As usual Giddings did his best to maintain party harmony, but only in the Reserve did the party show much life. Extensive campaigning by Hale and Julian in that area added greatly to the strength of the movement, and Hale gained one-third of his total Ohio vote from the six Reserve counties.[58] In the rest of the state, however, the Free Democratic vote was disappointingly small.

In other midwestern states the results brought little satisfaction. In Michigan, the long dormant anti-extension party revived enough to make nominations for some local contests. A state convention in Ann Arbor addressed by Giddings and Samuel Lewis helped renew interest, but the party made a poor showing in both the gubernatorial and congressional races. In Illinois, most Free Democrats supported the Whig candidates for Congress because of their strong opposition to the Compromise; however, in some districts there were separate third-party nominations also. Although Pierce swept the state, the Whigs, with Free Democratic support, won four of the nine Congressional seats. In Indiana, the Free Democrats benefited somewhat from Julian's candidacy, and the party began to revive after three years of inaction. Anti-Compromise sentiment was especially strong in Quaker districts in eastern Indiana, but in other areas third-party meetings were disturbed or broken up by opposition groups. Only in Julian's old district did the party nominate candidates for Congress and here the results were discouraging.[59] In none of these three states had third-party support been especially strong even in 1848. For the most part, the members had sought the security of the two-party system in the period between elections, and the party had virtually disappeared making the task even more difficult in 1852. Thus a lack of organization plus the

[58] Cleveland *True Democrat*, August 25, September 22, 1852; Smith, *The Liberty and Free Soil Parties*, 252-53; Roseboom, *The Civil War Era*, 271.

[59] Streeter, *Political Parties in Michigan*, 158; Cole, *The Era of the Civil War*, 110-11; Wright, "The Republican Party in Illinois," 105-6; Dale Beeler, "The Election of 1852 in Indiana," *Indiana Magazine of History*, XI (1915), 301-23, XII (1916), 34-52; Smith, *The Liberty and Free Soil Parties*, 253-57; *Whig Almanac, 1853*, 59-61.

general voter acceptance of the Compromise reduced the Free Democratic vote to a relatively small number of dedicated men.

The third-party campaign in Wisconsin received a tremendous boost from the visit of Hale and Julian to the state in October, but even this could not prevent the loss of the party's one seat in Congress. The Free Democrats nominated candidates in all three congressional districts but concentrated their efforts on the reelection of Charles Durkee in the southeastern part of the state. Durkee had won his second term in 1850 with the help of a Whig coalition, but in 1852 the presidential campaign made it impossible for the Whigs to endorse him again. In a bitter contest the Free Democrats, led by Sherman M. Booth, charged that the major parties had made a bargain whereby the Whigs would run a candidate simply to assure Durkee's defeat. Although Durkee ran well ahead of Hale in his district, he was defeated as the Democrats swept the state.[60] Unlike the campaigns in Massachusetts and Ohio, where factionalism had been a factor in reducing Free Democratic support, the party effort in Wisconsin was strenuous and united, but was simply not strong enough following its 1849 defections to resist the Compromise trend so prevalent throughout the North.

Thus in most northern states the third party had little to show for its efforts in 1852. It elected only three men to Congress, Giddings, Edward Wade, and Gerrit Smith, and the latter was more a Liberty man than a Free Democrat. In contrast, the party had elected twelve congressmen in 1848. In several other instances in 1852 it supported major party candidates who won election. In most states no third-party candidates gained seats in the state legislature, and in no state did the party hold the balance of power which had brought it limited success after the 1848 election. A combination of local issues, including factionalism and lack of organization, along with a general national weariness with sectional agitation together produced a lack of interest in Free Democratic candidates. Thus although the party's losses in the presidential vote were held to a minimum and many continued to

[60] Smith, *The Liberty and Free Soil Parties,* 254, 256; *Wisconsin Free Democrat,* October 13, 1852; Milwaukee *Daily Wisconsin,* October 13, 1852; Racine *Advocate,* September 29, October 20, 1852; Smith, "The Free Soil Party in Wisconsin," 136-37.

predict a bright future for the Free Democrats, results on the state level provided little encouragement.

The Free Democratic presidential vote in 1852 declined to slightly more than half of the Free Soil total of four years earlier, with about two-thirds of this loss resulting from the return of the New York Barn-burners to the Democratic party. In most other states also the Democrats gained more from the third-party decline than the Whigs, even though the Free Democrats had concentrated their attack on Pierce. This was partly because dissension among the Whigs had made their chances extremely poor from the start. As a result most Whigs who had joined the third party in 1848 continued in it in 1852, and in some areas new Whig converts joined. Many anti-extension Democrats, on the other hand, followed the example of the Barnburners in their desire for immediate office and, despite their distaste for the party's platform, returned to their original party. The lure of a prominent Democrat like Van Buren as leader of the party was now missing and many Democrats found Hale's appeal to be insufficient to keep them loyal to the third party. In the process they indicated that their free soil convictions were perhaps not as strong as those of the Whigs who voted for Hale. In addition, however, with so many people assuming that Pierce would be the winner right from the start, the Democrats had more incentive to return to the party and enjoy the spoils of victory. Whigs, on the other hand, realizing that their chances were poor and that their party was declining, were more inclined to stay with the Free Democrats. Thus practical politics as well as anti-extension convictions were important factors. The Hale-Julian vote included three major sources of support: those Whigs and Democrats who had left their party permanently in 1848; men who had been Liberty party members before 1848; and Whigs who withdrew from their party following the conventions of 1852.[61]

Tracing the origin of the Free Democratic vote in New York provides few surprises. The Hale vote declined to 25,000 from the Van Buren total of 120,000. With every prominent Barnburner endorsing Pierce in 1852, the third party was reduced to the old Liberty element plus Whigs who joined in either 1848 or 1852. The Democrats made

[61] Stanwood, *A History of the Presidency*, 257; Burnham, *Presidential Ballots*, 49; Smith, *The Liberty and Free Soil Parties*, 258.

their biggest gains in areas where the Free Democrats suffered the greatest losses. Some free soil Democrats may have supported Hale, but a comparison of voting figures indicates that the number was probably small. The example of St. Lawrence County, Preston King's stronghold, is representative of what happened throughout the state:

	1844	*1848*	*1852*
Democratic	6,008	614	5,584
Whig	4,672	3,667	4,570
Third Party	468	6,024	1,385

The best third-party showing came in counties in which Liberty candidate James G. Birney won strong support in 1844, indicating that the party had the full support of Liberty elements which had always been most firmly committed to antislavery principle.[62]

In Massachusetts, the Free Democratic strength declined by 10,000 votes, while the Democratic vote increased by more than 8,000 and the Whigs lost more than 8,000. A county-by-county comparison of the two elections shows that many who had supported Van Buren in 1848 followed the example of Marcus Morton and the Barnburners in returning to the Democratic party in 1852. As in New York, the Democrats gained most in those counties where the Free Democratic decline was greatest. The figures for Middlesex County are indicative of the results throughout the state:

	1844	*1848*	*1852*
Democratic	9,124	6,820	8,925
Whig	9,581	9,854	8,750
Third Party	1,718	5,964	4,231

A majority of the Massachusetts Free Democrats were now of the Conscience Whig and Liberty elements, although a substantial Democratic faction remained because of continued interest in the coalition.[63]

[62] Burnham, *Presidential Ballots,* 49, 632-46; *Whig Almanac, 1845,* 54, *1853,* 50.
[63] Stanwood, *A History of the Presidency,* 243, 257; *Whig Almanac, 1853,* 49-51; Bean, "Party Transformations in Massachusetts," 134. The breakdown of the vote by county in these two elections can be found in Burnham, *Presidential Ballots,* 510-12.

In the remainder of the Northeast, Pennsylvania and New Jersey had too small a third-party vote in either election to indicate any trend. In Tioga County, Pennsylvania, however, the area of Wilmot's greatest support in 1848, Free Democratic strength in 1852 was less than 8 percent of what it had been four years earlier, with the Democrats picking up almost all of the difference. In the New England states of Maine and Vermont the Democrats gained more at the expense of the third party while in Connecticut and Rhode Island the Free Democratic vote was too small to be indicative. In Hale's home state of New Hampshire, both major parties gained slightly at the expense of the Free Democrats. The third-party vote declined throughout the Northeast, and the figures indicate that the Democrats gained most from this loss. In some areas, the Whigs lost votes to both Democrats and Free Democrats. Disgusted by their party's platform and disillusioned with its future, some Whigs found Hale more to their liking than they had found Van Buren in 1848.[64]

The source of the Free Democratic vote in the midwestern states is difficult to determine because the rapid increase in population makes comparisons with earlier elections more complex. The westward movement and an increase in European immigration were largely responsible for the population growth. Both Democrats and Whigs increased their votes in 1852, but the former to such a great extent that it is probable that many free soil Democrats left the third party. On the other hand, the Whig increase was small enough in a few areas to indicate that some Whigs may have joined the Free Democrats. The decline of the third party's total vote in the Midwest from the 1848 election was about 20 percent, a figure which is even more significant in light of the great increase in population. The Free Democratic percentage of the total vote declined in each one of the six midwestern states and in two, Illinois and Wisconsin, the decline was by as much as 50 percent.[65]

In Illinois, a county-by-county study shows that the Democrats gained more from the Free Democratic decline than did the Whigs. Many of the Democratic votes lost to the Free Soilers in 1848 were regained in 1852. The figures from Cook County where the third party

<hr/>

[64] Burnham, *Presidential Ballots*, 318-20, 500-504, 624-32, 718, 720, 814-16; Stanwood, *A History of the Presidency*, 243, 257; *Whig Almanac, 1853*, 49-51.

[65] *Whig Almanac, 1853*, 56-61; Smith, *The Liberty and Free Soil Parties*, 258; Stanwood, *A History of the Presidency*, 243, 257.

was relatively strong in both elections are indicative of the trend throughout the state:

	1844	*1848*	*1852*
Democratic	2,027	1,622	3,767
Whig	1,119	1,708	2,089
Third Party	317	2,120	689

Comparative figures for Indiana and Michigan show roughly an equal increase by Whigs and Democrats at the expense of the Free Democrats. In Ohio, Hale did as well as or better than Van Buren in the Western Reserve areas, but the Whigs gained votes at a much faster rate in these counties than either of the other parties. Away from the Western Reserve, however, the Democrats gained more at the expense of the Free Democrats than the Whigs. The example of Hamilton County (Cincinnati) is indicative:

	1848	*1852*
Democratic	10,834	13,207
Whig	9,018	9,253
Third Party	1,986	684

In Wisconsin as well, the Democrats were the bigger gainers at the third party's expense. The example of Rock County is typical of much of the rest of the state:

	1848	*1852*
Democratic	491	1,691
Whig	1,300	1,509
Third Party	1,338	923

Finally, the vote in Iowa was not large enough to show any clear trend.[66] The decline of third-party strength throughout the Midwest was quite substantial and proved that many voters sought to avoid further sectional conflict. As in other parts of the country, improved Democratic chances and a less appealing third-party candidate attracted many anti-extensionists back to their old party.

The interest of Democrats in vigorous opposition to slavery had declined substantially from its peak, and the campaign of 1852 added

[66] Burnham, *Presidential Ballots,* 370, 678-96, 876.

further doubt as to the sincerity of their revolt in 1848. Their free soil activity seemed to decline proportionately with their increased chances for victory. Perhaps feeling they did not have as much to lose, Whigs, on the other hand, were more willing to stress principle and support Hale in 1852. In addition, Van Buren's candidacy, which had held some Whigs back in 1848, was no longer a factor. It would be primarily Whigs and Free Democrats who, not surprisingly, joined with a smaller number of Democrats to form the Republican party in 1854 and 1855. In the meantime, the Free Democrats labored on in 1853 and in some cases increased their strength as Whig fortunes continued to sag.

10

Aftermath:
From Free Democrats
to Republicans

The presidential campaign of 1852 had revealed several trends which would soon bring important changes in the political structure of the nation. The impending collapse of the Whig party, the southern orientation of the Democratic party, and the expanding appeal of the Free Democratic platform would combine to prepare the way for a new more broadly based northern party. The election of 1852 had been a relatively quiet one, as the great majority of Americans had ignored the pleas of Free Democrats and accepted the major party claims that the Compromise of 1850 had settled the outstanding sectional differences. But the next four years proved that the Free Democrats were correct in their contention that the Compromise, instead of settling anything had merely postponed a showdown between North and South. The Whig party, first to feel the effect of the crisis, seemed clearly to face extinction in the near future after a slow and agonizing decline. With the death of Webster and Clay the party now lacked effective leadership which could appeal to both North and South. At the same time, the Democratic party fell more and more under the domination of its southern wing. The South would virtually control the new Pierce administration, leaving many discontented men in the northern Democracy ready to revolt should the proper occasion arise.[1] The reaction of the Free Democrats to the events of 1853 and 1854 was a willingness to abandon their own party and become a part of

[1] Craven, *The Growth of Southern Nationalism*, 140.

a much larger movement designed in part to accomplish their own original purpose of containing slavery in the South.

Because of the changing political situation and despite its poor showing in the presidential race, the Free Democratic party emerged from the election of 1852 in a relatively strong position. It had not done as well as in 1848 but it had revived free soil interest somewhat from the apathy of 1850 and 1851. Its platform in 1852 had talked of economic issues such as tariffs, internal improvements, and homestead legislation, and had thus presented a broad appeal. The Free Democrats now expected to gain as the weakened and still feuding Whig party declined. Julian wrote: "The antislavery movement is bringing forth such visible fruits that the whole land must ere long witness and acknowledge its power. The Whig party is hopelessly prostrated." Joshua Leavitt predicted that the results of the election would make the Free Democracy the radical party which would "carry the country in four years if not eight."[2] Yet few Free Democrats denied that an anti-extension party much larger than their own was now possible.

The year 1853 brought a deceptive calm in sectional agitation. Although the Compromise spirit had won an impressive victory in Pierce's election, the forces of discontent were increasing everywhere. Over three hundred thousand copies of *Uncle Tom's Cabin* had been sold by the end of 1853 and sales were increasing. The South seemed in a defensive mood as it strove for sectional unity, while northern resistance to the Fugitive Slave Law continued to upset southerners. The situation seemed only to need a spark to bring the increasing tensions to a climax. This spark would not come until early 1854 when the introduction of the Kansas-Nebraska bill brought renewed agitation over slavery extension and the creation of a new political party. In the meantime, in 1853, the Whigs remained demoralized by their defeat and were inactive. The Free Democrats continued to agitate, however, and increase their influence. With no serious sectional debate in Congress to give them a forum for their program, they lacked the publicity they needed. With no nationwide or even congressional elec-

<hr>

[2] Julian to F. W. Bird, April 23, 1853, in Giddings-Julian Papers; Joshua Leavitt to R. H. Leavitt, November 12, 1852, in Leavitt Papers, Library of Congress.

tions, it is difficult to estimate the party's exact strength, but in this last year of its life it made the best showing in its brief six-year history.[3]

The Free Democrats were more successful in the Midwest in 1853 than anywhere else, and in Ohio and Wisconsin the party did especially well. With numerous Whigs joining the movement in 1852, the Ohio Free Democrats in that election had almost matched their vote of 1848. They felt that at last they had won a permanent place in Ohio politics. Wasting no time, they met in January, 1853, to nominate a candidate for governor for the fall election. The members assembled in a spirit of great enthusiasm, realizing that success could be imminent. The convention was one of great harmony, and past differences were almost forgotten. The delegates adopted a strong platform which included endorsement of free trade, temperance, and black suffrage. On the latter issue, the party in its national platform of 1852 had emphatically rejected equality for blacks as had the Ohio constitutional convention of 1850-1851, but the Ohio party under the leadership of Lewis, Giddings, and Chase was willing to take a much more advanced position. The members persuaded Samuel Lewis to run again for governor and passed resolutions commending both Giddings and Chase.[4] The delegates fully realized that if they could maintain party unity they could take full advantage of Whig apathy and become the second strongest party of the state.

The Free Democrats waged a strenuous campaign. Chase, Giddings, and Lewis visited every county in the state, including many that had never shown any interest in free soil. Often they emphasized temperance rather than slavery in their appeal for support, both because they were strong temperance advocates and because they knew it had great voter appeal. The Whigs, revealing their apathy, in a poorly attended convention avoided all mention of sectional issues. During the campaign there was widespread talk of fusion of the Free Democrats and Whigs because each realized it had no chance for victory by itself. Coalition tickets were arranged in some areas, and the Free Democratic

[3] Smith, *The Liberty and Free Soil Parties,* 261; Craven, *The Coming of the Civil War,* 323-24.

[4] Cleveland *True Democrat,* November 17, 1852, January 12, 19, 26, 1853; *National Era,* January 20, 27, 1853; Chase to E. S. Hamlin, February 4, 1853, in Chase Papers, Library of Congress; Roseboom, *The Civil War Era,* 275.

candidate for lieutenant governor withdrew in favor of the Whig. But
the Whigs were not yet ready to surrender their old party ties or to
endorse fully the Free Democratic views on free soil and temperance.
In addition, some Free Democrats such as Chase were less than enthusiastic over the proposed union, and the idea proceeded no further.[5]

The Chase faction, which had always been inclined toward Democratic fusion in the past, would find it very difficult to accept coalition
with a party whose ideas it had opposed for so long. Yet, with the
Democrats so firmly in power it would be fruitless to try to negotiate
a coalition with them. Thus to Chase, the future now lay in winning
over both Democrats and Whigs to the third-party point of view rather
than fusion with either party. "I am myself well satisfied that an
Independent Democracy, thoroughly organized and appealing alike to
Liberal Whigs and liberal democrats to unite in its action . . . could do
our work best," wrote Chase. With the political realities in mind and
his own future in the Senate at stake, even Chase was beginning to see
that future cooperation with the Whigs was more promising than ever
before. In this he was typical of most Ohio Free Soilers. Given the
rapidly changing structure of Ohio politics, by 1853 he had ceased
switching parties and trying to change the Democrats and sought
instead to persuade both Whigs and Democrats to join the Free
Democrats.[6]

The election returns gave the Free Democrats the best showing they
had ever made in Ohio. Lewis carried six counties and received more
than fifty thousand votes or about 18 percent of the total; the Democrats swept to an easy victory as expected, but the Whig decline was
staggering. The Whigs received only 30 percent of the vote with the
returns indicating that many had switched to the Free Democratic
party. The national party's defeat in 1852 and the lack of leadership
displayed by Ohio Whigs then and in 1853 had convinced many that
the Free Democrats could better represent their interests. The third
party in fact appeared to be in a good position to overtake the Whigs
and become the second party of Ohio. The Democratic sweep, how-

---

[5] Lewis, *Samuel Lewis*, 405-15; Cleveland *True Democrat*, June-November,
1853; Smith, *The Liberty and Free Soil Parties*, 268-74; Roseboom, *The Civil
War Era*, 276.

[6] Chase to E. S. Hamlin, February 4, July 21, 1853, in Chase Papers, Library of
Congress.

ever, did have the immediate result of costing the Free Democrats their seat in the United States Senate. Chase had naturally hoped that his party would hold the balance of power in the new legislature in order to give him a chance for reelection, but his hopes were to be shattered. Although the Free Democrats elected thirteen members to the legislature, the Democrats won an absolute majority.[7]

The ambitious Chase who constantly sought to enhance his own political position had wanted to return to the Senate to try "to redeem the state" from its connections with slavery. He saw the impossibility of reforming the state Democratic party when that party endorsed the Compromise in early 1854. Also, as the Pierce administration looked more and more to the South for direction, his dreams of an anti-extension Democratic party were further shattered. The Democratic legislature soon chose George E. Pugh to replace him in the Senate, thus giving Chase one more reason to seek Whig cooperation in the free soil movement. He would now be ready to support a coalition with the Whigs.[8] The election of 1853 had provided an important first step in the combining of Free Democrats and Whigs into a more general anti-extension party. "Thousands of Liberal Whigs separated from their party in 1848 and acted with the Independent Democrats," observed the *National Era*. "Thousands have this year followed their example; thousands more are now ready to join the new party."[9]

The situation in Wisconsin roughly paralleled that of Ohio as the Free Democrats and Whigs overcame many of their past differences and moved hesitatingly toward fusion. In a weak position in 1851, the Free Democrats had declined to nominate anyone for governor and had agreed instead to back the Whig candidate, L. J. Farwell. However, with the Whigs of Wisconsin so badly beaten in 1852, the third party was now in a much stronger position and would have more to say about the terms of any proposed union. Sherman Booth perhaps went too far when he announced that only if the Whigs dissolved their organization or adopted the Pittsburgh platform would the Free

---

[7] *Whig Almanac, 1854,* 62-63; Chase to Hamlin, December 21, 1853, in Chase Papers, Library of Congress.

[8] Chase to Edward Pierce, January 17, 1854, Chase to Hamlin, January 22, 1854, in Bourne (ed.), "Chase Correspondence," 252-56.

[9] *National Era,* December 1, 1853.

Democrats agree to cooperation. Nevertheless, had Governor Farwell been agreeable to renomination, fusion would have proceeded smoothly. When Farwell declined to run, the Free Democrats nominated one of their own members, E. D. Holton, and hoped the Whigs would endorse him. At first the Whigs chose their own candidate, but as their campaign lagged and party leadership failed to develop, just two weeks before the election they agreed somewhat reluctantly to support Holton.[10]

Already in a badly weakened position, the Whigs finally concluded that their differences with the Free Democrats were minor and that only through fusion could the Democrats be defeated. By agreeing to a strong anti-extension position and thus rejecting their national party's platform, the Whigs of Wisconsin in effect were demonstrating that there was little reason not to unite with the Free Democrats. In 1853, however, their action came too late to bring immediate success, but more important, the two parties had agreed to forget their differences and take common ground. This could only be regarded as a Free Democratic victory since fusion was achieved on the basis of the third party's position on slavery.[11] Coalition was rapidly becoming a reality in the two key states of Ohio and Wisconsin, where the Whigs had proven especially weak in resisting the Democrats and where the Free Democrats had shown themselves capable of filling this vacuum with strong anti-extension leadership.

In the other midwestern states the lack of statewide elections forestalled immediate cooperation of Whigs and Free Democrats. But everywhere the Whigs were stunned by their defeat of 1852, while the Free Democrats, encouraged by the prospects, continued to agitate. In Indiana, taking advantage of the Whig decline, the third party increased its vote in the spring elections of 1853 and strengthened its organization in the ensuing months. Under George Julian's leadership the party found new support in eastern Indiana and established itself as a permanent political force throughout the state.[12] Illinois, Michi-

10 *Wisconsin State Journal*, May 21, 1853; Smith, *The Liberty and Free Soil Parties*, 279-83.
11 *Whig Almanac, 1854*, 63; Smith, "The Free Soil Party in Wisconsin," 138-50.
12 Smith, *The Liberty and Free Soil Parties*, 263-64; Clarke, *George W. Julian*, 139; George W. Julian, *Speeches on Political Questions* (New York, 1872), 83-101.

gan, and Iowa Free Democrats followed the example of their midwestern colleagues and worked successfully to strengthen their party organization. In these states no fusion with the Whigs was attempted, but throughout the area the two parties became more tolerant of each other than ever before. For the most part, the Whigs refused to abide by their national convention's endorsement of the Compromise and awaited the proper opportunity to assume more advanced free soil ground. Under these circumstances complete fusion with the Free Democrats was just a matter of time.[13]

In the East there were fewer signs of agreement between Whigs and Free Democrats in 1853, and in some states relations worsened. In Massachusetts, the most important third-party state outside of the Midwest, the Whigs, long the dominant party, had resisted the national trend and won the election of 1852. The Whig inclination of the majority of voters had been strengthened by the party's willingness to take a relatively strong anti-extension stand, a situation which had naturally hurt the chances of the Free Democrats. Now, because of their continued control, the Whigs saw no need to cooperate with the third party. The persistent Free Democratic interest in a Democratic coalition and Henry Wilson's domination over his party also helped to prevent cooperation with the Whigs. Although the coalition had been defeated in 1852, it had, over Whig opposition, persuaded the voters to endorse a call for a state constitutional convention. The issue of a new constitution kept the political situation in Massachusetts in constant turmoil throughout 1853 and drove the Whigs and Free Democrats further apart.[14]

There was a definite need for reform of the Massachusetts constitution, a document which had been in effect since 1780. Originally written by John Adams, it had adequately met the needs of the Revolutionary Era but needed modification because of the many changes of the nineteenth century. The lower house had grown unwieldy and was malapportioned, heavily favoring rural areas. A general ticket system

[13] Cole, *The Era of the Civil War,* 219-20; Wright, "The Republican Party in Illinois," 133-41; Streeter, *Political Parties in Michigan,* 158-59; Smith, *The Liberty and Free Soil Parties,* 264-66.

[14] Pierce, *Charles Sumner,* III, 325; Bean, "Party Transformations in Massachusetts," 135.

allowed the Whigs to dominate Boston representation completely, and the absolute majority requirement meant that the legislature often had to decide the gubernatorial elections as well as those in many of the legislative districts. There were demands for other constitutional reforms, including, among others, general incorporation provisions and popular election of judges. The conservative constitution had blocked the way to change in many areas, but unfortunately many Democrats and Free Democrats viewed the convention more as a way to destroy Whig power than to enact any valuable and lasting reforms. Not all third-party men agreed with this aim, and the resulting struggle drove the Adams-Palfrey faction out of the party, leaving Henry Wilson in complete control. It also permanently shattered Wilson's coalition with the Democrats.[15]

Following voter approval of the convention call, elections were held in the spring of 1853 to choose delegates. The result was a large coalition majority in favor of reform. To Wilson this meant that final defeat of the Whigs was now possible: "Most of their [Whig] leaders know it — and they admit it — that the State has passed out of their hands. . . . The Free Soilers now have it in their power to place the party in a strong position — to take the control of affairs." The Boston *Commonwealth* optimistically predicted "the final overthrow of Whiggery in Massachusetts." Yet the election of delegates again drew attention to the continuing feud between the two Free Democratic factions. Almost every prominent politician in the state except Adams and Palfrey won election to the convention. Adams was defeated with the aid of the Irish voters in Quincy and as usual blamed the "rotten . . . treachery" of Henry Wilson for his misfortunes. Because of Adams' expected opposition to reform, Wilson was no doubt relieved to have him beaten, although he told Sumner: "I deeply regret the defeat of Adams but it could not be helped. I tried to induce the Irish to vote for him, but it could not be accomplished." Wilson, Dana, and Sumner would represent the Free Democratic leadership at the convention.[16]

---

[15] Samuel Shapiro, "The Conservative Dilemma: The Massachusetts Constitutional Convention of 1853," *New England Quarterly*, XXXIII (1960), 207-10; Donald, *Charles Sumner*, 245; Gatell, *John G. Palfrey*, 213-14.

[16] Shapiro, "The Conservative Dilemma," 211-12; Adams, Diary, March 7, 16, 1853, in Adams Papers; Wilson to Sumner, March 10, 1853, in Sumner Papers; Adams, *Richard Henry Dana*, I, 234; Pierce, *Charles Sumner*, III, 326-27.

The constitution produced by the convention represented a brazen attempt to destroy the Whig control over Massachusetts and place the coalition firmly in power. The provisions abandoned all property requirements for voting and office holding; limited the terms of some judges and required some to face popular election; and, in an open attempt to take power from the Whigs, abolished the general ticket system in Boston. Henry Wilson's complicated scheme to reapportion the legislature so as to lessen the influence of the cities, the centers of Whig power, was also accepted. Because Massachusetts had already removed most of its remaining discriminatory provisions against blacks, race was not an issue at the convention as it had been in Ohio. Blacks had long voted in Massachusetts, while in Ohio the Free Democrats had achieved little in that direction. The Massachusetts delegates rejected a much needed plurality provision for gubernatorial and congressional elections because it would have benefited the largest party — the Whig. Those supporting the coalition had little to be proud of in this partisan attempt to place themselves in power. Rarely had the Wilson group's emphasis on politics over principle been so obvious. One fair-minded Free Democrat, Richard Henry Dana, who played a very prominent role in the proceedings, became disgusted with the political maneuvering of the coalition and cooperated with the Whigs on many issues. Dana was far from happy with the finished product.[17]

In the fall elections of 1853 the voters had the opportunity to accept or reject the constitution in an issue that was closely tied to the prospects of the coalition. Henry Wilson, now in firm control of the Free Democrats, won his party's nomination for governor by a unanimous vote and would be elected by the legislature should the coalition gain control. For Adams, this prospect meant a partial withdrawal from politics. "If we are to have Mr. Wilson for Governor," he said, "I will make no lamentation at the desecration of an office which has seldom had very distinguished incumbents." Although not willing to campaign against Wilson, some Free Democrats were upset enough by the proposed constitution to speak out against it. Thus Adams and Palfrey,

---

[17] William G. Bean, "Puritan Versus Celt, 1850-1860," *New England Quarterly,* VII (1934), 74; Harrington, *Nathaniel Banks,* 17; Shapiro, "The Conservative Dilemma," 214-20; Shapiro, *Richard Henry Dana,* 68-83; Dana, Journal, November 21, 1853, in Dana Papers; Boston *Post,* September 23, 1853.

angered in part by their failure to win election to the convention in
the first place, worked with the Whigs to defeat the document and
further separated themselves from the Wilson wing.[18] Their continuing
clash with Wilson seemed more important than the likelihood of continued Whig ascendency should the two Free Democratic factions fail
to get together. Despite the need for third-party unity at this crucial
stage, the quarreling continued.

Palfrey led the opposition to the constitution by publishing a pamphlet attacking the changes in the document and thus giving new
strength to the faltering Whig drive. Adams followed with a speech
in Quincy in which he not only attacked the constitution but questioned the motives of Charles Sumner for supporting it and bowing
"to the iron rod of party." Adams later regretted this remark, for it
led to a cooling of relations with Sumner. He did not regret his opposition to the constitution, however. Even Henry Wilson found it impossible to defend the complicated apportionment scheme and said only
that it was a temporary solution. The Whigs now seized on the situation and circulated thousands of copies of the Palfrey and Adams
criticisms.[19]

Late in the campaign the coalition and the proposed constitution
received another devastating blow. On October 29, Caleb Cushing,
attorney general of the Pierce administration and long-time opponent
of the coalition, wrote an angry public letter in which he announced
President Pierce's firm opposition to the idea of cooperation with the
third party. Composed in dictatorial tones, the letter was soon dubbed
"Cushing's Ukase": "To support or vote for Free Soilers in Massachusetts is to give countenance and power to persons engaged avowedly
in the persistent agitation of the slavery question. . . . If there be any
purpose more fixed than another in the mind of the President . . . it is
that the dangerous element of abolitionism, under whatever guise or
form it may present itself, shall be crushed out." Free Democrats were

[18] Adams, *Diary*, September 8, 16, 1853, in Adams Papers; Shapiro, "The Conservative Dilemma," 223; Loubert, "Henry Wilson," 183.
[19] John G. Palfrey, *Remarks on the Proposed State Constitution by a Free Soiler
from the Start* (Boston, 1853); Boston *Daily Advertiser*, November 7, 1853; Palfrey to Dana, November 5, 1853, in Dana Papers; Adams, *Diary*, October 28,
November 8, 21, 22, December 5, 1853, in Adams Papers; Gatell, *John G. Palfrey*,
214-15; Donald, *Charles Sumner*, 248-49; Pierce, *Charles Sumner*, III, 338;
Shapiro, "The Conservative Dilemma," 223.

outraged; even Charles Francis Adams called it "the most monstrous document that was ever presented to a free people." Adams expected that the Democrats "would spurn, and hiss, and spew out of their mouths upon this manifesto," but the letter did have a serious effect. Many Democrats who were already inclined against cooperating with the third party used it as justification to withdraw their support and reject the constitution designed to place the coalition in power.[20]

As the election approached, the chances for both the coalition and the constitution dwindled. Marcus Morton joined in urging a repudiation of the document, while the Irish Catholics of Boston promised opposition because of the provision barring public funds for parochial schools. The Catholic press had long opposed the coalition because of the nature of many of the reforms it demanded and because many Irish were opposed to the third-party movement.[21] The results, not surprisingly, brought a crushing defeat for the coalition. The Whig candidate for governor far outdistanced his rivals, and Whig control of the legislature assured his election. In a surprisingly close vote the people rejected the constitution by only 4,800 votes out of the 130,000 cast. The document was supported in Free Democratic and rural areas but was defeated by solid Irish and Whig opposition in Boston. Although Wilson's 30,000 votes for governor meant that his party had held its own, the coalition had in effect been destroyed.[22] Free soil agitation in Massachusetts would now have to take place completely outside of the Democratic party, and the way was open for political cooperation from another source.

By the end of 1853 the Free Democratic party had served its usefulness in many parts of the East while it increased its power in the Midwest where the Whigs were much weaker and unable to provide opposition to the Democrats and where the Free Democrats were more united and organized and better able to take the initiative. In Massa-

[20] Fuess, *Caleb Cushing,* II, 139-43; Boston *Commonwealth,* November 2, 1853; Pierce, *Charles Sumner,* III, 339.

[21] Because of the frequent antagonism between recent immigrant groups and blacks, the Irish of Massachusetts typically opposed all aspects of the antislavery movement, including both abolitionism and anti-extensionism. Boston *Daily Advertiser,* November 22, 1853; Bean, "Puritan Versus Celt," 74-78.

[22] Pierce, *Charles Sumner,* III, 340-41; Dana, Journal, November 21, 1853, in Dana Papers; Shapiro, "The Conservative Dilemma," 224.

chusetts, the 1853 election had placed the Whigs so firmly in control
that they had no need to cooperate with other anti-extension groups.
With the coalition destroyed, the Free Democrats were confused and
weakened but ready to cooperate with any new free soil movement.
In New York, Democratic factionalism allowed the Whigs to return
to power in 1853, but there was little interest in a revived third-party
movement. The Whigs had no opportunity to recover their position in
other parts of the nation, however, and 1853 witnessed a further de-
terioration of the party organization.[23] The situation was finally ready
for the organization of the entirely new Republican party representing
purely northern interests. As indecision lowered the prestige of the
Pierce administration, all that was needed was the proper catalyst to
bring together anti-extensionists of all parties.

Senator Stephen A. Douglas provided the necessary stimulus in
January, 1854, when he introduced a bill to organize the territories
of Kansas and Nebraska. Repealing the ban on slavery in these areas
north of 36°30′ in effect since the Missouri Compromise of 1820,
Douglas's bill permitted the residents of the territories to determine the
status of slavery themselves. The immediate Free Democratic reaction
was an impassioned public letter written by Salmon P. Chase with the
help of Joshua Giddings and Charles Sumner, published on January
22, 1854, and entitled "Appeal of the Independent Democrats in Congress to the People of the United States." The letter, which Chase
called "the *most valuable* of my works," was signed by six members of
Congress, including Chase, Giddings, Sumner, Gerrit Smith, Edward
Wade, and Alexander De Witt. In exaggerated terms it labeled the
bill as "an atrocious plot to exclude from a vast unoccupied region
immigrants from the Old World and free laborers from our own States
and convert it into a dreary region of despotism, inhabited by masters
and slaves." Because the bill represented a repeal of the Wilmot Proviso principle in favor of popular sovereignty, thus giving the South
the possibility of another slave state, the Appeal could argue that
Douglas was willing to "permanently subjugate the whole country to
the yoke of slaveholding despotism." The authors urged the country
not to submit "to become agents in extending legalized oppression and

[23] Nevins, *Ordeal of the Union,* II, 74-76.

systematic injustice."[24] At the heart of the matter was the extension issue, which the third party had been warning the country about ever since the 1840s. Now at last the North suddenly agreed, and Chase's emotional Appeal became the point of departure for a new and more comprehensive anti-extension party.

While the bill was being debated in Congress, opposition developed throughout the North. Of the ten northern legislatures in session at the time, the five not controlled by the Democrats adopted resolutions of protest, while the legislature of Illinois was the only one to endorse the Douglas bill. In the congressional debates party lines weakened and sectionalism intensified as most southern Whigs supported the measure and many northern Democrats opposed it. With the bill becoming the burning issue of the day, old party labels appeared irrelevant. As Horace Greeley's New York *Tribune* noted, "The unanimous sentiment of the North is indignant resistance." The charges made by Free Democrats like Chase, Sumner, and Giddings that the Pierce administration had surrendered completely to southern demands for slave expansion were now accepted by northerners of all parties. The allegations were borne out in the movement to acquire Cuba as slave territory and were now brought home much more forcefully in the repeal of the Missouri Compromise. Many could now agree with the Free Democrats that the Compromise of 1850 had not been the final settlement that Whigs and Democrats had talked of. A movement began for the formation of a new northern party to oppose more effectively what northerners believed was the latest example of the power of the "slavocracy." The *National Era* spoke for many when it noted: "The North has a majority in Congress; let it use the power with which its numerical superiority invests it, to protect its rights and the cause of Freedom and Free Labor. . . ." The paper concluded that "the two old party organizations have outlived the issues which gave them birth."[25] Anti-extensionists of all three parties began now to think in terms of uniting

[24] *Congressional Globe*, 33rd Cong., 1st Sess., 175, 221-22; *National Era*, February 2, 1854; Chase to E. L. Pierce, August 8, 1854, in Bourne (ed.), "Chase Correspondence," 261.

[25] Malcom Moos, *The Republicans: A History of Their Party* (New York, 1956), 9; New York *Tribune*, March 2, 1854; *National Era*, February 16, 1854.

in a new organization which could better represent their interests and halt the spread of slavery.

On May 9, 1854, the day after the House took up the Kansas-Nebraska bill, some thirty northern representatives met in Washington to decide on the best course of action. Also present was Gamaliel Bailey, editor of the *National Era,* who helped to convince the gathering that the present party structure was no longer capable of stopping the spread of slavery. Only by forgetting the old parties, said Bailey, could an effective opposition to the South be created: "Let all sides and all classes, Whigs, Democrats and Free Soilers . . . unite in unselfish devotion to the cause of human rights." The Kansas-Nebraska bill and the reaction to it would, before many months, end the need for the Free Democratic party. The third-party position that Congress must prevent even the possibility of the extension of slavery in order to assure the territories for the possession of the small white farmer had become the position of the great majority of northerners. "If slaveholders are permitted to take their slaves into Nebraska and Kansas," one northern Whig told Congress in 1854, "the inequality and injury are to the free white men of the North and South who go there without slaves."[26] Excitement far exceeding that of 1848 would bring the new Republican party into being.

The Kansas-Nebraska Act became law in May, 1854, after passing the House by a close 113-100 margin. The three Free Democrats had joined with all forty-five northern Whigs and about half of the northern Democrats to resist Douglas's bill, but enough northern Democrats remained loyal to the administration to enable it to gain a majority. The bill's passage helped bring to a close the six-year history of the Free Soil–Free Democratic party, and the renewed opposition to the extension of slavery became the immediate task of the Republican party. The new party was created by a fusion of anti-extension Whigs, Democrats, and Free Democrats. Soon to replace the Whigs in the two-party system, it could not simply form around what was left of that party. Too many Whigs, especially in the East, stuck by their old

---

[26] Wilson, *The Slave Power,* II, 410-11; Andrew W. Crandall, *The Early History of the Republican Party, 1854-1856* (Boston, 1930), 47; Francis Curtis, *The Republican Party: A History of Its Fifty Years Existence and a Record of Its Measures and Leaders, 1854-1904* (New York, 1904), I, 179; *National Era,* June 22, 1854; *Congressional Globe,* 33rd Cong., 1st Sess., Appendix, 447.

organization and refused to recognize other groups. William H. Seward, whom many regarded as the next Whig presidential nominee, resisted a new party since he had so much at stake in the old. In Massachusetts, where the Whigs also enjoyed power, and in Pennsylvania, where they had recently been in control, they would not permit fusion except on their own terms. To northerners who had long opposed the Whig party, this attitude, its past inconsistencies on the slavery issue, and its present weak condition eliminated it as a possible nucleus of a new organization.[27]

Nor could the Free Democratic party realistically expect to appeal to all those who opposed the Kansas-Nebraska bill. For six years Democrats and Whigs had alternately ridiculed and ignored the entire third-party movement as it struggled to maintain its independence. The coalitions and bargains that many members entered into in 1849 had not enhanced the party's reputation, for many viewed the Free Democrats as men eager only for office and power. The party had perhaps become too familiar an organization. Rightly or wrongly its members were still looked on by some as dangerous agitators and fanatics. To join a party whose leaders they considered extremists would hardly be wise politics. A fresh approach was needed — one in which none of the anti-extension factions tried to dominate. As Bailey put it: "As to old Party names, the less harped upon the better until the Convention of free states settle that matter. What matters who lead in the movement — if in one State the Democrats; in another the People irrespectively of Party names? The Thing to be accomplished is Union on right principles, for the protection of Liberty."[28] A new party was needed without any restricting ties with existing parties or connection with past political defeats and mistakes. Only in this way could all anti-extension groups feel welcome.

The Republican party originated in the Midwest, where the Whigs were weakest and had the least to lose by abandoning their old organization, and where opposition to the Kansas-Nebraska Act was greatest. Fusion meetings were held and fusion tickets quickly arranged for the

[27] Nevins, *Ordeal of the Union,* II, 120, 316-23; Alexander, *Political History of New York,* II, 200-205.

[28] Smith, *The Liberty and Free Soil Parties,* 285-86; *National Era,* June 22, 1854.

spring and fall elections of 1854. Beginning with meetings in Ripon, Wisconsin, and Jackson, Michigan, the movement quickly engulfed both Whig and Free Democratic parties and attracted numerous anti-Nebraska Democrats. Chase and Giddings led their Ohio followers into the new movement at a convention in July. By the end of 1854 the Whigs as a major party in the Midwest existed only in Illinois. The Republicans' greatest successes in the region were the election of numerous congressmen in 1854 and the choice of Salmon P. Chase as governor of Ohio in 1855.[29]

In the East, the American or Know Nothing party complicated the transition from Whig and Free Democratic to Republican. Especially in Massachusetts, where the nativist movement captured control of the government in 1854, the situation was confused and in constant transition. Here numerous Free Democratic opportunists led by Henry Wilson joined the Know Nothings, while the old Conscience Whig element led by Adams refused to join. Wilson was elected to the Senate in 1855 by the Know Nothing legislature. The movement capitalized on the reform spirit and was a product of free soil, nativism, and anti-Catholicism. It was not until late 1855 that most New England anti-extensionists left the Know Nothings and joined the Republicans.[30] In New York, the Whigs persisted until early 1856 and attracted much fusion anti-extension support before being replaced by the Republicans. In Pennsylvania, David Wilmot and Galusha Grow attempted with limited success to form a fusion ticket in 1854. In New Hampshire, John P. Hale was returned to the Senate in 1855 by a fusion of anti-Nebraska forces. In some parts of the East, the Republicans met with even more immediate success.[31] Throughout the North the issue which brought people into the Republican party was the expansion of slavery, although the new organization also took over most of the Whig economic program as well as much of the unfortunate nativism which was so characteristic of the 1850s.

---

[29] Wilson, *The Slave Power*, II, 408-18; Smith, *The Liberty and Free Soil Parties*, 285-97; Roseboom, *The Civil War Era*, 280-82; Craven, *The Coming of the Civil War*, 344-45; Crandall, *The Early History of the Republican Party*, 20-26.

[30] John R. Mulkern, "The Know Nothing Party in Massachusetts" (Ph.D. dissertation, Boston University, 1963), 80-85; Bean, "Party Transformations in Massachusetts," 377-79; Duberman, *Charles Francis Adams*, 190-203; Donald, *Charles Sumner*, 268-69.

[31] Nevins, *Ordeal of the Union*, II, 323-46; Sewell, *John P. Hale*, 159-62.

The Free Democratic reaction to the events of 1854 indicated that most of them felt that formation of the Republican party represented the successful climax to six long years of agitation. Few mourned the death of their third-party organization and most were glad that they were now again a part of the two-party system. Bailey's *National Era* rejoiced that Whigs, Democrats, and Free Democrats were laying aside "their ancient and minor causes of difference" and uniting in a common political effort.[32] Many Free Democrats had long wished this and were relieved that they could reenter the two-party system without sacrificing free soil principle. Although they by no means controlled the new Republican party, they did have sufficient influence to help direct its policies and enjoy the political benefits. A few remained aloof for a time, such as Charles Francis Adams, who did so in part because of his continuing political and personal differences with Henry Wilson, but most other Free Democrats were active and influential participants in organizing the new party. The men who had led the third party for six years — Chase, Giddings, Bailey, Sumner, Hale, and Julian — eagerly embraced the Republican movement.

The new Republican party almost immediately became the minority party in Congress, achieving greater success in one year than the Free Soilers had attained in six. Yet, in addition to the nonsectional issues, the Republicans owed much to their anti-extension predecessor. In the ensuing years many of the important Free Soil leaders assumed even more prominent places in the Republican party. Joshua Giddings became a Republican in 1854 and continued in Congress until the late 1850s, playing an active role in the party's national conventions and assuming a diplomatic post under the Lincoln administration. Salmon P. Chase became the first Republican governor of Ohio and was an active aspirant for the Republican presidential nominations of 1856 and 1860. He then entered Lincoln's cabinet as secretary of the treasury and later became chief justice of the United States. Charles Francis Adams took little part in politics in the mid-1850s but entered Congress as a Republican in 1858. His most distinguished service came as Lincoln's minister to Great Britain during the Civil War. Gamaliel Bailey continued as editor of the *National Era* until his death

[32] *National Era,* June 22, 1854.

in 1859. His paper was one of the first to advocate the Republican position. Henry Wilson joined the Republican party after his brief support of the Know Nothings and served as a senator until he was elected vice-president in 1872. John P. Hale also served in the Senate as a Republican from 1855 to 1864. George W. Julian of Indiana was an early participant in the Republican party, serving as congressman for four terms during the 1860s. David Wilmot was one of the founders of the Pennsylvania Republican party and its first candidate for governor. He served in the Senate during the Civil War. Throughout the Civil War and Reconstruction periods Charles Sumner held the Senate seat first given him by the Massachusetts Free Soil coalition in 1850. Sumner was probably the most influential Republican senator during much of the period. Preston King returned to the anti-extension ranks during the Kansas-Nebraska controversy and achieved prominence in the Republican party as senator from New York.

On the other hand, the new party also included many of the more influential leaders who had previously refused to join the Free Soilers primarily for practical political reasons. Among them were such men as Horace Greeley, John Wentworth, William H. Seward, Hannibal Hamlin, and Abraham Lincoln. Nevertheless, the Free Soil leaders contributed significantly in the early years in terms of anti-extension leadership, and dedication. Collectively they comprised the element of the party which was most eager to stop the spread of slavery. While other elements often wanted to stress economic issues or other problems not related to anti-extensionism, the Free Soil faction attempted with some success to keep its old Wilmot Proviso principle in the forefront of the Republican platform. At the same time, although most of them were never devoted to the ideals of racial justice and equality and were eager to keep free blacks out of the territories, their influence did tend to temper the worst aspects of the racism of the other Republican factions.[33]

The Republican party came into prominence stressing the same issue that Free Soilers had been talking about since 1848 — opposition to the extension of slavery into the territories. Since 1848 the third

---

[33] See Foner, *Free Soil, Free Labor, Free Men,* especially, chaps. IV and VIII and Hans Trefousse, *The Radical Republicans: Lincoln's Vanguard for Racial Justice* (New York, 1969), especially chap. II.

party had agitated, but only a few had been willing to listen. But with the coming of the Kansas-Nebraska controversy, its position became that of a majority of northerners and it was no longer big enough to meet the needs of the anti-extension movement. The Free Soil party had perhaps been premature, but it, along with the abolitionists, had kept the issue of slave extension alive until the North was finally ready to listen. The Republican party thus had the advantage of building on an issue that the Free Soilers had helped to develop. In the long run, the new party succeeded where the Free Soil had not at least partly because of the difference in the temper of the times when each put forward its program. The Republican party also learned from the mistakes of the Free Soilers. It stressed local organization more and made a greater attempt to coordinate local and national issues. It endorsed the Whig economic program and appealed to nativistic fears. But for the most part, it took over almost completely the Free Soil platforms of 1848 and 1852. The major difference was that the North was ready at last to accept a new party fusing together elements of all political groups firmly opposed to the extension of slavery.

11

Political Expediency and
Free Soil Principle

The brief six-year history of the Free Soil–Free Democratic party reveals a unique blending of anti-extension principle and political expediency. On the one hand, many members of the third party were
often quite willing to sacrifice principle in order to strengthen their
political position. On the other hand, others were fully dedicated to
the containment of slavery and continued to defend that principle
even when political expediency dictated compromise. All Free Soilers
were motivated in part by what they regarded as increasing southern
influence in Congress as manifested in the annexation of Texas and
the movement to add further Mexican territories to the United States.
Yet many of them were equally desirous of using their protest movement as a means to increase their influence within the two-party structure. As northern opposition to the Mexican War increased with the
controversy over the extension of slavery, many who sincerely opposed
adding new slave regions combined with those who were more concerned with the political potential of an opposition movement to form
the Free Soil party.

The formation of the Free Soil party in 1848 was the direct result
of the refusal of either major party to risk antagonizing its southern
element by endorsing the Wilmot Proviso in its platform. The result was
that many northerners were willing to join a third party in protest
although they did so with a variety of motives. Many who endorsed the
Wilmot Proviso saw a real possibility of slavery in California and New
Mexico and with it more slave state votes in Congress. Many, including the frontiersmen already there, wanted to preserve the territories

for free white labor and thus prevent any contact with blacks, either free or slave. Some northerners seized on the Proviso as the most convenient and effective way to raise the moral issue of slavery everywhere. Slavery seemed secure and almost invulnerable where it already existed but not where it sought to gain a foothold. However unlikely it was that the people of California or New Mexico would go for slavery, the raising of the question could be used to denounce the moral evil of the institution everywhere. Although most who joined the Free Soil movement shared one or more of these motives most also had a purely political motive. For the Barnburners, the largest element, an intense desire to gain revenge on other elements of the Democratic party for wrongs done to them and their leader Martin Van Buren was one factor. Equally important was their hope of using the movement to regain control of the state Democratic party away from the hated Hunker faction. For the Conscience Whigs the third party might provide the necessary instrument to reassert their waning influence and eventually displace the cotton manufacturing element which was so influential within the Whig party. Many Barnburners and Conscience Whigs as well as some Liberty men had little desire to see a third party movement continue after the election, for they knew that real political influence came within the two-party structure.

The Free Soil campaign of 1848, like the entire movement, was characterized by the counter tendencies of anti-extension principle and political expediency. The only party to take a clear-cut stand on the Wilmot Proviso, the only real issue of the campaign, the Free Soilers took an openly sectional and ideological approach in a party system which had always tried to minimize sectionalism and ideology. While the major parties had appeal in all sections and had tried to avoid the slavery issue, the Free Soilers appealed primarily to northerners with their attacks on the slave system and their demands that it be localized. But in many other ways Free Soilers conformed strictly to the methods of traditional politics. Their nominating convention in Buffalo was characterized by maneuvering and manipulation typical of most major party conventions. The Barnburners were in firm control of the proceedings and were influential enough to dictate the nomination of their candidate, Martin Van Buren. Revenge on the national Democratic party and control of the state party always took precedence over the

Wilmot Proviso in Barnburner thinking. In return the New Yorkers
permitted the other factions to choose the vice-presidential candidate
and write the platform, being careful to make sure that the platform
would not be too advanced to antagonize Barnburner members. On the
issue of race the Free Soilers again had much in common with Democrats and Whigs. Few were willing to advocate racial equality, and the
party omitted from its platform any mention of the plight of the black
man in the North. Most members made it quite clear that their advocacy of the Wilmot Proviso was in part designed to keep all blacks out
of the territories and guarantee the new areas to the small white farmer.
As a result the black community of the North expressed very ambivalent and divided feelings about the Free Soilers. Some blacks were
willing to support them because they at least promised to halt the
spread of slavery. Others could not endorse a movement which opposed abolitionism and showed its racism by refusing to attack northern discriminatory laws. Only a few Free Soilers, including Giddings,
Bailey, and Chase, were willing to talk of racial equality, but even
they would not push it too hard and were always unwilling to consider
any form of social contact with blacks.

Despite its platform, which promised something for everyone, the
Free Soil party did not carry a single state in 1848. The most plausible
explanation of this disappointing showing was the persistence of the
two-party system. Americans had become accustomed to the tradition
of two nonsectional, nonideological parties, and unless a new party
could replace one of the old, it would have little chance. The Whigs
and Democrats had smoothly functioning and well-financed organizations around which to base a campaign, while the Free Soilers started
from almost nothing. Especially in state and local elections was the
party hampered by its newness. It failed to stress local issues and suffered from a lack of financial resources. Americans were reluctant to
leave an established organization for one with such poor prospects. In
addition, internal problems hampered the Free Soil group. The new
party had so many disparate elements that many could not feel comfortable in it. Whigs distrusted a party led by their old nemesis Martin
Van Buren. Democrats were ill at ease and had little in common with
the more principled and elitist Conscience Whigs. Not all Liberty men
could endorse a movement which ignored slavery in the South and

ignored the free black in the North. The conflict between the practical politician and anti-extension principle made the Free Soil task even more difficult, and many voters may have suspected that political expediency was the major motivation of the Free Soilers.

The years 1849 to 1851 revealed that for most, the Free Soil movement was a temporary expedient only, to be quickly abandoned if possible without loss of face. These years revealed a serious failure within Free Soil leadership. Without a national election or smoothly functioning organization to sustain the party, it quickly lost ground to its more experienced opponents. In addition, the Free Soilers often had little to say about state and local issues. To many, the spoils of office were an important consideration, and these people decided that continued isolation from the major parties would mean continued exclusion when the spoils were distributed. Not quite the dedicated reformers they professed to be, many advocated coalition or even fusion as the best way to attain anti-extension ends. In the process they often lowered themselves to the level of their competitors and appeared to be little more than office seekers. The haste with which the Barnburners reentered the Democratic party when they had a real chance to reassert state control proved again that politics rather than principle continued to control their actions. They quickly abandoned the Wilmot Proviso as they became Democrats again. Their example was copied in numerous other states as many seemed almost to wish the death of the third party. Many felt that little more could be gained from an independent Free Soil party and they were now eager to reenter the two-party system, where they had a greater chance for office. Although coalitions were successful in electing Chase and Sumner to the Senate, it was always at the expense of Free Soil identity. Men like Chase and Henry Wilson would gladly have given up a separate movement entirely if they could have enhanced their position in the process.

Yet not all Free Soilers were so quick to forget their platform of 1848. Especially in Congress, which became embroiled in an all-important sectional debate, the small group of Free Soilers overcame their differences and fought valiantly to prevent a sectional adjustment which in their minds was a surrender to slavery. Led by such committed anti-extensionists as Joshua Giddings, the party tried in vain to resist the Compromise spirit and the rejection of the Wilmot Proviso.

In the end, however, many Free Soilers, already inclined to return to their old parties, used the Compromise as further justification, asserting that the sectional issues had been settled. The year 1851 found the Free Soilers at their nadir, their leading principle rejected by Congress and their members deserting the party.

In 1852, the party made a slight resurgence but it failed to convince most that the Compromise was not the final settlement that Whigs and Democrats claimed it to be. The party's efforts to awaken northerners to the sectional dangers were received with apathy by most. Reduced to a smaller, more dedicated group, in contrast with 1848, free soil principle received more emphasis than political expediency. But as in 1848, the members were unwilling to expand their platform to include attacks on northern racism or slavery within the southern states as a small group of Liberty men demanded. The election results were not encouraging although the demise of the Whig party seemed imminent and with it a chance for the Free Soilers to move up. They could now negotiate out of strength rather than weakness, and their coalition attempts were vastly more successful in 1853 than those of previous years.

The Kansas-Nebraska bill of 1854 proved that the Free Soilers had been right that the Compromise of 1850 was not a final solution to sectional differences. It also proved that the Free Soilers were still motivated by the same combination of political expediency and anti-extension principle. As the members cheerfully gave up their old organization to become Republicans they did so with the feeling that they had reached the successful climax of six years of agitation. The new party, like the Free Soil party, stressed the Wilmot Proviso principle. Not surprisingly it ignored the issue of racial justice. The Free Soilers would provide an important element of leadership to the Republican party, for it was an organization in which most Free Soilers could feel very much at home. Expressing their own ideological views on race and the containment of slavery, the Republican party also offered something the third party never could — a place in the two-party system and with it the opportunity for political position.

Appendix A.
Free Soil Platform
of 1848

Whereas, We have assembled in Convention, as a union of *Freemen,* for the sake of Freedom, forgetting all past political differences in a common resolve to maintain the rights of Free Labor against the aggressions of the Slave Power, and to secure Free Soil for a Free People:

And whereas, The political Conventions recently assembled at Baltimore and Philadelphia, the one stifling the voice of a great constituency entitled to be heard in its deliberations, and the other abandoning its distinctive principles for mere availability, have dissolved the national party organizations heretofore existing, by nominating for the Chief Magistracy of the United States, under Slaveholding dictation, candidates, *neither of whom* can be supported by the opponents of Slavery-extension, without a *sacrifice of consistency, duty,* and *self-respect.*

And whereas, These nominations, so made, furnish the occasion and demonstrate the necessity of the union of the People under the banners of Free Democracy, in a solemn and formal *declaration* of their *independence* of the *Slave Power,* and of their fixed determination to rescue the Federal Government from its control:

Resolved, therefore, that we, the people here assembled, remembering the example of our *fathers* in the days of the first Declaration of Independence, putting our trust in God for the triumph of our cause, and invoking his guidance in our endeavors to advance it, do now plant ourselves upon the NATIONAL PLATFORM OF FREEDOM, in opposition to the Sectional Platform of Slavery.

Resolved, That Slavery in the several States of this Union which recognize its existence, depends upon the State laws alone, which can-

Source: Porter and Johnson (comps.), *National Party Platforms,* pp. 13-14.

not be repealed or modified by the Federal Government, and for which laws that Government is not responsible. We therefore propose no interference by Congress with Slavery within the limits of any State.

Resolved, That the PROVISO of Jefferson, to prohibit the existence of Slavery, after 1800 in all the Territories of the United States, Southern and Northern; the votes of six States, and sixteen delegates, in the Congress of 1784, for the Proviso, to three States and seven delegates against it; the actual exclusion of Slavery from the Northwestern Territory by the ORDINANCE OF 1787, *unanimously* adopted by the States in Congress, and the entire history of that period, clearly show that it was the settled policy of the nation, *not* to *extend, nationalize,* or *encourage,* but to limit, localize, and discourage, Slavery; and to *this policy* which should never have been departed from, the Government ought to *return.*

Resolved, That our fathers ordained the Constitution of the United States, in order, among other great national objects, to establish justice, promote the general welfare, and secure the blessings of Liberty; but expressly *denied* to the Federal Government, which they created, all constitutional power to *deprive any person* of life, *liberty,* or property, without due legal process.

Resolved, That in the judgment of this Convention, Congress has no more power to make a SLAVE than to make a KING; no more power to institute or establish SLAVERY, than to institute or establish a MONARCHY. No such power can be found among those specifically conferred by the Constitution, or derived by just implication from them.

Resolved, THAT IT IS THE DUTY OF THE FEDERAL GOVERNMENT TO RELIEVE ITSELF FROM ALL RESPONSIBILITY FOR THE EXISTENCE OR CONTINUANCE OF SLAVERY WHEREVER THAT GOVERNMENT POSSESS CONSTITUTIONAL POWER TO LEGISLATE ON THAT SUBJECT, AND IS THUS RESPONSIBLE FOR ITS EXISTENCE.

Resolved, That the true, and, in the judgment of this Convention, the *only* safe means of preventing the extension of Slavery into territory now free, is to prohibit its existence in all such territory by *an act of Congress.*

Resolved, That we accept the issue which the Slave Power has forced upon us, and to their demand for more Slave States and more Slave Territory, our calm but final answer is: No more Slave States and no more Slave Territory. Let the soil of our extensive domains be kept free, for the hardy pioneers of our own land, and the oppressed and banished of other lands seeking homes of comfort and fields of enterprise in the New World.

Resolved, That the bill lately reported by the Committee of Eight in the Senate of the United States, was no compromise, but an absolute surrender of the rights of the non-slaveholders of the States; and while we rejoice to know that a measure which, while opening the door for the introduction of Slavery into Territories now free, would also have opened the door to litigation and strife among the future inhabitants thereof, to the ruin of their peace and prosperity, was defeated in the House of Representatives, — its passage, in hot haste, by a majority, embracing several Senators who voted in open violation of the known will of their constituents, should warn the People to see to it, that their representatives be not suffered to betray them. There must be no more compromises with Slavery: if made, they must be repealed.

Resolved, That we demand Freedom and established institutions for our brethren in Oregon, now exposed to hardships, peril, and massacre, by the reckless hostility of the Slave Power to the establishment of Free Government for Free Territories — and not only for them, but for our new brethren in California and New Mexico.

And whereas, It is due not only to this occasion, but to the whole people of the United States, that we should also declare ourselves on certain other questions of national policy, therefore,

Resolved, That we demand CHEAP POSTAGE for the people; a retrenchment of the expenses and patronage of the Federal Government; the *abolition* of all *unnecessary* offices and salaries; and the election by the People of all civil officers in the service of the Government, so far as the same may be practicable.

Resolved, That *river* and *harbor improvements,* when demanded by the safety and convenience of commerce with foreign nations, or among the several States, are objects of *national concern;* and that it is the duty of Congress, in the exercise of its constitutional powers, to provide therefor.

Resolved, That the FREE GRANT TO ACTUAL SETTLERS, in consideration of the expenses they incur in making settlements in the wilderness, which are usually fully equal to their actual cost, and of the public benefits resulting therefrom, of reasonable portions of the public lands, under suitable limitations, is a wise and just measure of public policy, which will promote, in various ways, the interest of all the States of this Union; and we therefore recommend it to the favorable consideration of the American People.

Resolved, That the obligations of honor and patriotism require the earliest practical payment of the national debt, and we are therefore in favor of such a tariff of duties as will raise revenue adequate to defray the necessary expenses of the Federal Government, and to pay annual instalments of our debt and the interest thereon.

Resolved, That we inscribe on our banner, "FREE SOIL, FREE SPEECH, FREE LABOR, and FREE MEN," and under it we will fight on, and fight ever, until a triumphant victory shall reward our exertions.

Appendix B.
Free Democratic Platform
of 1852

Having assembled in National Convention as the delegates of the Free Democracy of the United States, united by a common resolve to maintain right against wrongs, and freedom against slavery; confiding in the intelligence, patriotism, and the discriminating justice of the American people, putting our trust in God for the triumph of our cause, and invoking his guidance in our endeavors to advance it, we now submit to the candid judgment of all men the following declaration of principles and measures:

I. That Governments, deriving their just powers from the consent of the governed, are instituted among men to secure to all, those inalienable rights of life, liberty, and the pursuit of happiness, with which they are endowed by their Creator, and of which none can be deprived by valid legislation, except for crime.

II. That the true mission of American Democracy is to maintain the liberties of the people, the sovereignty of the States, and the perpetuity of the Union, by the impartial application to public affairs, without sectional discriminations, of the fundamental principles of equal rights, strict justice, and economical administration.

III. That the Federal Government is one of limited powers, derived solely from the Constitution, and the grants of power therein ought to be strictly construed by all the departments and agents of the Government, and it is inexpedient and dangerous to exercise doubtful constitutional powers.

IV. That the Constitution of the United States, ordained to form a more perfect union, to establish justice, and secure the blessings of lib-

SOURCE: Porter and Johnson (comps.), *National Party Platforms*, pp. 18-20.

erty, expressly denies to the General Government all power to deprive any person of life, liberty, or property, without due process of law; and therefore the Government, having no more power to make a slave than to make a king, and no more power to establish slavery than to establish monarchy, should at once proceed to relieve itself from all responsibility for existence of slavery wherever it possesses constitutional power to legislate for its extinction.

V. That, to the persevering and importunate demands of the slave power for more slave States, new slave Territories, and the nationalization of slavery, our distinct and final answer is — no more slave States, no slave Territory, no nationalized slavery, and no national legislation for the extradition of slaves.

VI. That slavery is a sin against God and a crime against man, which no human enactment nor usage can make right; and that Christianity, humanity, and patriotism, alike demand its abolition.

VII. That the Fugitive Slave Act of 1850 is repugnant to the Constitution, to the principles of the common law, to the spirit of Christianity, and to the sentiments of the civilized world. We therefore deny its binding force upon the American People, and demand its immediate and total repeal.

VIII. That the doctrine that any human law is a finality, and not subject to modification or repeal, is not in accordance with the creed of the founders of our Government, and is dangerous to the liberties of the people.

IX. That the acts of Congress known as the Compromise measures of 1850, by making the admission of a sovereign State contingent upon the adoption of other measures demanded by the special interest of slavery; by their omission to guarantee freedom in free Territories; by their attempt to impose unconstitutional limitations on the power of Congress and the people to admit new States; by their provisions for the assumption of five millions of the State debt of Texas, and for the payment of five millions more and the cession of a large territory to the same State under menace, as an inducement to the relinquishment of a groundless claim, and by their invasion of the sovereignty of the States and the liberties of the people through the enactment of an unjust, oppressive, and unconstitutional Fugitive Slave Law, are proved to be inconsistent with all the principles and maxims of Democracy, and wholly inadequate to the settlement of the questions of which they are claimed to be an adjustment.

X. That no permanent settlement of the slavery question can be looked for, except in the practical recognition of the truth, that slavery is sectional, and freedom national; by the total separation of the General Government from slavery, and the exercise of its legitimate and constitutional influence on the side of freedom; and by leaving to the States the whole subject of slavery and the extradition of fugitives from service.

XI. That all men have a natural right to a portion of the soil; and that, as the use of the soil is indispensable to life, the right of all men to the soil is as sacred as their right to life itself.

XII. That the public lands of the United States belong to the people, and should not be sold to individuals nor granted to corporations, but should be held as a sacred trust for the benefit of the people, and should be granted in limited quantities, free of cost, to landless settlers.

XIII. That a due regard for the Federal Constitution, and sound administrative policy, demand that the funds of the General Government be kept separate from banking institutions; that inland and ocean postage should be reduced to the lowest possible point; that no more revenue should be raised than is required to defray the strictly necessary expenses of the public service, and to pay off the public debt; and that the power and patronage of the Government should be diminished by the abolition of all unnecessary offices, salaries, and privileges, and by the election by the people of all civil officers in the service of the United States, so far as may be consistent with the prompt and efficient transaction of the public business.

XIV. That river and harbor improvements, when necessary to the safety and convenience of commerce with foreign nations or among the several States, are objects of national concern, and it is the duty of Congress in the exercise of its constitutional powers to provide for the same.

XV. That emigrants and exiles from the Old World should find a cordial welcome to homes of comfort and fields of enterprise in the New; and every attempt to abridge their privilege of becoming citizens and owners of the soil among us ought to be resisted with inflexible determination.

XVI. That every nation has a clear right to alter or change its own Government, and to administer its own concerns in such manner as may best secure the rights and promote the happiness of the people; and foreign interference with that right is a dangerous violation of the law of nations, against which all independent Governments should protest, and endeavor by all proper means to prevent; and especially is it the duty of the American Government, representing the chief republic of the world, to protest against and by all proper means to prevent the intervention of Kings and Emperors against nations seeking to establish for themselves republican or constitutional Governments.

XVII. That the independence of Hayti ought to be recognised by our Government, and our commercial relations with it placed on the footing of the most favored nations.

XVIII. That as, by the Constitution, "the citizens of each State shall be entitled to all privileges and immunities of citizens of the several States," the practice of imprisoning colored seamen of other States, while the vessels to which they belong lie in port, and refusing to exercise the right to bring such cases before the Supreme Court of the United States, to test the legality of such proceedings, is a flagrant violation of the Constitution, and an invasion of the rights of the citizens of other States, utterly inconsistent with the professions made by the slaveholders, that they wish the provisions of the Constitution faithfully observed by every State in the Union.

XIX. That we recommend the introduction into all treaties, hereafter to be negotiated between the United States and foreign nations, of some provision for the amicable settlement of difficulties by a resort to decisive arbitration.

XX. That the Free Democratic party is not organized to aid either the Whig or Democratic wing of the great Slave Compromise party of the nation, but to defeat them both; and that repudiating and renouncing both, as hopelessly corrupt, and utterly unworthy of confidence, the purpose of the Free Democracy is to take possession of the Federal Government, and administer it for the better protection of the rights and interests of the whole people.

XXI. That we inscribe on our banner, FREE SOIL, FREE SPEECH, FREE LABOR, and FREE MEN, and under it will fight on and fight ever, until a triumphant victory shall reward our exertions.

XXII. That upon this Platform the Convention presents to the American People, as a candidate for the office of President of the United States, JOHN P. HALE, of New Hampshire, and as a candidate for the office of Vice-President of the United States, George W. Julian, of Indiana, and earnestly commends them to the support of all freemen and parties.

Appendix C.
Free Soilers in the Thirty-first
Congress (1849-51)

Senate	*House of Representatives*
JOHN P. HALE — New Hampshire	CHARLES ALLEN — Massachusetts
SALMON P. CHASE — Ohio	*WALTER BOOTH — Connecticut
	CHARLES DURKEE — Wisconsin
	JOSHUA GIDDINGS — Ohio
	*JOHN HOWE — Pennsylvania
	GEORGE JULIAN — Indiana
	PRESTON KING — New York
	*HORACE MANN — Massachusetts
	JOSEPH ROOT — Ohio
	*WILLIAM SPRAGUE — Michigan
	AMOS TUCK — New Hampshire
	DAVID WILMOT — Pennsylvania

* Elected with Free Soil coalitions and usually voted with the Free Soilers.

Appendix D.
Free Soil Votes on the
Compromise of 1850

Senate	Utah (July 31)	Texas (Aug. 9)	California (Aug. 13)	N. Mex. (Aug. 15)	Fugitive (Aug. 23)	D.C. (Sept. 16)
Chase:	N	N	Y	N	N	Y
Hale:	N	N	Y	NV*	NV	Y
Totals:	Y 32	30	34	27	27	33
	N 18	20	18	10	12	19
	NV 10	10	8	23	21	10

House	Texas-N. Mex. (Sept. 6)	California (Sept. 7)	Utah (Sept. 7)	Fugitive (Sept. 12)	D.C. (Sept. 17)
Allen	N	Y	N	N	NV
Booth	N	Y	N	N	Y
Durkee	N	Y	N	N	Y
Giddings	N	Y	N	N	NV
Howe	N	Y	N	N	Y
Julian	N	Y	N	N	Y
King	N	Y	N	N	Y
Mann	N	Y	N	N	Y
Root	N	Y	N	N	NV
Sprague	N	Y	N	N	Y
Tuck	N	Y	N	N	Y
Wilmot**	NV	NV	NV	NV	NV
Totals:	N 108	150	97	109	124
	Y 97	56	85	76	59
	NV 16	15	39	36	39

Source: Hamilton, *Prologue to Conflict*, 191, 195-200.
* Not voting.
** Wilmot would have voted with the other Free Soilers, but at the end of August decided to return to Pennsylvania to try to protect his seat in Congress from those who were trying to unseat him in the fall election. See Going, *David Wilmot*, 409-36.

Bibliographical Essay

The most important Free Soil sources are scattered among manuscripts found in libraries in several parts of the United States, and other primary sources such as newspapers and memoirs, as well as numerous secondary sources including monographs, biographies, articles, and unpublished dissertations. Following are comments on the sources which proved to be the most valuable in this study of the Free Soil party. A more complete listing may be found in the footnotes and the bibliography.

PRIMARY SOURCES

MANUSCRIPTS

No one manuscript collection can be singled out as the most important of the many revealing papers and letters left by the leading participants. By far the most useful for the Barnburner element of the party are the papers of Martin Van Buren (Library of Congress). Once the reader becomes accustomed to Van Buren's cryptic style and almost illegible handwriting, he finds a wealth of information on the events leading up to and including the Barnburner secession in 1848. Included among the former president's correspondents were most of the leading Barnburners as well as many Democrats outside of New York.

The Ohio element of the party is represented by several substantial sets of papers. Those of Salmon P. Chase (Library of Congress and Historical Society of Pennsylvania) are extensive for all phases of the party's six-year history and show much of Chase's attempts to maneuver himself into the best possible political position. The Joshua R. Giddings Papers (Ohio Historical Society) contain a wealth of valuable information surrounding the career of Chase's leading Free Soil rival. Included is a valuable diary covering 1848-49. The Joshua R. Giddings–George W. Julian Papers (Library of Congress) contain much correspondence between these two leading Free Soilers.

The Conscience Whigs of Massachusetts provide a more complete set of letters and diaries than any other element of the party. Most extensive and

important are the Charles Francis Adams Papers (Massachusetts Historical Society, microfilm) because they include not only many letters to and
from Adams concerning Free Soil matters, but a highly revealing diary
covering the entire period of the party's history. Adams's daily entries are
highly methodical and impersonal and show his somewhat elitist philosophy and his martyr complex concerning his role in the Free Soil party.
The papers of Charles Sumner (Harvard University) and John G. Palfrey
(Harvard University) include many letters which demonstrate their substantial roles in the Free Soil movement and the extensive infighting
among the Massachusetts participants.

Other collections worthy of note are those of the party's 1852 candidates. John P. Hale's (New Hampshire Historical Society) include significant letters surrounding his role in both presidential campaigns and
George W. Julian's (Indiana State Library) show both his role in Congress and the campaign of 1852.

Among those politicians who did not become Free Soilers the most
useful collections are those of John McLean (Library of Congress, Ohio
Historical Society), which reveal his maneuvering for the 1848 nomination, and William L. Marcy (Library of Congress), which are most helpful for the Barnburner-Hunker reunion of 1849.

NEWSPAPERS

Numerous Free Soil journals sprang up during 1848 and many established
presses endorsed the party in that year also. Of the few which remained
loyal for the entire six-year period, the most important was Gamaliel
Bailey's *National Era* (Washington) established in 1847. Bailey's accounts
and editorials deal with every aspect of the antislavery movement during
these years but are especially valuable for their coverage of congressional
debates and the role of Free Soilers in them. The newspapers of New
York are also essential in describing the Barnburner-Hunker maneuvers,
in part because some of the editors were themselves participants. The most
useful Barnburner presses are the New York *Evening Post,* edited by John
Bigelow and Wiliam Cullen Bryant, and the Albany *Evening Atlas,* edited
by James M. French and William Cassidy. The latter's leading rival, the
Albany *Argus,* edited by Edwin Crosswell, expressed the Hunker philosophy, while Horace Greeley's New York *Tribune* was indicative of the Whig
perspective. In Massachusetts, the most helpful are the Boston *Daily Whig*
which became the Boston *Republican* in 1848 and was edited by various
Conscience Whigs including Adams, and the Free Soil–Free Democratic

Boston *Commonwealth* controlled by Henry Wilson. The Boston *Atlas* presented the Cotton Whig point of view. In Ohio, the Ashtabula *Sentinel,* edited by Giddings's son Joseph, expressed the Giddings approach while the Cleveland *True Democrat* edited first by Edward S. Hamlin and later by James A. Briggs, also often sided with the Free Soilers. Wisconsin Free Soilers had a key journal in Sherman Booth's *Wisconsin Freeman* (Milwaukee). The abolitionist reaction to the Free Soilers is best seen in William Lloyd Garrison's *The Liberator* (Boston) and Oliver Johnson's *National Anti-Slavery Standard* (New York). The only newspaper which is indicative of the black perspective concerning third-party politics and the racism of most of the members is Frederick Douglass's *The North Star* (Rochester).

OTHER PRIMARY SOURCES

Several important published collections of letters and speeches are invaluable in a study of this kind. They include *The Collected Works of Abraham Lincoln* edited by Roy P. Basler (8 vols., New Brunswick, 1953) ; John A. Dix's *Speeches and Occasional Addresses* (3 vols., New York, 1864) ; *Letters of James Gillespie Birney, 1831-1857,* edited by Dwight L. Dumond (2 vols., New York, 1938) ; *A Compilation of the Messages and Papers of the Presidents, 1789-1897,* edited by James D. Richardson (11 vols., Washington, 1897). Especially valuable is Philip Foner's *The Life and Writings of Frederick Douglass* (4 vols., New York, 1950), which includes letters and editorials by Douglass concerning his reaction to the Free Soil movement. Equally relevant in this category are *The Works of Charles Sumner* (15 vols., Boston, 1874-95) which include numerous important speeches and letters pertaining to Free Soil matters and "Diary and Correspondence of Salmon P. Chase" edited by Edward G. Bourne et al. in the *Annual Report of the American Historical Association, 1902,* II (Washington, 1903) which contains numerous letters concerning Chase's election to the Senate in 1849.

In addition to the diaries of Adams and Giddings already mentioned, two important diaries have been published which contribute to an understanding of the movement. *The Journal of Richard Henry Dana* edited by Robert F. Lucid (3 vols., Cambridge, 1968) is especially significant because it includes Dana's highly revealing reaction to the Buffalo convention. *The Diary of James K. Polk* edited by Milo M. Quaife (4 vols., Chicago, 1910) shows the reaction of the determined president to the Free Soil movement and the effect it had on his administration.

Autobiographies and memoirs of leading political figures of the period also explain much about the Free Soil movement. Among the most significant are John Bigelow, *Retrospections of an Active Life* (5 vols., New York, 1909); Morgan Dix, *Memoirs of John Adams Dix* (2 vols., New York, 1883); Horace Greeley, *Recollections of a Busy Life* (New York, 1868); and, most useful, George W. Julian, *Political Recollections, 1840-1872* (Chicago, 1884) which reveals much about Julian's motives and philosophy. Also significant are the reminiscences of the Liberty leader turned Barnburner and then Democrat, Henry B. Stanton, *Random Recollections* (Johnstown, N.Y., 1885). One aspect of the black reaction to the Free Soil party can be seen in Frederick Douglass's *Life and Times of Frederick Douglass Written By Himself* (Boston, 1892).

General commentaries on the period include the semi-autobiography by Henry Wilson, *History of the Rise and Fall of the Slave Power in America* (3 vols., Boston, 1874) in which the author attempts to justify his often devious course. James Russell Lowell's *Biglow Papers* (Cambridge, 1848) reveals much about the temper of the times with its probing humor while L. E. Chittenden's *Personal Reminiscences, 1840-1890, Including Some Not Hitherto Published of Lincoln and the War* (New York, 1893) has some insights concerning the Barnburner role in 1848.

Numerous campaign documents are available for the 1848 contest. Most important is O. C. Gardiner's *The Great Issue or the Three Presidential Candidates* (New York, 1848), a Barnburner publication which reprints many of the Free Soil convention speeches and key letters of the leading participants. Oliver Dyer's *Phonographic Report of the National Free Soil Convention at Buffalo, New York, August 9th and 10th, 1848* (New York, 1848) gives a complete and relatively accurate account of the official actions of the convention. Campaign pamphlets attacking the Buffalo nominees especially in light of their earlier records include *Inconsistency and Hypocrisy of Martin Van Buren on the Question of Slavery* (1848) and *The Charles F. Adams Platform or a Looking Glass for the Worthies of the Buffalo Convention* (1848). Significantly, no similar publications for the Free Democratic convention and candidates in 1852 are available indicating the minor impact made by the party in that election.

The most important government document for this study is the *Congressional Globe* for the Twenty-ninth through the Thirty-third Congresses (1845-54). The Free Soil role in Congressional debates not only in 1850 but before and after covers a vital aspect of the movement which most historians have ignored. The *Whig Almanac,* a yearly publication of the New York *Tribune,* includes compilations of state and national election returns. The official platforms of the key parties involved in the 1844, 1848, and 1852 elections are included in Kirk Porter and Donald Johnson (comps.), *National Party Platforms, 1840-1960* (Urbana, Ill., 1961 [3d ed. 1966]).

SECONDARY SOURCES

BOOKS OTHER THAN BIOGRAPHIES

Two important studies bear directly on certain aspects of the Free Soil party. The old but still highly useful work by Theodore C. Smith, *The Liberty and Free Soil Parties in the Northwest* (New York, 1897) is a very thorough description of the two parties in states from Ohio west. Based primarily on newspapers of the period, it includes many significant insights as well as information not easily available elsewhere. Joseph G. Rayback's *Free Soil: The Election of 1848* (Lexington, Ky., 1970) is a highly detailed study of the key Free Soil campaign from the perspective of all three parties involved and stresses the slave extension issue. The book's major failings are the omission of the vital issue of race and its effect on the role of the Free Soilers in 1848 and the author's willingness to accept at face value the Barnburners' stated motives for revolt.

Three outstanding recent studies cover aspects of the relationship between the Free Soil movement and abolitionism. The best general study is Louis Filler's *The Crusade Against Slavery, 1830-1860* (New York, 1960), while Aileen Kraditor's *Means and Ends in American Abolitionism: Garrison and His Critics on Strategy and Tactics, 1834-1850* (New York, 1969) skillfully analyzes the theories of nonpolitical antislavery agitation held by the abolitionists of the Garrison school and carefully shows their relationship to the political approach of the Liberty and Free Soil movements. A book of essays edited by Martin Duberman, *The Antislavery Vanguard: New Essays on the Abolitionists* (Princeton, 1965) includes an invaluable one by the editor, "The Northern Response to Slavery," which suggests the possible motivations of those who endorsed the anti-extension movement.

The role of the Barnburners in the Free Soil movement is seen in two works. Herbert Donovan's somewhat dated *The Barnburners: A Study of the Internal Movements in the Political History of New York and of the Resulting Changes in Political Affiliations* (New York, 1925) covers the entire period of Barnburner activities through the reunion with the Hunkers in 1849 from the perspective of New York politics. Chaplain W.

Morrison's highly significant study, *Democratic Politics and Sectionalism: The Wilmot Proviso Controversy* (Chapel Hill, N.C., 1967) looks at the Barnburners from the perspective of national Democratic politics and carefully analyzes their decision to bolt the party. Equally important, Morrison skillfully explains the effect of the Wilmot Proviso on public opinion.

A somewhat dated although still satisfactory account of Massachusetts politics up to 1848 is found in Arthur B. Darling's *Political Changes in Massachusetts, 1824-1848: A Study of Liberal Movements in Politics* (New Haven, 1925). For the Conscience Whig movement this has been largely supplanted by Kinley J. Brauer's extremely useful study, *Cotton Versus Conscience: Massachusetts Politics and Southwestern Expansion, 1843-1848* (Lexington, Ky., 1967). Brauer carefully analyzes the factors which led to the Conscience decision to leave the Whig party in 1848.

The relationship of the issue of race to the Free Soil movement is seen in several studies. Leon F. Litwack's *North of Slavery: The Negro in the Free States, 1790-1860* (Chicago, 1961) is unsurpassed in showing the various forms of discrimination to which northern racism subjected the black man and the degree to which most abolitionists and anti-extensionists shared these attitudes. Eugene H. Berwanger's *The Frontier Against Slavery: Western Anti-Negro Prejudice and the Slavery Extension Controversy* (Urbana, 1967) treats the same subject in more detail for the regions from the Great Lakes to the Pacific coast. James A. Rawley's *Race and Politics: Bleeding Kansas and the Coming of the Civil War* (New York, 1969) accurately demonstrates the racism involved in the introduction and passage of the Kansas-Nebraska Act. The black perspective on northern racism is discussed by Benjamin Quarles's *Black Abolitionists* (New York, 1969). Quarles also notes the role of blacks in the third parties of the period.

Two recent studies show the important role of the former Free Soilers in the Republican party, both describing them as "radical" elements in the new party which fought successfully for the old Free Soil objectives. They are Eric Foner's *Free Soil, Free Labor, Free Men: The Ideology of the Republican Party Before the Civil War* (New York, 1970) and Hans L. Trefousse, *The Radical Republicans: Lincoln's Vanguard for Racial Justice* (New York, 1969). Foner contends that racism was not as pervasive or important in Republican ideology as actually was the case.

Free Soil politics are placed in the larger national political picture in several works. Milo M. Quaife's old but still useful study *The Doctrine of*

Non-Intervention with Slavery in the Territories (Chicago, 1910) describes the various approaches to the territorial issue. Richard P. McCormick's *The Second American Party System: Party Formation in the Jacksonian Era* (Chapel Hill, N.C., 1966) suggests reasons why the party system of the 1840s and 1850s left little room for an ideological party like that of the Free Soilers. A helpful statistical study of congressional voting behavior and the surprising degree of party loyalty in the face of growing sectionalism is provided by Joel Silbey's *The Shrine of Party: Congressional Voting Behavior, 1841-1852* (Pittsburgh, 1967). Holman Hamilton has written the most comprehensive history of the Compromise of 1850 in *Prologue to Conflict: The Crisis and Compromise of 1850* (Lexington, Ky., 1964) although it is somewhat brief on the Free Soil role in the debates.

BIOGRAPHIES

Of the many significant participants in the Free Soil movement, four of the most important still lack adequate published biographies. There has been no competent study of Martin Van Buren's career after his presidency. Nor is there a biography available of one of the most important and interesting Barnburners, Van Buren's son John. Perhaps even more serious is the lack of a recent study of the varied and shifting career of the leading Free Soil manipulator, Salmon P. Chase. Finally, there is no biography of Gamaliel Bailey, editor of the *National Era*. Two Barnburners do have biographies worthy of note. John A. Garraty's *Silas Wright* (New York, 1949), gives a complete picture of this key figure whose death in 1847 shattered the Barnburner hopes of remaining in the Democratic party. Charles B. Going's *David Wilmot, Free Soiler: A Biography of the Great Advocate of the Wilmot Proviso* (New York, 1924) provides an overly sympathetic account of Wilmot's career, but does include many relevant Wilmot letters not available elsewhere.

Most of the important Whigs who became Free Soilers have received scholarly and complete coverage by highly competent biographers. Among the most essential volumes, all of which include full accounts of Free Soil politics, are Martin B. Duberman, *Charles Francis Adams, 1807-1886* (Boston, 1960); Samuel Shapiro, *Richard Henry Dana, Jr., 1815-1882* (East Lansing, 1961); Frank O. Gatell, *John Gorham Palfrey and the New England Conscience* (Cambridge, 1963); and David Donald, *Charles Sumner and the Coming of the Civil War* (New York, 1960). Of special note is the biography by James B. Stewart, *Joshua R. Giddings and the Tactics of Radical Politics* (Cleveland, 1970), which is a sympathetic yet highly objective account of one of the key Free Soilers and adds much to our knowledge of the period. Patrick W. Riddleberger's *George Washington Julian, Radical Republican: A Study in Nineteenth Century Politics and Reform* (Indianapolis, 1966) adequately describes the life of the 1852 Free Democratic candidate for vice-president. Two biographies of Henry Wilson are now available but were published too late to be considered in this study. They are Richard H. Abbott's *Cobbler in Congress: The Life of Henry Wilson, 1812-1875* (Lexington, Ky., 1971) and Ernest McKay's *Henry Wilson, Practical Radical: Portrait of a Politician* (Port Washington, N.Y., 1971).

Of those Free Soilers with Liberty backgrounds, John P. Hale is the only one to have a biography of real value. Richard H. Sewell's *John P. Hale and the Politics of Abolition* (Cambridge, 1965) accurately shows Hale's relationship to the anti-extension movement. Several studies describe the motivation of key Liberty leaders who did not become Free Soilers. Betty Fladeland's *James Gillespie Birney: Slaveholder to Abolitionist* (Ithaca, N.Y., 1955); Ralph V. Harlow, *Gerrit Smith: Philanthropist and Reformer* (New York, 1939) and Bertram Wyatt-Brown's *Lewis Tappan and the Evangelical War Against Slavery* (Cleveland, 1969) reveal the roles played by key abolitionists. Benjamin Quarles's *Frederick Douglass* (Washington, 1948) and Philip Foner's *Frederick Douglass* (New York, 1964) are accurate portrayals of the leading black spokesman of the Free Soil period.

Among those Whigs who never became Free Soilers there are many useful biographies available. Included among the best are Glyndon Van Deusen, *William Henry Seward* (New York, 1967); Holman Hamilton, *Zachary Taylor: Soldier in the White House* (Indianapolis, 1951); Richard Current, *Daniel Webster and the Rise of National Conservatism* (Boston, 1955) and Francis P. Weisenburger, *The Life of John McLean, A Politician on the United States Supreme Court* (Columbus, 1937).

Several key Democrats also have biographies which describe their relationship to the Free Soil movement. Included are H. Draper Hunt, *Hannibal Hamlin of Maine: Lincoln's First Vice-President* (Syracuse, 1969); Ivor D. Spencer, *The Victor and the Spoils: A Life of William L. Marcy* (Providence, 1959); Don E. Fehrenbacher, *Chicago Giant: A Biography of "Long John" Wentworth* (Madison, 1957). Especially useful for the background of the Barnburner secession is the second volume of Charles Seller's comprehensive biography of James K. Polk, *James K. Polk, Continentalist, 1843-1846* (Princeton, 1966).

ARTICLES

The role of blacks in the antislavery movement and especially in third-party politics is discussed in several articles. They include: Howard H. Bell, "The National Negro Convention, 1848," *The Ohio Historical Quarterly*, LXVII (1958), 357-68; J. Reuben Scheeler, "The Struggle of the Negro in Ohio for Freedom," *Journal of Negro History*, XXXI (1946), 208-26; and Charles H. Wesley, "The Participation of Negroes in Anti-slavery Parties," *Journal of Negro History*, XXIX (1944), 32-74. Two revealing articles by Eric Foner describe the racist attitudes of the Barn-burners and the other Free Soil factions: "Racial Attitudes of the New York Free Soilers," *New York History*, XLVI (1965), 311-29; "Politics and Prejudices: The Free Soil Party AND the Free Negro, 1849-1852," *Journal of Negro History*, L (1965), 239-56.

Several aspects of the events leading to the bolt of the Conscience Whigs are clarified in two articles by Frank O. Gatell: "Palfrey's Vote, the Conscience Whigs and the Election of Speaker Winthrop," *New England Quarterly*, XXXI (1958), 218-31 and "Conscience and Judgment: The Bolt of the Massachusetts Conscience Whigs," *The Historian* (1958), 18-45. The politics of the Massachusetts coalition are best seen in Ernest A. McKay, "Henry Wilson and the Coalition of 1851," *New England Quarterly*, XXXVI (1963), 338-57 and Martin Duberman, "Behind the Scenes as the Massachusetts 'Coalition' of 1851 Divides the Spoils," *Essex Institute Historical Collections*, XCIX (1963), 152-60. Samuel Shapiro, "The Conservative Dilemma: The Massachusetts Constitutional Convention of 1853," *New England Quarterly*, XXXIII (1960), 207-24 shows the continuing factionalism among Massachusetts Free Democrats.

Ohio politics is satisfactorily covered in narrative fashion in the book-length article by Edgar A. Holt, "Party Politics in Ohio, 1840-1850," *Ohio Archaeological and Historical Quarterly*, XXXVII (1928), 439-591; XXXVIII (1929), 47-182, 260-402. Frederick J. Blue's "The Ohio Free Soilers and the Problems of Factionalism," *Ohio History*, LXXVI (1967), 17-32 discusses Free Soil divisions after the election of 1848. The Wisconsin third party receives fairly complete coverage in Theodore C. Smith's "The Free Soil Party in Wisconsin," *Proceedings of the State Historical Society of Wisconsin, 1893* (Madison, 1894), 97-162.

Two articles by Joseph Rayback are also worthy of note. "The Liberty Party Leaders of Ohio: Exponents of Antislavery Coalition," *The Ohio State Archaeological and Historical Quarterly*, LVII (1948), 165-78 describes the role of Chase and others in leading the Liberty party in the direction of fusion with the Free Soil movement. "Martin Van Buren's Desire for Revenge in the Campaign of 1848," *Mississippi Valley Historical Review*, XL (1954), 707-16 advances the highly questionable thesis that the former president's motives were much more honorable than political revenge and party control.

UNPUBLISHED DISSERTATIONS

Several unpublished Ph.D. dissertations reveal additional Free Soil information not otherwise available. Biographies of key Barnburners are provided by Ernest P. Muller, "Preston King: A Political Biography" (Columbia University, 1957), and Martin Lichterman, "John Adams Dix, 1798-1879" (Columbia University, 1952). Walter L. Ferree has written a thorough and highly competent study of New York Democratic politics: "The New York Democracy: Division and Reunion, 1847-1852" (University of Pennsylvania, 1953). A full account of Massachusetts events is available in William G. Bean's "Party Transformations in Massachusetts with Special Reference to the Antecedents of Republicanism, 1848-1860" (Harvard University, 1922). Less useful is Alto F. Whitehurst's "Martin Van Buren and the Free Soil Movement" (University of Chicago, 1932).

Bibliography

PRIMARY SOURCES
MANUSCRIPTS

Adams, Charles Francis. Massachusetts Historical Society (microfilm).
Appleton, Nathan. Massachusetts Historical Society.
Benton, Charles S. State Historical Society of Wisconsin.
Bigelow, John. New York State Historical Society.
Birney, James G. Library of Congress.
Blair, Francis P. Correspondence in Blair-Lee Papers, Princeton University.
Blair Family Papers. Library of Congress.
Butler, Benjamin F. Princeton University.
Chase, Salmon P. Library of Congress; Historical Society of Pennsylvania;
    New Hampshire Historical Society.
Corwin, Thomas. Ohio Historical Society.
Dana, Richard Henry. Massachusetts Historical Society.
Davis, Moses M. State Historical Society of Wisconsin.
Dix, John A. Columbia University.
Everett, Edward. Massachusetts Historical Society.
Flagg, Azariah C. New York Public Library; Columbia University.
Giddings, Joshua. Ohio Historical Society.
Giddings-Julian Papers. Library of Congress.
Hale, John P. New Hampshire Historical Society.
Julian, George W. Indiana State Library.
Leavitt, Joshua. Library of Congress.
McLean, John. Library of Congress; Ohio Historical Society.
Mann, Horace. Massachusetts Historical Society.
Marcy, William L. Library of Congress.
Morton, Marcus. Massachusetts Historical Society.
Palfrey, John Gorham. Houghton Library, Harvard University.
Polk, James K. Library of Congress.
Smith, Caleb B. Library of Congress.
Stanton, Edwin L. Library of Congress.
Sumner, Charles. Houghton Library, Harvard University.
Tappan, Benjamin. Library of Congress.

Tappan, Lewis. Library of Congress.
Van Buren, Martin. Library of Congress.
Wadsworth, James S. Library of Congress
Welles, Gideon. Library of Congress.
Wilson, Henry. Library of Congress.
Winthrop, Robert. Massachusetts Historical Society.

NEWSPAPERS

Albany *Argus*.
Albany *Evening Atlas*.
American Freeman (Milwaukee).
Ashtabula *Sentinel*.
Boston *Atlas*.
Boston *Commonwealth*.
Boston *Courier*.
Boston *Daily Advertiser*.
Boston *Daily Republican*.
Boston *Daily Whig*.
Boston *Post*.
Cincinnati *Weekly Herald*.
Cleveland *Daily Plain Dealer*.
Cleveland *Herald*.
Cleveland *True Democrat*.
The Colored American
  (New York).
Frederick Douglass' Paper
  (Rochester).
Kenosha *Telegraph* (Wisconsin).
The Liberator (Boston).
Madison *Daily Argus and Democrat*
  (Wisconsin).
Madison *Express* (Wisconsin).
Milwaukee *Sentinel and Gazette*.
Milwaukee *Daily Wisconsin*.

National Anti-Slavery Standard
  (New York).
National Era (Washington).
National Intelligencer
  (Washington).
New York *Daily Tribune*.
New York *Evening Post*.
New York *Herald*.
New York *Times*.
Niles' Register (Baltimore).
The North Star (Rochester).
Ohio Standard (Columbus).
Ohio State Journal (Columbus).
Ohio Statesman (Columbus).
Oshkosh *True Democrat*.
Pennsylvania Freeman.
Racine *Advocate*.
Southport *Telegraph* (Kenosha).
Washington *Daily Union*.
Washington *Globe*.
Weekly Chicago Democrat.
Wisconsin Argus (Madison).
Wisconsin Barnburner (Milwaukee).
Wisconsin Free Democrat
  (Milwaukee).
Wisconsin Freeman (Milwaukee).
Wisconsin State Journal (Madison).

Other Primary Sources

Addresses and Proceedings of the State Independent Free Territory Convention of the People of Ohio, Held at Columbus, June 20, 21, 1848. Cincinnati, 1848.

Angle, Paul M. (ed.). *Created Equal? The Complete Lincoln-Douglas Debates of 1858.* Chicago, 1958.

American Free Soil Almanac for 1849. Boston, 1849.

Autobiography of Thurlow Weed, ed. Harriet A. Weed. Boston, 1883.

Baker, George E. (ed.). *The Works of William H. Seward.* 5 vols. Boston, 1886.

Basler, Roy P. (ed.). *The Collected Works of Abraham Lincoln.* 8 vols. New Brunswick, N.J., 1953.

Benton, Thomas Hart. *Thirty Years View.* 2 vols. New York, 1857.

Bigelow, John. *Retrospections of an Active Life.* 5 vols. New York, 1909.

————— (ed.). *Writings and Speeches of Samuel J. Tilden.* 2 vols. New York, 1885.

Bourne, Edward G., et al. (eds.). "Diary and Correspondence of Salmon P. Chase," *Annual Report of the American Historical Association, 1902.* II. Washington, 1903.

Boutwell, George S. *Reminiscences of Sixty Years in Public Affairs.* 2 vols. New York, 1902.

Bowditch, William I. *Cass and Taylor on the Slavery Question.* Boston, 1848.

Calendar of the Gerrit Smith Papers in the Syracuse University Library, General Correspondence. 2 vols. Albany, 1942.

The Charles F. Adams Platform, or a Looking Glass for the Worthies of the Buffalo Convention. 1848.

Chittenden, L. E. *Personal Reminiscences, 1840-1890, Including Some Not Hitherto Published of Lincoln and the War.* New York, 1893.

Congressional Globe, 29th-33rd Congress.

Cralle, Richard K. (ed.). *The Works of John C. Calhoun.* 6 vols. New York, 1857.

Dana, Richard Henry, Jr. *Speeches in Stirring Times and Letters to a Son.* Boston, 1910.

Dix, John. *Speeches and Occasional Addresses.* 3 vols. New York, 1864.

Dix, Morgan. *Memoirs of John Adams Dix.* 2 vols. New York, 1883.

Douglass, Frederick. *Life and Times of Frederick Douglass Written by Himself.* Boston, 1892.

Dumond, Dwight L. (ed.). *Letters of James Gillespie Birney, 1831-1857.* 2 vols. New York, 1938.

Dyer, Oliver. *Great Senators of the United States Forty Years Ago (1848-1849) With Personal Recollections and Delineations of Calhoun, Benton, Clay, Webster, General Houston, Jefferson Davis, and Other Distinguished Statesmen of that Period.* New York, 1889.

————. *Phonographic Report of the Proceedings of the National Free Soil Convention at Buffalo, New York, August 9th and 10th, 1848.* Buffalo, 1848.

Fergus, Robert. "Chicago River and Harbor Convention: An Account of its Origin and Proceedings," *Fergus Historical Series,* No. 18. Chicago, 1882.

Foner, Philip S. *The Life and Writings of Frederick Douglass.* 4 vols. New York, 1950.

The Free Soil Question and its Importance to the Voters of the Free States. New York, 1848.

Free Soil Songs for the People. Boston, 1848.

Gardiner, O. C. *The Great Issue or the Three Presidential Candidates.* New York, 1848.

Giddings, Joshua R. *History of the Rebellion: Its Authors and Causes.* New York, 1864.

————. *Speeches in Congress.* Boston, 1853.

Goodell, William. *Slavery and Anti-Slavery.* New York, 1853.

Greeley, Horace. *Recollections of a Busy Life.* New York, 1868.

Hamilton, Luther (ed.). *Memoirs, Speeches and Writings of Robert Rantoul, Jr.* Boston, 1854.

Hamlin, E. S. (ed.). "Selections from the Follett Papers," Quarterly Publication of the Historical and Philosophical Society of Ohio. IX-XI (1914-1916), 71-100, 4-33, 5-35.

Hayes, John L. *A Reminiscence of the Free Soil Movement in New Hampshire, 1845.* Cambridge, 1885.

"The Herkimer Convention, The Voice of New York! Proceedings of the Herkimer Convention of Oct. 26, 1847 with Speeches of the Hon. David Wilmot of Pa., C. C. Cambreleng, John Van Buren and Others." Albany *Atlas,* Extra, November, 1847.

Hoar, George F. *Autobiography of Seventy Years.* 2 vols. New York, 1903.

"Home Letters of George W. Julian, 1850-51," *Indiana Magazine of History.* XXIX (1933), 130-64.

Inconsistency and Hypocrisy of Martin Van Buren on the Question of Slavery. 1848.

Journal of the Constitutional Convention of the Commonwealth of Massachusetts, Begun and Held in Boston, on the Fourth Day of May, 1853. Boston, 1853.

Julian, George W. *Political Recollections, 1840-1872.* Chicago, 1884.

————. *Speeches on Political Questions.* New York, 1872.

Lawrence, William R. (ed.). *Extracts from the Diary and Correspondence of the Late Amos Lawrence.* Boston, 1855.
"Letters of James K. Polk to Cave Johnson, 1833-1848," *Tennessee Historical Magazine,* I (1915), 209-56.
Liberty Almanac. Syracuse, 1844-45. New York, 1847-54.
Lowell, James Russell. *The Biglow Papers.* Cambridge, 1848.
Lucid, Robert F. (ed.). *The Journal of Richard Henry Dana.* 3 vols. Cambridge, 1968.
Mann, Horace. *Slavery: Letters and Speeches.* Boston, 1851.
Marshall, Thomas M. (ed.). "Diary and Memoranda of William L. Marcy, 1849-1851," *American Historical Review,* XXIV (1919), 444-62.
May, Samuel J. *Some Recollections of Our Antislavery Conflict.* Boston, 1869.
New York Hards and Softs: Which is the True Democracy? A Brief Statement of the Facts for the Consideration of the Union by a National Democrat. New York, 1856.
"Official Proceedings of the National Free Soil Convention, Assembled at Buffalo, N.Y., August 9th and 10th, 1848," *Buffalo Republic,* Extra.
Official Report of the Debates and Proceedings in the State Convention, Assembled May 4th, 1853. Boston, 1853.
Palfrey, John. *Letter to a Friend.* Cambridge, 1850.
———. *Remarks on the Proposed State Constitution by a Free Soiler from the Start.* Boston, 1853.
———. "To the Free Soil Members of the General Court of Massachusetts for the Year 1851." Boston, 1851.
Poore, Ben Perley. *Perley's Reminiscences of Sixty Years in the National Metropolis.* 2 vols. Philadelphia, 1886.
Proceedings of the Democratic and Free Democratic Conventions, Rome, August 15-17, 1849. Rome, N.Y., 1849.
Proceedings of the Democratic National Convention, Held at Baltimore, May 22, 1848. Washington, 1848.
Proceedings of the Democratic National Convention Held at Baltimore, June, 1852. Washington, 1852.
Proceedings of the National Liberty Convention. Utica, 1848.
Proceedings of the Utica Convention for the Nomination of the President of the United States Held at Utica, N.Y., June 22, 1848. 1848.
The Public Statutes at Large and Treaties of the United States of America. 76 vols. Boston, 1845-1963.
Quaife, Milo M. (ed.). *The Diary of James K. Polk.* 4 vols. Chicago, 1910.

Reunion of the Free Soilers of 1848 at Downer Landing, Higham, Mass., August 9, 1877. Boston, 1877.

Reunion of the Free Soilers of 1848-1852 at the Parker House, Boston, Massachusetts, June 28, 1888. Cambridge, 1888.

Richardson, James D. (ed.). *A Compilation of the Messages and Papers of the Presidents, 1789-1897.* 11 vols. Washington, 1897.

"Some Letters of Salmon P. Chase, 1848-1865," *American Historical Review,* XXXIV (1929), 536-55.

Stanton, Henry B. *Random Recollections.* Johnstown, N.Y., 1885.

Swisshelm, Jane Grey. *Half a Century.* Chicago, 1880.

The Syracuse Convention, Its Spurious Organization and Oppressive and Anti-Republican Action, Remarks of John Van Buren, Etc., Etc. Albany *Atlas* Extra, October, 1847.

Tuckerman, Bayard (ed.). *The Diary of Philip Hone, 1828-1851.* 2 vols. New York, 1889.

The Utica Convention: Voice of New York. Proceedings of the Utica Convention, Feb. 16, 1848, With Speeches of John Van Buren, George Rathbun, Etc. Albany *Atlas* Extra, February, 1848.

Van Buren, Martin. *Inquiry Into the Origin and Course of Political Parties in the United States.* New York, 1867.

Van Tyne, C. H. (ed.). *Letters of Daniel Webster.* New York, 1902.

Ward, Samuel Ringgold. *Autobiography of a Fugitive Negro: His Anti-Slavery Labours in the United States, Canada and England.* London, 1855.

Whig Almanac, 1845-1854. New York.

Whitman, Walt. *Gathering of the Forces,* I. Ed. Cleveland Rodgers and John Black. New York, 1920.

Wilson, Henry. *History of the Rise and Fall of the Slave Power in America.* 3 vols. Boston, 1874.

Winthrop, Robert C. "Speech of Hon. R. C. Winthrop of Mass.," February 21, 1850.

The Works of Charles Sumner. 15 vols. Boston, 1874-95.

Writings and Speeches of Daniel Webster. 18 vols. Boston, 1903.

SECONDARY SOURCES

Books Other Than Biographies

Alexander, De Alva Stanwood. *A Political History of the State of New York.* 4 vols. New York, 1906.

Benson, Lee. *The Concept of Jacksonian Democracy: New York as a Test Case.* Princeton, 1961.

Berwanger, Eugene H. *The Frontier Against Slavery: Western Anti-Negro Prejudice and the Slavery Extension Controversy.* Urbana, Ill., 1967.

Biographical Directory of the American Congress, 1774-1961. Washington, 1961.

Brauer, Kinley J. *Cotton Versus Conscience: Massachusetts Politics and Southwestern Expansion, 1843-1848.* Lexington, Ky., 1967.

Burnham, W. Dean. *Presidential Ballots, 1836-1892.* Baltimore, 1955.

Campbell, Stanley W. *The Slave Catchers: Enforcement of the Fugitive Slave Law, 1850-1860.* Chapel Hill, N.C., 1970.

Catterall, Helen T. (ed.). *Judicial Cases Concerning American Slavery and the Negro.* 5 vols. Washington, 1936.

Cole, Arthur Charles. *The Era of the Civil War, 1848-1870.* Vol. III of *The Centennial History of Illinois,* Clarence W. Alvord (ed.). Springfield, Ill., 1919.

Crandall, Andrew W. *The Early History of the Republican Party, 1854-56.* Boston, 1930.

Craven, Avery. *The Coming of the Civil War.* Chicago, 1942.

———. *The Growth of Southern Nationalism.* Vol. VI of *A History of the South.* Baton Rouge, 1953.

Curtis, Francis. *The Republican Party: A History of Its Fifty Years' Existence and a Record of Its Measures and Leaders, 1854-1904.* 2 vols. New York, 1904.

Darling, Arthur B. *Political Changes in Massachusetts, 1824-1848: A Study of Liberal Movements in Politics.* New Haven, 1925.

Dictionary of Wisconsin Biography. Madison, 1960.

Donoghue, James R. *How Wisconsin Voted: 1848-1954.* Madison, 1956.

Donovan, Herbert. *The Barnburners: A Study of the Internal Movements in the Political History of New York and of the Resulting Changes in Political Affiliations.* New York, 1925.

Duberman, Martin (ed.). *The Antislavery Vanguard: New Essays on the Abolitionists.* Princeton, 1965.

Dumond, Dwight Lowell. *Antislavery Origins of the Civil War in the United States.* Ann Arbor, 1939.

———. *Antislavery: The Crusade for Freedom in America.* Ann Arbor, 1961.

Dunaway, Wayland Fuller. *A History of Pennsylvania.* New York, 1935.

Ellis, David, et al. *A Short History of New York State.* Ithaca, N.Y., 1957.

Filler, Louis. *The Crusade against Slavery, 1830-1860.* New York, 1960.

Foner, Eric. *Free Soil, Free Labor, Free Men: The Ideology of the Republican Party before the Civil War.* New York, 1970.

Foner, Philip S. *Business and Slavery: The New York Merchants and the Irrepressible Conflict.* Chapel Hill, N.C., 1941.

Geary, Sister M. Theophane. *A History of Third Parties in Pennsylvania, 1840-1860.* Washington, 1938.

Guetter, Fred J., and McKinley, Albert E. *Statistical Tables Relating to the Economic Growth of the United States.* Philadelphia, 1924.

Hamilton, Holman. *Prologue to Conflict: The Crisis and Compromise of 1850.* Lexington, Ky., 1964.

Hatch, Louis Clinton. *Maine, A History.* II. New York, 1919.

Hesseltine, William B. *The Rise and Fall of Third Parties from Antimasonry to Wallace.* Washington, 1948.

Hickok, Charles T. *The Negro in Ohio, 1802-1870.* Cleveland, 1896.

Kraditor, Aileen S. *Means and Ends in American Abolitionism: Garrison and His Critics on Strategy and Tactics, 1834-1850.* New York, 1969.

Lader, Lawrence. *The Bold Brahmins; New England's War Against Slavery: 1831-1863.* New York, 1961.

Lane, Brother J. Robert. *A Political History of Connecticut During the Civil War.* Washington, 1941.

Litwack, Leon F. *North of Slavery: The Negro in the Free States, 1790-1860.* Chicago, 1961.

Logan, Rayford W. *Haiti and the Dominican Republic.* New York, 1968.

Ludlum, David M. *Social Ferment in Vermont, 1791-1850.* New York, 1939.

McCormick, Richard P. *The Second American Party System: Party Formation in the Jacksonian Era.* Chapel Hill, N.C., 1966.

McKee, Thomas Hudson. *The National Conventions and Platforms of all Political Parties: 1789-1900.* Baltimore, 1900.

Martin, Asa Earl. *The Anti-Slavery Movement in Kentucky Prior to 1850.* Louisville, 1918.

Merkel, Benjamin. *The Antislavery Controversy in Missouri, 1819-1865.* St. Louis, 1942 (dissertation abstract).

Miller, Douglas T. *Jacksonian Aristocracy: Class and Democracy in New York.* New York, 1967.

Moos, Malcolm. *The Republicans: A History of Their Party.* New York, 1956.

Morrison, Chaplain W. *Democratic Politics and Sectionalism: The Wilmot Proviso Controversy.* Chapel Hill, N.C., 1967.

Mueller, Henry R. *The Whig Party in Pennsylvania.* New York, 1922.

Nash, Howard P., Jr. *Third Parties in American Politics.* Washington, 1959.

Nevins, Allan. *Ordeal of the Union.* 2 vols. New York, 1947.

Nichols, Roy Franklin. *The Democratic Machine, 1850-54.* New York, 1923.

O'Connor, Thomas H. *Lords of the Loom: The Cotton Whigs and the Coming of the Civil War.* New York, 1968.

Paul, James C. *Rift in the Democracy.* Philadelphia, 1951.

Pease, Theodore C. *The Frontier State, 1818-1848.* Vol. II of *The Centennial History of Illinois.* Springfield, Ill., 1918.

Petersen, Svend. *A Statistical History of the American Presidential Elections.* New York, 1963.

Pierce, Bessie Louise. *A History of Chicago.* 3 vols. New York and London, 1937, 1940, 1957.

Porter, Kirk H., and Johnson, Donald Bruce (comps.). *National Party Platforms, 1840-1960.* Urbana, Ill., 1961.

Quaife, Milo M. *The Doctrine of Non-Intervention with Slavery in the Territories.* Chicago, 1910.

————, and Glazer, Sidney. *Michigan: From Primitive Wilderness to Industrial Commonwealth.* New York, 1948.

Quarles, Benjamin. *Black Abolitionists.* New York, 1969.

Quillin, Frank U. *The Color Line in Ohio: A History of Race Prejudice in a Typical Northern State.* Ann Arbor, 1913.

Rawley, James A. *Race and Politics: Bleeding Kansas and the Coming of the Civil War.* New York, 1969.

Rayback, Joseph G. *Free Soil: The Election of 1848.* Lexington, Ky., 1970.

Roseboom, Eugene H. *The Civil War Era, 1850-1873.* Vol. IV of *The History of the State of Ohio.* Carl Wittke (ed.). Columbus, 1944.

————. *A History of Presidential Elections.* New York, 1957.

Schlesinger, Arthur M., Jr. *The Age of Jackson.* Boston, 1945.

Silbey, Joel. *The Shrine of Party: Congressional Voting Behavior, 1841-1852.* Pittsburgh, 1967.

Smith, Theodore C. *The Liberty and Free Soil Parties in the Northwest.* Vol. VI of *Harvard Historical Studies.* New York, 1897.

Stanwood, Edward. *A History of the Presidency from 1788 to 1897.* Boston and New York, 1898.

Streeter, Floyd Benjamin. *Political Parties in Michigan: An Historical Study of Political Issues and Parties in Michigan from the Admission of the State to the Civil War.* Lansing, 1918.

Thomson, Alexander M. *A Political History of Wisconsin.* Milwaukee, 1902.

Trefousse, Hans L. *The Radical Republicans: Lincoln's Vanguard for Racial Justice.* New York, 1969.

Van Deusen, Glyndon. *The Jacksonian Era, 1828-1848.* New York, 1959.

Van Dusen, Albert E. *Connecticut.* New York, 1961.

Weisenburger, Francis P. *The Passing of the Frontier.* Vol. III of *The History of the State of Ohio.* Carl Wittke (ed.). Columbus, 1941.

BIOGRAPHIES

ADAMS, C. F. Adams, Charles Francis, Jr. *Charles Francis Adams.* Boston, 1900.

————. Duberman, Martin B. *Charles Francis Adams, 1807-1886.* Boston, 1960.

ADAMS, J. Q. Clark, Bennett Champ. *John Quincy Adams, "Old Man Eloquent."* Boston, 1932.

————. Bemis, Samuel Flagg. *John Quincy Adams and the Union.* New York, 1956.

BANCROFT. Nye, Russel B. *George Bancroft, Brahmin Rebel.* New York, 1944.

BANKS. Harrington, Fred Harvey. *Fighting Politician: Major General N. P. Banks.* Philadelphia, 1948.

BENTON. Smith, Elbert B. *Magnificent Missourian: The Life of Thomas Hart Benton.* Philadelphia, 1958.

BIGELOW. Clapp, Margaret. *Forgotten First Citizen: John Bigelow.* Boston, 1947.

BIRNEY. Fladeland, Betty. *James Gillespie Birney: Slaveholder to Abolitionist.* Ithaca, N.Y., 1955.

BLAIR. Smith, William Ernest. *The Francis Preston Blair Family in Politics.* 2 vols. New York, 1933.

BOWDITCH. Bowditch, Vincent Y. *Life and Correspondence of Henry Ingersoll Bowditch.* 2 vols. Boston, 1902.

BRYANT. Bigelow, John. *William Cullen Bryant.* Boston, 1890.

BUCHANAN. Klein, Philip Shriver. *President James Buchanan: A Biography.* University Park, Pa., 1962.

CALHOUN. Wiltse, Charles M. *John C. Calhoun, Sectionalist, 1840-1850.* Indianapolis and New York, 1951.

CASS. McLaughlin, Andrew. *Lewis Cass.* Boston and New York, 1899.

————. Woodford, Frank B. *Lewis Cass: The Last Jeffersonian.* New Brunswick, N.J., 1950.

CHASE. Hart, Albert G. *Salmon P. Chase.* Boston, 1899.

————. Schuckers, Jacob William. *The Life and Public Services of Salmon Portland Chase.* New York, 1874.

————. Warden, Robert B. *An Account of the Private Life and Public Services of Salmon Portland Chase.* Cincinnati, 1874.

CLAY. Poage, George R. *Henry Clay and the Whig Party.* Chapel Hill, N.C., 1936.

CUSHING. Fuess, Claude M. *The Life of Caleb Cushing.* 2 vols. New York, 1923.

DANA. Adams, Charles Francis, Jr. *Richard Henry Dana, A Biography.* 2 vols. Boston, 1890.

————. Shapiro, Samuel. *Richard Henry Dana, Jr., 1815-1882.* East Lansing, 1961.

DOUGLASS. Foner, Philip S. *Frederick Douglass.* New York, 1964.

————. Quarles, Benjamin. *Frederick Douglass.* Washington, 1948.

EARLE. Bronner, Edwin B. *Thomas Earle as a Reformer.* Philadelphia, 1948.

FESSENDEN. Jellison, Charles A. *Fessenden of Maine, Civil War Senator.* Syracuse, 1962.

FILLMORE. Rayback, Robert J. *Millard Fillmore: Biography of a President.* Buffalo, 1959.

GARRISON. Nye, Russel B. *William Lloyd Garrison and the Humanitarian Reformers.* Boston, 1955.

GIDDINGS. Julian, George W. *The Life of Joshua R. Giddings.* Chicago, 1892.

————. Stewart, James B. *Joshua Giddings and the Tactics of Radical Politics.* Cleveland, 1970.

GREELEY. Van Deusen, Glyndon G. *Horace Greeley, Nineteenth-Century Crusader.* Philadelphia, 1953. See also LINCOLN AND GREELEY.

GROW. DuBois, James T., and Mathews, Gertrude S. *Galusha A. Grow, Father of the Homestead Law.* Boston, 1917.

HALE. Sewell, Richard H. *John P. Hale and the Politics of Abolition.* Cambridge, 1965.

HAMLIN. Hamlin, Charles Eugene. *The Life and Times of Hannibal Hamlin.* Cambridge, 1899.

————. Hunt, H. Draper. *Hannibal Hamlin of Maine: Lincoln's First Vice-President.* Syracuse, 1969.

HOAR. Storey, Moorfield, and Emerson, Edward W. *Ebenezer Rockwood Hoar: A Memoir.* Boston, 1911.

JULIAN. Clarke, Grace Julian. *George W. Julian.* Indianapolis, 1923.
———. Riddleberger, Patrick W. *George Washington Julian, Radical Republican: A Study in Nineteenth Century Politics and Reform.* Vol. XLV of *Indiana Historical Collections.* Indianapolis, 1966.

LEMOYNE. McCulloch, Margaret C. *Fearless Advocate of the Right: The Life of Francis Julius LeMoyne, M.D., 1798-1879.* Boston, 1941.

LEWIS. Lewis, William G. W. *Biography of Samuel Lewis, First Superintendent of Common Schools for the State of Ohio.* Cincinnati, 1857.

LINCOLN. Herndon, William H., and Weik, Jesse W. *Abraham Lincoln: The True Story of a Great Life.* New York, 1892.

LINCOLN AND GREELEY. Horner, Harlan H. *Lincoln and Greeley.* Urbana, Ill., 1953.

LOWELL. Duberman, Martin. *James Russell Lowell.* Boston, 1966.

MCLEAN. Weisenburger, Francis P. *The Life of John McLean, A Politician on the United States Supreme Court.* Columbus, 1937.

MANN. Williams, E. I. F. *Horace Mann, Educational Statesman.* New York, 1937.

MARCY. Spencer, Ivor D. *The Victor and the Spoils: A Life of William L. Marcy.* Providence, 1959.

PALFREY. Gatell, Frank Otto. *John Gorham Palfrey and the New England Conscience.* Cambridge, 1963.

PIERCE. Nichols, Roy Franklin. *Franklin Pierce: Young Hickory of the Granite Hills.* Philadelphia, 1958.

POLK. McCoy, Charles A. *Polk and the Presidency.* Austin, 1960.
———. Sellers, Charles. *James K. Polk, Continentalist, 1843-1846.* Princeton, 1966.

SEWARD. Bancroft, Frederic. *The Life of William H. Seward.* New York, 1900.
———. Seward, Frederic W. *Seward at Washington as Senator and Secretary of State: A Memoir of His Life with Selections from His Letters.* 3 vols. New York, 1891.
———. Van Deusen, Glyndon. *William Henry Seward.* New York, 1967.

SEYMOUR. Mitchell, Stewart. *Horatio Seymour of New York.* Cambridge, 1938.

SMITH. Harlow, Ralph Volney. *Gerrit Smith: Philanthropist and Reformer.* New York, 1939.

STANTON. Thomas, Benjamin P. and Hyman, Harold M. *Stanton, The Life and Times of Lincoln's Secretary of War.* New York, 1962.

STEVENS. Current, Richard N. *Old Thad Stevens: A Story of Ambition.* Madison, 1942.

SUMNER. Donald, David. *Charles Sumner and the Coming of the Civil War.* New York, 1960.

———. Pierce, Edward L. *Memoir and Letters of Charles Sumner.* 4 vols. Boston, 1894.

TAPPAN, L. Wyatt-Brown, Bertram. *Lewis Tappan and the Evangelical War against Slavery.* Cleveland, 1969.

TAYLOR. Dyer, Brainerd. *Zachary Taylor.* Baton Rouge, 1946.

———. Hamilton, Holman. *Zachary Taylor: Soldier in the White House.* Indianapolis, 1951.

TILDEN. Bigelow, John. *The Life of Samuel J. Tilden.* 2 vols. New York, 1895.

———. Flick, Alexander Clarence. *Samuel Jones Tilden: A Study in Political Sagacity.* New York, 1939.

TUCK. Corning, Charles R. *Amos Tuck.* Exeter, N.H., 1902.

VAN BUREN. Alexander, Holmes. *The American Talleyrand: The Career and Contemporaries of Martin Van Buren, Eighth President.* New York, 1935.

———. Shepard, Edward M. *Martin Van Buren.* Boston, 1888.

WADE. Riddle, Albert G. *The Life of Benjamin F. Wade.* Cleveland, 1886.

———. Trefousse, Hans L. *Benjamin Franklin Wade: Radical Republican from Ohio.* New York, 1963.

WEBSTER. Current, Richard N. *Daniel Webster and the Rise of National Conservatism.* Boston, 1955.

WEED. Van Deusen, Glyndon G. *Thurlow Weed, Wizard of the Lobby.* Boston, 1947.

WELLES. West, Richard S. *Gideon Welles. Lincoln's Navy Department.* New York, 1943.

WENTWORTH. Fehrenbacher, Don E. *Chicago Giant: A Biography of "Long John" Wentworth.* Madison, 1957.

WHITMAN. Allen, Gay Wilson. *The Solitary Singer: A Critical Biography of Walt Whitman.* New York, 1955.

WHITTIER. Bennett, Whitman. *Whittier: Bard of Freedom.* Chapel Hill, N.C., 1941.

WILMOT. Going, Charles Buxton. *David Wilmot, Free Soiler: A Biography of the Great Advocate of the Wilmot Proviso.* New York, 1924.

WILSON. Nason, Elias, and Russell, Thomas. *The Life and Public Services of Henry Wilson.* Boston, 1876.

WINTHROP. Winthrop, Robert C., Jr. *A Memoir of Robert C. Winthrop.* Boston, 1897.

WRIGHT, E. Wright, Philip Green and Elizabeth Q. *Elizur Wright, The Father of Life Insurance.* Chicago, 1937.

WRIGHT, S. Garraty, John Arthur. *Silas Wright.* New York, 1949.

———. Gillet, R. H. *The Life and Times of Silas Wright.* 2 vols. Albany, 1874.

———. Hammond, J. D. *The Life and Times of Silas Wright.* Syracuse, 1848.

YANCEY. Du Bose, John W. *The Life and Times of William Lowndes Yancey.* Birmingham, 1892.

ARTICLES

Appleton, William S. "The Whigs of Massachusetts," *Proceedings of the Massachusetts Historical Society.* Second Series, XI (1896, 1897), 278-82.

Baker, Florence Elizabeth. "A Brief History of the Elective Franchise in Wisconsin," *Proceedings of the State Historical Society of Wisconsin, 1893.* Madison, 1894, 113-30.

Bean, William G. "Puritan Versus Celt, 1850-1860," *The New England Quarterly,* VII (1934), 70-89.

Beeler, Dale. "The Election of 1852 in Indiana," *Indiana Magazine of History,* XI-XII (1915-1916), 301-23, 34-52.

Bell, Howard H. "The National Negro Convention, 1848," *The Ohio Historical Quarterly,* LXVII (1958), 357-68.

———. "National Negro Conventions of the Middle 1840's: Moral Suasion vs. Political Action," *Journal of Negro History,* XLII (1957), 247-60.

Blue, Frederick J. "The Ohio Free Soilers and the Problems of Factionalism," *Ohio History,* LXXVI (1967), 17-32.

Boucher, Chauncey S. "In Re That Aggressive Slavocracy," *Mississippi Valley Historical Review,* VIII (1921), 13-79.

Brewer, W. M. "Henry Highland Garnett," *Journal of Negro History,* XIII (1928), 36-52.

Carmen, Harry J., and Luthin, Reinhard. "The Seward-Fillmore Feud and the Disruption of the Whig Party," *New York History,* XXIV (1943), 335-57.

Cochran, William C. "The Western Reserve and the Fugitive Slave Law," *Western Reserve Historical Society Collections,* CI (1920), 9-220.

328   *The Free Soilers*

Duberman, Martin. "The Abolitionists and Psychology," *Journal of Negro History*, XLVII (1962), 183-92.

———. "Behind the Scenes as the Massachusetts 'Coalition' of 1851 Divides the Spoils," *Essex Institute Historical Collections*, XCIX (1963), 152-60.

Dumond, Dwight. "Race Prejudice and Abolition, New Views on the Anti-Slavery Movement," *Michigan Alumnus Quarterly Review*, XLI (1935), 377-85.

Dyer, Brainerd. "Zachary Taylor and the Election of 1848," *Pacific Historical Review*, IX (1940), 173-82.

Fishback, Mason M. "Illinois Legislation on Slavery and Free Negroes, 1818-1865," *Transactions of the Illinois State Historical Society, 1904*. Springfield, 1904, 414-32.

Fishel, Leslie. "Wisconsin and Negro Suffrage," *Wisconsin Magazine of History*, LXVI (1963), 180-96.

Foner, Eric. "Politics and Prejudices: The Free Soil Party AND the Free Negro, 1849-1852," *Journal of Negro History*, L (1965), 239-56.

———. "Racial Attitudes of the New York Free Soilers," *New York History*, XLVI (1965), 311-29.

Fox, Dixon Ryan. "The Negro Vote in Old New York," *Political Science Quarterly*, XXXII (1917), 253-67.

Gatell, Frank Otto. "Conscience and Judgment: The Bolt of the Massachusetts Conscience Whigs," *The Historian* (1958), 18-45.

———. "Palfrey's Vote, the Conscience Whigs, and the Election of Speaker Winthrop," *New England Quarterly*, XXXI (1958), 218-31.

Geiser, Karl F. "The Western Reserve in the Antislavery Movement, 1840-1860," *Proceedings of the Mississippi Valley Historical Association, 1911-12*. Cedar Rapids, 1912, 73-98.

Graebner, Norman A. "James K. Polk: A Study in Federal Patronage," *Mississippi Valley Historical Review*, XXXVIII (1952), 613-32.

———. "Thomas Corwin and the Election of 1848: A Study in Conservative Politics," *Journal of Southern History*, XVII (May, 1951), 162-79.

Harrington, Fred Harvey. "Nathaniel Prentiss Banks, A Study in Anti-Slavery Politics," *New England Quarterly*, IX (1936), 626-54.

Hicks, John D. "The Third Party Tradition in American Politics," *Mississippi Valley Historical Review*, XX (1933), 3-28.

Holt, Edgar A. "Party Politics in Ohio, 1840-1850," *Ohio Archaeological and Historical Quarterly*, XXXVII (1928), 439-591; XXXVIII (1929), 47-182, 260-402.

Hubbart, Henry Clyde. " 'Pro-Southern' Influences in the Free West, 1840-1865," *Mississippi Valley Historical Review*, XX (1933), 45-62.

Hubbell, John. "The National Free Soil Convention of '48 Held in Buffalo," *Publications of the Buffalo Historical Society*, IV (1896), 147-62.

King, Ameda R. "The Last Years of the Whig Party in Illinois, 1847-1856," *Transactions of the Illinois State Historical Society*, XXXII (1925), 108-54.

Learned, Henry Barrett. "The Sequence of Appointments to Polk's Original Cabinet: A Study in Chronology, 1844-1845," *American Historical Review*, XXX (1924), 76-83.

Litwack, Leon F. "The Abolitionist Dilemma: The Antislavery Movement and the Northern Negro," *New England Quarterly*, XXXIV (1961), 50-73.

————. "The Federal Government and the Free Negro, 1790-1860," *Journal of Negro History*, XLIII (1958), 261-78.

Lofton, Williston H. "Abolition and Labor," *Journal of Negro History*, XXXII (1948), 249-83.

Ludlum, Robert P. "Joshua R. Giddings, Radical," *Mississippi Valley Historical Review*, XXIII (1936), 49-60.

Luthin, Reinhard H. "Abraham Lincoln and the Massachusetts Whigs in 1848," *New England Quarterly*, XIV (1941), 619-32.

————. "Salmon P. Chase's Political Career Before the Civil War," *Mississippi Valley Historical Review*, XXIX (1943), 517-40.

Lynch, William O. "Antislavery Tendencies of the Democratic Party in the Northwest, 1848-1850," *Mississippi Valley Historical Review*, XI (1924), 319-31.

McKay, Ernest A. "Henry Wilson and the Coalition of 1851," *New England Quarterly*, XXXVI (1963), 338-57.

Mintz, Max M. "The Political Ideas of Martin Van Buren," *Proceedings of the New York State Historical Association*, XLVII (1949), 422-48.

Peck, Charles H. "John Van Buren, A Study in Bygone Politics," *Magazine of American History*, XVII (1887), 58-70, 202-13, 318-29.

Persinger, Clark E. "The 'Bargain of 1844' as the Origin of the Wilmot Proviso," *Annual Report of the American Historical Association, 1911*, I. (Washington, 1913), 187-95.

Price, Erwin H. "The Election of 1848 in Ohio," *Ohio Archaeological and Historical Society*, XXXVI (1927), 188-311.

Rayback, Joseph G. "The American Workingman and the Antislavery Crusade," *Journal of Economic History*, III (1943), 152-63.

————. "The Liberty Party Leaders of Ohio: Exponents of Antislavery Coalition," *Ohio State Archaeological and Historical Quarterly*, LVII (1948), 165-78.

————. "Martin Van Buren's Break with James K. Polk: The Record," *New York History*, XXXVI (1955), 51-62.

————. "Martin Van Buren's Desire for Revenge in the Campaign of 1848," *Mississippi Valley Historical Review*, XL (1954), 707-16.

Riddle, Albert G. "The Election of S. P. Chase to the Senate, February, 1849," *The Republic*, IV (1875), 179.

————. "Recollections of the Forty-Seventh General Assembly of Ohio, 1848-1849," *Magazine of Western History*, VI (1887), 341-51.

————. "The Rise of Antislavery Sentiment on the Western Reserve," *Magazine of Western History* VI (1887), 145-56.

Riddleberger, Patrick W. "The Making of a Political Abolitionist: George W. Julian and the Free Soilers, 1848," *Indiana Magazine of History*, LI (1955), 221-36.

Roach, George W. "The Presidential Campaign of 1844 in New York State," *Proceedings of the New York State Historical Association*, XXXVI (1938), 153-72.

Scheeler, J. Reuben. "The Struggle of the Negro in Ohio for Freedom," *Journal of Negro History*, XXXI (1946), 208-26.

Sewell, Richarl H. "John P. Hale and the Liberty Party, 1847-1848," *New England Quarterly*, XXXVII (1964), 200-223.

————. "Walt Whitman, John P. Hale, and the Free Democracy: An Unpublished Letter," *New England Quarterly*, XXXIV (1961), 239-42.

Shapiro, Samuel. "The Conservative Dilemma: The Massachusetts Constitutional Convention of 1853," *New England Quarterly*, XXXIII (1960), 207-24.

Shriver, Edward O. "Antislavery: The Free Soil and Free Democratic Parties in Maine, 1848-1855," *New England Quarterly*, XLII (1969), 82-94.

Smiley, David. "Cassius M. Clay and John G. Fee: A Study in Southern Anti-Slavery Thought," *Journal of Negro History*, XLII (1957), 201-13.

Smith, Theodore C. "The Free Soil Party in Wisconsin," *Proceedings of the State Historical Society of Wisconsin, 1893*. Madison, 1894, 97-162.

Stenberg, Richard R. "The Motivation of the Wilmot Proviso," *Mississippi Valley Historical Review*, XVIII (1932), 535-41.

Townshend, N. S. "The Forty-Seventh General Assembly of Ohio — Comments Upon Mr. Riddle's Paper," *Magazine of Western History*, VI (1887), 623-28.

Vroman, Mason. "The Fugitive Slave Law in Wisconsin with Reference to Nullification Sentiment," *Proceedings of the State Historical Society of Wisconsin, 1895.* Madison, 1896, 117-44.

Wesley, Charles H. "The Participation of Negroes in Antislavery Political Parties," *Journal of Negro History*, XXIX (1944), 32-74.

Williams, Mentor L. "The Chicago River and Harbor Convention, 1847," *Mississippi Valley Historical Review*, XXXV (1949), 607-26.

UNPUBLISHED DISSERTATIONS AND THESES

Bean, William G. "Party Transformations in Massachusetts with Special Reference to the Antecedents of Republicanism, 1848-1860," Ph.D. dissertation, Harvard University, 1922.

Boom, Aaron. "The Development of Sectional Attitudes in Wisconsin, 1848-1861." Ph.D. dissertation, University of Chicago, 1948.

Bradford, David H. "Background and Formation of the Republican Party in Ohio, 1844-1861." Ph.D. dissertation, University of Chicago, 1947.

Cole, Albert J. "The Barnburner Element in the Republican Party." M.A. thesis, University of Wisconsin, 1951.

Fair, Clinton. "Internal Improvements and Sectional Controversy." M.A. thesis, University of Wisconsin, 1937.

Ferree, Walter L. "The New York Democracy: Division and Reunion, 1847-1852." Ph.D. dissertation, University of Pennsylvania, 1953.

Goldfarb, Joel. "The Life of Gamaliel Bailey, Prior to the Founding of the *National Era;* The Orientation of a Practical Abolitionist." Ph.D. dissertation, University of California at Los Angeles, 1958.

Lichterman, Martin. "John Adams Dix, 1798-1879." Ph.D. dissertation, Columbia University, 1952.

Loubert, J. Daniel. "The Orientation of Henry Wilson, 1812-1856." Ph.D. dissertation, Boston University, 1952.

Mulkern, John Raymond. "The Know Nothing Party in Massachusetts." Ph.D. dissertation, Boston University, 1963.

Muller, Ernest P. "Preston King: A Political Biography." Ph.D. dissertation, Columbia University, 1957.

O'Connor, Thomas Henry. "Cotton Whigs and Union: The Textile Manufacturers of Massachusetts and the Coming of the Civil War." Ph.D. dissertation, Boston University, 1958.

Solberg, Richard W. "Joshua Giddings, Politician and Idealist." Ph.D. dissertation, University of Chicago, 1952.

Stampp, Kenneth M. "Opposition to Slavery in the Upper South, 1808-1860." M.A. thesis, University of Wisconsin, 1937.

Whitehurst, Alto L. "Martin Van Buren and the Free Soil Movement." Ph.D. dissertation, University of Chicago, 1932.

Wright, John S. "The Background and Formation of the Republican Party in Illinois, 1846-1860." Ph.D. dissertation, University of Chicago, 1947.

Index